Cheryl
Milner
356-3462

THE POLITICS OF INFORMATION MANAGEMENT

Policy Guidelines

Paul A. Strassmann

Books by Paul A. Strassmann
INFORMATION PAYOFF
THE BUSINESS VALUE OF COMPUTERS

The Information Economics Press • New Canaan, Connecticut

Editor: Vera Dolan

Production Coordination and Design: Enoch Sherman, Renaissance Publishers

Graphics and Composition: Paul A. Strassmann

Illustrations: John Klossner, Klossner Studies

Printing: R. R. Donnelley & Sons

Order directly from Publisher:

THE INFORMATION ECONOMICS PRESS

P.O. Box 264

New Canaan, Connecticut 06840-0264

Fax: 203-966-5506

Printed in the United States of America
2 3 4 5 6 7 8 9 10

Library of Congress Cataloging-in-Publication Data
Strassmann, Paul A.
    The Politics of Information Management
    1. Politics   2. Information Technology
    3. Business Management   I. Title
    1995   658.4
Library of Congress Catalog Card Number 93-80110
ISBN 0-9620413-4-3

Return-on-Management™, R-O-M™ and Information Productivity™ are registered trademarks of Strassmann, Inc.

TABLE OF CONTENTS

Table of Contents v
List of Illustrations xiv
Acknowledgments xvii
Introduction xxiii
      Why "Politics"? xxiii
      Scope xxiv
      Content xxv
      A Discipline of Information Politics xxvii
      Precursors xxix
      The Value of Information Politics xxx
Part I Governance 1
  1 What Is Policy? 3
      Using Policy 3
      Avoiding Policy-Making 5
      Politics vs. Policy 6
      Policy and Success 7
  2 Framework 9
      Information Politics, an Element of
         Information Management 10
      Business Plan Alignment 11
      Implementation Matters 12
  3 Definitions 15
      Information Management 15
      Executive Ownership 18
      Delegation 18
      Information Systems 19
      Information Technology 20

	Stealth Technology	21
	Technology Management Roles	21
4	Roles	23
	Information Effectiveness	23
	Unstable Leadership	25
	Political Realities	26
	The Onlookers	27
	A Long View	28
5	Making Policy	31
	Priorities	31
	Policy Innovation	32
	Conflict Resolution	33
	Economics and Politics	33
	Local Politics	34
	The Totalitarian Taint	35
	Balance of Power	36
	The Politics of Choices	37
	The Politics of Control	38
	Transition Politics	39
	Distribution of Power	41
6	Federation	43
	U.S. Constitutional Model	45
	Information Constitutional Model	45
	Layers of an Information Constitution	47
7	Architecture	51
	Favoring External Information Sources	52
	Design for Complexity	53
	Configuration Management	54
	Lessons from History	56
	Software as Federated Governance	57
	Networking Choices	57
	Hub Networking	61
	Web Networking	63
8	Organization	67
	Decentralization vs. Centralization	67
	Choices in Dividing Authority and Budgets	69
	Merits of Alternatives	70
	Distributing Tasks	71
9	Scope of a Constitution	73
	Why a Constitution?	73
	Limits	75
	Inclusion Principles	75

    Exclusions 76
    Drafting a Constitution 77
    Local Initiatives 79
10 Institutions 81
    Separation of Powers 82
    Executive Level Staff 82
    Conflict Resolution 84
    Involvement of Auditors 86
    What Can Go Wrong 86
    A Long Journey 88
11 Model Constitution 89
    Statement of Goals 89
    Statement of Principles 92
    Responsibilities at the Enterprise and Business Levels . 96
    The Information Management Policy Board 97
    Responsibilities of Information Systems Managers . . . 99
    Responsibilities of Operating Managers 100
    Planning and Finance 101
    Contracting Out 102
    Care for Customers of Internal Information Services 103
    Data Management 105
    Information Configuration Policies 106
    Decentralization Policics 107
    Personnel Development Policies 108
    Systems Design Policies 109
    Design Principles 110
    Technology Advancement 112
    Reuse 113
    Telecommunications 113
    Risk Management 115
    Technology Acquisition 115
    Security 116
12 Concept of Operations 119
    Mission Concepts 120
    Enterprise Level Concepts 122
    Enterprise Level Checklist 122
    Process Level Concepts 124
    Process Level Checklist 125
    Business Level Concepts 127
    Business Level Checklist 127
    Application Level Concepts 129
    Application Level Checklist 129

Local Level Concepts 130
Local Level Checklist 133

13 Standards 135
The Politics of Standards 135
Standards Compliance 139
Making Standards 139
Managing Standards 141
Standards Topics 143
Standards Documents 145
Standards as Governance 147

14 Governance Cases 149
Debates About Consolidation 149
The Case of Customer Account Numbers 150
Data Malfeasance Cases 151
The Case of Joint Cooperation 153
Lessons Learned 154

Part II Observations **157**

15 Analogies 159
The Leninist Option 161
The Cold War and Computers 163
New Challenges 164
What Has Changed 166
Technology Agendas 167
Management Agendas 168
Reconciling the Agendas 170

16 History 171
Underlying Concepts 172
The Elitist View 172
The Populist Reaction 175
The Mainframe Theocracy 177
The Minicomputer Hierarchy 177
The Microcomputer Revolution 177
The Age of Cooperative Alliances 178
The Age of Information Democracy 178
The Pharaoh and His Scribes 179
From Theocracy to Hierarchy 182
The Rise of the Barons 182
The Working of the Invisible Hand 183
The Expense of Baronial Possessions 185
The Monopoly Crumbles 186
Me, Myself and I 188
The Reformers 190

The Counter Reformation 191
Working at Home 192
17 Privacy 197
Personal Privacy 197
Property Rights 199
Organizational Privacy 201
Information Intrusion 204
Corporate Implications 206
Encryption 207
The Faustian Bargain 208
18 Security 211
Global Barriers 214
Enterprise Barriers 215
Process Barriers 217
Business Barriers 217
Application Barriers 217
Local Barriers 218
19 Reengineering 221
Origins of Reengineering 221
Overhead Cost Reduction 223
Total Quality Movement 224
Industrial Engineering 225
Application of Reengineering 225
Dictatorial Characteristics 226
Deductive vs. Inductive Reasoning 227
The Deduction of Best Practices 228
Disregarding Experience 230
Haste and Reengineering 231
Public Sector Reengineering 232
The Extremist Strain 233
The Extremist Point of View 234
Morality in Warfare and Commerce 236
Revolutionary Changes 237
20 Process Improvement 241
Improvement Through Cooperation 243
Node Trees 243
Process Flow Simulation 244
Organizing Business Process Improvement 248
Emerging Trends 249
21 Software 253
Software Process Improvement 253
Software Independence 254

Software as Inheritance 255
Legacy Software 256
Legacy Systems 257
Migrating Legacy Systems 258
The Flight From Mainframes 259
22 Reuse 263
Software Portability 263
Technology Recycling 265
Software and Business Reorganization 266
Disruption as Rationale for Change 267
Reuse as a Political Agenda 269
23 Learning 271
Cost of Errors 271
Dissipation of Knowledge 272
Collective Knowledge 273
Organizational Learning 274
Profitability of Employee Development 274
Organizational Memory 275
Learning as a Continuum 278
Education for Information Systems 278
Learning Assistance 280
Distance Tutoring 281
The Costs of Ignorance 282
Education as a Business 283
A Knowledge Based Theory of Labor 283
24 Tools 287
Technology Obsolescence 288
Protecting Long Term Assets 289
Prolonging Software Life 289
Responsibility and Accountability for Software Assets 290
The Development Environment 291
Problems with Software Maintenance 293
Articulating Systems Requirements 294
Manufactured Software 295
Openness 296
Dimensions of Open Systems 296
Significance of Open Systems 297
Part III Leadership 299
25 Objectives 301
Goals vs. Objectives 301
Objectives and Customer Satisfaction 303
Cost Reduction Objectives 304

Setting Objectives 307
Example of Poorly Targeted Objectives 309
Basic Beliefs 310
Too Many Objectives 311
Focus 312
Examples of Information Systems Objectives 313
26 Roles 315
Identifying Excellence 316
Outsourcing as a Loss of Identity 318
Identity 321
Signs of Failure 322
Patterns of Failure and Success 324
The Roots of Failure 325
The CIO's Image 327
The CIO Disorientation 329
Pragmatic vs. Mandarin CIO 331
CIOs in Charge of Reengineering 331
Loss of Power 333
27 Charter for the CIO 335
A Functional Summary 335
Duties and Authorities 337
Principles for Guiding CIO Actions 338
Ownership of Infrastructure Assets 341
Is the CIO Like a CFO? 343
Managing 344
Claims 345
Political Astuteness 346
Technology Adventurism 347
Building Support 348
Governance Before Action 350
28 Innovation 351
Home Grown Innovation 351
Let the Professionals Manage 352
Control Only What Matters 352
Take Unoccupied Territories First 353
Alliances and Benefits 354
Innovation Is Experimentation 355
Entrepreneurship 356
Entrepreneurs 356
Funding Innovation 357
Diversifying Innovation 357
Suppression and Stimulation 359

29 Survival 361
    All Short-Term Decisions Become Long-Term 362
    Establish Credibility 364
    Solve Critical Problems 366
    CIO Prospects 368

Part IV Recollections **371**
30 Industry 373
    General Foods 373
    Kraft 376
    Xerox 378
    The Xerox Information Services Division 381
31 The Road to CIM 383
    The Origin of CIM 385
    Early CIM Efforts 391
    The Executive Level Group 396
    CIM Principles 398
    Role of Command, Control, Communications
       and Intelligence 401
    Creating the Corporate Information Function 403
    Innovation Calls for Unconventional Thinking 404
32 Implementing CIM 407
    Information Policy Board 411
    From "Grand Design" to Migration Systems 412
    Gold Nuggets 416
    Creating Policies 417
    Technology Improvement Programs 421
    Implementing Business Process Improvement 423
    An Information Management Doctrine for Defense . 429
    CIM Rules 430
33 The Politics of CIM 437
    The Flawed Acquisition Process 438
    Cutting Down the Scope of Acquisition Programs . . 441
    Resisting a Common Infrastructure 444
    Command and Control Functional Analysis 446
    Data Processing Installations 450
    Central Design Organizations 451
    Workstations and Terminals 452
    Long Distance Networks 453
    Condition of the Defense Information Infrastructure 454
    Creating a DoD Information Infrastructure 455
    The Defense Information Infrastructure Proposal . . . 458
    Security Risks 460

The Politics of Infrastructure Building 461
CIM Lessons 463
A Postscript 465
Part V Perspectives **467**
34 Prospects 469
Externalizing Information Politics 469
Information Services Utilities 471
Effect on Careers 472
Business Procedures as a Political Act 473
Politicophobia 474
Politics Before Technology 476
Technocratic Utopianism 477
Anarchy 478
Monarchy 478
Feudalism 479
Federalism 480
35 Diversity 483
Information-Based Societies 484
Industrial-Based Societies 484
Materials-Based Societies 485
Diversity in Governance 485
Future of Information Politics 486
The Universality of the Telephone 487
Governance and Standards 489
The Universality of Computer-Based
    Communication 492
An Historical Perspective 494
A Technology Perspective 495
Information Technology as a Global Political Force . . 496
A Global Perspective 497
Political Integration 498
Concluding Remarks 501
Glossary 503
Index 511

LIST OF ILLUSTRATIONS

Figure 1.1 Policy Without Governance 4
Figure 2.1 Elements of Information Management 9
Figure 2.2 Elements of Information Superiority 10
Figure 3.1 The Context of Information Management 15
Figure 4.1 Unpredictable Leadership 26
Figure 4.2 Clear Roles and Responsibilities 28
Figure 5.1 Simplicity is the Clearest Policy 36
Figure 6.1 Federation Is a Way of Balancing Power 43
Figure 6.2 A Federated Governance Model 46
Figure 7.1 Configuration Management 54
Figure 7.2 Distributing Computing Power 58
Figure 7.3 An Information Hermit 59
Figure 7.4 Virtual Reality 60
Figure 8.1 Conflicts Within an Information Structure 68
Figure 8.2 Differences Between High and Low Productivity 70
Figure 9.1 If It Is Not Written, It Is Not Policy 79
Figure 10.1 Settling Disputes, Contemporary Bureaucratic Style 85
Figure 11.1 The Visionary Consultant 90
Figure 11.2 Governance That Adapts 93
Figure 11.3 Network Control Tasks 114
Figure 12.1 Explaining the Concept of Operations 119
Figure 12.2 Experimental Prototyping 131
Figure 13.1 Introducing a New Standard 138
Figure 15.1 Growth in Global Computing Power 160
Figure 15.2 Soviet Style Computing 162
Figure 15.3 Differences in Computer Management 163
Figure 16.1 A Clash of Cultures 175

Figure 16.2 Acquiring Skills for Information Technology 177
Figure 16.3 The Paperwork Factory 179
Figure 16.4 A Brief Political History of Information Technologies 180
Figure 16.5 People as Computer Peripherals 180
Figure 16.6 U.S. Information Cottages 193
Figure 17.2 A New Method for an Old Trade 200
Figure 17.3 Direct Connection from Customer to Supplier 202
Figure 18.1 Organizing for Security 212
Figure 18.3 Security Barriers 216
Figure 19.1 Business Process Analysis 224
Figure 19.2 Some Reenginering Choices 235
Figure 20.1 Downsizing 242
Figure 20.2 Top Branches of a Node Tree Diagram 244
Figure 20.3 Sample of a Workflow Diagram 245
Figure 20.4 Cost Comparison of Alternatives 246
Figure 20.5 Simulating Processing Time 247
Figure 20.6 Simulating Staff Utilization 248
Figure 21.1 Ready for Reincarnation 255
Figure 22.1 Software Portability 264
Figure 22.2 Computer Progress as Cause of Computer Trash 265
Figure 22.3 Hardware Obsoletes Faster Than Knowledge to Use It . . .268
Figure 23.1 Preservation of Knowledge 276
Figure 23.2 A Knowledge Repository 277
Figure 23.3 Computer-Assisted Training 281
Figure 24.1 Long-Term and Obsolescent Assets 287
Figure 24.2 Signs of Obsolescence 288
Figure 24.3 Separating Development from Execution 292
Figure 25.1 What is a Realistic Goal? 302
Figure 25.2 Example of Unit Cost Reduction Indicators 305
Figure 25.3 Example of Declining Administrative Costs 307
Figure 25.4 Leadership by Press Release 309
Figure 26.1 A View of Outsourcing 320
Figure 26.2 A Potentially Fatal Misunderstanding 327
Figure 27.1 A Map Is Useful Only If You Know Where You Are 335
Figure 28.3 Innovation Needs Incentives 358
Figure 29.1 CIO Succession Planning 362
Figure 30.1 Corporate Contests, 1970s Style 380
Figure 31.1 Defense Cost Reductions and CIM 388
Figure 31.2 Functional Cost Reduction Tasks for 1990-1997 389
Figure 31.3 Services Cost Reduction Tasks for 1990-1997 389
Figure 31.4 CIM Share of DoD Cost Reduction Tasks 390
Figure 31.5 Paying Too Much Attention to Computer Problems 392

Figure 31.6 Early CIM Efforts 394
Figure 31.7 A Comptroller's Systems Concept 395
Figure 31.8 The CIM Model, in Order of Priority of Decisions 400
Figure 32.1 After Policy Comes Implementation 409
Figure 32.2 An Evolutionary Migration Schema 413
Figure 32.3 Migration Tree for Selected Financial Applications 415
Figure 32.4 Master Diagram for Business Process Improvement 424
Figure 32.5 Map of Process Improvement Tasks 426
Figure 32.6 Ft. Sill Engineering Management Processes 427
Figure 32.7 Ft. Sill Business Process Activity Costs 428
Figure 32.8 Cost Reduction Potential in Business Process Analysis 428
Figure 33.1 The Traditional DoD Systems Acquisition Process 441
Figure 33.2 The Preferred Acquisition Process 442
Figure 33.3 Benchmarking Data Center Labor for Savings Potential . .451
Figure 33.4 Savings to Fund Modernization .455
Figure 34.1 Shift in Literacy as a Political Force 480
Figure 35.1 Let Your Agents Walk the Information Channels 492

ACKNOWLEDGMENTS

The precise time of the birth of the idea of this book can be traced to about 11 a.m., December 18, 1991. That morning I was asked to address a group of officers from the Army, Navy, Marine Corps and Air Force as well as key officials from the Office of the Secretary of Defense about systems integration. Until then my usual presentations to similar groups covered the pending reductions in the Defense budget, the need to consolidate redundant facilities and the urgency of systems modernization. My fiscal logic, influence over expenditures, as well as reasoned arguments in favor of upgrading obsolete systems were usually impeccable. Yet, I knew that the audience would be primarily concerned with the organizational consequences of any proposals that I was ready to talk about. The minds of the audience would be full of apprehensions about the intrusion of headquarters civilians on the prerogatives of military services. The formally announced agenda would be only of secondary interest.

Two days before the presentation I informed my sponsors that instead of talking about *Corporate Information Management*, the latest Defense buzzword, I would address the age old issue of organizational politics. The title of my December 18 talk thus became *The Politics of Information Management*. The slides in that presentation included, for the first time, an outline of an *Information Constitution* and an illustration of *Layers of Information Governance*.

To my surprise, the reaction to my comparisons between the "architecture" of information systems and the structure of constitutional governance were favorable. Consolidation and the integration of systems did not necessarily abolish the jealously guarded autonomy. Defining the integration of systems in terms of layers of governance, applying a due process for reconciling differences, creating institutions for the separation of powers and delegating all powers not expressly retained to those who would benefit from systems, echoed already familiar themes that every American accepts as the foundation of a democratic society. When I got finished with the presentation, several officers suggested that the talk deserved a book of its own. In haste, I agreed to do it.

While I was fully engaged in my tasks at the Department of Defense, there was no time to write anything except an unending stream of memoranda, commentaries and presentation outlines. At night, I saved bits of ideas about information governance, as my work became increasingly involved in drafting policy proposals that would leave a legacy of sound information management principles. The greatest help, and by far the most informed criticism in this effort, came from my good friend Ron Knecht, then Special Assistant to my boss, Duane Andrews, Assistant Secretary of Defense. Ron is one of the foremost experts in the sublime art of drafting policies and decision memoranda which look at consequences beyond the horizon of current power plays and set in place conditions for future constructive advances. I owe much to Ron for these lessons.

Subsequently, I worked for a year with Rudy Alexander, an AT&T Corporate Vice President and head of the AT&T CIO transition team, in testing the commercial applicability of what I have learned about formally defining the respective roles of corporate staffs, operating units, standards and enterprise integration. I am indebted to Rudy and his able staff for the opportunity to debate and refine my original concepts of governance.

The dedicated writing of this book did not start until about a year ago, when I began condensing megabytes of accumulated material. Originally, I intended to write a concise book of less than 180 pages. It would be patterned after Niccolo Machiavelli's *The Prince*, completed in

1513 and the first Western book devoted to a realistic description of the practice of politics. Contrary to the unfairly maligned reputation of Machiavelli, I found the format and contents of his book of immense historical interest. Niccolo was a retired senior civil servant, who had served many princes of the state and church. After he retired he felt it would be useful to describe his experiences in realistic terms, instead of the then prevailing language clothed in vague abstractions.

Whether it was a difference in the document creation capacity between Machiavelli's goose quill pen and my Macintosh, or the enormous expansion in the complexity of governance between 15th century Florence and 20th century Washington, I could not imitate the brevity of *The Prince*. After condensing the notes into seven hundred pages of text, my children advised me to quit writing. As a compromise, I split my notes into a trilogy, of which this is the first installment. I apologize for the inexcusable length of this treatise, but much of it is due to the fact that the same people who counseled me to keep it short kept asking me to further clarify particularly controversial passages. As my final concession to readability, I yielded to my son Steven's insistence to get some illustrations into the book. I agreed to engage the services of John Klossner, whose work is found throughout the book and on the cover. Working with John was an absolute delight, because he readily caught some of the fine points suggested in the text.

To oblige the casual readers who likes simple summaries, this book has a different epigram placed at the beginning of each Chapter. That makes it theoretically possible to claim an understanding of the essence of this work in less than two minutes! However, limiting the number of epigrams was troublesome. About fifty more of them would have been omitted until my son-in-law, Peter, noticed that they would make an excellent Glossary. He suggested that I pattern it after the work of the American satirist, Ambrose Bierce (1842-1914), whose *Devil's Dictionary* amused several generations who did not always take the fancy jargon of politicians and preachers too literally. The Glossary is a further acknowledgment that all politics has an element of irony, where even learned expositions should never be taken as seriously as they are offered.

The following friends have contributed generously with their critique: Eric Boehm, Peter Dolan, Anne Eddy, Sam Harvey, Ron Knecht, Richard LaLonde, Barbara McNurlin, Mike Mestrovich, DuWayne Peterson, Dan Ryan, Steve Schanzer, Jim Schweitzer, Ed Sibley, Bob D. Steele, Herb Spirer, Owen Wormser and Mike Yoemans. Peter could be relied on to provide a different perspective on my categoric assertions. Anne was merciless in correcting my errant sentence structure and I regret she could only edit Part I. Barbara insisted that I shorten my long sentences. Ed despaired about my mixing a memoir with a more respectable academic text. Herb's sharp mind found several unforgivable inconsistencies. Owen checked out a number of my observations. Ron read the text three times and every time found something to correct. However, none of these critics can be blamed for any of the inadequacies, which are all mine.

On the production side, this home-made, home-produced and home-managed exemplar of a fully integrated cottage industry would not be possible without the involvement of my friend Enoch Sherman, who made sure that I could enter and exit the mysteries of the QuarkXPress desktop publishing software without wrecking the jumbled composition of text, footnotes, headers, footers, indexes and graphics. The principal editor of this book is my daughter, Vera, whose occasional exclamations of "Oh, Dad, how can you say that without statistical evidence?" have kept my ideas disciplined to reasonably provable assertions.

Everything that I have ever written has been with the blessing, discussion and support of my lifetime partner and friend of forty years, Mona. She is also the publisher of whatever I write, as well as conceiver of the best bunch of chattering and irreverent in-house information systems consultants any father could ever wish to have. I am grateful to Mona and to my children, Vera, Andrew, Steven and Eric — whom we all miss very much — for the love and stimulation they have given to me, which made all the explorations easy to do and exhilarating to write about. They are a constant reminder to me of the privilege of living in a free and prosperous society, the United States of America. It is a joy and blessing that has been denied to my parents, who perished exactly fifty years ago. It is to my parents' memory that I am dedicating this tribute to the continuation of the heritage of personal liberty and justice in an information-based future.

Paul A. Strassmann
New Canaan, Connecticut
October 1, 1994

INTRODUCTION

Computerization is the conduct of management by other means.

Why "Politics"?

The title of this book contains the word "politics" because this term describes, perhaps more aptly than any other, what information management is mostly about. Information management is the process by which those who set policy guide those who follow policy. Politics concerns power, and applying an understanding of power to the management of information technologies is not only appropriate, but timely. The proliferation of computers has now reached a stage of development where they are shaping relationships between suppliers and customers in business, as well as how public institutions relate to private organizations and individuals.

The fundamentals of politics were debated by the Greeks over twenty-five hundred years ago. The traditional forum for dealing with matters of policy has been the parliament, the council, laws and decrees. The medium has been the spoken and written word, restricted by geography, time delay and scope. What is different now are the enormous capabilities of communications technologies to address issues of public governance and business organization that have confounded mankind in how to organize for diversity while preserving unity where it matters:

- How may organizations allow for individuality when cooperation is an absolute necessity?
- How may groups promote local initiatives when the economy is global?
- How may organizations promote innovation without destroying the accumulation of past knowledge?
- How may individuals who do not have computer skills be protected in a world where power flows to those who control the sources of information?

This book deals with information governance within business organizations where the market economy prevails. I have little to say about managing information technologies where government controls the economic and social life. I am interested in making economically self-supporting organizations more viable. In most cases competitive service organizations are superior to government-enforced monopolies in getting people to cooperate, in delivering efficient results, and in creating customer value-added.

Scope

Information management seeks to answer the same questions as those raised in politics. The management of information defines how you organize. Politics defines how you govern. Organization is synonymous with power, and so is politics. Where control over information changes the alignment of power, information politics appears. Whether that turns out to be constructive is something that must be resolved through information management. Who gets what data and who converts data into information? Who balances the competing interests of leaders and followers? Who benefits from the ownership of information? Who controls the information technologies that are essential for running any enterprise? On what basis do you make information management decisions? Who will make them, why, how, and at what cost?

This book addresses questions that are especially of concern to an estimated two million general managers who have suddenly found themselves making decisions about the purpose, scope, costs, and characteristics of information systems. If this book merely discussed information technology, it would be of interest to less than hundred-thousand computer managers, but it does not limit itself only to that topic. With the proliferation of computers, information systems have become an inseparable element of all management acts. Only the technical aspects of such decisions can be safely delegated to computer and telecommunication specialists. Computerization is the conduct of management by other means, and therefore cannot be delegated, but must be retained as an essential managerial skill.

Managing information systems is primarily a matter of politics and only secondarily a matter of technology. Therefore, the purpose of this book is to view information management from the standpoint of information politics. I shall discuss how the introduction of computers alters the possession and distribution of information in public and commercial organizations. I will show how the inevitable conflicts that accompany computerization can be chanelled into productive outcomes.

Computers offer new options for creating, distributing, retrieving and preserving information. They make access to sources of knowledge easier, faster and for less cost than ever before. Computer networks now pass information directly to customers, employees, and citizens to make decisions previously requiring intermediaries. As result, old relationships are severed as new ones are created. Whenever that happens, there will be conflicts that require resolution if we are to take advantage of the enormous power of information technologies.

Content

In this book I will show how the introduction of computers has exacerbated intraorganizational friction between the information haves and the information have-nots. Such conflicts have always existed, but now they have become more dramatic because they strike at the livelihood of the single largest and most prosperous occupation al grouping of the postindustrial economy: the professionals, administrators and managers. I will describe how computerization, overhead reduction and organization politics have become inextricably intertwined. Automating information handling has hastened the disintegration of specialized functions which have been the basis for managing large and complex industries and continue to be the basis for running public sector enterprises. In many respects, the insertion of computers into the industrial-age organization is analogous to the introduction of firearms into the feudal fiefdoms. Cannons, once seen as a means for strengthening the power of feudal sovereigns, turned out to be the means for accelerating their demise.

In 83 percent of the 204 major U.S. corporations I recently examined, the budgets for information technology now exceed their economic value-added.[1] Meanwhile, information coordinators – executives, managers, expediters, accountants, lawyers, and analysts – have become the main consumers of information technology as a means to strengthen their intraorganizational power. Unless information technology is productively used to gaining external competitive advantages, it will become the cause of unemployment for an entire class of office workers. Competition from enterprises that have mastered the use of computers for achieving dominance will drive the laggards in information management out of business. To counter those threats, competitors who do not understand computers will react by engaging in a prolonged series of overhead cost cut-backs that may increase profits temporarily but will not restore the viability in an arena in which information has become a means for survival.

The economic theme of my message is that the costs of coordination can easily exceed the costs of production in a modern enterprise. The costs of administration are now, with rare exceptions, greater than the value-added by shareholders, greater than the costs of capital assets, and greater than the expenses for direct labor. Computerization has become the primary means for overhead reduction which results in diminished power for a large segment of the corporate bureaucracy. Putting such a power shift into effect cannot be successfully handled

---

1. This data will appear in my forthcoming book, *Business Alignment*, The Information Economics Press, 1995. Economic value-added is profit after taxes minus compensation for shareholder capital.

merely by installing advanced information technologies.[2] This is a change that must be addressed by redistributing control over access to information, and that is what makes it a political issue, often with security implications.

A Discipline of Information Politics

My purpose is to establish information politics, when practiced constructively, as a discipline that enables the transformation of the workplace from excessive managerial coordination to widespread empowerment of customers, suppliers and producers of services. I hope that studies in information politics will identify new ways how computerization can succeed without humiliating or destroying the self-respect of people who have been serving their organizations in the best way they know. Constructive information politics offers lessons in preserving the billions of hours of accumulated know-how that are suddenly economically dispensable.

Most importantly, a study of politics offers insights into the importance of the balance of power in all affairs. When you redistribute responsibility and control to others, you must also reallocate accountability and expertise for taking action. Information governance must possess a balanced symmetry between management practices and the design of information systems. When clear and simple principles support such a symmetry, all participants in the information community will be in a position to provide a constructive critique from their point of view. It is the lack of such a balance that causes problems, because each situation would then require a reinterpretation of complex regulations and precedents before anybody could act. The demise of the Spanish empire in America is largely attributable to such a lack of balance. Local governors who commanded enormous resources were nevertheless bound by vague and inconsistent regulations that required

---

2. Even the U.S. government has difficulties in this respect. The Information Infrastructure Task Force (IITF) of the National Performance Review program has published a report *Reengineering Government Through Information Technology*, Report to the Vice President of the United States, 1993. It places computerization ahead of policy. It favors the means ahead of the ends.

written approval from Spain before any action of significance could take place in the colonies.

My understanding of information politics originates in the historical tradition of always seeking successful evolutionary adaptation to changing conditions. I reject radical proposals to reap gains from computerization at the price of destroying what ultimately matters most to the survival of an enterprise – trust, commitment, and morale. I believe that the enhancement of productivity by means of information technologies is first and foremost a matter of improving the "governance" of institutions rather than technological gains. I will argue that information systems management, currently thought to be unique because of its heavy reliance on technological means, is only an extension of information politics and not an independent discipline of management.

The limit of the scope of any organization, whether public or private, lies in the organization's capacity to coordinate the utilization of its resources. Since effective coordination is what information management strives to achieve, mastering increasing diversity is a challenge that every information manager must meet. I will address how to improve the effectiveness of information management, with or without computers.

However, transforming hierarchical systems to cope with diversity through deliberate, gradual and structured organizational learning is not popular. Many information technologists have not abandoned the idea that standardization and centralized designs by experts will extend the viability of centrally planned information systems for a few more years. Lurking behind much of the networking, integrating, downsizing, reengineering, and client/server talk are unreformed technocrats who keep speaking the language of technology instead of the more controversial dialect of power politics. One of the purposes of this book is to help readers recognize computer-camouflaged centrist thinking dedicated to keeping unresponsive structures in place just a little bit longer.

Impeding innovation is one of the time-proven ways for postponing necessary change, at least temporarily. In due course, barriers to progress that offers an economic advantage will always break. The penalty for holding back the tide of advancement is paid by those who resist, without any adaptation, to the end. The recent wholesale dismissals of legions of managers and administrators is the result of the inattention by chief executives to the opportunities of making steady improvements in information management practices over the last twenty years.

Managers and administrators who do not learn while there is time to do so are the losers when the revolutionaries who offer radical technology solutions assault the established order. Such takeovers frequently occurred in companies when an entire generation of managers who ran tabulating equipment departments retired to make room for computer experts. Similarly, an entire generation of mainframe technical managers began to report to chief information officers with political skills when the scene shifted from technology push to customer pull. The same experiences will happen to the present chief information officers when their power base is contracted out to information services suppliers. This will happen when operating executives discover that information politics is so essential to their own jobs that they cannot delegate information management to a specialist any more.

I will propose making knowledge-based organizations more viable by adapting to information driven organizations the federalist thinking of Thomas Jefferson, James Madison and John Adams. This view suggests that the politics of information management concerns the balancing of conflicting interests somewhere between centralized control and decentralized execution. The management of information is then seen as a federated arrangement for cooperation by delegating the maximum authority over technology to those who actually need to use information so that they may remain competent managers.

Precursors

My first book, *Information Payoff – The Transformation of Work in the Electronic Age (1984),* explores the social and economic circumstances in which businesses will operate in the 1990s. I conclude that the payoff from the electronic age will come from improved ways for expanding what individuals can accomplish with the aid of computers, not from automating existing work. The main theme is that to make people more productive, work flow requires redesign. I further conclude that computer-assisted deployment of people based on customer needs will become the organizing principle for office work in the electronic age.

The second book, *The Business Value of Computers – An Executive's Guide (1990),* examines reasons why some organizations are more productive than others, irrespective of their spending on computers. It concludes that economic viability, defined in terms of management value-added, is the most appropriate measure by which to judge the effectiveness of computer investments. The book describes the consequences of applying capital-based ratios in evaluating the efficiency of enterprises. Return-on-assets or return-on-equity ratios are misleading for judging the value of the majority of enterprises where information management costs exceed the costs of capital. The main theme of the book is that the global economy is in transition from the industrial era, in which success has been measured by the productivity of capital, to an age in which enterprises should be evaluated by the effectiveness of their information-handling capabilities.

My recent involvement as the director of the U.S. Department of Defense, the world's largest computer complex, is not the reason this book is titled *The Politics of Information Management.* Readers expecting attention to the quirks of Washington personalities, will not find it here. Managing information systems for the U.S. Department of Defense is not an experience that you can duplicate in the private sector. The benefit to the readers lies in the lessons learned undertaking the most extensive business process redesign ever conceived.

The Value of *Information Politics*

Read this book as a sequel to the *The Business Value of Computers.* If management of information is indeed the key to the economic success for any enterprise in the twenty-first century, then you will find practical suggestions for deploying information resources. My hope is that you will highlight some of the paragraphs for subsequent follow-up. A measure of the utility of this book will be the number of paragraphs you will mark for further action. I trust you will find a few noteworthy nuggets that will increase your worth to those who expect from you an awareness of what information management can accomplish in making people more effective.

PART I

GOVERNANCE

*Laws and institutions must go hand in hand
with the progress of the human mind*

Thomas Jefferson, 1816.

I

WHAT IS POLICY?

Policy is what you do, not what you say or write.

Policy (from Greek, to display, to make known) defines organization, power, and accountability. As a result, in government, as well as in business, policy-makers are distinguished from policy-followers by influence, privilege and rank.

Corporate policies are the business equivalent of public law. They define acceptable conduct of groups and individuals. They set norms that shape orderly relationships. Much of the politics within organizations arises from a desire to influence the formulation and promulgation of policy. Organizational politics makes it necessary to establish an orderly process for the establishment of policies so that a board, executive committee or corporate staff may assert control over investment in information systems by legitimate means.

Using Policy

Few organizations possess an understandable collection of guidelines to constructively channel the conflicts that occur when information must be shared across business functions and the distribution rules are absent or unclear. Every action involving the distribution of authority over computer systems implies a policy decision, whether or not it is recorded on paper. For example, policy is implicit if there are no restrictions about purchasing a microcomputer from a mail-order house, loading it with database software and generating data for widespread

3

distribution. Policy is implicit if users cannot alter what is seen on a screen unless central staff make the changes. Policy is also implicit if the general manager of a billion dollar business can purchase several five-thousand-dollar devices only after filling out pages of forms and then having to wait several months for approval.

Ultimately, policy is not what one writes but what the followers actually do. The sole purpose of conceiving and publishing policies is "to display, to make known" guidelines to acceptable conduct what people can be expected to follow. Individuals cannot arbitrarily make up their own rules if they wish to live in an orderly community. Similarly, individuals or departments cannot have unlimited discretion to interpret information management policies unless the corporation wishes to deliberately foster disorder.[3] Unrestrained privilege to do as one pleases has a price in inhibiting cooperation or taking advantage of specialization.

Figure 1.1 Policy Without Governance

---

3. There are popular thinkers who advocate such discretion. See Tom Peters, *Thriving on Chaos: Handbook for a Management Revolution*, (New York: Alfred A. Knopf, Inc., 1987).

Where there are no corporate policies to guide information management, computer executives will be in peril when making long-term technology choices. Policy decisions are essential before one can embark on technical designs that give information systems a long life. Coming up with an information policy is comparable to drafting a constitution that protects society from the opportunistic acts of a transient administration.

In this book, I distinguish management policies from technology policies. Each type of policy requires different approaches in formulation and implementation. Management policy-making takes precedence over technical policy matters; this is therefore my principal focus.

Avoiding Policy-Making

Top corporate executives traditionally have taken the position that information management policy is a matter for technical experts to take care of. If executives do not trust their own experts, which is too frequently the case, they hire consultants presumed to be unbiased. By doing so, they are practicing policy-making avoidance because policy is the top executives' first and foremost responsibility.

Computer executives usually think that developing information management policies is the same as publishing a company's information strategy plan. I have reviewed dozens of such documents in recent years. These plans set forth technology directions, not governance policies that could solve some of the fundamental conflicts that keep obstructing progress. Resolving policy conflicts is too sensitive a matter for exclusive handling by the technical establishment. Information technology strategy plans in the absence of business policies are symptoms of policy-making avoidance by top executive management.

Academics tend to shun this topic because it is too difficult to collect research data about policy-making that meet the publishing criteria of academic journals. Occasionally, consultants circulate opinion surveys that touch on this topic inconclusively. I do not trust the validity of such surveys. It is foolish to expect that chief executives officer of public corporations would be willing to admit to dissent within their own ranks. It is unrealistic to expect them to talk candidly about their internal conflicts with complete strangers. It is naive to expect some-

one to document their doubts by filling out a questionnaire that could become a quotable record. There is no conceivable gain to an executive in responding to surveys that could be later embarrassing. Opinion surveys are not fact; they are a reflection of what someone wishes others to believe. Chief executive officers, and particularly chief information officers who are most likely be looking for new jobs soon, have every reason to respond to questionnaires in the most self-serving terms they can possibly claim.

Lawyers avoid giving policy-making advice and dealing with intraorganizational conflict unless it involves potential litigation. The absence of clear policy is useful in a legal defense because it gives ample room to obfuscating issues. Perhaps exposure to potential litigation explains why clear information policy has so few proponents. Lawyers for the for a complaining party, and especially for the government, have been known to cite violations of the defendant's own internal policies as evidence of managerial malfeasance.

The only professionals who insist on written policies are auditors, who require text against which to cite violations. The potential discomfort resulting from handing a scourge the auditors, like threats of congressional hearings, gives computer executives every incentive to keep policy statements as ambiguous as possible.

As a result of abdicating policy-making, avoiding or ignoring research, minimizing legal exposure, and confusing the auditors, the executives charged with managing information end up without meaningful guidelines for their missions. Avoidance for the purposes of self-defense becomes a self-made trap.

Politics vs. Policy

Politics is the art of the feasible. When policy pronouncements vacillate between conflicting agendas, management must be supremely skillful or it will surely fail to carry out its responsibilities. Politics is also the art of dealing with realities that contradict lofty policy pronouncements, such as the expansive "visions" which can emanate from top executives.[4] Politics is what you live by if you are the manager who must implement these sometimes flaky visions, without adequate resources to deliver what the higher-ups have already promised to the public.

Policy is the capacity of top management to explain what is an attainable goal and to make sure that implementation will occur. Policy, especially if translated into control over budgets, is the best means of resolving conflicts between the espoused values of the corporation and the motives of business units or individuals striving to achieve whatever they believe is right whether for the corporate good or for themselves. In the absence of policy, business units and individuals will divert energies from supporting stated corporate goals to improvising whatever they think is best.

Much of the success of information policy rests on its clarity. Computer staff can safely deliver superior results only if they are executing an unambiguous information policy. Fuzzy objectives and ill-defined means lead to confused execution. Under such conditions it may be a matter of luck by blundering into success if what is delivered matches what management alleges that they always wanted.

Policy and Success

To manage information successfully, policy makers must set forth explicit principles for information governance and secure cooperation by engaging everyone in a discussion as to their implications. Full disclosure of the rules for governing must indicate who will deliver what results and how policy will be enforced.

While discussing the proposed policies, all managers must come to understand how the policies will affect their roles and responsibilities. Therefore, policy pronouncements should be made only after allowing for adequate time and consideration, especially if they publicize the rules

---

4. Twenty five years ago, top executives of Xerox made widely advertised pronouncements that they would pioneer an all-encompassing "architecture of information" for managing office work. Hardly anything was ever delivered by Xerox. Current efforts to make the information highway all things to all communication needs extends far beyond that which can be organized by the federal government.

of information governance. Despite many ambiguities and compromises, one reason the U.S. constitutional principles have endured so well is that the lengthy debates of the Constitutional Convention served as the civic forum for laying the foundations for the new republic.

When examining the consultants' current polls about the anxieties of information technology managers, one discovers that their main worry is their capacity to link what they actually do to what their enterprise needs. In the absence of policy-based governance, organizations will operate as an unruly collection of factions that pull in opposing directions. No wonder that computer people, who thrive on formally structured statements, will hesitate to commit themselves to an action plan under such conditions. Out of desperation, and often out of ambition, they may decide to become corporate policy makers instead of sticking to their traditional roles.

Is it possible for information technology managers to make sound corporate policy on their own? I believe that is neither feasible nor advisable, in the long run. Corporate policy setting takes place in the executive suite. Policy is the outcome of a bargaining process among those who wield power, such as what occurs during the allocation of budgets across the entire organization. Negotiations about budgets and organization charts must be settled before discussions can begin about how the deployment of information technologies can come into play.

2

FRAMEWORK

Control of the sources of information is the essence of all managerial power.

Information politics, which to me means the same as information governance, is part of a much larger scheme whose purpose should be to deliver superior business results. As outlined in Figure 2.1, information technology and information management are supporting elements of business planning, functional planning and productivity planning, not something apart:

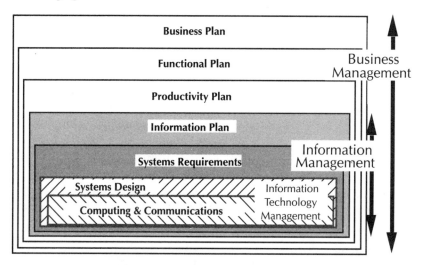

Figure 2.1 Elements of Information Management

Information management only has value within the context of business management. You cannot justify information management as an isolated activity. The benefits of investments in information technology can be assessed only as seen from the standpoint of a business plan.

Many consultants delight in compiling elaborate checklists of best information management practices on the basis of intellectually attractive concepts. Analysts then assign points for compliance with each prescribed practice on the checklist. The points are added to come up with a measure of information management excellence. I do not think that such ratings are of much use unless you first accumulate evidence whether or not a particular business management practice is frequently found in businesses that show exceptional economic success over an extended time. The highest rated information systems establishment will be a failure if business management is faulty.

Information Politics, an Element of Information Management

The topic of information politics covers the goals, policies, practices and organizational ideas about how to strengthen local decisions while the entire enterprise cooperates for information superiority.

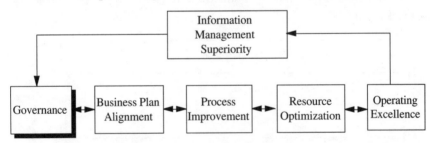

Figure 2.2 Elements of Information Superiority

I place governance – information politics – ahead of all other attributes of information management, because if you do not get that right everything else will not make up for this fundamental flaw. Politics is not only a way to exercise authority, but it is also an art for achieving corporate consensus.

To make information politics equally applicable to the commercial and public sectors, I define it as the institutionalization of a governance process that guides how individuals and groups cooperate. Without a general consensus about the principles and policies of who does what, when and how, you cannot create a foundation on which to construct information superiority. If you do not have a generally accepted understanding of relationships and do not possess the means for resolving disputes, most of energies will be diverted to internal conflicts instead of coping with external challenges.

This book will devote most of its text to the governance element of information management. It will explore topics which have not yet received adequate attention in books or articles that deal with information management issues. It recognizes that politics is a more popular term than governance, although I will be using these terms interchangeably. I will also try to fill in gaps in understanding how the introduction of computers has sown discord among managerial staffs who previously attended to other matters. Contention over control of computers deserves thorough discussion, especially because computers are now treated by employees as personal possessions. Seizing control over computers has captured the attention of every corporate bureaucrat even though such efforts have placed them into direct conflict with everyone. I will illustrate where the cmotional attachment of employees to their computers can be chanelled into constructive directions.

Business Plan Alignment

Following governance, the next step in the sequence shown in Figure 2.2 of attaining information superiority is the alignment of information management with the business plan. Without such congruence, the economic viability of all information systems plans will always remain questionable. The desired outcome of the alignment process is the identification of any gaps and inconsistencies that would occur if the planned computer projects go on without changes in direction. Alignment also calls for the identification of those changes in policy that could potentially generate the greatest economic gains.

The sequel to this book, *Business Alignment*, is well on its way to completion. It will contain answers to the following questions:

- Does information technology improve corporate economic performance?

- How do executives know if information technologies are deployed efficiently and effectively?
- What methods ensure that information technology projects are deployed for maximum gains?
- Should management increase or decrease the information technology budget?

Analyses presented in this sequel benefit from the recent widespread acceptance by financial analysts of Economic Value-Added (EVA) as the appropriate measure of business performance.[5] EVA is computationally identical to Management Value-Added, which is the numerator of the *Return-on-Management*™ productivity ratio discussed in *The Business Value of Computers.* The conceptual difficulty that many executives had in accepting Management Value-Added was addressed by the firm of Stern Stewart & Co., who have widely promoted and popularized this concept. Annually they publish a computation of EVA values for the top 1,000 U.S. corporations.[6]

Whereas *The Business Value of Computers* showed results based on private data, *Business Alignment*, will disclose the *Information Productivity*™ ratios for over 200 U.S. corporations.[7]

Implementation Matters

Much of the distrust and disappointment with information technology originates in a widespread preoccupation with the technical details of implementation. These matters include process improvement, resource optimization, project planning, and technical operations of data centers and networks. Implementation problems are easier to understand because their impact is immediately visible. The technical details of

---

5. G.B. Stewart, *The Quest for Value*, Harper Business, 1991. The book thoroughly discusses why neither profit, earnings per share, return on investments, nor revenue growth are valid measures of business performance. This conclusion was also the central theme in my book *The Business Value of Computers*, The Information Economics Press, 1990.

6. For further details see Stern Stewart Management Services, *Performance 1000 Database Package*, New York, 1993.

7. *Information Productivity*™ is an approximation of the *Return-on-Management*™ ratio.

implementation receive management attention, especially in cases of failure, when everyone can become an expert.

Vendors, the trade press, consultants and university computer science departments find it more rewarding to address implementation matters. Nevertheless, recent surveys of information systems managers reveal an increasing awareness that something may be amiss not with implementation but with the direction that information management is taking.[8]

The greatest obstacle to achieving information superiority is the practice of making frequent radical changes in matters of business governance and alignment, sometimes annually. Improvising what ought to be a long-term commitment every time there is a revision in the organization chart dissipates resources. This destroys the confidence of those engaged in implementation. When goals, policies, and standards are volatile, you cannot expect your people to make a determined effort to get something accomplished. Uncertain leaders will have uncertain followers.

I do not belittle the importance of good tactics and sound implementation. Only after establishing the long-lasting policies that shape value-creation and asset-preservation is it possible to focus on the three tactical tasks of process improvement, resource optimization, and operational excellence.

Superior strategies may deliver poor results if the implementation is poor. However, sound implementation cannot prevent failure when the strategies are flawed. Faulty strategies will persist for a long time, because they become deeply rooted in habit, culture and power structure. Defining governance and alignment – the strategic processes – therefore must always take precedence in all information management planning, because defective tactics are easier to fix. Many strategic elements will influence the ways in which an enterprise benefits from

---

8. A June 1993 *Dataquest* mail survey of 780 information systems managers on five continents shows that a large number listed "improve customer focus" in better serving the business needs of their respective organizations as their top 1993–1996 goal.

information management. The most difficult of these is establishing information governance policies.

3

DEFINITIONS

Only people can be productive, not computers.

Before we can establish information policies, we must first define their underlying concepts. The terms most frequently confused are information management, information systems, and information technology. These terms are not interchangeable, and the policies addressing each of them are different. Figure 3.1 shows the context of these terms.

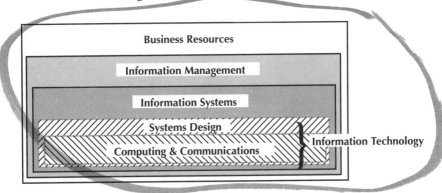

Figure 3.1 The Context of Information Management

Information Management

I take a broad view of information management. The generally accepted approach identifies it as something that relates only to computers. If you accept that view, you will miss perhaps as much as 80 percent of the

expenses used in coordinating information. Information management is an activity that does not depend entirely on computers. Before exploring the uses of information technologies on business missions, such as increasing sales or expanding market share, you must be able to demonstrate that your information management is effective. There is no point in computerizing ineffectiveness.

The purpose of information management is to allocate, simplify, reduce costs, increase effectiveness and boost the quality of all information processes, whether or not they are automated. Information management includes coordinating suppliers, employees, and customers in tasks including managing, training, counseling, coordinating, recording, and reporting. It excludes the physical production, handling and delivery of goods or services to paying customers.[9]

Information management cost is mostly made up of payroll, allocated benefits, and occupancy charges of people who are not directly involved in the production and delivery of goods and services to paying customers. Often it carries the designation "overhead." The largest amount of activity consists of preparing and attending meetings. In addition to employee time, information management includes all purchases that support overhead labor, such as telephones, computers, magazine subscriptions, legal services, and travel expenses to meetings and educational conferences.

Once information management costs are removed from all other organizational expenses, what remains are direct costs incurred in delivering products and services to customers. Information management expenses arise from activities that customers cannot readily identify as providing value-added. That is why information management expenses are also known as indirect expenses.

This definition is much broader than that used in most organizations. It includes every person classified as an information worker. It also covers part of the activity of production and service workers when they are engaged in work that is of no direct value to a paying customer,

---

9. In the information services business, resources consumed while generating revenues are direct costs, not information management costs.

such as filling out forms and attending training sessions. A manufacturing firm may have over half of its value-added tied up in information management.

Companies and public-sector organizations do not disclose their information management or overhead expenses because they fear that the costs may reflect poorly on their management. They are probably right in being defensive, since these costs invariably exceed profits, shareholder value-added, or economic value-added. In many cases, I find it possible to estimate these costs by looking at the accounting "Sales, General and Administrative" category [S.G.&A.] in published financial statements. This number understates true overhead costs, especially if plant, branch and divisional overhead are included in the cost of sales, but it provides useful insights nevertheless.

Institutions, especially those which are bureaucratic, tend to label overhead activities with prestigious designations, such as "strategic information visioning." Their objective is to acquire the broadest franchise for claiming the widest possible territory.[10] The federal government recently announced information resource management policies, laws and regulations with the intent of streamlining bureaucracy regardless of form, content or technology. Not surprisingly, the new information resource executives turned out to be computer managers in a new disguise. They preside over shrinking hardware budgets, manage contracts and hold onto control of mainframe computers while looking for ways to expand their administrative roles.

Information management must be pursued under a deliberate plan. Since it is one of the pillars of competitive superiority, such a plan must encompass all information-handling, knowledge preservation, communications and learning functions. Such a definition makes information management synonymous with the practice of business management. Confusing information management with information technology is the primary reason why a comprehensive information

---

10. That is how simplification becomes business process reengineering, budget cutting turns into reinventing the government, some clerks are renamed senior executive occupational requirements analysts, and undertakers are now bereavement counselors.

management design that integrates overhead activities with those that serve customers is rare. As long as information management is not seen as an essential part of the art of management, a chief executive officer (CEO) may find it attractive to abdicate this responsibility to technical specialists. Such neglect explains better than any other rationalization why computers do not always deliver the expected results.

Executive Ownership

Information management is what binds an enterprise together. It makes possible the coordination of diverse actions to outsmart and outrun competitors. Whether such coordination occurs by computer, mail or messenger pigeon is only a matter of relative cost advantages and speed. The CEO must ensure that information management is pervasive and inseparable from all other managerial functions. Competent information management is essential not just for growth but also for survival. It is a key prerequisite to attaining competitive excellence, regardless of the type of business, geography or culture.

Executives should not avoid the responsibility for information management by renting, contracting, outsourcing, subletting or delegating it to suppliers or consultants. Information management is intrinsic to exercising the powers of executive management. It is, in fact, one of the essential ingredients of their leadership roles.

You may rent, contract for, outsource, sublet, license, and delegate information technology but not information management. You can manage with artificial limbs, kidney dialysis, or a heart transplant but not without your own native-grown brain.

Delegation

The worst thing a CEO can do is to hire a chief information officer (CIO) with the intention of delegating responsibility for information management to an expert. This is an abdication of essential powers because information management is inseparable from the essence of every managerial act. Suppliers can deliver many elements of information system and technology support services, especially if the home-grown solutions are uneconomic. The accountability for information management should not ever be passed on to anyone who is not also responsible for customer care and for financial performance.

Information management is similar to personnel management. You can hire a personnel vice president to administer the formal personnel processes. But you should never allow the personnel department to take over from operating managers the responsibility for acquiring, motivating, developing, promoting and firing people. The CIO should be someone who has a thorough understanding of how the enterprise works. Give to him or her the responsibility for making sure that enterprise information systems are effective and efficient. But, do not expect the CIO to pick where and how to apply information systems. That is a decision only general management is qualified to make.

Information Systems

One of the primary objectives of enterprise-wide information systems management is to secure the integration, reliability and security of all information processes. Information systems encompass all information processes that depend on a formal procedure for completion. For example, a clerk recording inventory on a clipboard is part of an information system. A truck dispatcher talking with a driver over the radio about schedules is an element of an information system. I did not mention computers in these examples because information systems do not necessarily require computers. Some of the most effective information systems are not automated, such as a bookie keeping track of several hundred bets and payoffs on slips of paper. Egyptian scribes had elaborate information systems in place five thousand years ago.

Information systems include all personnel, facilities and services associated with the creation, processing and distribution of information following a prescribed procedure, without necessarily applying any computers. Information systems expenses definitely include the costs of those who operate computer devices, including the time of anyone who creates inputs, receives outputs, or corrects errors. A system possesses structure, procedures, rules, and routines. In the absence of those attributes, any other information activity is merely an element of other information management costs.

Information systems costs also encompass the cost of personnel engaged in managing, communicating, training, counseling, coordinating, recording, processing and reporting information processed by formally established procedures. Formally established channels of information include: office automation, data collection, data entry, automatic and direct capture of information products or information services from factory, process control, communications switching systems, and research-and-development support systems. For the sake of emphasis let me repeat that all training costs, including the time to correct errors associated in any way with systematized work, should be included in the costs of information systems. Often these costs will exceed the expenses for information technology. Never exclude the consideration of these elements when making an evaluation of the life-cycle costs for information systems. Improved training and quality may be more important than any advantages gained from advanced technology.

The definition of information systems excludes all unstructured informal activities such as meetings, counseling, presentations, coordination, reading mail and reports, speaking on the phone, and casual discussion, because these are part of general information management. For the same reason, it excludes the operation of devices, such as: copiers, duplicators, typewriters, electric pencil sharpeners, facsimile machines, answering devices, voice telephones and mail room devices unless they are elements in a systematic workflow sequence.

Information Technology

Information technology includes everything in support of information systems, such as: computer operations, network operations, information retrieval services, automated library services, programming, and all voice, data, video and radio telecommunications. It also involves systems design that includes systems engineering, database design and configuration management. The scope of information technology also extends to commercial information services, such as contract programming, software purchases, maintenance services, and consulting services.

Some of the most severe damage to the smooth functioning of a modern firm arise from a firm's inability to manage information technology discontinuities and incompatibilities. In the absence of enterprise-wide technical integration, messages sent by facsimile will be inaccessible to computers, mail received by post will get lost within filing cabinets, and electronic mail will not reach those who need it. Production units will find out about engineering changes only after they order obsolete parts. Factory floor statistics will not match corporate summary numbers. Top management will never hear why key customers run to the competition. From today on, what matters is not so much the choice of information technologies as the capacity to manage the integration of its enormous diversity.

Stealth Technology

A special form of information technology is its "stealth" activity. As microcomputers and local networks proliferate, we find that a large number of people otherwise classified as financial analysts, traffic expediters, secretaries, special assistants, and even "special specialists" function as software installers, local-area network troubleshooters, hotshot programmers, or widely sought after computer gurus who deliver answers quickly without bothering with project authorizations. The size of this population is anybody's guess. Estimates vary, but I have never heard of one that is less than 20 percent of the official information technology workforce.

Stealth information technology personnel receive much respect and are eagerly supported and requested during budget exercises. Their value is similar to the ballast on balloons. Such people are dismissed first when there are mandatory head-count cuts. When only long-tenure and high level personnel remain, engineers and administrators find themselves doing those jobs, including becoming their own secretaries.

Technology Management Roles

One of the most frequent mistakes made by information technology executives is in misunderstanding the boundaries within which they operate. The CIO usually receives unquestionable jurisdiction over information technology. Often CIOs also have the responsibility for delivering information systems projects. They must see to it that such projects go well, although the CIOs' roles are unclear when it comes to responsibility for startup and full implementation. Planning and budgeting for training and security - some of the largest expense items - is usually poor; this gives rise to disputes over when information technology makes the transition to information management.

Trouble arises when the CIO intrudes on operating management prerogatives over matters related to information management. Without clearly understood rules of governance, the CIO will fall into a trap from which escape is possible only by promotion into the ranks of operating executives or, more often, into the ranks of the temporarily unemployed. That is why definitions are an essential underpinning of all governance, because they are the basis for describing the scope of jobs that can be accomplished by competent people. Jobs that escape definition call for a miracle, forgetfulness, or just plain fraud for anyone to demonstrate success.

4

ROLES

Politics is the art of getting and retaining power.

Defined organizational relationships make it possible for an information systems executive to succeed in doing his job. Active involvement of top corporate executives in information policy-making elevates the politics of managing information technology from squabbles to purposeful design. Good policy-making gives the information manager a fair chance of surviving, and his only chance of excelling in the delivery of expected results.

Information Effectiveness

After more than a decade of studying a large number of companies, I could not find any direct relationship between shareholder returns and the amount a firm spends on information technology.[11] This discovery led to the conclusion that although computers were important, managerial competence in balancing all resources ultimately determined if computers provided any benefits. Management comes always first, and technology only second whenever one finds a dysfunctional information systems organization. Exceptionally effective applications of computers do not depend entirely on the level of expense, technical sophistication, degree of innovation, or brilliance of the systems staff. What matters is

---

11. P.A. Strassmann, *The Business Value of Computers*, Chapter 7.

not the technology, but how it is applied. Winning companies concentrate their information resources on tasks that directly affect value-added for which customers are willing to pay a premium price. Companies that dedicate their information resources principally to internal coordination and control instead of deployment for the benefit of external customers do not realize the benefits, regardless of the technical excellence of their applications.

A sensible approach to evaluating the information effectiveness of a company should never start by examining data centers or checking the elegance of the computer software. It should begin by asking what share of the budget supports services that customers recognize as value-added. In other words, the test of information excellence is to determine what the Marine Corps calls the "tooth-to-tail ratio." When you go off to war, what is critical is the relative power of your "teeth" compared with your "tail," which is overhead.[12]

Any activity is amenable to such evaluation. For instance, take a ubiquitous procedure such as handling travel. What is the ratio of total travel expenses to the total cost of authorizing travel and approving expense reports? It just happens that the Department of Defense has numbers on this. "We spend about $2 billion on travel each year...and another $2.4 billion processing the travel orders."[13] That is a tooth-to-tail ratio of 0.83. Based on my research findings, I expect well managed organizations to show that ratio to be anywhere from 8 to 20. It appears that there are about 3,900 DoD clerks making sure that nobody who sleeps in their rented station wagon instead of a hotel will charge the government for accommodations.

You do not improve information effectiveness by programming computers to check useless procedures. A basic principle of good information policy is to make clear that operating managers, not the chief information executive, are accountable for their own information effec-

---

12. The current composition of the Russian army makes it less threatening as a conventional force because when they cut their headcount by 60 percent they kept most of the officers and every administrator. They have more than one officer and administrator for every soldier.

13. Lt. Gen. Thomas McInerney, head of the Defense National Performance Review study, as quoted in *Federal Computer Week*, April 11, 1994, p.42

tiveness. This idea may appear so obvious that it does not need restating. Yet, in large organizations, the question of who is responsible for information management and who is responsible for information technology are often mixed up. Such confusion is most common when the chief information executive (CIO) aspires to assume the leadership roles for improving everybody's work flow.

Major changes in information management can be implemented successfully only by those who have direct responsibility for operating results. Establishing the dividing line between information management and information technology should be the first on the agenda for defining workable roles and responsibilities.

Unstable Leadership

Reports about the comings and goings of top information executives appear weekly in the computer trade press. The job tenure of a CIO is short these days, with an average time on the job estimated by a number of consulting surveys at less than three years. Computer executives with national recognition often lose their jobs and end up with another firm that was searching for someone with a completely different orientation towards computers. Because CEOs keep changing what they consider important, unemployment among technically competent chief computer executives is relatively rare. Experts with technical expertise usually take turns in the CIO seat with people known for their reputations as control-minded administrators. Salaries escalate after each round because the same small pool of talent is merely being swapped around.

The outcasts in autumn become the heroes of spring. You surely know instances where evicted exiles turned out to be the princes of another executive team. There are probably more hero-to-outcast and outcast-to-hero tales about computer executives than in any other professional occupation.[14] Perhaps the only exception to this is the fate of

---

14. A reviewer of this passage asked what clauses would I advise a prospective CIO to seek in an employment contract. Established governance rules are as good a safeguard as anything that a lawyer could draft for a job description.

political appointees after a change in the party controlling the White House.

Figure 4.1 Unpredictable Leadership

Unstable leadership in the information management function reflects more on the inability of top management to articulate a coherent information policy than on the qualification of whoever occupies the position of the CIO. For this reason, a principal concern when drafting an information policy should be its expected stability and long-term consistency.

Policies that take a relatively short two- to four-year view are accommodations, not rules of governance. Unless top executives are willing to invest the effort to decide how they wish to shape the fundamental roles of information governance for at least a decade ahead, they will be almost certainly wasting the careers of at least three CIOs in rapid succession.

Political Realities

The new information executive who attempts to take over information management policy-making will run into ambushes manned by long-tenured corporate executives or permanent civil servants who are skilled in guessing where the leadership may be heading. Good, explicit policy-making sanctioned by the executive committee provides a new information executive with protection such as air and artillery cover does for a force that is landing on a beach under hostile fire. When the new incumbent in the CIO position becomes isolated, he must have policy cover or he will get blasted away.

Information executives must have the sanction of top management policy before setting in motion programs that will support business needs. Information executives should not seek inspiration from the latest technological fad or from magazine headlines, but track with care the political mandates emanating from the top of the organization, provided that they reflect the realities of the approved business plans.

It is regrettable that the pace of information technology over the last ten years has become inhibited not because of a lack of its capabilities but because of intramural skirmishes between computer system personnel arguing the merits of centralization versus decentralization, and between computer technicians and their customers. Much of this infighting took place because of the absence of coherent corporate information policies. The policy vacuum explains much of the failure in productivity growth that should have been attributable to information technologies. Assets that should have been converted into productivity were ground up in aborted intraorganizational conflicts.

The Onlookers

Top operating executives, unsure of their roles in an area where they had little prior experience, have shown a tendency to observe passively the intramural jockeying between CIOs and everyone else. Chairmen and presidents, mayors and governors, chiefs of staff and department heads have traditionally not assumed what should have been one of their central roles, namely, asserting control over information policy-making.

LIVESTOCK
DIRECTIONAL
CONSULTANT

REGIONAL GRASSLAND
ENGINEER

REGIONAL LIVESTOCK
OPERATIONS AND ANALYSIS
MANAGER

Figure 4.2 Clear Roles and Responsibilities

Essentially, all management is information management. Whether management executes it with computers or by other means is irrelevant. A policy vacuum at the top will create conditions where even projects of demonstrable competitive merit will linger indefinitely without purpose or direction.

A Long View

The principles that govern the creation, dissemination and sharing of information determine how every civilization functions. One way to understand the historical limitation on social progress is to study the possession and distribution of knowledge under pharaohs, shahs, emperors, kings, popes and presidents. What becomes apparent is that policies that inhibit the spread of knowledge set the limits of how far a society can advance.

Every society depends on cooperation for prosperity and the accumulation of wealth. Only by collaborating internally and with other organizations does productivity growth become possible. Cooperation springs forth from sharing of information, which itself requires open channels of communication that are free of political inhibitions.[15]

Information is the vehicle by which an organization shares common goals with its employees, customers, and suppliers. Information is the means for managing the missions of an enterprise. Top executives must articulate shared goals because that is the basis of their legitimacy. The responsibility of leaders to be also information managers is inescapable. When it comes to guiding the uses of the most revolutionary tool ever developed for getting people to work together, the obligation to declare information policies becomes a matter of highest priority.

---

15. The word communication comes from the Latin communis, which means sharing. This has nothing to do with communism, an ideology that has perfected some of the most destructive forms of information denial.

5

Making Policy

Policy is to management what law is to governance.

The political aspects of an information policy will determine how an organization's information technology programs will succeed. To that end, it is necessary to acknowledge the political dimensions of information technology by fitting it into a corporation's existing business planning process. Often this means repackaging technical proposals into a form that looks like material that the decision-makers always have been accustomed to seeing. Information technology managers must learn to give up parading technical elegance if the Board of Directors is interested primarily in financial results and potential liability exposure.

If a corporation allows each operating unit to chase after customers without coordination, the use of a standard data dictionary will have little value because it will not alter how the individual businesses will operate in the marketplace. If local tellers and loan officers do not do anything other than enter data into standard applications, information technology managers need not propose distributing computing capacity, because there will be no need for local personnel to use it for processing their own information. Fit the technology to the reality of politics, not *vice versa*.

Priorities

Information policy-making should receive adequate attention from top management to contain organizational politics within constructive channels. Explicit policy-making will not happen unless it is initiated by the CEO and has a stated purpose, such as delivery of a governance document — an information "constitution." In the absence of that, your policies will arrive by default, which is typically a solution favored by managers who do not add economic value to an enterprise. Ambiguity in policy favors the power of the entrenched bureaucrats, because everyone has to keep running back to them for an interpretation of what to do next.

Policy-making is too important to be delegated to *ad hoc* negotiations in committees and task forces, because that can only lead to acrimonious exchanges in the absence of clear guidelines. In internal conflicts the wounded ones have ways of inflicting vengeance whenever their turn comes during another reorganization. There is a Washington saying that "friends come and go, but enemies accumulate, because they have longer memories."

In the absence of clear rules of governance, top executives and key managers will divert much attention to waging civil wars instead of concentrating on fighting competitors. The CEO owes to all managers minimal ambiguity in establishing information management principles. As one of the principal responsibilities, the CEO must answer the classic questions about the fundamentals of governance: How do we balance separate and often competing goals and values within our organization? How may we make the trade-offs and on what basis?

Policy Innovation

It is encouraging is to see that eventually — which is sometimes longer than one can wait — organizations end up making the right moves, though they were originally met with overwhelming resistance. If the assessment of a competitive situation is realistic, an organization will ultimately come around and implement what was proposed, even though it will now be labeled as novel and politically correct. There is no escape from the pressures of the marketplace, where customers increasingly value information-rich services in competitive contests. Therefore, projects that first take care of customers will prevail, even though the originators may not be around to receive the credit. For this reason, it is better to introduce innovation experimentally, gradually, and wherever local conditions are ripe to try innovation on a small scale, rather than make a direct attack on an entrenched opposition.

In any business, all extraordinary gains originate from long term innovative ventures. It is good information policy to have a set of rules that are unusually permissive to innovation. A society that exiles its innovators wastes its most precious assets. However, there is another aspect to such loss. Innovators are usually impatient and loath to accept the argument that all fundamental changes require a reasonably long time to gestate. Therefore, one of the objectives of good policy-making is to create conditions that protect, over a long term, people dedicated to seeking new ventures instead of pursuing only opportunistic solutions.

Conflict Resolution

As noted earlier, much of the energy that could be translated into productivity gains becomes fuel for internal contests over the control of computers. The political maneuvers practiced in these collisions would be understandable to any courtier in a medieval kingdom. In the last thirty years it has been common to see projects and careers evaporate when the new and potentially powerful players in the organization — the information executives — became engaged in intramural warfare for positions of influence. Without a policy to guide ways to resolve such conflicts, much valuable talent goes to waste. It is the role of information governance to anticipate conflict and delineate boundaries beyond which transgressions of corporate policy will not be tolerated.

Economics and Politics

Medieval feudalism rested on two joining pyramids of church and state, consisting of an array of lords, abbots, barons, bishops, dukes and squires, with loose rules defining their prerogatives. Presiding over all was the emperor or the pope, each with contested claims to privilege and might. Business initiatives, when allowed, were a matter for local negotiation, which made them subject to unpredictable vetoes from conflicting jurisdictions.[16] With the rise of industrialization, there was an increase in interdependence between government and business, which in turn gave rise to the growing power of the national state pursuing commerce and industry. The locally autonomous feudal fiefdoms collapsed because the local potentates could not compete against the financial strength of large aggregations of commerce.

There are many similarities between the rise and collapse of feudalism and the patterns of information management in large enterprises. Just as in medieval times, the mainframe feudal lords have been unable to cope with huge increases in demand for services when minicomputers and microcomputers showed up. Such analogies are useful because they imply that, in due course, every untenable political position, regardless of how powerful, is vulnerable to destruction by economic forces that do not tolerate gross inefficiencies for long. Anyone who experiments with information politics must understand that it is impossible to violate economic realities with impunity for any extended time. Since the economics of supporting distributed microcomputers has now acquired a high cost penalty, it is only a matter of time until the prevailing politics of uncritical and unconstrained decentralization will give way to some re-centralization of network control.

Local Politics

In currently developed countries, two centuries after the demise of feudalism, we are now at the threshold of a civilization that leverages knowledge as its principal source of economic power. The centrally managed nation-state is no longer viable in achieving efficiency in producing wealth. The spread of information technologies allows operations to be distributed globally while local and small-scale units have learned how to adapt to rapidly changing conditions.[17]

The failure of socialism was the failure of centrally managed super-states in coping with the diversity and complexity of technolog-

---

16. The Pentagon saying "There are many who can say no but hardly anyone who can make a yes stick" would ring familiar to any twelfth century merchant.

17. Singapore, Switzerland, and Hong Kong are ranked among the most prosperous and competitively aggressive commercial communities in the world.

ically advancing societies. Unfortunately, many of those computer executives who had managed centralized information technologies over the past thirty years have never abandoned the idea that computers will ultimately make a centrally planned organization practical. Much of the current predilection favoring local computing autonomy originates in reaction to the excesses of centrally dictated computing. It is a revolt against heavy-handed central control, the penalty for which is a disregard for enterprise-wide integration.

Anyone who wishes to practice information politics must understand that local computational autonomy is here to stay. To sustain the enterprise-wide integration of information systems, one has to recognize the local aspirations for information independence and work with them instead of against them.

The Totalitarian Taint

Centrally managed computer establishments are suspected of having a totalitarian bias by the owners of personal computers. The genesis of this view can be traced to the way that technology developed during the 1950s and 1960s. One can still hear intensely adverse feelings about computer managers as stated in a recent confidential survey of business executives. This included a comment that, "The information technology areas are the last remaining vestige of Stalinist centralist bureaucracy in the Western world."

Opinions like this provide a good excuse to corporate executive committees to dissolve central computing organizations, outsource telecomputing services, and empower each business unit to reach for self-sufficiency in information management. A committee of the managers of independent units, supported by a powerless staff, would then look out for any common interests, such as adhering to standards.[18] Counter-revolution, not economics, inspires such moves that inhibit the capacity to achieve corporate-wide cooperation.

---

18. Over the last few years recommendations like this have been frequently delivered by consultants to large companies and government agencies. Consultants do not usually read each other's reports and therefore the conclusions may truly reflect the spirit of the times.

Balance of Power

The time has come to apply policy-making to the politics of balancing rigid order against anarchy. Principles are needed that guide us in what to favor and what to avoid while we search for a compromise between extremes.

Should you satisfy all of your global computing demands from a single data center? Should all of the programmers be in the same building, under the same management as a way to stimulate professional development? Should you encourage employees to find whatever computing resources are convenient to take care of their computation needs, even if that means disregarding company-operated computer services? The answers to these and similar questions are unique, because each organization is unique and therefore the balancing act must be unique.

Figure 5.1 Simplicity is the Clearest Policy

The central issue is one of control. How much control is mandatory to avoid chaotic conditions? How much coordination is necessary to conserve shared resources? How much intrusion protection is essential for safeguarding the security of systems? Since governing and controlling cost money and slow things down, how can top management be sure that they have found a practical answer to Thomas Jefferson's dictum that "whoever governs least governs best"?

These questions are what executives ought to answer, preferably in an open debate, because that is more likely to accelerate understanding and acceptance. For an inspiring example of compelling arguments and well-reasoned passion, refer to the *The Federalist Papers*.[19] They illustrate what it takes to embrace the diversity of opinions concerning the powers of central or local governance. Every chief executive should read these documents for lessons in crafting lasting rules of governance.

The Politics of Choices

There are two aspects to control over technology. One concerns how to apply the technology. Operating people, who depend on computing to get their jobs done, must have a decisive say about the technology they use. Technology choices should not force a production scheduler to accept an order entry system that generates erroneous delivery instructions. Ideally, any well motivated and properly trained employee should have the guaranteed right to pull the plug on any computer application that could harm or damage the enterprise.[20] Who can pull the plug, when, and, under what circumstances is clearly a political decision. Addressing such situations belongs in the rules of governance.

Another aspect of control over technology concerns the power to choose which technologies are best for the organization. That includes decisions such as selecting operating systems, compilers, hardware configurations and network management software. Such choices should come from consistently reliable experts in order to allow operating management to concentrate on using computers instead worrying about technical decisions. Everyone cannot have the unrestricted freedom to choose their own local area networks, electronic document standards, location of their archival files or data formats. Otherwise, the result would be chaos. Who makes technology choices, when, and under what

---

19. Alexander Hamilton, James Madison, John Jay, *The Federalist Papers*, First published 1787. Edited by Clinton Rossiter, Penguin Books, 1961
20. A version of Isaac Asimov's first law of robotics.

circumstances is clearly a political act. This also belongs in the rules of governance.

The Politics of Control

The persistence of internal clashes about information management are a sure sign of weak policy-making. An organization can either sanction some measures of control through formal rules of corporate governance, or abandon such an idea in favor of just about everybody pursuing autonomous initiatives. Where a power vacuum exists, managers will seek to assert their own initiatives in dealing with information technologies. When that interferes with the assumed prerogatives of others, organizational squabbles will arise. It is a basic lesson of politics that seizure of power will take place whenever there is a neglect of governance.

One of the principles of physics is that nature abhors a vacuum. Similarly, bureaucrats abhor a vacancy in the power structure whenever that involves control over information. If there is confusion about policies concerning the handling of information, at least one manager will attempt to exploit such ambiguity. If there are several managers involved, prepare for another round in the unceasing turf wars that are the essence of bureaucratic posturing for budget increase.[21]

The most ineffective remedy for dealing with policy ambiguity is to lump together warring units and make them report to the same manager. This is how sales specialists are reassigned to product divisions in order to gain product focus. When that does not work, the same people are redeployed into geographic districts to strengthen customer focus. The possibilities for organizational reshuffling are infinite. The players can rearrange reporting relationships for fighter planes, bombers and helicopters; tanks, infantry and special forces; computers, peripherals and information services. Each new arrangement on the organization charts comes with plausible explanations until the next reorganization contradicts what came before. Unless there is a demon-

---

21. I like the Washington, D.C. term "jurisdictional altercation," which shows that even street gang expressions can be clothed in pompous bureaucratic terminology.

strable, long-term economic advantage in any such redistribution of control, I call such activity "organizational hijacking of the weak by the strong."

Without governance, tradition or an established institution, any mutual dependency will create conflict in competing for money and priority. There is no one way to optimize organizational structure within its own boundaries. There will be always someone who must depend on someone else. An abundance of reorganization activity is a sure sign that the instability has its origin in top management's lack of resolution.

An interesting question is whether or not organizational opportunists should receive encouragement. Are they innovators who stimulate learning or are they villains who agitate to create chaos in order to expand their influence by engaging in bureaucratic forms of piracy? Are they like predatory fish added to a fish pond in order to intimidate the lazy feeders? Should a corporation engage a succession of aggressive executives to reverse a steady managerial decline?

When working as a consultant, I have to decide if a particular organization is attempting to move towards adventurism or stagnation. In bureaucratic contests, each party accuses the other of one of these behaviors. One must look for evidence. Does the proposed change in information management demonstrably support the stated objectives of the enterprise? Does it replace one choice of information technology by another without reasonable prospects of noteworthy improvements in the creation of business value?

If an organizational change does nothing except rearrange the names on the organization chart, I recommend against settling any dispute by reorganization, and certainly not by changing the flows of information to suit personalities. In most instances, you can achieve a better result by keeping everyone's position intact, but changing the rules under which they work together.

Transition Politics

One of the most persistent conflicts confronting information executives is who owns the central computer and communication "utility." A politically astute CIO can balance competing interests by relying on long-range cash flow forecasts to evaluate the merits of each option. Unfortunately, the differences between the consolidators and the distributors of computational power typically cannot be resolved using purely financial rationale. These confrontations are simply proxies for the contest between advocates of local independence fighting against the powers of central coordination.

A better solution to these corporate versions of civil war is to resort to principles of governance where commercial and security arguments take precedence over political motivation. Governance rules must offer a compromise that allows the retention of local autonomy without compromising the needs of the company. Such an approach would prevent a dispute from ever requiring top executive intervention.

Let me give an example to illustrate that local autonomy and social responsibility are not necessarily at odds. If you have an ancient car in your garage and want to play with it there, the Motor Vehicle Bureau should not care what you do with it. That protects individual interests. However, in order to drive that vehicle on a street, it is necessary to follow rules of safe transportation for everyone. That protects the community.

What you do in your bedroom with your Macintosh is nobody's business. That protects individual interests. However, to communicate with others requires observation of protocols that not only address security, but also follow conventions, such as message formats, data integrity and authentication of commands. That protects the community.

Choosing whether or not to consolidate divisional data centers under corporate control is a complex proposition. If long-term economics dictates consolidation and will not compromise security, then go on with it. However, you must establish safeguards so that timely and low cost service for local level operations will not capriciously change. The act of moving control of organizational assets from the local to a higher level of authority should include the corporate equivalent of an enforceable political treaty among all parties. Such formal agreements promote acceptance and assurance, which are political motives. This reflects the fact that consolidation of information technology, in any form, is first and foremost a political act .

Distribution of Power

The history of civilization is full of examples where societies exchange some less important freedoms with the ones they would like to gain. The price for being a hermit or anarchist, both of whom insist on complete social independence, is the severing of social ties.

Whenever one wishes to address the question of control over computing resources, one of the most difficult political issues is the emotional attachment most office workers have for their personal computers. Most new computing assets now being installed in offices are for individually operated microcomputers. Office workers have a sense of ownership of their machines as a way to enhance their skills and preserve the privilege of using information technology for personal purposes. Therefore, they will resist any encroachment on their sense of technological independence.

Totally autonomous local area networks rarely offer cheaper computing power when compared with leaving some of the difficult network management tasks for central administration. Exorbitant support costs driven up by enthusiastic amateurs have created maintenance communes whose support costs exceed the hardware cost advantages from local processing. An organization must find politically and emotionally acceptable answers to the aspirations of individuals for independence, privacy and self-directed experimentation while leaving to experts what they can do best. Otherwise, purely economic arguments for a more balanced distribution of responsibilities for local network administration will fail. The art of politics is as much a matter of dealing with perceptions as with economic interests.

I do not believe that *ad hoc* negotiations with local information communes can result in agreements on how to rearrange the control over microcomputers. In the absence of sound and well established rules of governance, all negotiated settlements will be temporary improvisations. Such agreements are subject to unilateral abrogation whenever a party finds it advantageous to do so.

When information steering committees are appointed without rules of governance sanctioned by the executive committee and without budget authority, friction over the allocation of information resources and priorities increases. When a king allows his nobles to interpret for themselves all agreements, you can bet that the nobles will find justification for whatever they wished to do anyway. Discussion in any information steering committee should be subject to oversight at the executive level and preferably by the corporate executive committee. There must be a clear line of authority to reinforce compliance with corporate objectives, in case discussion wanders off to parochial agendas. The politics of information governance requires a process that transcends the authority of individual interests.

The distribution of power over information resources should be consistent with the processes of budgeting, planning and performance evaluation. If profit accountability is in the hands of business unit executives, but subject to enumerated rights reserved by the corporation, such as in finance, legal, public relations and management appointments, then information governance should follow a similar pattern. Information governance would then delegate to local operations all information management responsibilities except those specifically reserved by policy to the corporation.

6

FEDERATION

It is the balance of power, not centralization or decentralization, that matters.

To deal with the inherent conflicts between autonomous business units and headquarters, which happen in most large organization nowadays, the management of information should operate as a multi-layered federation.

Figure 6.1 Federation Is a Way of Balancing Power

The federation is a form of government in which sovereign power is balanced among a central authority and a number of constituent political units. This is distinct from a confederation, in which elements unite for a common purpose without giving up any sovereignty. In a confederation, or a league, all authority remains with the units unless they agree to delegate specific roles to a collective body. In a federation, central authority is independent of the units. The United States of America is a federation, NATO is a confederation. The recent vacillation of the IBM corporation between federated and confederated forms of organization are an example of the damage that can be incurred if the fundamental arrangements of governance relationships remain unresolved.

Many corporations claim to be federations, but operate as confederations. When that happens, a chief information officer with a federation mission can never succeed, regardless of what he may try to do.

Federation governance follows the principle that everything which is not retained under a constitution-like process is automatically delegated. In a federated structure, managers at headquarters concentrate only on decisions that concern enterprise-wide interests. Everything else passes on to the next echelon, which may be a group, division, region, district, branch or team. In this way, everyday operations are not hindered by higher level oversight. In a federated form of organization it is desirable for each layer to retain only the coordinating authority that is essential.[22]

Throughout my career, I have spent much time preparing organizational charters, conceiving architectural reference models, drafting statements of principles, issuing declarations of information policy goals, preparing statements of responsibilities and generating corporate standards manuals. Most of this work did not make much difference, in resolving major conflicts because it tried to describe, in excessive detail,

---

22. One person's decentralization is another's centralization. I remember visiting a regional vice president of Kraft, who complained about corporate staff usurping most of his decision-making privileges. When the conversation turned to the delegation of responsibility to branch managers, his still memorable comment was, "I do not deputize my authority to anyone."

procedures for passing information up and down organizational layers and functions. It was an enumeration of the minutiae without any context. It was all pine needles without a pine forest.

Computer people are description-compulsive about anything that concerns their work. They are that way because their work is mostly procedure- or process-oriented. They engage in more elaborate descriptions of their procedures and methods than anyone else, with the exception of the tax authorities. Their insistence on receiving an exhaustive definition of every conceivable step in what is expected of them has not served them well. For instance, the typically elaborate manuals that prescribe who does what to whom during a phased program management sequence has earned systems analysts the deserved reputation of being impossible to communicate with. By the time comprehensive documentation of systems requirements is complete, conditions have changed sufficiently to make the specifications unreliable.

U.S. Constitutional Model

The simplicity of the U.S. Constitution has much to offer as a template for information policy guidance. It represents a point of view that addresses the governance of complexity by concentrating only on the fundamentals, while leaving everything else for resolution by means of a due process wherever that is appropriate.

To make autonomous, knowledge-based organizations viable in an increasingly interdependent world requires an adaptation of the federalist thinking of Thomas Jefferson, James Madison and John Adams. They conceived a master plan to endow a new nation with principles that since have endured extremely well as communities evolved from an agrarian society to a postindustrial global power. The U.S. constitutional model enabled this country to be guided in its transformation from a monarchy to a layered political system that balances national, state, local and individual interests.

Information Constitutional Model

An information constitution follows the principle of layered governance, where everything not specifically reserved under a constitution-like due process is delegated.

Every organization should come up with its own way to layer its information schema. It is inconceivable that exactly the same structure would fit every organization. Figure 6.2 displays a conceptual model consisting of seven layers, which is as complex as any information governance should ever get.

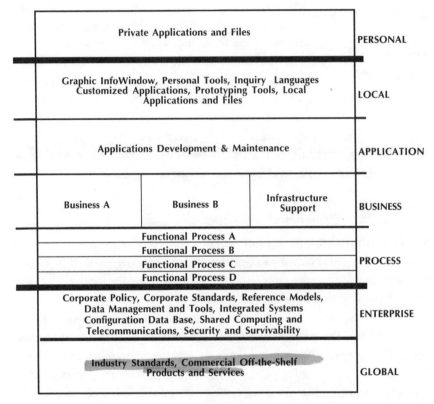

Figure 6.2 A Federated Governance Model

Small organizations should require just three layers (global, process, and personal), whereas giant multinational corporations may need the full hierarchy to fit their diverse needs. However, a word of caution is in order. Whenever the layered model is first unveiled, there will always be a demand for additional layers to satisfy some claimants' wishes. I found that seven layers were sufficient to embrace the world's second largest information-processing organization, the Department of

Defense. Therefore, resist any attempts to add further complexity as a way to create unique privileges.

When thinking about the structure of information governance, remember that the world's largest integrated information-processing organization is the Catholic Church, with only three layers between the pope and the parish priest. The astounding information efficiency with which the church has maintained continuity over centuries, not to mention it having the lowest overhead of any global organization relative to its size, is a testimonial to the value of long-term policy, clear governance and superb information doctrine.[23]

The Soviet Union used to be the largest centrally-run information system, but its policies reflected practices of a self-absorbed, conspiratory gang. Its governance existed only on paper, and its information doctrine denied information to everyone, including its own managers. No wonder the Soviet Union disintegrated in the largest information implosion in history. Governance based on violence, self-delusion and lies cannot function for any sustained period in the modern times.

Layers of an Information Constitution

With the warning that there is no such thing as a standard constitution, the following is an illustration of how you may define the attributes of individual layers of governance:
- Level 1: **Global.** All functions, services, and standards that assure the interoperability of the enterprise with suppliers, customers and technology vendors;
- Level 2: **Enterprise.** All services and standards that define the rules of governance to assure economic viability, integration and interoperability of internal information systems;
- Level 3: **Functional Processes.** All functions that assure a integration of shared activities, regardless of business function, location or business specialization. Func-

---

23. "Doctrine" is defined as fundamental principles by which an organization guides the actions of its members in support of stated overarching objectives. A doctrine is authoritative, but requires individual judgment in how to apply it.

tional processes cut horizontally across all elements of
a hierarchic, or vertically structured organization;

- Level 4: **Business.** All systems that are unique to the products
  or services delivered by an autonomous organizational
  unit;
- Level 5: **Application.** All features that support the specific
  operating needs of individual or groups performing
  similar tasks;
- Level 6: **Local.** All features that are unique to individuals or
  groups for which higher level standard processes are
  inadequate;
- Level 7: **Personal.** All data that individuals may want keep private without prior consent.[24] Personal privacy has two
  components that should be considered. The first is
  peer-to-peer expectation of privacy, which should be
  the norm, since we sometimes shut doors and lock
  our desks. The second one is privacy from examination by an authorized official to audit the conduct of
  business. The second kind of privacy cannot be
  allowed if a business requires accountability and security.

Customized versions of these layers already exist in some form or
other in many organizations. These include versions for telecommunication networks, software engineering systems, systems integration
plans, data center operations and security procedures. One of the most
ambitious efforts I have seen is the mapping of all of these relationships,
including personnel qualifications and implementation schedules, onto
a huge spreadsheet in an attempt to lay out the entire governance framework as seen from different points of view.

I find such efforts ambitious and helpful in discovering any inconsistencies, except when they become incomprehensible. For discussions

---

24. This level does not concern what people may do with personal communicators or laptops
that are the individual's private property. Level seven covers exemptions, if any, for individuals
to use the property of their employers to record private information. From the standpoint of
network security and protection of information assets, such an exemption creates insurmount-
able problems, even though as a general practice everybody nowadays considers the use of their
personal computer in the office as a generally accepted entitlement.

with executives, I usually offer something that looks like a legal draft of a charter. This is a more acceptable format for those accustomed to reading and thinking about political matters in a familiar format.

In addition to the definition of governance as a legal treaty, whenever I draft an information "constitution" I also include a cook-book-like reference manual which defines operational authorities as a comprehensive checklist of who is responsible for what. Most people prefer to have a handy guide for determining who can be expected to get something accomplished. Such a reference makes disputes brief, and this is the reason that constitutional governance works.

7

ARCHITECTURE

An exclusively technical solution is form without substance.

Corporate and government bookshelves are filled with dust-covered architectural plans conceived by task forces, consultants, and vendors. These are idealized technological concepts that rarely link their schema to the power structure they are supposed to support. There can be no enterprise architecture without a direct connection to governance. The authors of architectural documents that discuss only technologies confuse form with substance. Technical definitions of how information will be distributed must be always consistent with definitions of who will be in control.

A technical information systems architecture tells us how to build information systems. Governance tells us how a human organization that already exists can become successful and have the capacity to adapt to change. These are not separate but intertwined relationships that are clearly interdependent.

A technical information systems architecture deals with the connections among physical and programmed elements. Governance deals with interactions among human beings. In information-rich organizations these are not separate but symbiotic relationships.

A technical information systems architecture is typically imposed unilaterally and enforced by technological means. Governance, in the sense used here, must be a reflection of a social consensus that results from multiparty and negotiated compromise.

A technical information systems architecture provides a framework for the capture, storage and manipulation of data. Only governance can define how information should be organized so that it can be converted into organizational knowledge.

Implementation of a technical architecture should take place only after establishing clear political governance, because it would be otherwise constructed on a shaky foundation. Politics always comes before technology. Drawing up an information constitution should always precede decisions about launching major new investments in computers.

In the last decade IBM has suffered major losses in market share because they tried to impose a well-reasoned technical architecture on an environment that had became increasingly varied. Customers demanded solutions that fitted rising aspirations of individuals for computing independence. That lesson should be heeded by anyone who gets the commission to write yet another technical architecture document.

Favoring External Information Sources

Complex organizations, just like biological organisms, have evolved by finding ways of minimizing resources and energy consumed for internal coordination while coping with external threats. Touching a red hot iron ought to trigger a faster response than noticing a fire across the street. The same is true of organizations that rely on computers to manage much of their information. A basic principle of an information architecture should be a strong bias toward giving priority to processing external information that concerns revenue before processing internal information that concerns control. Competitive forces are intended to overcome external threats, whereas bureaucratic forces are essential to control and ensure internal coordination. Both forces are important, except that external effects are swifter and potentially more devastating.

A typical enterprise receives an avalanche of data every day. The crew in an air traffic control center may be receiving ten thousand data items per minute. Under battlefield conditions, an Army corps may have to sort out more than a million data items per minute. The peak hour transaction workload for a major airline reservation system is approaching four thousand transactions per second. The New York stock exchange recently traded fifteen thousand shares per second. The Clearing House Interbank Payment Systems (CHIPS) each day handles more than one trillion dollars.

Perhaps the most important measure of the capabilities of an information design is its reaction time, which is the delay between a threat occurring and the time that the organization reacts to it. Information systems should be tuned to respond to external signals in preference to internal ones.

Design for Complexity

The capacity to translate external signals into appropriate responses determines how well an organization will cope with external challenges. The capacity to analyze signals will set the speed of its adaptive reflexes. The ability to make decisions on the basis of incoming information will determine how much money an organization can afford to invest in internal coordination. The design of information systems tells us where things go, how they should fit and how they related to each other, but does not prescribe how to put them together.

An enterprise design framework should document much more than the way that computer systems pass messages to each other. The information flow diagrams of an enterprise are perhaps the most reliable ways of explaining how it coordinates for action. The information structure determines an organization's capacity to create economic value under competitive conditions, since every competitor is racing to become swifter and smarter. The master systems design document should reveal more about how an organization responds to adversity than the organization charts.

There is no such thing as a standard enterprise architecture. Enterprise design is as unique as a human fingerprint, because enterprises differ in how they function. Adopting an enterprise architecture is therefore one of the most urgent tasks for top executive management. Fundamentally, an information framework is a political doctrine for specifying as to who will have what information to make timely decisions. Never delegate creating the enterprise master design plan for information systems to computer experts, for they will judge it only on its technical merits.

Scarcely anything has been published that could tell executives what such an architecture involves. In this book, I describe a systems structure template that does not reflect the needs of any particular corporate or public sector unit. This template is presented as a check-list for decisions by top management. It is a list of topics that authors of an enterprise design document would have to consider. These topics addresses questions that usually come up when CEOs ask about recommended practices for information management.

Configuration Management

It takes more than standards to ensure that hardware, software, and telecommunications provide an organization with responsive information handling capabilities. Every organization that owns several hundred computers needs a model to explains how information originates, how it becomes useful, and how it is preserved for subsequent use as organizational memory.

Figure 7.1 Configuration Management

Unfortunately, the word "architecture" is perhaps the most overused term in current conversations among systems experts. It covers almost every conceivable effort used to bringing some semblance of order into an environment where improvisation and inconsistencies prevail. Because of overexposure, the term architecture has ceased to have meaning beyond its narrow technical use in specifying computer and telecommunications standards.

A better description of what is meant by architecture is what engineers call configuration. A configuration model is a set of rules which describes valid combinations of elements that may be assembled into a system. A system configuration is the result of applying configuration rules. A system configuration model offers a much richer set of rules than "architecture" which deals with fixed structures. My objection to the architectural analogy is its lack of dynamic concepts. Architecture, in its traditional sense, also does not have an evolutionary dimension. The concept of systems configuration management offers the following:

- A static system configuration model defines the components of the system. It includes a description of the "objects" that make up the system.

- A configuration relationship model defines how "objects" in the system relate to each other and the attributes of these relationships.

- A configuration dynamic model describes the dynamic attributes of objects and relationships, such as making modifications, scaling up operations and migrating into a different technological environment.

I find the the generally used building construction metaphor incapable of offering useful insights into some of the most important issues of contemporary technical design for information systems, such as dealing with object oriented programming, establishment of knowledge repositories, computer-managed training, adoption of "*open*" systems" and shifting communications to multimedia.[25] I believe that when the power of configuration management becomes more apparent, the rising

---

25. The purpose of "open systems" is to make portability and interoperability feasible. Portability refers to the ease with which a software system or hardware component can be transferred from one hardware or software environment to another. Interoperability is the ability of two or more computer systems and their software to exchange information and use the information that has been exchanged.

demands for network computing will make this concept an essential discipline for dealing with the complexity of software and hardware.

Lessons from History

I have always searched among successful human social institutions for lessons in successful information system management. Instead of the traditional building analogy depicting systems as frameworks and structures, I find that information management reflects relationships that are more like social covenants. Information systems resemble tribal cultures more than something built out of bricks and mortar. In studying the effects of systems on organizations, the discipline of anthropology is more appropriate than the practice of electrical engineering.

Over the centuries, humankind has been experimenting with a variety of ways how to organize their communities. Our collective experiences include theocracies, monarchies, anarchies, democracies and dictatorships in many forms. So far, the most robust framework for preserving individual freedoms while creating wealth is a constitutionally governed federation.

Complex organizations cannot operate as centralized dictatorships. Nor can they survive in anarchy. The most stable and adaptable forms of complex organizations are federated covenants which I have found suitable for every organization I have ever worked with or studied. The essence of this approach is the assignment of specified information management responsibilities to designated layers within an organization. These responsibilities relate to each other by a set of rules that define an information constitution document. Like every constitution, it is subject to elaboration, amendment and evolution as conditions change.

Constitutional principles suggest that one can find a successful balance between the power of the state and the freedom of individuals. Complex societies require several layers of government, with each performing assigned functions so that changes can affect one layer at a time without overhauling everything whenever conditions change. When communications engineers approached the design of the world's telephone and data communications networks, the only time-proven solution was to set it up as a layered federation of protocols with each layer assigned specified tasks.[26]

Political power in federations is not centralized, but neither is it decentralized. Federations depend on a defined process for delegating power and preserving privileges. This requires trust, stability, long term commitment and acceptance of evolutionary innovation that is shared among the participants rather than a destabilizing revolution that is dictated from a single authority.

Software as Federated Governance

If software is a form of organizational memory and a way to define how people work together, then a systems model that defines the ownership and control over software makes it possible to view organizations that are neither centralized nor decentralized. Federations are a superior form of organization, especially if their scope reaches across national, cultural and economic boundaries. In the federated model, software assets reside where they can do the most good, which includes the possibility that you may have multiple copies of software and data at several locations. However, databases must be able to maintain integrity regardless of hardware changes, and be independent of different ways of examining simultaneously the data from different geographic locations. The federated model offers this capability because it prescribes how changes to hardware, displays and networks can occur independently.

Networking Choices

All business is based on internal collaboration among employees or external cooperation with customers and suppliers. Organizing networks to connect these computing clients is one of the key decisions for configuration management.

The language for describing various network configurations options is not precise. Frequently used catch phrases, mostly of an advertising origin, hide more than they reveal. You will find references

---

26. The OSI (Open Systems Interconnection) telecommunication protocols are a prime example of how to define technical rules for governing computer communications.

to master-slave architectures, which is a pejorative for central computing. If you happen to be selling peer-to-peer networks you will apply the catchall phrase "client-server," which has lost all meaning and therefore can be mentioned with a complete disregard of consistent logic. You will hear about distributed function solutions, remote data management architectures, virtual network connectivity and distributed intelligence solutions. In the future one can expect that imaginative advertisers will keep adding to this collection of terms to make their solutions appear unique. The following illustration shows that systems configurations are not only a matter of hardware, but largely a matter where the control over application programs and software resides.

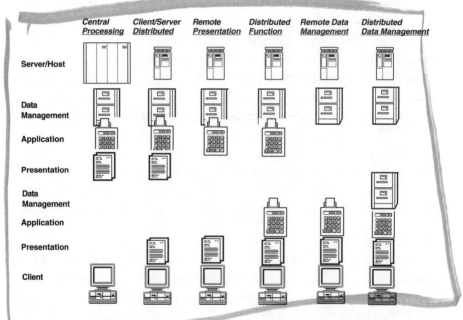

Figure 7.2 Distributing Computing Power

All configurations are constructed from combinations of three styles of governance processes:

- Dictator relationships. A host process tells some other process exactly what to do. For example, a microcomputer that drives a printer, a communications controller that drives a modem, and a mainframe that

drives a display terminal all exhibit dictator relationships with their subordinates. Do not let anybody sell
you the idea that only IBM mainframes exhibited dictatorial behavior. The server you install in your
department as proof of your emancipation from the
central computer slavery is likely to be as dictatorial to
your local clients as what you had before. The difference is political, not architectural. The difference is
that you now control the server, but somebody else
owns the data center.

Figure 7.3 An Information Hermit

• Hermit relationships. Nobody tells you what to do
and you do not tell anybody what to do. For example,
you get the largest and most powerful microcomputer
your desk and budget can stand. You read *Byte* magazine, *PC Week* and get free copies of *MacWorld*.
Once in a while you pass a disk to somebody with
whatever computations you have completed. Quite
often, you beg, borrow or even purchase disks to feed
your machine with new software. It is this social isolation that gives this relationship its name. Do not let
anyone sell you the idea that hermits become socially
active citizens as soon as they sign up on *Internet*, or

when they start roaming on the "information high-way." As soon as you give anyone, regardless how well connected, a powerful computer with plenty of memory they will act as hermits much of the time. The server you buy for your department, as a way to stimulate group participation, will sit idle while your fellow hermits manipulate their spreadsheets one more time.

The most constructive form of this relationship is when children play and learn with assistance of computers. Computer-aided learning is by far more sympathetic, attentive, and interesting than most teachers. In its asocial form, hermit computing fosters personal isolation with possible excursions into "virtual reality" when the real world becomes unpleasant. When hermit tendencies veer towards fanatic pursuits they take the form of anarchist behavior, such as cracking networks that belong to authorities.

Figure 7.4 Virtual Reality

- Peer relationships. I work with you and you work with me to make information more useful. It is hard to tell who makes which contribution. Authorship is diffused as we cooperate on getting work accomplished. Your machine has a great deal of computing power, but if you need more there is always some other place where you can get more. Your machine has some data, but if you need information you can always get it somewhere on the network. Do not let anyone sell you the idea that only their brand of configuration will assure peer-to-peer relationships. In passing new data to a file server, a microcomputer will assume a dictatorial role. When checking up on prior actions in your own files, your peer-to-peer machines become hermits.

All arguments that to use a single label for describing governance processes of information networks are simplistic. The architectural analogy which assumes that there is a meaningful description such as split-level, colonial, skyscraper, or ranch implies that the construction of systems is similar to forms made of brick or mortar. To understand a systems configuration requires an understanding of behavior that is human and dynamic. Buildings designed by architects are static. Network systems exhibit relationships which alternate between dictatorial, hermit, and peer forms. Buildings stay put.

Next time you need to explain to your Board of Directors what they will get for the next hundred million dollars worth of client/servers, or whatever other buzzword may be currently fashionable, you should talk in terms of relationships, behavior, control, politics and power. That will spell out the configuration of your network better than any diagram that shows how machines, files, telephones and satellite dishes are connected.

Hub Networking

From the standpoint of network configuration, there are some forms that are used frequently. The oldest computer networking configuration, dating from the mid 1960s, is a hub-spoke set-up. The mainframe is the hub and all terminals receive data, intelligence, and support through fixed spokes. The clients at the end of the spokes receive information, in a tightly prescribed manner only if they ask for it, and if the central computer can respond.

Except in cases that are highly organized and stylized, such as in banking and airline reservation systems, the hub-spoke configuration has many disadvantages. All traffic must be hauled across the country and even between continents to and from the central machine. It may take about $100 million per year to operate a hub that can support a peak load of 2,000 to 4,000 transactions per second.[27] There are many organizations where over 10,000 electronic stations could hit the hub simultaneously. Therefore, there are capacity, safety, and economic limits where central computing can serve enterprise-wide needs. The widespread adoption of minicomputers in the late 1970s lowered the cost and the complexity of networking for small groups. Nevertheless, the hub and spoke arrangement remained unchanged. The local hub now commands a smaller set of spokes and became a client to the central hub as necessary.

The hub-spoke design of networks is not dominant any more. Local computing is incredibly cheap and does not require maintaining large exclusive central hubs for the sake of economy in making use of computers, files, and communications switching equipment. Memory, especially archival memory, is inexpensive and compact. You do not have to hoard data at a hub to make the best use of it.

Exclusive central computing hubs are vulnerable because they concentrate all security risks. If a hub fails, everything fails. Therefore, the days of hub-controlled networks are fading away except in cases requiring expensive computing services, such as supercomputing, for difficult scientific calculations. This is true even in those cases where you must keep a master record up-to-date at all times, such as stock

---

27. The Spring 1994 purchase price of an IBM ES/9000 Model 511 TPF capable of processing about 3,500 transactions per second was $27.9 million. As a general rule, for large on-line processing operations the computer costs are less than 15% of data center charges. To that you have to add cost of memory peripherals, telecommunications and considerable systems engineering support labor costs. See "TCP-A Benchmarking," *Datamation*, May 1, 1994

market quotations. Modern databases make it possible to replicate data at several sites while keeping them in synchronization at all times. As soon as it is economically feasible, you should abandon the central hub-spoke design and start retraining the technical managers who would otherwise resist networking. Politically, managers who control central computational hubs are in an untenable position. They cannot possibly hold on to their positions much longer as economics, response time and reliability favor the distribution of computing power to multiple sites that can take over each other's functions at short notice.

Web Networking

Webs are spun out of fine threads, but they get their strength from clever design and a capacity to overcome local failures. Much of the promotion of client-server methods implies that by distributing existing computing power you gain in economy and reliability. If you leave the existing hub network in place without altering database management practices, and locate the new servers at the ends of the existing hubs, your support costs as well as risks will increase. Your costs will increase because you will have many more data centers to attend to. Your risks will also increase because your points of vulnerability will be greater.

When it comes to computing, I believe that all networked computers are created equal. Some may be richer, some may be poorer in terms of power, functions, or resources. However, I consider it a matter of good prudence that all computing resources should be able to connect to each other by multiple routes. Each computer should be able to reach others by at least two and preferably three physically independent paths. The routing should not be done at hubs, but at points of origin by inserting into each message destination-seeking instructions. The traditional way to connect people, such as in the telephone system, linked dumb and low cost handsets with very expensive and enormously smart central switches. In web networking, the network is passive and the switches are cheap while the messages and the stations are very intelligent.

Network stations should be treated as equals and not as separate classes of superior "clients" attended by inferior "servers" because the stations are now supercomputers. These distinctions are not just a linguistic quibble. They are a matter of distinction that are reflected in how network privileges and network organizations are put together.

Web networking supports cooperation among groups that organize and dissolve rapidly. It could be design engineers on separate continents reaching agreement on the layout of a circuit board. It could be an infantry commander coordinating close air and artillery actions. It could be a group co-authoring a report. It could be a negotiation. It could be working out details of a purchase with a stock broker. It could be an act as simple as placing an order for merchandise. Who will talk to whom, with what device, over what telecommunications link, is unpredictable and therefore cannot be specified in advance in the same way as you would design structural members of a building.

The fundamental premise behind web networking is that regardless of the amount of automation involved in a transaction, there is always a human being who will be accountable for what happens. Web networking is not only a matter of software design, but also a reflection of managerial practices how to handle exceptions, errors, security, and responsibility for data integrity. The politics of web networking is a reflection of how an organization views relationships among employees, customers and suppliers. The master-slave, hub-spoke configuration enforces subordination and centralization of knowledge and control. This form is medieval, authoritarian and totalitarian. Peer-to-peer computing over web networks does not in itself guarantee cooperation, but surely makes it possible. It is egalitarian, with all of its faults and freedom to engage in wasteful foolishness.

I favor web network configurations because they embody the principles of free enterprise, choice and individual responsibility in dealing with an electronically connected community. It also happens to be the most economically sound solution to computing in most cases, but not necessarily on account of its superior technical configuration. The superiority of web networking resides in its social and political context. It makes it possible to view every computer as a mini-business that can choose when, how and at what price to participate in acts of cooperation with information suppliers who offer the best deal. An economist would classify participants on a web networks as "perfectly rational consumers." Customers on a global web network would have instant, perfect knowledge of all prices, capacity and quality of service. The customers would be in a position to make the optimum purchasing decision, which is the dream of every economic theoretician, since computers have no practical limit on the amount of analysis that can be done to find the best solution.

Do not become enamored of peer-to-peer networking presentations from vendors and consultants. They will offer to you a technically easy escape either from your obsolete central computers or your microcomputer mess if you only buy their particular version of networking. A totalitarian mentality can nullify any potential benefits from decentralized computing. Continued adherence to central prerogatives in switching and control will make peer-to-peer solutions expensive toys. In making networking choices you must remember they reflect differences in managerial style, policy and politics.

Before you embark on a totally distributed networking configuration, make sure you understand what managerial changes will be necessary to make the technology work for you instead of against you.

8

ORGANIZATION

Complex organizations require complex governance.

Can information workers be trusted to use electronic access to information wisely and safely?[28] Is the world ready for employee autonomy in the information workplace? Will the distribution of information confer responsibility as well as power? With the adoption of federated principles of governance, the answers to these questions may be all "yes." Except for highly specialized occupations, information workers are using only only a fraction of their intrinsic abilities. When you consider the potential of skill augmentation offered by expert systems technologies, the gap between machine-aided human potential and what people actually do in their jobs is becoming wider. The question then remains how to organize work to capture their presently underutilized talents.

Decentralization vs. Centralization

The word decentralization has ceased to describe the organization of work flow in a manner that avoids all hierarchy. Unlike factory workers, information workers (with the exception of clerks performing repetitious tasks) have not been under a regime that tightly prescribes every job step. Most of the work in the office is not subject to prescriptive controls

---

28. Information workers is an occupational grouping defined by the U.S. Department of Labor.

at all. Anthropologists who have studied office work report that what office workers do is not what analysts' flow-charts assert.[29] Much of what actually occurs in office work is difficult to describe by formal means.

Most people who operate computer terminals have little slips of paper that remind them what to do when official procedures do not work.[30] Even in well-disciplined organizations, such as in insurance companies, banks or government bureaus, much of the work effort is expended in tackling problems that no computer program addresses and that no procedural manual defines.

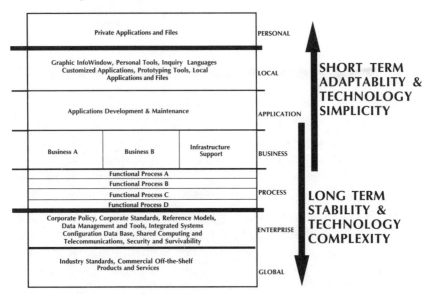

Figure 8.1 Conflicts Within an Information Structure

The alternative to decentralization is not necessarily centralization in the same way that a measure of disorder does not require specifying what every person must do at all times. As suggested in Figure 8.1, systems must allow people at the local level to add their own enhance-

---

29. Based on research from the Xerox Palo Alto Research Laboratory.
30. One of the most sensitive command stations in the world, requiring a general officer's continuous attendance, had 5"x 7" index cards laminated to the desk. These cards displayed handwritten notes about which buttons to push.

ments to standard information systems. These additions should be the products of clever local discoveries, not interference with the integrity of applications. Notes on these little slips of paper that people write for themselves provide an opportunity for improving the quality of the support that computer systems could provide.

Information workers should be working on what they find relatively easy to do for the good of the organization, which includes taking advantage of their workplace knowledge. Freeing people to define their own choices how to use computers is feasible only if they do not have to become computer experts. Technical configuration should prescribe the retention of the tough technical decisions at the upper layers of the federation, where the employment of dedicated computer experts makes the most sense. What is left, should be relatively easy to do in teaching a personal computer how to respond to an individual's wishes.

Choices in Dividing Authority and Budgets

There are decisions that are required at the enterprise level of a federation, such as those about long-term investments. Deciding where to place airports, bridges, tunnels, roads, sewers, power lines and water supplies is not something that can be left to each individual homeowner in an urban society.

Similar systems decisions involve choices about data management, network design, information security, selection of software engineering tools, and distribution of computing assets. Depending on the permanence and size of the capital investments — such infrastructure choices — should stay as close as possible to the authority that usually makes long term commitments of corporate assets.

Adapting services to local conditions should occur wherever the action actually takes place. Deciding how to pave the driveway, where to plant roses, what furniture to place in the living room, what bathroom fixtures to install, and whether or not to spend money on copper plumbing should not be determined by complete outsiders.

Similar systems decisions involve choices about the size and color of display screens, hardware configuration, selection of applications, composition of inquiries, training, and one-of-a-kind report formats. It is preposterous to insist that office workers, who otherwise influence thousand dollar decisions, go through time-consuming approvals for minor modifications that they could make themselves in a few minutes.[31]

The federated approach partitions accountability and responsibility. As with all negotiated solutions, the approach is open to abuse. Successful federations answer for themselves the question of what share of the information management budget remains under local control and what is central. An information management budget where more than two-thirds of the discretionary decisions are at the corporate level can be hardly designated as a federated solution. This is centralized management, despite claims to the contrary.

If the enterprise level infrastructure consumes less than ten percent of the total information technology budget, then it may warrant calling it a balanced federation. The fewer resources that require support from federation sources, the fewer reasons there are to argue about it.

Merits of Alternatives

No conclusive evidence is yet available about the relative merits of centralized *versus* decentralized approaches to governance. My only guidance comes from the information industry's most comprehensive survey about the structure and costs of U.S. information organizations.[32] The results show a bias against excessive distribution of information assets:

Company Structure	17 High Productivity Companies	36 Low Productivity Companies
% of CIOs reporting to the CEO	6%	19%
% of companies with centralized MIS	59%	22%
% of IT staying in Business Units	26%	38%

Figure 8.2 Differences Between High and Low Productivity

---

31. The most extreme example of such inconsistency is in the U.S. Department of Defense. Captains and Majors require elaborate cost justifications and up to eight levels of signatures to buy a laptop computer costing less than $2,000. This piece of equipment costs less than an artillery shell or a few minutes' worth of jet fuel for a bomber. It also can cause less damage.
32. *1993 Computerworld Premier 100* survey. Data provided courtesy of editors of *Computerworld.* This information must be used with caution, since most of the answers were generated by central staffs.

Information Productivity™ in these cases is defined as an approximation of the Return-on-Management™ calculations in which "Management Value-Added" came from public source information published by the consulting firm of Stern, Stewart as "Economic Value-Added" (EVA™) and "Management Costs" came from public Securities Exchange Commission disclosure reports as the Sales, General and Administrative expense (S.G.&A). High productivity companies were defined as organizations with a positive Information Productivity™ index, whereas all low productivity companies had a negative index value. The 1992 output value-added of companies with negative productivity was less than their inputs.

The findings offer a few surprises:

- High productivity organizations have a smaller fraction of CIOs reporting to the CEO.

- High productivity organizations continue to rely on predominantly centralized Management Information Systems (M.I.S.) activities.

- High productivity organizations have moved less of their staffs to business units.

These suggest that high productivity organizations may follow a conservative approach when distributing computing power. Decentralization may be progressing less rapidly than one would expect from reading computer periodicals.

Distributing Tasks

There are many feasible ways for distributing information technologies efficiently between the enterprise and local levels of authority. It is the purpose of governance to provide generally accepted rules to channel contention about authority and privilege into a balanced resolution. It is also one of the purposes of governance to protect and preserve resources for reuse over an extended time while ensuring that there are ample funds available to take care of temporary needs.[33] Governance must safeguard data whose usefulness is measured in decades while allowing ready access to a few lines of code that execute a one-of-a-kind inquiry.

Long-term considerations are becoming more urgent as the global economy progresses. The spread of computer literacy increasingly favors local solutions. The long term and the short term converges much faster nowadays. Looking at the current rate of technological development, I find that technological revolutions that used to take a century now become surpassed in only ten years.

If in doubt about where to reach a balance between concentrating resources on long term and centralized tasks *versus* short term and local choices, opt for the short term solutions that meet immediate customer needs. For decisions that could go either way, bend in favor of local options. People who are closest to your customers can see trouble coming sooner than anyone at headquarters, who only read about it later in reports, customer complaints, the press or the auditors' statements.

---

33. The contention about what share of the Gross National Product (GNP) should be considered from the "public sector" (e.g. enterprise level of governance) and what should be in the "private sector" (e.g. the local level of governance) has been the central theme of political disputes for more than 200 years. It is a matter of record that in the last thirty years, the highest rates of economic growth have been shown in countries where the lowest share of the GNP is in the public sector. During the same period centralist governments (mostly socialist) have been either bankrupted or have steadily lost economic viability.

In a socially advanced, mature and peaceful community, the assets devoted to the public infrastructure ought to be a small fraction of the total wealth of its citizens. I am intrigued by the budget of Singapore with government expenditures at 16.4% of the GDP as contrasted with 35%-55% ratios for the U.S.A. and European Economic Community countries. Public sector employment in Singapore is only 7.6% of total employment, and falling, while their GDP growth consistently exceeds 6% per annum. Public sector employment in the U.S.A. now exceeds total manufacturing employment.

9

SCOPE OF A CONSTITUTION

A constitution is policy that endures over many changes in management.

Why a Constitution?

Complex organizations require complex rules to avoid enthusiastic chaos. There are at least ten thousand organizations in the world that operate large information complexes with annual budgets exceeding $10 million. These systems rely on databases, communications, terminals, application software, and properly trained people to work in different departments, at diverse geographic locations. Even a small company with only a hundred interconnected microcomputers is likely to have over ten applications with a thousand distinct data elements. Consequently, the small company will have up to a million different ways of fouling up internal operations.

The purpose of law is to define acceptable rules of conduct. Civilized society is based upon legal constraints on conduct that enable individuals to lead their lives without undue interference from others. As long as the formulation of such rules follows a socially acceptable due process that permits change for adapting to new conditions, laws need not be a burden. Order only becomes an impediment when someone perverts it for destructive purposes. A constitution becomes a liability if it imposes an order that most people recognize as injuring their interests.

An enterprise constitution articulates fundamental principles that should have a horizon of many decades. An information management constitution should not become encumbered with the baggage of bureaucratic interests seeking an opportunity to insert words into the text to protect their entrenched prerogatives.

Following the pattern of the framers of the U.S. Constitution, the resolution of short-term conflicts should be a straightforward matter of interpretation once the fundamental principles are in place. A constitution defines the assumptions, concept of operation, policies, principles, and processes for judging individual situations. The purpose of an information constitution is to lay out the foundation for making long-term investment choices. An information constitution reduces the risks of long-range projects. It builds confidence in lasting commitments. It inhibits the use of short-lived power plays to substitute expedient solutions and the opportunism of speedy decisions for lasting improvements.

Chapter 11 presents a prototype of an information constitution to reveal the complexity of relationships that comes into play when defining how to manage business information. If the coverage of critical topics in an information constitution is incomplete, the various stakeholders will resort to their own cunning to pursue whatever they think is best for them.

In our prototype you may find that descriptions may be too detailed or cover too many topics. You may prefer to see a few broad declarations, which give to anyone sufficient freedom to interpret these generalities as it is convenient. Except in the case of simple organizations, such as individual proprietorships, a one page policy statement about information management directions is inadequate. Even worse, a terse and nebulous vision statement emanating from the CEO may leave everyone more confused than before. Everybody will claim the authority to pursue whatever directions they happen to favor based on interpretations of what the vague directions are assumed to mean.

There is no need for a formal constitution for microcomputers serving only a few persons. A formal document is a necessity for complex organizations where conflicts arise about goals, policies, budgets, and ownership. An information constitution is one of the principal remedies for destructive information politics.

Limits

Constitutions operate within boundaries. This book addresses the politics of information management and its subcategories, information systems and information technologies. I will not deal with managing business resources, formulating business strategy, planning organizational design or engaging in an exploration how to compete through better information management.[34] Those matters are suitable for the stage set by top operating management because they involve business politics, not information politics.

Inclusion Principles

To define the scope of information management, you must remove all costs that are directly attributable to the production of goods and services. What remains is the information cost of coordination of the enterprise internally, as well as the information costs of cooperation with suppliers and customers. I define all expenses for internal and external coordination as information management costs.

As technologies become tightly coupled with real-time control of factories and machines, the previously easy distinction between an *embedded* and a *management information* systems becomes blurred. Identical technologies may be regarded differently in different organizations. Sometimes there are regulatory implications that influence how a business deals with these distinctions.[35]

---

34. These topics will be covered in my book, *Business Alignment*, The Information Economics Press, May, 1995.

35. In the U.S. Department of Defense you can receive a Warner exemption from the onerous provisions of the Brooks bill which regulates the acquisition of administrative information systems. You can get a Warner exemption if you can show that you will be using a computer on a combat-related mission. Having as many computers and networks as possible classified under the Warner exemption is a much admired skill in the Pentagon. I believe there should be a Brooks exemption, not vice versa, because all defense information systems ought to support combat and not bureaucracy.

There is also the matter of jurisdiction: who controls what. For example, when analyzing the total information management expenditures of Federal Express, it is possible to classify the computer in the truck or on the driver's belt as either part of an *embedded* logistical system, under the control of the vice president of customer services or as a *management information* system under control of the CIO. My approach is to defer the matter of making the distinction to the judgment of the end-use customer.[36] If the customer gets directly perceived value from a computer system, then the system is *embedded.* If not, then it is a *management information* system. In the case of FedEx, the computers on the delivery person's belt and in the truck are *management information,* because they help the company manage delivery services and the customer does not care how that is accomplished.

Exclusions

Embedded computers are found in factory robots, commercial avionics, weapons guidance, process controllers, servo-mechanisms, and laboratory instrumentation. Microprocessors, which now have power equivalent to that of mainframes twenty years ago, are now embedded in most machines, appliances, and devices.

This book does not deal with the economics, organization, accountability or principles that apply to *embedded* computers. For instance, the electronics that control automobile ignition and the avionics that guide airplanes are excluded. Also excluded are computers that are part of a production process, such as real-time process control in a petrochemical plant, delivery of revenue-generating computer services, and industrial robots. Such computing machinery is directly involved in making products and are a direct cost of goods and services, whereas information management is always and indirect cost, or *overhead.*

Information management is the cost of coordinating the acquisition, production and customer delivery processes. It is the automation of managerial work. You must, however, include as an element of information management those standards that will allow the embedded

---

36. Following the precedent in the *Bible*, 1 Kings 3:24 (the King Solomon judgment).

devices to shake hands with a management information system and pass intelligible messages back and forth. An example is the black box that sends signals from a factory robot to the production scheduling system, informing it of task completion.

The scope of information management should also exclude information technology products and services used in generating revenues from external customers. For instance, if you are in a time-sharing or communications line-switching business, the computers that perform these functions are production equipment and not management information systems. If you are in the stock-brokerage business, a large portion of your information technology is production equipment.

The scope of information management excludes all engineering, research, and development that are a direct cost of products and services. For example, computer-aided devices that draw the masks for custom, very-large-scale-integration semiconductors (VLSI) are essential production equipment not management information systems. In a semiconductor plant, computers are production equipment, since they are used for process control and testing finished products. The same reasoning applies to laboratory equipment that supports product development, including programmers' workstations in companies that build software for commercial sale.

Drawing the distinction between *embedded* and *management information* systems is crucial. The harsh reality of the competitive place dictates the deployment of *embedded* information technologies. If the competitor offers automatic banking teller stations or bar-scanning checkout counters, you better install them too. If the capabilities of your embedded computers are inferior, that market place will let you know that quickly, and without much forgiveness.

The uses of information technologies in support of *management information* is largely dictated by information politics. If your management information systems are inferior, the people who caused to have it constructed to begin with, will try to keep it going indefinitely.

Drafting a Constitution

For a diversified international corporation or multi-agency government department, it is necessary to first define the authority that belongs at the highest level. For instance, an international auditing firm consisting of independent partnerships must state the unifying principle that binds the organization. Similarly, when you define governance for nearly autonomous institutions such as the Army, Navy, Marine Corps, and Air Force, you must first cite what binds them together before you can define what they may do separately. You should not draft constitutions from the bottom up, but from the top down. Constitutional conventions are difficult, because in most cases they call for giving up some of previously held privileges to the federation, rather than gaining local privileges by delegation from the federation.

Because federations involve the yielding of power, do not convene low-level employee working groups to draft the principles of a federation. The chances are that they will have no authority except set up obstacles on behalf of the potentates who prefer the *status quo.* Do not hire consultants to tell the CEO how to define the roles of information management in his company.[37] The consultant cannot possibly know enough about the subtleties how people and principles may interact. The debates about a constitution are one of the highest forms of organizational learning. That grows from discussions among managers and not from interviews with consultants, who are readily perceived as scouts for the CEO's agenda.

Learning that lasts matures through doing, not through listening. The most senior executives, as a group, should conceive of and preferably author the fundamental statements of the information policy themselves. Only after the top executive councils reach agreement about the fundamentals should these statements pass to others for elaboration. The essentials of any information constitution document should express the principles in simple terms. Initially they do not have to be in their final form.[38] As teams begin working on details, it will be necessary to go back to the top executives for further clarification.

---

37. I am amazed by CEOs who keep hiring consultants to advise on organization of systems, whose reputation is based exclusively on articles in business journals while having never managed a business organization.
38. Even the Ten Commandments came in two drafts.

Figure 9.1 If It Is Not Written, It Is Not Policy

To get any constitution understood and accepted requires lengthy debate and, ultimately, must be a negotiated compromise. Therefore, how you organize the constitutional writing process is as important as the substance of the text. The debates about the implications of the information constitution should reflect the spirit of the proposals. You cannot declare a commitment to local autonomy when the CEO releases an information constitution without the involvement of those ultimately affected.

Local Initiatives

Is it possible for an organizational unit to conceive its own rules of governance if there is no guidance from headquarters? The example for making good use of local constitutions while gaining valuable political experience comes from the American colonies. The colonials' experience in first conceiving, and then implementing innovative constitutional ideas is important. For example, the Commonwealth of Virginia had established its own rules about the separation of Church and State prior to the U.S. Constitutional convention. Such rules were of great value when the time came to draft the U.S. Constitution. Since most organizations have not even begun to compile their principles of governance beyond technical standards, they should not hesitate to start learning how to remove unnecessary conflicts by drafting formal governance principles.

No effective community can operate without commonly declared and generally accepted rules of governance. Whenever possible, the scope that defines an information constitution should be as forward-looking as circumstances allow. In the wilderness every small garden carries the promise that someday there may be a cultivated countryside.

10

INSTITUTIONS

*Without verifiable results management promises are
only desires.*

The dynamics of information technologies, especially the rapidly changing demands for new services, make it difficult to write anything that
has the same stability as constitutional law. Over the next few decades,
many of the current liabilities arising from the proliferation of computers, such as security risks and privacy intrusion, will become intol-
erable. Declaring rules of information governance will not suffice. Even
after protracted debates, what is issued as official policy will be immediately subject to challenge. Those who draft an information constitution will have to form additional institutions that can respond to
disputes, misunderstandings, and even rebellions, because that is in the
nature of all information politics.[39] The very volatility of the information environment makes it necessary to strengthen the capabilities of
two organizational units, the executive level staff and the auditors.

---

39. My favorite insurrection is the 1794 "Whiskey Rebellion" in western Pennsylvania.
Although nominally an opposition to taxes, it was a test of the new U.S. Federal government
to enforce its laws. As soon as an organization promulgates its "enterprise level architecture," you
can expect "COBOL," "Ada," "ISDN," "Unix" and "Windows" rebellions.

Separation of Powers

The principle of the separation of the judiciary from the executive and legislative branches is as sound in corporate governance as in public policy. Using the constitutional analogy for government:

- The equivalent of the legislative branch of information governance is the information management policy board. This board may appoint working groups to gather advice on technical, standards or implementation matters. However, there shall be only one source of authoritative policy decisions. None of this precludes the appointment of an executive staff as well as advisory councils at the process, business or local levels to interpret policy for use within their respective areas of influence.

- The equivalent of the executive branch of information governance are the information systems delivery organizations placed respectively at the enterprise, process, business, application or local levels of governance.

- The equivalent of the judiciary branch of the information governance is vested exclusively within the audit organization.

- The representatives of the governance processes are all managers, because all management is information management.

Executive Level Staff

The alignment of information systems with business plans calls for a powerful and expert executive-level staff. A small number of experienced professionals are essential to provide seasoned guidance in managing a portfolio of information management projects. These people must assure top management that long-term goals are being met while delivering superior service at the local level.

Currently, many companies are debating the relative advantage of contracting out their information systems. Regardless of how the financial advantages may direct the decision to outsource information services, an executive-level information management staff must remain the competency for preserving a corporation's information-handling capabilities.

Central staff executives who enjoy ready access to top management have the tendency to recommend in crisis seizing direct control over operations. Harassed executives have a proclivity to yield to such easy solutions. If the emergency fix becomes a long-term power position, the takeover of operations by corporate staff will disrupt the balance of relationships and tilt control toward centralization, without adequate safeguards. Combining the role of chief of the executive-level staff for information systems with the job of running data centers, programming, and telecommunications may have been a good solution twenty years ago, when the scope of such a job was minor relative to the power of marketing or manufacturing executives.[40] When the central systems staff first entered into the corporate arena, it had the expertise to control already scarce corporate information technologies. At that time, making information systems decisions and systems ownership were concentrated in the same hands. Such a concentration of power is now untenable because most of the information processing capacity and control have been distributed to business operations. Recent concepts of operations I have seen in many companies prohibit central staff from having direct control over information systems operations.

Currently, individual divisions, departments, and agencies have acquired the means to control their own information management processes and information systems capabilities. A large corporation must now attain its information management objectives through an amalgam of alliances, agreements, and accommodations that recognize the distribution of sufficient control over information management. To

---

40. In the 1970s, for a period of four years I held the position of global chief staff officer for all information management in Xerox as well as the job of general manager of the information services division in the U.S. which operated most computing, telecommunications and programming services. That arrangement could not last. After that I moved into the position of global chief staff officer for information management and administration for Xerox and all its subsidiaries.

balance the many interests yet order to support corporate systems integration requires creating conditions for equilibrium. In politics that is called a balance of power.[41]

It is essential to establish an independent central executive staff responsible for maintaining a viable balance between enterprise-wide and local information systems. To maintain the needed checks and balances, the central staff cannot have ownership of any large portion of the information systems empire. When CIOs become empire builders, it is just a matter of time before local interests overwhelm them. In an ensuing palace coup many benefits of the empire will fall into decay. The corporation is likely to regress to the chaotic conditions prevailing prior to the CIO starting on the path towards empire building.

Conflict Resolution

Those who have an information constitution will need a conflict resolution process. Established lines of accountability should prevent most major conflicts. However, there may be situations that are open to liberal interpretation, no matter how well the constitution document is written. To settle matters rapidly that may otherwise escalate into a conflict, top executives must find speedy and effective ways to deal with questions about interpreting rules and standards. There must be a graceful way to separate enterprise privileges from local, and *vice versa*. Viable constitutions depend on a formal process that enables interpretations to become precedents, and precedents to become accepted policy.

Any conflict resolution process must have a legitimate forum for interpreting the original intent of approved policies. It is not enough to assert that an organization wishes to have *open* systems and transparent communications. The extent to which local organizations adhere to such policies depends on having someone capable of conducting thorough and unbiased fact-finding.

---

41. For the most eloquent exposition of this idea see Henry Kissinger, *Diplomacy*, Simon & Schuster, 1994, especially Chapter 31.

Figure 10.1 Settling Disputes, Contemporary Bureaucratic Style

An information management policy board reporting directly to a member of the executive committee should be in a position to sort out most of the management issues and resolve policy conflicts arising over differences of opinion about technical matters.[42] However, since such boards are usually composed of a peer group they are unlikely to engage in unbiased fact-finding. The affected members of the board would protect their constituencies, which diminishes the authority of the board to look after enterprise-wide interests. The board also should not involve itself in uncovering violations of information policies or anything that looks like policing actions. For that an expert professional staff is best. These personnel should be best placed in the audit department that needs such expertise to understand the complexities of information systems. Consulting firms are also well suited for monitoring compliance with corporate information policies, especially if this involves matters of systems integrity and security.

---

42. Members of the information management policy board should be operating executives who are clearly senior in representing major consumers of information services. Preferably, they should be in line for succession to the top job in their respective functions. The membership of the policy board should exclude information systems executives. They can be organized into an information systems policy board to deal with technical and implementation matters.

Involvement of Auditors

Over the years I have helped form expert technical teams within audit departments. These teams have performed the necessary fact-finding about such matters as the adequacy of systems planning, the trustworthiness of investment justification, the adequacy of testing prior to installation, and the safeguarding of information security. When outside experts were needed, the corporate auditors hired them, not the systems managers.

The first time I helped create an expert audit group, we reaped unexpected benefits.[43] Our most promising systems supervisors were rotated into two year assignments with specialized information audit teams. These employees gained a better perspective about the broad scope of information management than if they had remained on the technical career ladder for all advancement. The auditors, in turn, acquired exceptional talent who would not have otherwise considered working in auditing.[44] On the basis of this experience, I was able to promote a personnel development program for many systems managers at Xerox which included a stint in the audit department.[45] A high percentage of these professionals presently serve as chief information officers of other corporations.

Using the audit organization to validate claims avoids exposing members of the information management policy board to disputes that devalue their corporate roles. Technical competence within the audit department uncovers potential disasters sooner than an overoptimistic computer project manger might be willing to disclose to anyone.

What Can Go Wrong

The worst possible situation when drafting a constitution is to lapse into inaction for an extended period of time while partial drafts are circulating among top executives. Such delays could take many years.

---

43. In 1965 at the National Dairy Products Corporation, later renamed the Kraft Corporation.
44. Professional auditors are usually recruited with good academic credentials but not necessarily with systems experience. Moving people back and forth between systems and auditing enhances the development of promising talent in both organizations.
45. Under the personal guidance of the chief auditor.

Although this is always a sign of poor executive leadership, it often happens. Whenever such delays occur further progress is arrested into inaction. Meanwhile, alert managers will be carving up defensible fiefdoms for themselves instead of concentrating on the business.

The next worst situation is a mandated governance schema that frames the latest organization chart as rigid guidance for all future governance. Information infrastructures, like sewers, roads, pipelines, and airports, must be sufficiently flexible to meet a wide range of needs and accommodate future growth. They cannot be ripped out every few years, or completely redesigned while still under construction. If all governance is specified for the instant gratification of recently appointed executives and if all infrastructure investments are short-lived, then much of the information technology budget will be used up only on survival needs, and maybe not even on all of those. The organization will not start accumulating the benefits of a continuous stream of investments to sustain long term growth through a steady accumulation of knowledge.

Many attempts to build an information infrastructure by *policy-du-jour* directions remind me of the story my grandfather used to tell about a farmer who kept pulling out his young apple trees every year to re-examine the roots. The farmer didn't understand why he never got any apples.[46]

While a reluctant organizations languishes in procrastination or short-sightedness, a smart competitor with an identical computer budget, will be able to allocate a concentrated share of available funds to information capabilities that keep accumulating. Meanwhile, the improvising opponents will waste his energies in erecting and then disassembling a succession of flimsy information skeletons. The opportunists will never build up the necessary capacity to fend off an attack from the determined opponent, when it finally comes.

---

46. The recommendations of the General Accounting Office to congressional committees are examples of systems direction by frequent re-inspection.

A Long Journey

The path towards information governance is difficult. It may take many years before you have a comprehensive model for guiding individual acts. However, I cannot conceive how top executives can align their information systems with business plans unless they have also put into place a framework by which individuals and organizational units can cooperate while minimizing the debilitating effects of contentious politics.

Conceiving, discussing, announcing, and working under the guidance of an information constitution is not only desirable but essential. The systems capabilities that an organization acquires in this way will shape the benefits of computerization more than any other influence. Governance will always surpass technology as the most critical success factor. That is the most important lesson of all information politics.

II

MODEL CONSTITUTION

Government that governs the least will survive the longest.

This chapter offers a prototype of an information constitution for a diversified organization.[47] A constitution sets forth a decision-making process that endures over time. Since each organization is unique, its constitution must be customized to fit the specific circumstances. The example in this chapter shows a prototype constitution which explains the roles of central enterprise management while at the same time allowing for the strengthening of local initiatives. The prototype presented here seeks to balance between a central staff who desire corporate-wide standardization and the local operators who aspire to greater flexibility and independence.

Statement of Goals

Goals should be set forth by the chief executive officer of an enterprise. If possible, they should be endorsed by the board of directors, especially if they propose significant increases in the resources that will be devoted to information management.

------

47. By diversified I mean a corporation or government agency made up of several profit centers, operating units or autonomous functional departments. Usually there is a headquarters staff unit to coordinate this diversity. The annual information technology budget is typically over $10 million.

Frequently goal statements sound as though they were textbook abstractions or recent buzzwords from a management magazine. Even though they may reiterate currently fashionable phrases, such pronouncements will not inspire anyone. Operating managers dismiss statements that sound like platitudes because they cannot envision how to apply generalizations that cannot be somehow related to action. Goals should stretch thinking but stop short of describing utopia.[48]

Figure 11.1 The Visionary Consultant

48. There is a giant, highly diversified global corporation that alleges its goal is "To Lead the World in Everything We Do." Realistically that is unfeasible considering the number of businesses and geographic markets it is engaged in, so managers find it difficult to decide what to focus on. This vision is not taken seriously by anyone except the public relations department.

A useful statement of goals is more like a checklist of achievements that a CEO wishes his organization would attain at some point beyond the current planning horizon. If a company makes plans that deal with the future up to five years out, then its goals should address the next six to ten years. If management can articulate what an enterprise should look like within ten years, then statements of goals should reach out for aspirations that may be fifteen to twenty years away.

Since information management goals are company- and industry-specific, I cannot provide a generic model. However, information systems goals have many commonalities across a range of corporations. The following information systems goals could be realistic for a high technology international corporation with a four-year business plan already in place:

¶ Our decentralized business units shall become fully responsible for the benefits and the costs of information technology they deploy in their operations. They will assume full accountability for delivering the productivity gains derived from information technologies, as committed in their business plans.

¶ Our competitive advantage shall be supported with information technology solutions that offer the most effective information-handling capabilities in this industry.

¶ We shall make information productivity one of the key indicators of performance and include it in all periodic performance evaluations.

¶ We shall make it possible for our people to satisfy the majority of their communication needs using electronic means.

¶ Our employees, suppliers, joint-venture partners and customers shall be able to contact us anytime, by computerized means, to obtain the needed information.

❡ Our employees shall work more effectively as well as communicate and cooperate electronically better than any of our competitors' employees.

❡ Our information systems shall integrate communications, computing and systems support functions automatically by means that do not require personal intervention, except in cases involving information security.

❡ Our voice, data, video, and image information systems shall be interoperable and secure so that employees will be able to retrieve, on an authorized computing device, a display of information from any authorized information source.

❡ Our information systems shall enhance the information productivity and work quality of employees, suppliers, contractors, and joint venture partners.

❡ Our enterprise-wide information systems shall share resources effectively and efficiently through adoption of common standards, common data, and common software capabilities.

To manage an enterprise as an integrated, interoperable and low cost organization, compatible management processes and shared resources are needed. The following sections define how it may be feasible to achieve that objective.

Statement of Principles[49]

The difference between goals and principles is that goals are hardly ever attained in their entirety, whereas principles are propositions that someone can test for conformity on a committed schedule. With regard to principles, you are either in compliance or you are not. Goals should

---

49. This section reflects most of the recommendations of the Department of Defense Executive Level Group, of which I was a member prior to my appointment in the Department of Defense.

not change, and even if they do, that should happen only after lengthy deliberation and testing. Goals should be open to enhancement but not to complete reversal. Any corporation that changes its goals every five to ten years should be suspected of having confused leadership.

Principles should never violate goals. The Ten Commandments are principles, not goals. The U.S. Constitution sets forth principles, not goals. Principles require constant amplification to keep up with evolution towards increased complexity. Here are examples of statements of principles:

Figure 11.2 Governance That Adapts

¶ We shall manage information through centralized control over standards, efficiency, security and the sharing of assets.

¶ We shall manage information through central policy direction and decentralized execution to assure responsiveness, quality, learning and innovation.

¶ We shall require eliminating redundant tasks and then simplifying all information processes prior to building new applications.[50]

¶ We shall enhance existing information systems whenever the need arises for additional automation instead of opting for new systems development as the preferred choice.

¶ We shall subject existing and proposed business methods to risk-adjusted cost-benefit analyses using for comparison the best public and private sector results.

¶ We shall prove and validate new business methods in pilot installations prior to full scale implementation.

¶ We shall use common applications software for all information systems that perform the same function, unless verifiable proof exists that some functions should remain unique.

¶ We shall hold operating managers at all levels accountable for all benefits and costs of developing and operating their information systems.

¶ We shall develop and enhance information systems according to standard enterprise-wide methods in order to enhance the speed of such development and realize benefits swiftly.

¶ We shall pursue a policy of small, incremental system development before considering any investments in large and comprehensive programs.

---

50. Eliminating redundant processes, such as hand carrying disks from one application to another, or running conversion software to make messages understandable to another application, is what integration tries to accomplish.

¶ We shall develop and enhance information systems using standard process models that document business methods.[51]

¶ We shall make computing and communication networks transparent to the information systems that rely upon them.[52]

¶ We shall adopt company-wide data definitions and standards for all data.

¶ We shall acquire information services through competitive bidding that considers internal as well as external offerings.

¶ Our information services shall meet the criteria of being proven,[53] interoperable, scalable,[54] low cost ,and well supported, and have clearly defined migration strategies toward further technological evolution.[55]

¶ We shall enter data into the information system only once, at the point of origin.

¶ We shall assign to our data elements safeguards that assure close to zero errors at points of origin.

---

51. See Integration Definitions for Functional Modeling (IDEF0) and Information Modeling (IDEF1X), Federal Information Processing Standards 183 and 184 respectively, National Institute of Standards and Technology, December 21, 1993.

52. Transparency is the capacity for applications to exchange data, images or voice regardless of the physical medium over which the exchange takes place and irrespective of the computer technology used to process such transactions.

53. Proven means that the information services must have had sufficient prior operational use to reduce technology risks to a minimum. Relying on proven technology suggests not adopting the first software releases or purchasing computer products that have just emerged from development.

54. Scalable means that the information services are capable of at least a thousand-fold expansion in capacity.

55. Low cost means less than ten percent of the prospective development cost of a replacement at the time conversion becomes necessary. With hardware and software technologies currently experiencing two to four year life-cycles, a well-defined migration strategy should assure at least a ten year life and provide a path for low-cost conversion afterwards.

¶ We shall facilitate, control, and limit access to our information according to universally applicable security principles.

¶ We shall protect our information assets against deliberate attack by technically experienced adversaries.

¶ We shall safeguard our information against unintentional or unauthorized alteration, destruction, or disclosure.

¶ We shall standardize our graphic presentation format for communication between users easy and to enhance learning in the use of applications.[56]

Responsibilities at the Enterprise and Business Levels

Policies are derived from the established goals and principles. They describe the means to achieve the stated goals. The credibility of an information management executive will grow with the number of effective policies that make it possible for people to concentrate on getting on with their jobs, instead of arguing about privileges or the minutiae of technical preferences.

¶ The corporate executive committee shall consent to and issue all corporate information management goals, principles, policies and objectives.

¶ The chief information officer shall be a senior executive who reports to a member of the corporate executive committee. The CIO will be responsible for independently assessing whether the information management plans are aligned with the approved business plans.

¶ The chief information officer shall be responsible for long range human resource planning for personnel

---

56. I define easy as the ability to learn how to use an application in a matter of minutes, not hours. It may take more time to learn a particular system, but the basic style of graphic presentation should be consistent across all applications.

involved in information management, including the skill and career advancement of information technology personnel.

¶ The chief information officer shall report at least annually, to the corporate executive committee on the state of information management. This report must document whether current information assets are enhancing or detracting from the economic value-added to shareholders.

¶ The staff of the chief information officer shall manage and coordinate only enterprise-level programs. All other projects and operations, shall be managed by personnel as close as possible to where the service is used.

¶ Each business unit shall appoint a business unit information officer with responsibility for that unit's information management paralleling in scope the roles and responsibilities of the corporate chief information officer.

¶ The business unit information officer shall be responsible for assessing the alignment of the business unit's information management plans and resources with the approved goals, principles, policies and objectives of the business unit as well as the corporation.

The Information Management Policy Board

¶ The corporate executive committee shall appoint an information management policy board.

¶ The corporate executive committee shall define the authority of the information management policy board and may overrule its decisions.

¶ The corporate executive committee shall delegate to the information management policy board the authority for developing and proposing corporate information management standards. However, the corporate executive committee will retain the authority to issue standards as corporate policy and to address instances where there is non-compliance with enterprise-wide standards.

¶ The responsibilities of the information management policy board will include:

- Oversight of pricing for all inter-unit information services;[57]

- Oversight of corporate projects that are financed out of enterprise funds;

- Endorsement of information processing standards and all technical standards proposed by an information technology council which serves as a subcommittee of the information management policy board;

- Approval of an information configuration framework that encompasses all levels of the organization;

- Endorsement of information security policies and review of all reports on violations of security standards;

- Evaluation of intelligence about progress by competitors in information management; and,

- Oversight of centrally managed personnel development and training programs.

These responsibilities may be modified, subject to approval by the corporate executive committee.

¶ Decisions by a majority of the members of the information management policy board becomes effective immediately. Disputes shall be settled by the corporate executive committee.

---

57. Particular attention shall be given to setting allowable overhead charges for activities such as internal billing, training, education and long range technology investments.

¶ The information management policy board shall define the rules for corporate-wide sharing of information capabilities, such as sharing software, using common corporate data, assuring telecomputing interoperability and adopting best business practices. The rationale for sharing corporate-wide capabilities with be minimizing life-cycle systems costs for the corporation and not necessarily for each business unit.

¶ The information management policy board shall publish criteria against which information technologies must qualify to be declared as *open* systems solutions that are consistent with the approved enterprise configuration master plan.

Responsibilities of Information Systems Managers

Regardless of the organizational level, all information systems managers - defined here as all managers who control information systems - shall adhere to the following principles:

¶ Information managers shall be responsible for providing superior responsiveness to customer needs, enhancing the value of information products and services, and supporting employees to increase their productivity and the quality of their work.

¶ Comparisons of actual results against those proposed in the business plans and budgets shall be used to evaluate information managers' contributions.[58]

¶ Information managers shall be responsible for authorizing access to information bearing in mind security requirements. They will be also accountable for any lapses in information security.

---

58. As measured by "Management Value-Added," which is identical to "Economic Value-added," also known as EVA™.

¶ Information managers shall be responsible for providing training and assistance to all users of information services, even when such support originates from vendors.

¶ Information managers shall comply with corporate policies regarding security, safety, survivability, technology sharing, technology investment planning, data integrity, data access, applications interoperability, and cross-functional integration.

Responsibilities of Operating Managers

Every operating manager needs to be a manager of information resources, because information management is potentially the most efficient means for coordinating all work. Operating managers may or may not use computerized information systems for that purpose.

¶ Operating managers shall be responsible for ensuring that information systems deliver results as planned or better. They shall be accountable for both the costs and benefits of their information resources. They will measure their information productivity and report on their progress in achieving committed objectives.[59]

¶ Operating managers shall be accountable for the planning, design, implementation, quality and operational performance of all information systems necessary to support their missions.

¶ Operating managers shall be responsible for granting security access to information.

¶ Operating managers shall be accountable for surpassing their organization's competitors in the effectiveness of their information systems.

---

59. Benefits and costs are measurable when they affect the business plan. If the effect on the business plan is not demonstrable, the use of information resources makes no difference and their use should be questioned.

¶ Operating managers shall use information management to realize competitive gains and enhance economic value-added.

¶ Operating managers shall be responsible for assuring that employees understand how to apply information systems effectively while meeting or exceeding quality standards.

Planning and Finance

¶ Business plans must show how information systems contribute to achieving planned operating results.

¶ Business plans shall include information systems implementation plans that are consistent with the stated financial and operating targets.

¶ Support services, whether provided from shared facilities or managed locally, shall adhere to standard cost accounting practices. Service providers shall benchmark their costs and performance against the best organizations, regardless of industry.

¶ Activity-based standard costing shall be used in billing for information services. Services shall be priced and billed by activity that consumes information services, as recognized by the customer, as opposed to those defined by information technology.

¶ The established practice of billing by computer resource units, central processor time, number of tape mounts and kilo packets shall not be used.[60] Invoices shall indicate only those elements the customer can control, such as the volume of transactions, the number of data elements queried, the length of transmis-

---

60. This practice prevents comparing costs and measuring productivity gains. Metering and then billing for such details is expensive and it also alienates the internal customer.

sions or the number of sites for which support has been contracted for.

¶ Overhead surcharges on pass-through billings for contractor-supplied services shall be allowed only if justified by value-contributing services.[61]

¶ Information services shall be competitively priced and reflect the rapidly declining unit costs of information technologies.

¶ Favorable comparisons with the most efficient among similar commercial services shall be demonstrated after discounting competitive prices for profit and marketing expenses.

¶ At least a twenty percent annual decline in unit costs charged to customers shall be realized over a period of several years. Management will examine at least a five year track record of cumulative cost reductions to confirm that this policy is followed.

Contracting Out

¶ Information processing and software development shall be contracted out only if quality, cost, security and service standards are equivalent to or better than those found within the organization.[62] All bids shall be evaluated against fully allocated internal costs instead of directly budgeted expenses.[63]

---

61. For a number of years it was a standard practice of data center managers to mark up their telecommunication bills by as much as fifty percent to cover other losses or to support promotional overhead. Customers have figured this out and now contract for their own services which makes` systems integration more difficult.

62. This proviso assumes that security will not be compromised and that these applications are not a source of unique competitive advantage

63. For instance, many costs dictated by corporate policy such as personnel, executive offices, legal counsel, finance and accounting are never fully charged to cost centers. A commitment to outsourcing services should recognize that all fixed overhead costs are ultimately variable.

❡ Services shall be subcontracted not only to commercial sources but also to other company units or affiliated organizations that have demonstrated competitive excellence.[64]

❡ Resources for information services shall not be expended by business units on systems that in any way duplicate services available from another business unit or from commercial source.[65]

❡ Analytic methods based on economic value-added shall be used to justify discretionary expenditures for information management projects in excess of limits set by the information management policy board.

Care for Customers of Internal Information Services

❡ Personnel at points-of-use shall determine the acceptability of the human-machine communication and the quality of the performance features of all information systems.[66] They shall evaluate the quality, utility, responsiveness, and effectiveness of the information systems on which they depend.

❡ Information management shall operate on the principle of assigning single point accountability for the successful completion of every information management services task.[67] The organization that has the single

---

64. When benchmarking such services against commercial prices, disallow marketing and product development costs from the commercial bid in order to come up with comparable operating costs.

65. It can be wasteful for every business unit to be autonomous and completely self-sufficient in all of its information services. Checking for possible duplication should precede making any new investment.

66. Point-of-use is where the eye or ear of a decision maker receives information from an information system. This could be anywhere and could involve a variety of electronic means including voice, displays, simulation, or direct projection to the retina of the eye.

67. If there is a malfunction, the point-of-use customer should not be obliged to contact multiple sources such as communications, hardware, software and training experts. There should be only one phone number a customer calls to get complete resolution of a question or problem.

point of accountability shall have the capacity to perform every diagnostic test and draw on all required
expert assistance to correct any defects and answer any
customer queries.[68]

¶ Approaching zero defects shall be established as the
achievable quality standard for information services.[69]

¶ Customer satisfaction shall be measured only as seen
from the customer's point of view, and not as defined
by the providers of services.[70]

¶ Every customer complaint shall be accounted for.
Every corrective action shall be recorded and reported
to the organization that has been assigned the responsibility for auditing compliance with policies, principles and standards.

¶ Process improvements that result from error corrections shall be routinely reviewed jointly by information systems and operating management in order to
avoid frequently repeated mistakes that originate from
error-prone business procedures, inadequacies in
training or mistakes in applications design.

---

68. Single point accountability means that it is clear who is accountable for assuming zero
defects in every product or service. Single point accountability is an essential element of system
design.

69. With the enormous expansion in the number of transactions processed through computers 99.9 percent reliability — once considered the standard in data services — is no longer good
enough with the enormous expansion in the number of transactions processed through computers. Consider the following consequences of systems that have 99.9 percent reliability:

 • A national pharmaceutical system issues twenty thousand incorrect drug prescriptions per year;

 • The postal system loses sixteen thousand pieces of mail every hour,

 • Medical organizations perform five hundred incorrect surgical operations each
week, and,

 • The system would drop on the floor fifty newborn babies every hour
(Source: *Computerworld,* February 15, 1993

70. Do not accept reporting on responsiveness as seen from the standpoint of the service organization, such up-time in the computer room. What matters is the response time, as seen by the
customer, when requesting a data display.

¶ All customers of information services shall be provided with facilities, tools, and training to evaluate the quality, price and utility of the organization's providers of information services.

Data Management

¶ All information acquired or created by employees while conducting business, except that which is specifically exempted as personal or private, is a corporate resource.[71] The intellectual or property rights to all corporate information produced while on the company payroll belongs to the corporation.

¶ Business units or local management may receive a temporary authority to become custodians of enterprise-level data. In such cases, the methods, rules and conditions of custody cited in corporate information management policies and standards will apply.

¶ All corporate data elements shall be entered into the information system only at authorized points of origin. All subsequent uses of such data elements shall rely on copies of the original entries. Methods for positively identifying the originating source of all corporate data elements will be included in all systems designs.

¶ Calculated summaries and aggregations of data, such as totals and subtotals, shall be derived only from original data entries to maintain information integrity at all times. Summary data obtained by other means shall not be entered into the information system, except as authorized.

---

71. The exemption for private information applies only if the rules of governance allow the retention of personal information in the organization's files.

❡ The points of origin, authorization, security, context and definition of all data shall be documented using standard data model description methods.

Information Configuration Policies

Information management shall follow levels of accountability, which describe the information management master plan. Definitions of a seven-level structure are:[72]

* Level 1: Global. All functions, services and standards that assure the interoperability of the enterprise with suppliers, customers and vendors of information technologies;

* Level 2: Enterprise. All services and standards that set the rules of governance to assure the cost effectiveness and interoperability of information systems;

* Level 3: Functional Processes. All functions that support common business processes and assure horizontal integration of activities, across the entire enterprise, that have interrelated work flows regardless of location or business;

* Level 4: Business. All systems that are unique to the products or service delivered by an autonomous organizational unit;

* Level 5: Application. All systems features that uniquely satisfy the operating needs of personnel who perform similar tasks;

* Level 6: Local. All systems features and practices that are unique to individuals or groups who require modifications of the standard processes not provided by higher organizational levels;

* Level 7: Personal. All data that individuals wish to keep private.

The purpose of the assignment of levels to the master systems configuration framework is to define the applicability of policies and standards. Configuration management calls for close adherence to stan-

---

72. The choice of seven levels reflects what I estimate to be the maximum amount of complexity that is manageable. It is always preferable to have fewer than seven levels. William of Occam (1285-1349) was right when he asserted that whatever can be done well with less is better. Levels can be eliminated by delegating authority. Stalin ran a large federation, except all seven levels of authority were within the Kremlin. The Soviet Union disintegrated when the Kremlin could not effectively control what was going on locally.

dards at higher levels while providing maximum flexibility at the local and personal levels.

¶ A formal management process, administered by the information management policy board, shall define the application services performed at each level of the master design framework.

¶ Information management functions that are not expressly reserved for a higher level shall be delegated to the next level. The information management policy board shall not delegate what has been already reserved for enterprise level accountability. Only the corporate executive committee has such authority.

¶ The chief information officer shall be responsible for keeping track of unresolved interpretations of the principles of information management governance and bring them to the attention of the information management policy board without delay. The CIO shall also be responsible for resolving any incidents that interfere with the capacity of the organization to react to competitive actions or expose the enterprise to jeopardy, especially when they involve matters of information security.

Decentralization Policies

¶ Information processing capabilities shall be available at the local and personal levels, except for those services expressly reserved for operations at the business, process or enterprise levels.

¶ Operating decisions about communications capabilities, document management, computing resources, applications support and training shall be made wherever local management has discretionary powers over budgets and performance.[73]

¶ Designing screens, creating local applications and making ad-hoc inquiries shall be done by point-of-use personnel, provided they use only standard software tools provided for this purpose.

¶ Adequate resources shall be made available to operating managers for local training, integration and innovation needs.

Personnel Development Policies

The development, motivation and retention of information technology and management experts are keys to success for any organization that strives for information superiority. Rapid innovation rates accelerate the technical obsolescence of information professionals. The resources and care devoted to enhancing the value of personnel must receive concentrated attention from the corporate executive committee and be on the agenda of the information management policy board for scheduled reviews.

¶ The corporate executive committee shall review at least annually an independent assessment, and preferably from a consulting firm, of the quality of the personnel who support information management services.

¶ The information management policy board shall monitor the progress of all personnel development programs that concern information management.

¶ A professional corps of information managers and technical experts shall focus on innovation and business value creation irrespective of any outsourcing of computer services to commercial providers. The chief

---

73. The objective is to place accountability for costs and benefits where information management has the greatest impact.

information officer of the enterprise shall be accountable for this activity.

¶ Certification by an authorized professional organization for minimum technical qualifications shall be
required of all systems personnel, especially for information managers responsible for systems projects.

¶ Collegial and peer group electronic communications
shall be established for all information systems personnel, regardless of geographic location or organizational level.

¶ Every information management professional shall
share knowledge, cooperate in finding solutions to
problems, identify opportunities for improvement,
promote innovation and assist personnel who have
less developed skills. This shall be accomplished by
establishing and maintaining a secure information
communications network.

¶ Standard computer-aided systems engineering tools
and standard project management methods shall be
applied in planning, management and implementation of systems projects.[74]

¶ Distance learning and on-line services shall be used
to improve the affordability and timeliness of information systems training. Remote diagnostics for just-
in-time tutoring shall be available for all applications.
Distance learning, tutoring and distance applications
support shall be a feature of all applications.

Systems Design Policies

The quality of systems designs determines the benefits systems can
deliver. Poor systems design will produce failure, even if implementation

---

74. Training costs can escalate enormously in the absence of standard tools and practices.

is technically superior. With a good systems design, there is a chance that even poor implementations can recover after corrective actions.

¶ Systems integration shall be established as the core competency of the systems development organization. Systems integration is the capacity to build low cost, secure and technically interoperable systems according to rules that follow the prescribed systems standards for each level of the enterprise.

¶ Full systems integration capabilities for the enterprise will be demonstrable when any authorized individual can easily share information without regard to application, operating system or computer hardware.[75]

¶ Integration services shall be available within each organizational level, which will promote the reuse of standard software and data models. The enterprise information systems integration staff will assist in adopting integrated systems engineering methods and help in distributing for general use successful adaptations of local applications.

Design Principles

¶ Standard software tools shall be supplied to local personnel to increase the range of choices available to them, within the constraints imposed by architectural standards. These tools will enable experimental prototyping of local variants or additions to existing standard applications.

¶ Software tools shall become available at all levels of the architecture for constructing unique local appli-

---

75. Integration is a simplification of design that improves efficiency of developing and maintaining systems at least tenfold. What happens to redundant staff if there is such an enormous gain in productivity? They will require retraining and upgrading to enable them to offer new services, such as business process improvement or application support, to a larger and more sophisticated population of computer users.

cations and databases. Data originating from one level shall not enter a higher level without first complying with standards prescribed for the higher level.

¶ Locally developed applications shall be encouraged, provided that they comply with the master systems design framework and security standards. These duplications must not introduce nonstandard data definitions for further distribution outside their local scope.

¶ The best of locally developed applications shall be considered for migration to higher levels to become enterprise, business, or functional level systems. Criteria for their selection shall include: low operating and maintenance costs; features that satisfy a list of required new functions; a systems design possessing the best prospect of being upgraded; and a design that complies with *open* systems standards.

¶ The design of any major new application shall be authorized only after the completion of business process improvement studies that trace the work flow of the existing business processes and compare it with what is proposed.

¶ All new application developments or major software enhancements shall follow an evolutionary path towards *open* systems that conform to the approved enterprise standards.

¶ The cost of information systems operations shall be reduced by avoiding periodically printed reports, eliminating all printing except for local exception reporting, and using tools so that customers may specify their own output formats.[76]

---

76. These recommendations reflect a fundamental switch from the technology push approach of information generation to the customer demand pull method of operation.

¶ Design costs and implementation schedules shall be reduced by making widely accessible a repository that stores customer-conceived templates of useful system solutions.

¶ Contractors, consultants and suppliers engaged in the development of new corporate applications must comply with the approved corporate design standards and procedures so that their work is reusable elsewhere and does not keep up a dependency on maintenance services from the original designers.

Technology Advancement

¶ The systems specification process shall be accelerated by designing while prototyping.

¶ Applications shall be rapidly enhanced by means of add-on modular features in preference to redesigning or modifying the application itself.

¶ The design cycle shall be shortened by using leading-edge users to conduct experimental testing of pilot applications. The systems staff shall be frequently rotated from technical design tasks to the operating environment through short term and diversified assignments involving direct communication with revenue-producing customers.

¶ Experimental installations of leading-edge technologies shall surpass the most advanced competitors. The rapid pace of innovation makes the most advanced technologies also the most economical to operate. Early pilot demonstrations of the commercial feasibility in new technologies shall be funded to assemble a portfolio of opportunities that offer potential competitive advantages.[77]

Reuse

¶ Accumulated process knowledge from legacy systems shall be salvaged through reverse engineering and redesign.

¶ Data element, software component, software object, and business process reuse shall be maintained using distributed but centrally coordinated configuration catalogs of all systems designs.

¶ A standard graphic systems work flow description notation shall be used throughout the organization. This symbolic notation shall be at a sufficiently comprehensible level so that any operating manager, without extensive technical training, will be able to understand systems proposals using these methods to comprehend the contemplated changes in business procedures.

¶ Developers, contractors, consultants, and suppliers shall segregate the software development environment from the software execution environment to increase software portability from an existing operation to a totally new computing system.[78]

Telecommunications

¶ A shared telecomputing network shall be capable of securely delivering voice, data, image, and video information on demand, anywhere and anytime in a high quality, timely and cost-effective manner which

---

77. There are too many gadgets coming into market to make comprehensive experimentation affordable. Therefore, forming a small expert staff to engage in technology intelligence will pay off.
78. Software execution is also known as the "run-time" environment.

also assures privacy and the protection of the information that is conveyed.

¶ Dependence on local support personnel shall be reduced through central online diagnostics, remote help desk support, and network control services, as illustrated in Figure 11.3.

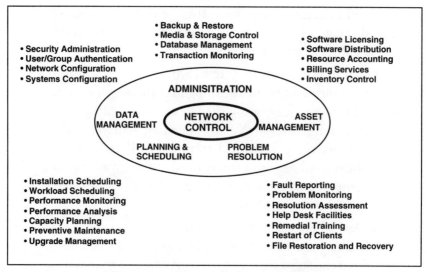

Figure 11.3 Network Control Tasks

¶ A communications redundancy classification shall be assigned to every personal computers, workstation, gateway, server or communications switch on the network. This classification shall determine how many alternate communication channels must be available for traffic to move without disruption if a network failure occurs. This classification will also guide the decision how and when to replicate local data bases to backup sites.[79]

Risk Management

❡ System designs shall use multiple identical databases to assure survivability under conditions of failure.

❡ Application designs shall use local databases to improve transaction response times and minimize the dependence on communications links.

❡ Applications shall be location and data source independent. In the event of a local disaster, it shall be possible to reconstitute operations from an alternate site without deterioration of customer services. Formal actuarial methods shall be used to determine the economic affordability of risk protection.

Technology Acquisition

❡ Commercially available technologies, services and software shall be used. Modification of vendor-maintained commercial software will not be allowed except where the ability to make modifications is a standard option of the software.

❡ The adoption of *open* systems shall be enforced by procurement guidelines that specify which standards must be met.

❡ Consultants or contractors shall use only prescribed standard software development and maintenance tools. Acceptance tests will assure that purchased or contracted for software remains portable, and will assure independence from having to continue the consultants' or contractors' engagements after contract completion.

❡ Applications shall not be dependent on hardware, operating systems, systems engineering tools, man-

---

79. Replication is a concept in database management where two or more data bases remain exact copies of each other while simultaneously processing different applications.

agement methods or computer languages that are available only from a single source of supply.

Security

❡ Computing power shall continue to be available anywhere within the organization, on short notice, regardless of any disruptions of services. A continually tested and independently certified contingency plan shall be documented on the basis of criteria set by the information management policy board.

❡ Information services support for customer-support operations shall be restored, within a specified time period, subsequent to any incident of physical destruction caused by natural disaster or professionally executed sabotage.[80]

❡ Only essential services shall be maintained when a specified fraction of facilities, defined by the information management policy board, become inoperable.

❡ All workloads shall be shifted geographically within the enterprise or to commercial providers as the need arises to meet emergencies. The information management policy board shall specify how rapidly this must occur.

❡ Software revisions for critical applications shall be subjected to an independent change management and

---

80. Our financial institutions are choice targets for disruption of service. For example, the Chicago Mercantile Exchange asserts that in 1993 it traded $100 trillion dollars of currency, equity indexes and commodities (*Wall Street Journal*, March 30, 1994, p.A17), which is an average trading volume of $670 million per minute. Recently I visited the network control center of one of the top U.S. banks. The CIO pointed out that the lit screens were clocking transactions of half a billion dollars per minute during a sudden rush in trading. The general lack of restricted access controls, and the relative ease with which unauthorized personnel can gain access to unattended computers to make false trades, should be of great concern.

control process that tracks all software change actions and monitors test results.

¶ At least two independent levels of authorization shall be used for granting network access privileges to any software repository or for making software modifications in critical corporate applications.[81]

¶ Dual security access authorizations to confidential databases shall be required in all cases where the alteration of such databases would have severe consequences.

¶ Multilevel security software and hardware shall permit the acquisition, display and manipulation of secure as well as open information in a single display, without compromising security.

¶ Redundant network control centers and archival data repositories at fully protected sites shall be established and continually tested.

¶ Data network services, including online data network diagnostic capabilities for local area networks, shall have the capacity to achieve rapid service restoration of local computing facilities from a remote site.

---

81. The software repository is the most likely place for someone to tamper with computer applications to avoid detection.

12

CONCEPT OF OPERATIONS

The proof of a workable system is found in everyday conduct.

Many laymen are uncomfortable reading anything that looks like a legal document. They look to lawyers for interpretation of clauses that may not be clear. The trouble with most corporate policy documents, including the ones that I authored years ago, is that they look and sound like arcane legalese. Managers prefer a language that clearly states who does what to whom. I call such statements concept of operations guidelines.

Figure 12.1 Explaining the Concept of Operations

Concept of operations statements require tailoring to fit each organization. Political compromises, the assignment of responsibilities, and the authority for expenditures will be different in each situation. Because I have been asked repeatedly what such a document might look like, here is an abbreviated version.

Mission Concepts

¶ The purpose of the **global** level of the information management configuration is to enable an enterprise to share information with institutions, partners, customers, suppliers and contractors. The information system of an enterprise is not entirely self-sufficient. Managing seamless transfers of secure information to and from points outside the boundaries of an enterprise will be one of the most complex issues of corporate governance in years to come. How and when to allow the transfer of information to and from the enterprise will determine what information passes to other levels.

¶ The purpose of the **enterprise** level of the information management configuration is to supply operating managers at all levels of the organization with the necessary tools, data, software, and standards to develop and maintain business-specific applications. The policies that govern the management of data will guide the creation, distribution, and access to databases and data repositories.

¶ The purpose of the **process** level of the configuration is to integrate information systems across similar functional processes within the enterprise. Finance, accounting, personnel, and benefits administration are the most likely candidates for shared computer applications that are independent of business or geographic units. Functional processes represent *horizontal* integration, whereas business processes emphasize *vertical* integration. Most of the political friction encountered in information management matters stems from the contest between *horizontal* and *vertical* proponents. In the long run the horizontalists will prevail because *vertical* business structures are unstable due to continuous reshuffling of organization charts, whereas the *horizontal* information flows represent the realities of the ongoing business and remain relatively stable regardless of what happens as result of the latest reorganization announcement.

¶ The purpose of the **business** level is to enable local managers with limited resources to readily adapt applications that support the specific, unique needs of their business missions. For example, there is no reason to integrate spare-part inventory systems for submarines and tanks, or toasters and tractors. These are separate and distinct businesses, with different patterns in timing, costs, geography and customer demand.

¶ The purpose of the **application** level of information management is to facilitate rapid installation of new applications and enable quick modifications to existing systems. The application level inherits from higher levels those standards that address data definitions, data models, application templates, software components, software tools, network connections, computing facilities, and graphic interfaces. The purpose of this inheritance is to minimize the effort necessary to deliver new applications.[82]

---

82. Well over 80 percent of the labor costs associated with application development and maintenance are caused by the need to define elements that would already exist if you had global, enterprise, function, and business layers in place. I expect that the current handcraft approaches to application management to evolve towards factory-like assembly methods of software components.

¶ The purpose of the **local** level is to adapt those technology elements passed on from higher levels to meet the needs of employees and customers at point-of-use. Differences in training, language, culture, habit, work organization, security, and affordability make it necessary to abandon the idea that applications can be specified which fit everybody's needs, everywhere, at all times.

¶ The purpose of the **personal** level is to protect the privacy and confidentiality of information which is originated by an individual for personal uses only. This information shall be accessible only at the discretion of the originating individual. Private files on a local disk drive may contain data people value and do not wish to have exposed without their consent. Technical safeguards should permit the use of encryption and a protected partition of memory for storing private information. Just about every information management policy textbook avoids discussing this issue.

Enterprise Level Concepts

Activity at the enterprise level focuses on decisions that have consequences up to twenty-five years into the future, such as research and development. In case of information systems, once data definitions and data elements receive endorsement, they should remain in place for a long time, independently of technology or usage.

Activity at the enterprise level maintains technology policies, standards, reference models, data management tools, integrated systems, as well as database and software configurations. To reap the benefits from *open systems*, costly technologies must remain in place for well over a decade.

Enterprise Level Checklist

Enterprise level actions shall be supervised and approved by the corporate executive committee. These actions include:

¶ Determine which corporate-wide business processes require enterprise-level systems integration.

¶ Prescribe information systems integration methods.

¶ Mandate information security and systems recovery standards.

¶ Announce information message and media interchange standards.

¶ Advance the application of information management standards.

¶ Specify data reliability and information quality performance measures.

¶ Declare information configuration management rules and models.

¶ Operate secure data and software repositories.

¶ Acquire, maintain, protect, and distribute data models.

¶ Fund the acquisition, maintenance, and distribution of software objects.

¶ Acquire information systems integration methods and tools.

¶ Maintain the master network configuration management controls, including software and hardware for enterprise-wide assets.[83]

¶ Administer contracts for telecomputing networks purchased from vendors.

¶ Oversee the procurement, leasing, and maintenance of software licenses.

---

83. Configuration management is to information systems as the master parts list is to manufacturing. Both relationships define which components belong where. The absence of configuration management is one reason current information systems are not interoperable and largely unmanageable.

¶ Ensure conformance with approved information management standards is audited.

¶ Administer a corporate wide development and training program for all technical personnel engaged in information management activities.

¶ Conduct finance, budget and planning reviews of all information management plans and programs with life-cycle expenditures that exceed an amount set by the corporate executive committee.

¶ Approve the information management sections of each business plan.

¶ Operate enterprise-wide telecomputing facilities that are essential to delivering corporate-wide applications.

¶ Direct information security reviews and evaluations through an independent organization.

¶ Accumulate and evaluate all systems intelligence about competitors' gains in information systems capabilities. These assessment must be reported to the information management policy board.

Process Level Concepts

Every process level systems organization shall deliver "one stop" services to its customers, which means that the customer will not have to negotiate separate arrangements with programming, data center, telecommunications, training and maintenance services. The process level systems services will also include project management, information systems engineering, transition planning, database conversion, quality assurance, as well as software acquisition and testing services. Also included are the development and delivery of all applications software, except when delegated to lower levels.

The process design organizations shall remain geographically and organizationally integrated with their customers, preferably in proximity to personnel who specify systems requirements.

The ultimate mission of process level data centers shall be to function as data and backup repositories and not as sites for executing applications.

For each application level site there shall be at least two data centers from which to restore applications services without loss.

All data centers shall have the capability to take over each other's functions on a timely basis by means of high-capacity transmissions according to a regularly tested emergency backup plan. Each major data center shall connect to others by means of at least two independently routed circuits to facilitate load sharing at peak hours.

The master software and archival data repository shall be located at sites that fully meet physical and operational security standards.

At least one data center shall be operational in a standby and fully secure mode. Such arrangement will provide the capability to shift critical work load, under emergency conditions, to a remote site that does not share similar disaster exposures.

Any changes in the configuration of operating systems, database software or hardware at a major data-center facility shall require dual authentication from a higher level.[84]

Process Level Checklist

Process level actions shall be reviewed by the corporate executive committee. These include:

¶ Develop and maintain functional flow diagrams of corporate-wide management and business processes.

¶ Plan and manage the migration of legacy software and databases for use across all business functions.

---

84. How can you be sure that an individual who is signing on to a computer is indeed the one he claims to be? Passwords are particularly unreliable and relatively easy to figure out, especially if you look inside the top drawer desk for the card that most office workers keep for easy reference. For more sophisticated break-ins, there are software packages available for making informed guesses about likely passwords. From a security standpoint, the adoption of a credit-card-sized "smart card" with a built-in microprocessor is likely to become a practical means to identify people. For sensitive transactions security procedures may require additional authentication checks, such as voice-prints.

¶ Prepare plans for removing or consolidating all applications that duplicate corporate functional processes.

¶ Manage organizations which design, implement, and maintain applications that control and manage the functional level databases.

¶ Operate data center services that manage corporate functional databases.

¶ Manage, from one or more control points, distributed information processing centers and wide area communications networks that support functional processes whenever such consolidation is economically justified.

¶ Maintain network configuration control, including software and hardware for applications under functional control.

¶ Issue applications access privileges to lower level administrators.

¶ Report quality and performance measures, that include capacity utilization, service quality, unit cost trends, and response time.

¶ Manage information systems integration services for the application and local levels.

¶ Test the application and local level systems for conformity with functional process information systems models and standards;

¶ Select software objects for inclusion in the enterprise level software repository;

¶ Keep records of hardware, software, and communications configurations to enable reconstituting operations from backup sites in case of a disaster;

¶ Identify problems that may impair the performance of the functional services. For each problem prescribe remedies and oversee their administration;

¶ Manage joint information systems development opportunities with allied or affiliated organizations, such as financial services organizations, suppliers, customers, and government agencies.

¶ Collect and evaluate all systems intelligence about competitors' gains in information systems capabilities and report findings to the secretary of the information management policy board.

Business Level Concepts

The role of business level management is to be fully accountable for the business results and improvements in productivity of the business unit.

The business unit shall be accountable for costs, benefits, and quality of all information services, regardless of where the operations take place.

Business unit executives shall ensure that all incidents of information systems malfunctions are routinely reported as a measure of overall business performance.

Business unit executives shall record all corrective actions taken for each incident of systems failure.

Business unit management shall be responsible for supporting information workers as they perform an increasing variety of tasks.

Business unit management shall pursue a policy of computer-aided work enhancement to encourage access to information by individual workers regardless of geographic, organizational or functional lines of authority.

Business Level Checklist

Business level actions shall be reviewed by a business information review council, appointed by the general manager of that business. These actions include:

¶ Coordinate application and local level information systems.

¶ Manage a business level systems integration service to assure interoperability and integrity of all information for that business.

¶ Plan and budget information management programs to support approved business objectives.

¶ Define information systems requirements and manage the acquisition of information products and services.

¶ Assign diagnostic capabilities for single-point problem resolution for that business.[85]

¶ Maintain network configuration management records for business-wide information assets, including software and hardware.

¶ Delegate the granting of network access privileges to the local level while retaining the authority to authenticate access to online data.

¶ Monitor conformity with information security and data center recovery standards.

¶ Issue network access control privileges to local level administrators.

¶ Monitor compliance with information media interchange standards.

¶ Monitor and report on the quality of information network performance.

¶ Assure systems survivability and recovery from backup sources.

¶ Collect and evaluate intelligence about superior applications of information technologies in unrelated businesses which may be useful.

---

85. For further discussion of this matter, see Paul A. Strassmann, *Information Payoff*, Free Press, New York, N.Y., 1985, pp. 130-135.

¶ Explore opportunities for joint development with other corporate units, affiliates, alliance partners and commercial sources. Such initiatives should accelerate the introduction of superior information technologies at a lower cost.

¶ Collect and evaluate all systems intelligence that may be useful about competitors' gains in information systems capabilities and report findings to the secretary of the information management policy board.

Application Level Concepts

Every application level organization shall support "one stop, nonstop" assistance for local levels. Such assistance includes installing applications, transition planning and startup, programming new options, report generation, and customizing standard services.

Budget guidelines shall specify allowances for staffing maintenance, training, and application assistance services. Actual support costs shall be compared with support ratios found in comparable commercial operations.

Application level support organizations shall have direct electronic access to their customers' local level servers. They will offer remote diagnostics, online tutoring, applications backup and capacity management services.

Any deviations from approved enterprise level standards shall require prior higher level approval to avoid technical and administrative incompatibilities at the local level.

Application Level Checklist

Application level actions shall be reviewed by the appropriate information board. When applications serve diverse businesses, each organization will appoint representatives to a joint applications review council. Actions taken at the application level include:

¶ Plan, develop, test, deliver and maintain application software, including training and start-up assistance services.

¶ Manage application technical support and help desks for inquiries from functional and local assistance centers.

¶ Participate in planning and managing the migration of local applications to any other level.

¶ Distribute application software and modifications from the applications repository to local level servers. Application level software shall not be allowed to operate at the personal level because local level services must retain control over the integrity of all applications;

¶ Provide training for local personnel in using tools that adapt general applications to local conditions .

¶ Maintain records of all information systems malfunctions, quality defects and subsequent corrective actions.

¶ Stimulate innovative uses of existing applications.

¶ Identify local level innovations as candidates for enterprise-wide use;

¶ Identify threats from competitors' gains if the competitors demonstrate superior use of a similar application;

¶ Explore opportunities to improve existing applications with new productivity-enhancing features.

Local Level Concepts

The purpose of the local level information systems management is to stimulate innovation and speed up adaptation to unique conditions.

Wherever possible, control over the management of information shall be placed at the local level.

The value of encouraging local experimentation is to test prototypes for quick and widespread adoption. Ultimately, such prototypes will become new standard applications. A good test for determining if an innovative prototype should become an established standard is noting whether imitations spread through informal channels.

Figure 12.2 Experimental Prototyping

Protect and nurture flashes of homegrown brilliance within the local level until such time as successful prototypes are ready for testing, documentation, auditing and approval for general use. This saves local initiatives from the burden of having to comply with standards for achieving interoperability with higher levels of the system configuration.

Search for clever ways to retrieve data, routines that take advantage of unique local talent, customized applications that solve local problems in an unexpected manner, original ideas and *ad hoc* simulations.

An application does not qualify for the local level if it creates data for subsequent use elsewhere. For example, it is acceptable for a local branch office to create a customer status tracking application. However, if the information from this application passes into a business level summary report, it becomes subjects to the standards that apply to business level applications.

Data defined at the local level shall not be incorporated into any consolidated reports but must always remain tagged to identify it as of nonstandard origin.

The mission of local servers is to deliver rapidly developed applications to local customers, preferably in a matter of hours.

Administrative productivity and effectiveness arise from the ability to obtain data from multiple sources. The mission of local systems support personnel is to organize the retrieval of data from any source.

All application servers shall have the capability to restore, by remote command, application services supporting local level workstations.

Place application servers in physical proximity to points of use to avoid excessive dependence on public network communications. Servers shall be able to take over each other's functions in realtime by means alternate transmission links. Each server shall connect to any other by means of at least two alternatively routed circuits capable of supporting business operations at degraded service levels if necessary under emergency conditions.

Application servers shall be reconfigured for hardware or software upgrades only when authorized and authenticated from a higher level.

Commercial suppliers shall be required to stock standby servers for fully operational replacement within a specified time, which must never exceed twenty-four hours.

All physical maintenance and equipment upgrading shall take place from secure maintenance facilities to prevent local tampering with security safeguards. Only trusted third party organizations will be allowed to perform equipment maintenance, if that involves insertion of diagnostic programs that can alter software configuration in any manner, or making any change in the hardware configuration. Local operating personnel shall not be allowed to perform equipment or software maintenance tasks that involve changes in configuration.

Local Level Checklist

Local level actions shall be reviewed by the appropriate information review council. These actions include:

- ¶ Manage the physical integrity, service responsiveness, applications availability, and security of local servers.

- ¶ Manage local area networks and assure their connectivity to wide-area networks, including the maintenance and installation of all network connections.

- ¶ Manage and be accountable for the security access to local level networks from on-site or remote personal computers, including off-site portable equipment.

- ¶ Administer information systems hardware and software configuration changes at the local level, subject to higher level approvals to safeguard compatibility, integrity and security.

- ¶ Conduct exercises to test application and local level disaster survivability and backup.

- ¶ Approve service requests for telecomputing equipment, network installation, and related facilities.

- ¶ Maintain inventories of all equipment and networks assigned to local servers.

- ¶ Perform only defined minor repairs on locally installed equipment. Exceptions shall require higher level authentication and authorization.

- ¶ Order replacement equipment or plug-in replacement components from approved suppliers.

- ¶ Request support services from functional, business or application level centers.

- ¶ Lease equipment and license software exclusively from the enterprise level at commercially competitive rates.[86]

---

86. Leasing relieves local management of the need to employ a large acquisition staff.

¶ Place requests for downloading and remote testing of software from the application level.[87]

¶ Enforce the prohibition against export of any personal software directly from the privately reserved memory space to the local server.[88]

¶ Report on the condition of equipment and networks connected to the local servers.

¶ Define local information analysis and reporting needs using standard report generation tools.

¶ Define data input formats for local option applications using standard form generating tools.

¶ Formulate one-of-a-kind information queries using standard inquiry tools;

¶ Develop and experiment with innovative uses of standard applications;

¶ Program local applications that do not duplicate functions performed at higher levels;

¶ Create local databases for exclusive local use. Do not allow the transmission of data acquired expressly for local use to any higher levels except where authorized;

¶ Identify threats and opportunities to the enterprise information management network from local sources.

¶ Collect and evaluate all systems intelligence about competitors' gains in information systems capabilities and report findings to the secretary of the information management policy board.

---

87. Workstations connected to the local area or wide area networks receive all operating and applications software through the local server, not by means of an on-site installation.
88. This assumes that the rules of governance allow such a practice.

13

STANDARDS

*Standards are a compromise between chaos and
stagnation.*

Standards, like concepts of operations, are an extension of information
policies. They represent accumulated experience as well as a codification
of past compromises. Their purpose is to reduce the number of options
to preferably only one, provided that the choice can be accepted
throughout the enterprise. Standards restrict selection yet increase
autonomy, because they make it possible to design information systems
without having to worry about every option out of thousands of possible combinations. Standards are useful if they simplify decisions, but
not if they require continuous guessing about which are the right ones.

The Politics of Standards

One problem with standards is politics. There is no such thing as a standard that offers the optimum solution for everyone. Another problem
with standards is that most of them are non-standard and that there are
so many of them. All standards are negotiated compromises between
vendors who favor exclusivity and customers who wish to attain permanent universality in everything they use. Committees that create
standards represent interests that jockey for privileged positions, similar to what you find in any parliamentary democracy. A vendor who
enjoys sufficient market share can also impose *de facto* standards, just as
in a popular dictatorship. Only if the standards-setting process involves

broadly based participation and competition, is it possible to end up with something that deserves widespread acceptance.

Before executives make a decision about which standards to adopt for their organization's systems, they should know something about its origins, especially because this may require an investment of millions of dollars. It is always good advice to keep away from standards that are imposed by market muscle, even though that may appear to be the most expedient course in the short run.[89] Trust the participative process for arriving at consensus, even if it is painful, uncertain and takes time. Trust demand-pull more than vendor-push.

Before you pick a standard you ought to know who holds any proprietary interest in its perpetuation. Do not adopt hardware or software solutions where a dominant vendor possesses the market power to extract exceptional profits from having established a widely accepted solution. Do not commit to standards which try to encompass too much, because they may be overtaken by opportunistic solutions that offer limited yet workable answers. When picking standards for adoption, while the direction of a technology is still unsettled, you should not make those decisions on technical merits alone. By the time you have sufficient knowledge as to which solution survives, your investments in the wrong choice may be already too large. A political assessment of the power of the respective vendors and the track record of the standards organization should strongly influence your choice.

Just because a standard is conceived as *open* by an international committee does not necessarily guarantee that it should be followed. Take for example the Open Systems Interconnection (OSI) communications protocol. From an engineering standpoint it is the ideal solution. It includes just about every feature you could possibly think of. It was this striving for perfection that made it lose to a much simpler and wildly successful protocol (TCP/IP) that sprung forth from experimentation on the Internet. While the OSI committees met to debate the finer points of how to make their complicated solutions fit every-

---

89. Remember that at one time adopting whatever IBM did was considered to be the safest choice as well as the accepted standard.

one, the TCP/IP community proceeded testing and implementing what worked, and worried about standardization later. Potential OSI vendors were reluctant to commit to its implementation, whereas TCP/IP offered a ready clientele. TCP/IP, despite an initial U.S. government mandate to the contrary, remained a commercial success because users trusted it. Nobody could monopolize TCP/IP since it offered a public and not a proprietary solution.

As a lesson in standards selection, consider the advisability of adopting Ethernet® as a networking standard in 1980. That would have been a relatively safe choice, because Xerox made its patents and know-how available for a license fee of less than $200 to anyone. It did not take much time for a number of vendors to offer versions of Ethernet.

Xerox simultaneously invented the first commercial document print format for laser printing.[90] Xerox made it a tightly held proprietary solution to strengthen its then dominant position in laser printing. Adopting the Xerox document print format would have been an unwise choice in 1980. When a start-up firm organized by ex-Xerox researchers, Adobe Systems Corporation, came up with a document print standard available to anyone for a relatively small license fee, laser printing manufacturers adopted it immediately. Shortly thereafter, the Xerox print standard lapsed into oblivion. Customers who originally bought Xerox desktop laser systems abandoned them in favor of solutions that offered compatible software solutions from multiple sources of supply.

The choice of the Ada language in the Department of Defense is an example of how an effort to create a standard, regardless of its theoretical merit, will not work. Ada has not been enthusiastically embraced by U.S. non-defense federal agencies, state and local government, or any other government in the world. Industrial and academic uses have been negligible or non-existent. It is an example of an unsuccessful attempt by a few specialists to impose a standard that was too slow in delivery and too isolated from the commercial development mainstream to receive widespread acceptance. The proponents of Ada did not follow the enormously successful methods of commander (and later Rear

---

90. The precursor of PostScript®.

Admiral) Grace Hopper engaged the cooperation of industry and promoted the widespread acceptance by computer professionals to COBOL. Purchasing power, which the Department of Defense was relying on to promote Ada, is not an adequate substitute for popularly accepted leaders like Grace Hopper.

Figure 13.1 Introducing a New Standard

You will always be confronted by special interest groups that attempt to get their preferred practices blessed as a way to make it harder for others to compete.[91] Standards can enforce a legitimized monopoly or create a proprietary marketplace opportunity. Which result occurs depends on the standards' intent and construction. Pick standards that favor competition, which suggests to me that at least two well-established alternative sources of supply should be available. Do not declare as a binding standard an operating system or communication protocol that is available from one vendor, regardless of its popularity. A standard that is implemented for the benefit of only one vendor

---

91. The choice of the Ada compiler as the only mandated computer language sanctioned by the Department of Defense constitutes a restraint that favors contractors who specialized in doing primarily defense systems work.

is not a standard, but a marketing tool for extracting high profits. Deliberate carefully about the economic benefits before you commit to standards that apply only to government and that have not been accepted for general commercial use.

Standards Compliance

Every time you adopt a standard that binds your entire organization for years to come, you have committed a political act. When there is an incident of non-compliance within your organization, you must take action to enforce the standard with the full weight and prestige of the corporate office. Such actions are political events, because deliberate deviations from approved corporate standards subverts the authority of those who pronounce them. Violators usually get away with impunity. I do not know of any CEO who would place on the agenda of an executive committee discussion of a non-conforming use of the UNIX operating system by an operating unit that is stuck with a transition from IBM's CICS software.

To legitimize acceptance of standards, you must establish a due process for debating, ratifying, and then implementing standards. Your constituency is no longer your own technical organization. You must also deal with vendors, suppliers and consultants who over the years addicted your organization to their proprietary habits.

Do not promulgate standards if you cannot organize and enforce their use. Announcing enterprise-wide standards is similar to declaring that henceforth there will be only one religion. Unless you already have many followers, any unilateral and precipitous declaration will be an opportunity to stage a popular rebellion, regardless of the merits of the standard. If you launch standards without first gaining widespread support, your standards manual will join many others collecting dust or generating ecologically useful heat. Just to be on the safe side and to make sure everyone gets the message, do not forget to arrange for sufficient purchasing power to back up your declarations.

Making Standards

Without formally endorsed standards, information technology policy-making is unworkable. However, currently there are hundreds of competing technology standards generated by a variety of quasi- official standards bodies. Some of them have limited applicability, such as government standards. Others reflect the ambitions of new associations, such as the European Economic Community or X-Open. Many standards have become a means for competition for influence among trade associations that claim to represent the identical membership. Standards are also instruments of national industrial policy, such as in the recent disputes between European and American telecommunications companies, and between Japan and the U.S. about manufacturing automation.

Regardless of how much you would like to avoid making choices between ECMA (European Computer Manufacturers Association) standards and those endorsed by CBEMA (the U.S. Computer and Business Equipment Manufacturers Association), you must take the recommendations of you standards advisory subcommittee one way or another about what to adopt. Somebody in your organization will surely protest whatever decision you make if that person already had chosen a different direction. This is when the matter ceases to be a technical issue and becomes one of political accommodation. The economic interests of your business should dictate your choices of standards, which in turn should always support anyone who advances the interests of multi-vendor systems that are reasonably independent of technology or source of supply.

There are also *de facto* standards. These occur when some manufacturer, by virtue of an early product entry, establishes a software or hardware standard. Most of the computers in your firm already use the *de facto* software. Meanwhile, a respected international standards organization announces a new *open* standard. What you decide to do next has far reaching implications. If you endorse the new *open* solution, many in your organization will have to convert from the old to the new and ask you to pay the bill.

Can you afford remaining locked into a sole source of supply and be at its mercy for software upgrades when it suits that manufacturer? Are you going to take some money from the corporate till to pay for conversion to an *open* systems solution? No matter what you do, it will have political repercussions when the word gets around that one way of extracting money from the corporation is to be a technological deviant. This is why early commitments to standards are preferable to after-the-fact policy announcements. You can penalize the deviants only after they know about your policy and have disregarded it.

Making decisions about which standards to adopt is equivalent to the emotions arising when committing to root canal work. You do not like it, you cannot neglect it and you must do it. The best you can say about standards is to announce them as an integral element of governance policies that can demonstrate how technology standards and architectural choices are related. If possible, avoid announcing standards one at a time. Publish them as you reveal the details of your firm's enterprise model and show how governance and standards are essential to its realization.

Managing Standards

All the senior information management executives I know have tried to avoid entangling themselves in discussions involving technical standards. Often these involve fine points of minute distinction that only specialists can comprehend. I have never met standards specialists who endorsed another's view without elaborate reservations, which always made it difficult to judge what was best.

Over the years I have always had standards specialists on my staff, sometimes simply as a precaution against having to agree to something I did not have the time to explore. I found the personalities of our standards experts gentle, but singularly boring and uncommunicative. Their primary distinction was a large travel budget to meeting places such as Maui in January, Vermont in August, and the French Riviera in October. The people representing us at such meetings worked as individual contributors and never as part of a team. They saw their lone activity as a welcome relief from the turmoil at corporate headquarters.

Unless you assign to your standards people questions you expect them to answer, you will end up with indecipherable proceedings of meetings that nobody in your organization will read. You must manage standards projects as you would any other activity by assigning specific tasks that have deadlines. Your organization must continuously make decisions about which technology to adopt. What about NT versus

UNIX? What about IDEF versus Yourdon? When to switch to ATM? Are Lotus Notes *open* or not? Should we stick only with Intel microprocessors?

Your standards team members must make recommendations based on the best information available at the time when you must provide guidance to your organization. Your standards people should anticipate what choices your people will have to make, before they make them. You do not need standards people to tell you that a standards body has finally endorsed a standard after years of deliberations. A standard is useless if it becomes valid long after events have eliminated your chance of adopting it, especially if your organization had already committed much money in the wrong direction.

Your standards organization must find out what upcoming decisions depend on their advice. Your standards team should be part of the systems engineering organization that acquires your software tools, not merely ambassadors of good will who attend professional meetings to keep you informed. The primary criteria for accepting recommendations from your standards staff should be always economic. As a matter of routine ask them to prepare life cycle cost estimates for alternative options. The answers you get may not be clear, but at least this approach will place before you a written statement of the assumptions your people make behind their preferences or guesses.

Standards are relatively easy to establish when nobody has yet committed themselves, especially where broad-based participation and informed consent are involved in making the choice. Established standards are very hard to eliminate after they have shaped training, work habits and have caused an accumulation of large sunk costs.

To use standards effectively in making informed technology choices, you should consider how you staff your standards team. I would mix the standards staff with my technological avant-garde instead of my rear guard. You can assert technological leadership if your standards are linked with your principles of governance and systems architectures, instead of allowing them to remain a matter of individual preference of anyone who becomes enamored with a particular vendor or consultant.

Standards Topics

Here is a partial list of standards that you ought to have in place to increase interoperability and the sharing of information resources:

- Configuration management of hardware and software assets.
- Identification, cataloguing, and formats for reusable software components.
- Database administration methods, including models, data dictionaries, and definitions.
- Telecommunications protocols and network monitoring definitions.
- Computer-aided systems engineering methods.
- Standard systems management tools, including project management methods, project reporting and quality assurance testing.
- Definitions for describing work flow processes and representing information management requirements.
- Evaluation and testing metrics for system design, including evolutionary development and pilot testing.
- Open systems compliance verification and interoperability testing.
- Migration and reengineering methodologies.
- Integration of cross-application and cross-organizational software.
- Visual man-machine interfaces to minimize training and conversion costs.
- Program documentation, style manual for training documentation, and user instructions independent of applications and languages.
- Software objects.
- Measurement standards for making competitive comparisons (e.g. benchmarking) meaningful.

- Document and engineering data interchange formats.
- Information network security procedures, including threat assessments, contingency scenarios, security exercises under conditions of simulated emergencies, database integrity safeguards and security clearance methods for access to corporate databases.
- Safekeeping corporate information assets against unauthorized alteration, destruction, and disclosure.
- Archiving and recovering electronic information under emergency conditions.
- Software maintenance testing, access control by maintenance programmers, monitoring of database cloning, access authentication, and controlling software integrity under emergency conditions.
- Linkage between internal and external systems, such as direct electronic exchanges of documents and drawings, and electronic dissemination of information.
- Direct electronic transmission of information to and from financial intermediaries, government, contractors, and suppliers to avoid the cost of reentering data.
- Business process redesign methods, notations, and process flow repositories.
- Functional systems requirements which precede any computerization.
- Transaction metrics, such as response time, transaction reliability, systematic error analysis, and recording cumulative maintenance costs.
- Intra-corporate e-mail and work-group interoperability, including document, graphic, voice, and video formats.
- Prototype contracts for vendors, consultants and suppliers, with special emphasis on protecting the orga-

nization's own patents, trademarks, copyrights, confidentiality and security.

- Health matters, such as physical stress, potential electromagnetic emissions and ergonomics.

- Preferred systems design practices that are favorable to effective human-machine functioning, such as use of color, screen resolution, standard help routines, access to training, and in-process tutorial support.

- Personal privacy for personal e-mail and personal files on local workstations, if that is allowed.

- Capability assessment practices for employee training and personnel development programs.

Standards Documents

Standards are not something that you announce in memoranda or post on bulletin boards. There must be standards documentation that serves not only as a reference source, but also as training materials. Understandable standards manuals have exceptionally complete indexes and reference notes that reveal how the preferred practices fit together. The current custom of randomly assigning the writing of different standards to different people produces a hodge-podge of three-ring binders that invites non-compliance. The production of standards documents, like the authoring of policy matters, calls for professional skill and editorial dedication.

The structure, organization, indexing, maintenance, distribution, and production of standards documents should be consistent across organizational activities that range from naming conventions of data center tasks to the formats of long range strategic plans. Standards documents should be a part of an integrated repository of knowledge that encompasses all information management. Draft, review, approve, and distribute standards documents through the same network that you use for electronic conferences, e-mail, or electronic bulletin boards.

The following is a partial list of documents that make up an integrated standards collection:

- Organizational manuals that define responsibility for the execution of information technology policies.
- Procedures that state how internal customers may exercise control over expenditures.
- Documentation of the boundaries, scope, and accountability for implementation of information systems projects.[92]
- Documents that demonstrate how current business plans depend on the execution of information technology management.
- Standards that define the policy-formulation, policy-declaration and policy enforcement processes.[93]
- Cost accounting standards that explain how fixed and variable costs are attributed to activity-based charges for services.
- Standards for measuring and tracking the cost-effectiveness of information technology investments, including analytic practices and forms.
- A budget manual with procedures, forms, and guidelines for status reporting.
- Acquisition policies that guide the procurement of information technology assets and services. These must include standards for information technology resource inventories and methods used to keep track of configuration management.

---

92. Interorganizational strife would diminish if there were a quick and effective way to publish the new arrangements after each reorganization. Reorganizations are typically a redistribution of functions and thus amenable to graphical portrayal by showing objects dragged into a new collection. Such documentation would relieve the chaos that prevails every time a new and improved structure is announced. Standards can be seen as one way to define the configuration of management tasks.

93. Policy enforcement includes the activities, procedures, and practices of the systems audit department.

- Standards for documenting life-cycle effectiveness and costs of applications, the pricing of information services, milestone reviews and operational testing.

- Systems integration standards specifying the migration path options for legacy systems.

- Standards and procedures for managing shared resources, such as corporate data centers, central design units, corporate telecommunications networks and corporate services such as e-mail, video-conferencing, voice mail, executive information systems, and group-support services.

Standards as Governance

In most organizations, standards either do not exist or they reflect limited efforts to put together a body of knowledge without much consistency or continuity. I have never seen a systems manual that is over ten years old and that is still up to date. Usually what you find are book cases filled with binders that are products of ambitious efforts that perish as soon as a new management team arrives to authorize a new series of three ring binders.

One of the primary purposes of an information management policy board is to authorize and approve the products of work groups that define standard practices that have good continuity and comprehensive coverage.

An enormous amount of good will can arise from making the process of selecting enterprise standards an Olympic competition for excellence rather than a committee compromises that may not be workable. Every organization has the potential for coming up with practices that deserve widespread imitation. Make sure that your standardization efforts possess a spirit of cooperation, a sense of mutual respect as well as financial incentives for those who have conceived practices that end up being emulated. It certainly makes sense to spend more money on educating people how to use standards and less on the expense of publishing them.

Identifying, deliberating, approving and implementing standards are critical indications of whether information governance is constructive or whether it slows down progress. Therefore, investing in a long range standards education program should be one of the priorities for establishing lasting principles of governance. It requires generous funding. Aligning your standards with the governance principles deserves appointing only promising leaders to standards management posts. They will acquire skills of great value for progressing to any senior systems management position. Make the standards program the main channel for promising careers, not a backwater.

14

GOVERNANCE CASES

There is no quick long term fix.

Debates About Consolidation

There is a classic dispute about governance that keeps executives and consultants occupied much of the time. Should you centralize data centers under a single corporate utility, should you decentralize everything to divisional control or should you contract for services from a vendor?[94] Is the proposed centralization just a power grab by a newly appointed CIO or does it serve a purpose that is consistent with approved plans? Is the proposed decentralization just a disguised plot to shelter an exceptionally profitable division that does not wish to share costs with other operating units?[95]

In most situations, arguments favoring both consolidation and separation are equally convincing. The problem with both positions is they look backwards and not forward to changes that could make the arguments irrelevant.

The rapidly growing complexity of information technology is leading to a situation where the only choice that matters is selecting the

---

94. Data centers need not be owned. They can be run by a vendor.
95. Corporate information services divisions are notorious for overcharging the more profitable divisions so that weak customers and corporate projects may be funded out of the surplus.

personal computer used to reach and retrieve all information. Future computing will resemble more the interdependence of people living in a metropolis than life on a deserted island. The debates about consolidation *versus* distribution will disappear, because soon all computing power and resources will scatter to many places. Even today, a transaction may bounce around the globe, visiting many computer sites, before its completion. Most of the time, companies will complete their transactions on networks they do not control directly and may not even know where they are, just as with voice telephone calls.

The company's concerns should be improving enterprise-wide cooperation at the lowest cost, not about who will actually own dedicated computing facilities. If your policies reward cooperation, people act differently in debates about the merits of data center consolidation. Instead of dealing with the past, everyone will focus on the most effective means to make the transition to where the organization needs to go in the next decade.

In situations involving the perennial centralization *versus* decentralization debate, you should seek the most economical way to own as few of the rapidly obsoleting data processing assets as possible. Whether you are in the candy or the rocket businesses, the economic value-added will come from the competitive superiority of products, not from mastery of data center administration. Concentrate on educating your organization about how to use information technologies effectively, regardless of who possesses them. When the time comes, your people should have the skills to know what they need, and when they need it.

Unless there are some overwhelming financial advantages to either the centralization or decentralization of your data centers (which I doubt, although there are exceptions in instances of chronic neglect) you should make your decision based on what will contribute best to the development of your employees' information management skills. Always place the capabilities of your people ahead of the capabilities of your information technologies.

The Case of Customer Account Numbers

The stated corporate goals of this organization called for integration of critical functions across the entire enterprise, such as instituting global management of multinational customer accounts. However, corporate policy was not explicit about how to accomplish that.

Corporate management made highly publicized pronouncements about acting as a single global unit capable of supporting its multinational clients with standard billing, pricing, and advertising. Meanwhile, corporate management continued to yield to local potentates the power to continue doing business as they wish every time there was a confrontation between global and national interests. This included unhindered autonomy for every country manager in designing, developing, operating and maintaining unique order entry, billing and marketing systems.

The corporate marketing executive in charge of coordinating multinational accounts suggested that the only way to create global cohesion was to assign customer account numbers directly from corporate headquarters. The numbering of customer accounts was then declared a systems matter, in the opinion of the marketing staff. The corporate systems steering committee then got the job of figuring out how to do it.

If you place on the systems agenda a problem that is fundamentally an organizational matter, you will get the failure you deserve. A steering committee was formed consisting of the marketing representatives from individual countries. They never found a source of funds that would support the resources necessary to implement a workable global account numbering scheme.

Coordinating global businesses effectively has worried boards of directors of just about every major corporation for a long time. A coding scheme cannot enforce globalization wherever parochialism prevails. The numbering of international accounts should be a detail included in a comprehensive package that addresses revised principles of marketing and administrative governance.

Data Malfeasance Cases

The mandate that all data management practices must be reflected in standard data models will be a source of much controversy. Usually, local business units have much latitude in how and when they enter data, since higher levels in the organization mostly see summaries. This gives local operations opportunities to make corrections that favorably reflect on their reported performance results. Here are a few examples of flexible practices which strict data modeling would inhibit:

- Sales personnel will postpone order entry in the last week of a quarter if they already met their sales quotas, and the marginal gains from the commissions for exceeding the quota are less than not meeting the sales quota in the next quarter.

- A customer is encouraged to order in excess of requirements so that salespeople meet their revenue quota and collect their commissions. The customer will be free to cancel the order afterwards. If such practices involve quantity discounts and physical return of merchandise, this will be a very costly way to make the necessary adjustments.

- Entering data in non-standard ways occurs often in tax manipulations. Inventories are build up prior to tax assessment days and corresponding sales show up after the tax deadline. Over a number of years that can greatly distort the record of actual earnings.

- Earnings are open to manipulation by being flexible about data entry cut-offs at the end of an accounting period. Orders received in the first week of a month can show up as sales in the prior month. In this way, the local accountant can smooth the reported revenues, since the month of May could be twenty-eight days long in one year and thirty-three days long in another when making year-to-year comparisons.

- One of the greatest opportunities for mischief is in manipulating the credits for returned merchandise. There are many ways to handle the timing, pricing, and accounting for loss. In the absence of defined business rules and data models, returns become an opportunity to make the local numbers look better in reports to top management.

These practices illustrate why autonomous managements will find data models too confining. They will fight data management standards, although their real motive will be to retain their latitude to manage the numbers that top executives will use in judging operating results.

The Case of Joint Cooperation

The Army, Navy, Marine Corps and Air Force manage, budget, plan, recruit, and promote their own military personnel. No joint steering committee with the task of coming up with an integrated defense information system can deliver anything other than a conglomeration of existing Army, Navy, Marine Corps or Air Force systems features that will preserve the traditions of their unique methods and practices. Under such circumstances, the best one can expect are treaty-like agreements to prescribe the electronic transmission formats that the services will pass back and forth. However, such compromises will not produce a joint, non-redundant, low cost and interoperable system. It would be like supplying a town with electricity by running extension cords from house to house across streets and sidewalks.

National military goals may declare the necessity for the military services to have a unified approach to data, communications, security and systems integration in the battlefield. National military goals may also declare the need for seamless coordination of combat actions regardless of military department or functional specialization so one could see deployment, air support, intelligence, logistics, medical and personnel information on the same laptop. However, the nation will never get a workable resolution of national military policy through a steering committee co-managed by Army, Navy, Marine Corps and Air Force information executives. Before that becomes feasible, the military must have an explicit process for planning, budgeting, funding and acquiring systems that support commanders on joint missions.

In the absence of clear commitment with funding and enforcement from policy-making leaders, the best one can hope for is to obtain agreements that authorize inserting hardware and software translators on top of existing patchwork fixes. In this way the military may overcome the most painful systems incompatibilities, yet create new ones. The new additions will breed added complexity, making joint interoperability not only more expensive, but also more fragile on the battlefield.

Matters left undefined by policy should not be passed on for resolution by individuals charged with preserving parochial interests. Irresolution will only exacerbate intraorganizational friction, diminish incentives for voluntary cooperation and bring about compromises falling far short of what is possible. Getting several parties to stop what they are doing and contributing funds to joint ventures also does not work. If a joint project fails, the party that contributed the most will suffer the most adverse consequences. Such disappointment will make the prospects for future cooperation even more discouraging.

It is the responsibility of top defense executives to declare the rules of governance, such as a joint information management doctrine, that will guide the design and fielding of systems benefiting from a joint defense infrastructure. The sharing of common functions does not preclude retaining those distinctions that are unique to each service. Forcing cooperation through the consolidation of hardware acquisition practices will make inter-service conflicts only worse, because joint interoperability is primarily a matter of standards, configuration management, and software and not something that can be achieved by everybody toting around the identical brand of personal computers. Information management decisions in the absence of a joint information management doctrine are like a drama without a plot. The actors will go through the motions without giving the audience an understanding what the performance is all about.

Lessons Learned

- Policy must always lead information management.
- Never make decisions about software, computing, and telecommunications until you have top level policies, experienced managers, proven organizations, generally accepted measures of performance and conceptual models of operations in place.
- Apply financial incentives and perform detailed technology planning only after you have laid out a plan showing how the pieces fit together.

- Deciding on business methods should always come before discussing the technical merits of individual applications.

- Never engage in a major project without first deciding on measures of successful performance.

- Build business process models before you consider revising systems and applications.

- Make sure that you have an organization that has demonstrated an ability to take on an undertaking of comparable scope as the new venture calls for.

- Do not expect enthusiastic systems people to do a job that should be done by experienced business executives who have operating responsibility and undiluted accountability for implementing the recommended change.

PART II

OBSERVATIONS

The Faster We Go the Closer We Have to Examine the
Signs That Guide Us

15

ANALOGIES

The strange may be understood through the familiar.

History books will record two epochal events as shaping the last half of the twentieth century. They are the end of the cold war and the advent of the first information-based society in the U.S.

By the early 1990s, the U.S. had less than five percent of the world's population and operated more than half of the world's computer capacity. The U.S. supplied three fourths of the worldwide computer software market. Europe had only twenty percent of the critical software market and Japan only four percent. U.S.-based companies now ship seventy percent of the personal computers in the world. U.S. firms also dominate the computer services industry, which is the fastest growing segment of the systems business and exceeds the value of computer hardware sold each year.[96]

---

96. *Fortune*, April 18, 1994, p.64. Software and computer services now account for $204 billion in business purchases worldwide.

The U.S. is the first society that has more than half of its work-force in information occupations.[97]

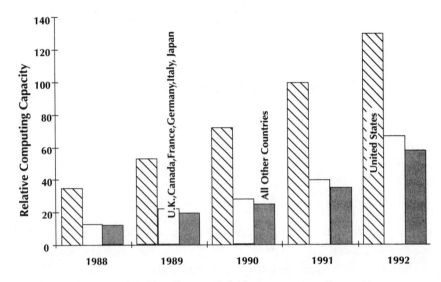

Figure 15.1 Growth in Global Computing Power[98]

In the past, societies and individuals learned to cope with the risks of a hostile world by adopting the following measures:

- Augment resources. From the ancient granaries to the accumulation of financial capital, building up surplus capacity was always the preferred way to minimize adversity.

- Contain the unexpected. From the digging of irrigation canals to the suppression of dissidents, the impo-

---

97. According to the April, 1990 report from the U.S. Department of Labor, Bureau of Labor Statistics (USDL 90-220), for a total employment of 117.3 million employees:

	Employment(millions)	% of Total
Managerial and Professional	30.5	26%
Technical, Sales and Administrative	36.9	31%
Information Workers	67.4	57%

In 1960, total U.S. employment was 54.2 million, with only 43% information workers.
98. "The Growth of Computing Power," *Fortune,* December 13, 1993, p. 68

sition of order has always kept changes from disrupting established hierarchies.

- Improve information capability. From the invention of language to the building of computers, learning has offered a way to adapt to the unexpected.

Historically, acquiring capital and controlling markets has been the principal means for safeguarding economic security from adversity and from competition. This simple prescription is no longer sufficient. The U.S. already has accumulated enormous amounts of physical assets, but that is no longer adequate to sustain economic growth. Power through enforced control of the markets is also no longer tenable. Economic competition has become global, and it is impossible to prevent new players from entering the marketplace.

The U.S. is the first society to experiment with containing risks by shifting from accumulating capital and market power to increasing dependence on information. The U.S. is pioneering development of an information-based society to cope with the challenges of the post-industrial, post-cold war world order.

The Leninist Option

In the last seventy-three years, another experiment took place to manage the risks of social evolution, traversing a totally different path of historical development from that pursued by the U.S.A. For a while, almost half of the world's population subscribed to the view that information should be under the tight control of an elite exclusively possessing a vision for guiding the transition into the future.

States that followed Marxist-Leninist precepts of central political control over information failed as their managerial capacity collapsed as soon as they tried to satisfy consumer needs beyond the bare necessities. The disintegration of the Soviet Union is a textbook case of why rigidly prescribed information handling, especially when aggravated by police methods, will invariably fail. The Soviets crippled their information systems and thus lost the capacity to deal with the rising complexity of a modern state.[99]

Figure 15.2 Soviet Style Computing

The Soviet Union was not the only failure caused by bankrupt management of information. Current bureaucracies in every country offer opportunities for further study. They hope to deal with their information risks by strengthening controls. They are unable to exploit the ample resources already under their management. They substitute regulating prices, supply and demand for letting a free flow of information shape the allocation of resources. These are not totalitarian countries, but some major U.S. corporations, as well as most U.S. government agencies.

---

99. In 1982 I presented in Moscow to a committee of the USSR Council of Ministers a tutorial on information management. In two four-hour lectures, they received a then shocking description of how fast the U.S. was computerizing in order to decentralize decision-making. What some of the Soviet officials wanted to do was precisely the opposite. They were laying plans to have computers make all the supply and demand calculations in Moscow ministries, all the way to the retail level. I showed why such an idea was not technically feasible.

Later on, some of the people associated with Gorbachev published my 1984 book about the transformation of work in the electronic age in Russian, under the title *Information in the Era of Electronics*, Economika, 1987. The book shows how poorly managed organizations become worse if they install information technologies to accumulate malfeasance faster.

In the case of the Soviet Union, there was nothing else to do except end this tragic hoax that had cost the lives of tens of millions. In the cases of Western ossified corporations or government institutions, there is no other way to end their regimes except through bankruptcy or by salvaging their losses through increased taxes.

The Cold War and Computers

There are similarities between the winning of the cold war and establishing computers as the basis of an information-based society. Both the cold war and the widespread acceptance of computers took place at the same time, starting in the late 1940s and culminating in the early 1990s. Both developments experienced distinct stages, trying to deal with rapidly changing opportunities while slowing progress to allow the old order to last just a bit longer. There were casualties during each transition, with the difference that the U.S. had a sufficiently flexible economy to finish each round faster and with less damage than the Soviets.

Figure 15.3 Differences in Computer Management

In the cold war, we first had to deter bombers delivering atomic weapons, later deal with ballistic missiles, then cope with wars waged by proxy and at last face the prospects of a massive air-land attack in

Europe. The cold war ended with the adversary disintegrating from within because it did not have the staying power to last another round.

The introduction of computers in the U.S. first concentrated on mechanizing accounting, later expanded to automating offices as if they were paperwork factories, then attacked clerical office work and finally addressed the integration of information flows throughout the enterprise. In establishing the computer as the centerpiece of the information society, we first had to learn how to convert simple business processes to punched-card accounting, later scale that up to data processing centers, then distribute computing power throughout the organization and finally face the challenge of making widely distributed information processing function successfully with tens of millions of personal computers. The affirmation of computers as the basis for a twenty-first century advanced civilization finally occurred when knowledge workers adopted them as their personal means to enhance occupational skills.

Eight of the ten major players who started in the computer manufacturing race have disappeared. Of these original computer manufacturers, those who are still around are crippled. Wherever government intervened to keep computer manufacturers alive, such as in Europe, the odds of survival were even worse. It is a credit to the strength of the competitive economy that each round brought new players to the table, so that the computer innovation cycle still continues at an accelerating rate.

In the cold war, each escalation cycle led to larger commitments until one of the adversaries gave up. In the information revolution, each escalation cycle led to escalating commitments in rising computer budgets in organizations until there was enough momentum built up to keep further development going, perhaps indefinitely. The difference here is that the politics of the cold war were mostly destructive, while the politics of building an information society is mostly building new wealth.

New Challenges
Our cold war generals succeeded beyond their fondest dreams. Even as late as 1980, nobody would have believed that their opponent would disappear as a threat without clouds of radioactive fallout. Are the vic-

tors now ready to relax because the contests that occupied them for over forty years no longer exist? The opposite is true, for everywhere there are now more threats to national security than before.

Instead of facing a single source of danger, advanced societies now have to deal with an onslaught of multiple and unforeseen difficulties. For the first time in forty years, the global alliances that have been held together under the threat of annihilation are now questioning how to deal with the dangers of low-intensity warfare, terrorism and global high-tech criminality. This is why I am now concentrating on information warfare as a new discipline of information management.

Computer executives who spent their careers in spreading automation likewise succeeded beyond their fondest dreams. Even as late as 1980, very few considered it plausible that knowledge workers would soon have enormous amounts of computing and communication power at their disposal.

As with international relations, information management in the 1990s is also in turmoil. The dismal financial performance of one time leaders of the computer industry, such as IBM, Phillips, Sperry, Digital Equipment, Siemens, Fujitsu and Bull (and those who disappeared as major systems manufacturers, such as General Electric, RCA, Honeywell, Burroughs, Prime, National Cash Register, Olivetti, and Xerox) indicate that all is not well.

Economic analysts offer many reasons for the current state of affairs. Some blame excess capacity, others fault shifts in technology. Capacity is not the issue, because there have been many historic periods of excess capacity for industries which recovered when the demand reappeared. Technology is also not the culprit, because that has always changed at a rapid pace. What is unprecedented now is that, for the first time in forty years, corporate managements are resisting making computer investments because most of them are unsure they will realize any payoff.

An 1993 Andersen Consulting survey reports that of 800 senior executives polled from 220 FORTUNE companies, eighty-one percent ranked their organizations' payback from computers minimal or average.[100] The fact is that the current growth rate of corporate information technology investments is less than half of the rate in the early 1980s.

What Has Changed

The payoffs from computers are there, as they have always been for those who aligned information technology plans with business plans. What has changed are the perceived higher levels of risk. This change in thinking has its origin in two developments that have altered the rules that previously determined the development of the first thirty-five years of the computer age:

- Computing technologies are now everywhere. Fifteen years ago there were fewer than a half million computers in the world that were tended by about a half million experts. Soon we will have about 250 million computers in the world, attended by at least 100 million individuals whose ambition is to apply information technologies to earning a better income for themselves.

- The effects of information processing technologies are now pervasive. Fifteen years ago, it was possible for an organization to know its information processing expenses, and to a lesser extent, the benefits. At present it is practically impossible to determine the total information processing costs. The benefits escape tracking completely.

The risks of technology investment payoffs are now much greater than before because of the scope of computerization. The influence of computers, once controllable and confined to a few projects, is now everywhere. The costs used to be easy to estimate since they mostly involved expenses for technology purchases from a vendor who rendered detailed invoices. At present, the total expenses are unknowable

---

100. *Computerworld,* October 18, 1993

because most of them are spent on retraining the workforce and correcting errors. That which is difficult to understand increases perceived risk.

Currently, the benefits of information technologies are also very hard to pin down. They are certainly not attributable to faster calculations but to improvements in workflow, changes in customer relationships and the ability of people to enlarge the scope of their work. The total effect of information technologies is observable only as changes in overall organizational productivity. However, organizations have notorious difficulties in defining their productivity. That which is difficult to measure increases apprehension about making mistakes.

Technology Agendas

Increasing top corporate executives' doubts about the benefits of computers have changed the agenda in discussing the effect of information technologies. Conversations used to be simple and direct among vendors, consultants, the trade press and buyers of information technologies. Now, conversation includes diverse topics such as:

- Mainframe downsizing;
- Client/server computing;
- Microsoft Windows *versus* X-Windows Motif;
- Distributed processing;
- Relational databases;
- Enterprise computing;
- Cooperative processing;
- Object oriented programming;
- Reengineering legacy systems;
- Electronic distribution of information;
- Information infrastructure;
- Multimedia;
- Open systems; and
- Groupware.

None of the above subjects were on the technology agenda ten to twenty years ago, even though they are pressing issues right now. Present conversations also concern whatever is the latest transition from something to something else. For example, you would hear about transitions from:

- Emphasis on hardware to safeguarding software;
- Proprietary to *open* systems solutions;
- Procedural to object programming methods; and
- Host/terminal to client/server architecture.

This list goes on indefinitely because it is profitable for the computer industry to extend it. The computer trade press gets most of its revenues from advertisements about the latest information technologies. Consultants and vendors constantly keep searching for the latest hot topic to open opportunities for seizing bigger contracts and gain market share. However, from the executive's standpoint, the problem is that the information highway from every *from* to every *to* has a costly toll station at each point of entry and exit. In many companies, the road itself essentially has not changed. The problems are organizational and managerial, not technological.

Management Agendas

Corporate executives who must approve new computer projects are focused on issues beyond technology decisions. The need to:

- Realize the business value from information systems investments.
- Make the information systems organization responsive to business needs.
- Assure the interoperability of information within the firm and with suppliers and customers.
- Decentralize information processing for local adaptability to changing needs.
- Customize resources to fit individual capabilities and diversity in the workforce.

- Accelerate processes for rapid response to increasing complexity.

- Reduce overhead costs through sharing of information.

- Install leading-edge applications for competitive advantage.

- Improve organizational learning and accelerate employee training.

- Assure survivability and continuity of information management in case of disasters, and

- Establish security for safeguarding the reliability and integrity of information.

Their interest in transitions is founded on the premise that it is not technology, but the practice of management that needs changing. To take advantage of computers, management orientation is shifting from:

- Centralized definitions to decentralized control over data.

- Incremental improvements in isolated departments to large scale business process redesign across the entire enterprise, and

- Project control to enterprise information management.

This list keeps growing because information management policies and practices are now inseparable from most general management problems and issues. The neat separations of concerns that once belonged to computer specialists *versus* those taken care of by executive management do not exist any more. Management is information management and vice versa. This is apparent from the recent increase in attention to computers in business magazines.[101]

---

101. I used to dread Mondays because my office mail included several "How about this?" executive queries with a clipping from the latest *Business Week* story about some new information systems development. Xerox corporate staff used to call that MBWF - Management by *Business Week* Fad. The *New York Times, Forbes, The Economist* and *Fortune* magazine now routinely cover technical details about the latest developments in computers.

Reconciling the Agendas

How do you reconcile the frequently changing list of technology agendas with unresolved executive-level issues? You cannot tackle each problem one at a time. The issues are just too numerous and interrelated to be guided by improvised decisions concluded without a coherent framework. The topics are also not random, although they may appear that way if you listen to conversations held by the technologists.

New resistance to maintaining the historically high rate of investment in computers stems from the incompatibility between the technology and executive agendas. Executive interests have remained remarkably the same for over thirty years, while technology fads have come and gone in seven year cycles. Executives, like citizens who supported the cold war, are now looking for their equivalent of the peace dividend in terms of an assured payoff. They are not now receiving such benefits in ways they can understand and explain.

Executives are unwilling to fund yet another cycle of information technology conversions and investments, regardless of how attractively they are advertised, unless their perceptions of assured gains improve. The only way to do that is to place the executive agendas ahead of the technology agendas.

16

History

The future is built on what has happened before.

The diagram most frequently drawn in popular books about computers to demonstrate the progress of computing shows the increasing number of transistors placed on a chip as years go by. Such graphs often also display MIPS (million instructions per second) per chip for every year since 1965. Straight lines on semi-logarithmic paper portray the doubling of calculating capabilities every eighteen months. For readers who are more technically oriented, experts will oblige by plotting communication transmission speeds in bits per second or tabulate millions of bytes of memory per dollar over time.

I find the technical measures of progress interesting but not particularly useful when I talk with business executives interested in profitability. MIPS, semiconductor packing densities or bytes per square inch tell us nothing about relationships. Technology is not an adequate indication of those revolutionary forces that change how people relate to each other. It is like calculating engine horsepower in order to understand drive-in movies, commuting and shopping centers. Engine torque does not tell you anything about how people choose whether they will use motorcycles, boats, automobiles, buses or airplanes to get to places they want to go.

Underlying Concepts

The origins of this book go back to 1957, when I got my first job that required immersion in organizational conflicts.[102] In the years since then, I was never sure how my technology plans would turn out because of the problems that emerged every time I started installing well con-ceived and formally approved computerization programs. It always came as a surprise that well-laid plans could go awry for no apparently good reason except for something I kept dismissing as mere company politics.

During the early years of computerization those of us who man-aged automation believed that we were the scouts of the coming infor-mation age. Whether we were trailblazers, explorers, pioneers, forerunners, precursors or pathfinders, our self-esteem was boosted by romantic notions that we could bring about progress faster and with less pain if only the politicians would give us a seat in the boardroom and if everyone would become computer literate. From positions of power and with the aid of properly enlightened executives, it was sup-posed to be easy to overcome resistance to something we considered to be intrinsically good and useful.

The Elitist View

In the beginning it was acceptable for IBM to teach top corporate exec-utives Boolean algebra, principles of programming and elements of data-base design. Popular academics preached that if executives would somehow learn to think like computer people, integrated management information systems would follow in short order. Their model was that only a computer-literate philosopher-king could advance computeriza-tion in the workforce without much opposition. This model invariably

---

102. As the Assistant Comptroller for Planning and Analysis and member of the executive committee of Burns and Roe, an engineering firm engaged in nuclear power and defense sys-tems.

included a chief information officer who would whisper in the king's ear where to turn and when to jump.[103]

I remember meetings of chief computer executives of major corporations to which Jim Rude, then Pillsbury VP of systems, brought along Terrence Hanold, his CEO, to talk about computers. Hanold liked to work with computers and appeared in business magazines as the prototypical modern executive. His interests reinforced the theory that if you could only get the CEO to become directly involved with computing, the era of a systems-driven corporation could not be far away.

The romantic interpretation of the situation in Pillsbury was a mistake. Enlightened leadership was not sufficient to deliver the promised land of integrated systems. The much talked about relationship between Hanold and Rude did not last. Both left when profits fell precipitously.

The elitist view of computerization dominated corporate thinking for thirty years. An outgrowth of this attitude was a movement to install executive information systems [EIS] in expensive war rooms close to the CEOs' offices. One of the most heavily promoted EIS systems turned out to be nothing more than graphic renditions of a spiral bound, two-hundred page monthly data book, in color. That EIS cost over $150,000 in capital per executive plus over $30,000 in annual maintenance expenses. The only difference between the EIS and the old paper volume costing four dollars was the saving in executive time searching for information. Whatever time was saved was not worth the ten hours of training in EIS literacy that was the prerequisite for EIS membership.[104]

---

103. The CIO designation came later with the general inflation of all titles. To be corporate director or VP of information systems was good enough for the first twenty years of the computer age. The CIO is not and never was the Chief Information Officer. Almost in every instance he has little to say about public relations, advertising, market research, employee training, the company library, the mail room, copying machines, the print shop and filing cabinets, just to mention a few sources of important corporate information.

104. The demonstration of this EIS also started the wrong way. The executive in charge could not sign on. Network control informed him that the old passwords were now void and the new passwords were in his EIS mailfolder.

There is still no proof that corporations with elaborate executive information systems will enjoy superior profitability over those which do not. The available evidence shows that the only thing that really matters is superior information support for the people who deal directly with customers.

The elitist view about the style of systems leadership ended up making the information systems professionals the most difficult corporate function to manage.[105] That view does not seem to have changed much. For instance, in February 1992, a government agency asked seventy operating executives for candid views about what they thought their information technology should support. Here are a few choice extracts:

- "We have still have not got our information technology areas under control."
- "The only way to keep these wonks under control is to lock them in a cage and throw away the key."
- "Information is a strategic resource and fundamental to the achievement of our goals, but the information technologists' policies and directions are not well understood by one hundred percent of my peers."

Those computer executives who were elitists ended up without a political constituency in their respective organizations, especially when their enterprises stopped expanding. Part of that was envy of the well-advertised prosperity of the computer people. Much of it was distrust and fear as to when the elitists would turn into henchmen to eliminate jobs through automating white collar jobs. The early association of computer executives with the job-cutting bias of reengineering reinforced popular apprehensions, and made the computer experts politically vulnerable to defenestration.[106]

---

105. American Productivity Center and Cresap, McCormick & Paget, *Positioning Corporate Staffs for the 1990s*, Cresap, McCormick & Paget, Chicago, 1986.
106. A term widely used in Central Europe to describe the fate of the losers in palace revolutions. From the Latin "fenestra," or windows. In the old castles all windows were high above the ground.

Figure 16.1 A Clash of Cultures

The Populist Reaction

The theory of progress through computerizing the executive suite for omniscience came to an end when information workers revolted in the early 1980s against the computer establishment. Instead of being guided into the office of the future by the masters of the data centers, office workers seized the initiative. They acquired personal computers, mostly without much participation of the certified experts. Instead of trickling innovation from the top of the hierarchy downwards, the large scale adoption of computers took place from the bottom upwards. Instead of a planned progression led by acknowledged experts, the automation of the office became a spontaneous experiment led by quick-study amateurs. Instead of placing typists and secretaries into word-processing centers that conformed to the data processor's views of organization, the secretaries responded by getting most professionals to start doing their own typing and filing while the secretaries were learning the mysteries of DOS.

From a technical standpoint, the world migrated from many thousands of computer shops to millions. Indeed, over one hundred million people now act as if they were computer people - reading about megabytes, RAMs and the concurrency feature of this or that operating system. There are now more computer journals than sex magazines at most airport shops in the U.S. and at London's Heathrow airport.

The computer romantics of the past thirty years achieved more than they had hoped. The world has become more like them. However, they failed because they ended up as followers instead of leaders. The flagships of the romantic era, Sperry, IBM, GE, Nixdorf, Bull and RCA, failed to grow their customer base. Xerox, perhaps the most prolific originator of ideas about the *office of the future*, has for all practical purposes disappeared as a supplier of integrated information systems.

What similarities are shared by the computerization leaders of the 1970s who ended up as followers by 1990? They all missed the rapid transformation from centrally managed technologies to individually managed initiatives. They lost their constituencies to organizations that were swift, more adaptable and cheap. IBM, DEC and Xerox continued to cater to an orderly and limited group of customers willing to pay premium prices, while computer market share had shifted to small, locally managed independent entrepreneurs on small budgets. The failure was political and comparable to a defense establishment that insists on fighting with bombers, submarines, aircraft carriers and heavy tanks while the opponent shifts to guerrilla ambushes with nothing more than mortars, rifles and hand grenades.

Each transition in the brief history of information technology, from machine accounting to computers, from computers to minicomputers, from minicomputers to microcomputers and from computers as calculators to computers as consumer appliances was full of missed opportunities. Those who were dominant during one phase relinquished their position of leadership during the next round.

The only discipline that inquires into the underlying causes of the rise and fall of institutions is political history. In this book we shall continue an examination of the political forces that altered the course of information systems executives who still thought that they were in control. We shall explore why people kept steering with determination along a course that led to a dead end.

The Mainframe Theocracy

One of my favorite explanations of the progression of the computer revolutions is Figure 16.2, which shows how long it takes a literate person to learn how to operate a computer and how many people in the world are acquiring such skills.

During the early years of computing, it usually took about ten years of training before someone was competent enough to instruct a computer to accomplish something useful. The number of people who actually wrote programs during the early 1960s was very small - not much over 50,000 in the world.

The Minicomputer Hierarchy

After 1970, the number of people qualified to communicate with computing machines expanded to over 500,000. Operating systems and the relative ease of gaining access to minicomputers brought computer literacy to all sorts of people who were not even considered to be computer professionals.

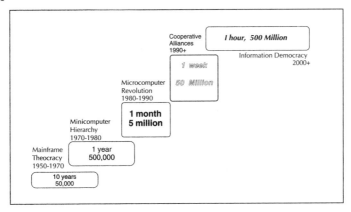

Figure 16.2 Acquiring Skills for Information Technology

The Microcomputer Revolution

The explosive proliferation of computer skills to over 5 million people by the mid 1980s resulted from the introduction of devices sold through retail stores. The ranks of purchasers of microcomputer devices are estimated to be growing now at the rate of twelve percent per year.[107] By the late 1980s, one could become quite proficient in customizing a wide range of standard applications without the benefit of much formal training. Millions took up programming as a part time occupation. Professional programmers now account for less than one tenth of the total population who may claim that they program as a professional occupation.

The Age of Cooperative Alliances

The most exciting developments are taking place right now as attention is shifting to connecting isolated computers, television sets, cable and electronic games into a global network. There are over one hundred fifty million computers installed in the world, with over fifty million people able to instruct them in performing specific tasks. The current shipment rate of new equipment is exceeding forty million computers per year, of which more than half replaces obsolete equipment as customers acquire additional capacity to make communications easier. It takes little time to adapt standard software packages to custom use. Applications are readily available through every conceivable outlet, including newspaper stands.

The Age of Information Democracy

I think the big breakthrough in computerization is still ahead of us. It will transform computers from being office equipment to ubiquitous appliances that integrate functions previously offered separately by the telephone, television, cable, videotape, radio, record player, typewriter, answering machine, facsimile, paging device, security alarm, appliance controllers and mail. This new device is sufficiently friendly that it takes negligible amounts of training to make it do whatever you wish. Every literate person living in a post-industrial society would become a master of his or her personal communicator.

The arrival of the era of information democracy is approaching. All possessors of an information appliance will have equal opportunities

---

107. Bruce Caldwell, "Who Needs Programmers?," *InformationWeek*, April 25, 1994, p. 27.

to learn whatever previously was accessible only to those who occupied positions of information privilege.

The Pharaoh and His Scribes

I use Figure 16.4 in executive presentations to explain the evolution of information technologies from centralized control to greater local autonomy.

During the first twenty years of computerization the approach to designing the flow of information came from Frederick Taylor's ideas of almost a century ago about factory efficiency. Accordingly, to overcome the chaos of error-prone paperwork, computer analysts saw their jobs not much differently than industrial engineers. They broke up paperwork steps into programmable sequences of transactions. Their objective in designing the computer system was to monitor the flow of the data. Wherever possible, the computer captured as many of the sequential processing steps as possible.

Figure 16.3 The Paperwork Factory

As on the factory assembly line, automation could not do everything. Human intervention was necessary to complete steps not easily amenable to programmable logic.

There are always office processes that lack the flexibility demanded by business variety. To cope with this, programmers kept adding exceptions to what were originally simple standard methods. Exceptions devoured computer machine cycles, ate up memory and crowded magnetic storage media. To manage that, computer departments kept buying enormous increases in processing capacity. During the 1960s and 1970s, it was not unusual to double raw computer power every year. The promised cost reductions did not always materialize. Clerical personnel, who previously made the old systems function by working around standard procedures, became increasingly demoralized as they became appendages to unforgiving computer routines.

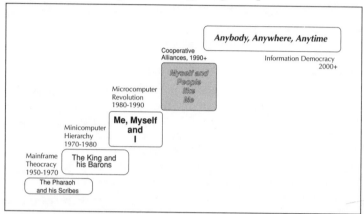

Figure 16.4 A Brief Political History of Information Technologies

Meanwhile, top management demonstrated their unquestioning faith in computerization by hiring additional computer staff and raising budgets for data centers. With the need to reduce clerical headcount because of the proliferation of administrative rules, operating managers found it advantageous to continue transferring even the most trivial clerical tasks to computers. They did not mind doing this since they did not pay for the central computer monopoly services managed under the tutelage of the corporate comptroller.

Figure 16.5 People as Computer Peripherals

As with all imperial and theocratic regimes, computer managers saw safety and economy in computing power as synonymous with predictability and control of the business. In the beginning, that made sense because the primary beneficiaries of computerization were the accountants and comptrollers who owned the largest clerical departments. Their world had to be predictable and controllable, and there the computers found their natural habitat. If there were such an academic discipline as "bureaucratic ecology," mainframe computerization of the financial functions would be its perfect environment. Computers and financial management became one and the same. IBM thrived in this environment because its internal culture mirrored perfectly the habits of its major customers. They were selling what they were acting out within their own firm. Early leaders in computer technology, such as the engineer-dominated UNIVAC and Control Data Corporation, would never get in tune with the executives who made the key purchasing decisions. Which just proves that any politician who wants to be elected is well advised to wear, at least occasionally, the same clothing as the electorate.

As with all cases of unconstrained monopoly, the financial systems become increasingly dysfunctional and unresponsive. The "scribes" – now called programmers and analysts – became absorbed in attending to the minutiae of the automated processes. Ever larger investments to recruit even more programmers and analysts to overcome processing failures had only a limited success. The clerical workers, who knew the most about the small details, understood that aiding computerization was not only unwelcome by the computer people who subscribed to academic theories about work, but often dangerous to their own employment prospects.

It was not until 1970 that organizations learned enough to be able to avoid some of the most frequent hazards of automation. They opted for centralizing data processing to eliminate the risk that clerks would make work adjustment decisions that did not fit standard procedures. As streams of paperwork became consolidated, previously informal and clever local handling of customer exceptions stopped. Consequently, the dissatisfaction of operating executives with computerization grew during a period of the greatest expansion of information processing power.

From Theocracy to Hierarchy

Much of the dissatisfaction with the computer monopoly was political and not an issue of economics. Power was shifting from the traditional manufacturing and marketing executives to the financial comptrollers. By the beginning of the 1970s, corporations began to see overt information contests between decentralized marketing executives and the centrally directed financial establishment. A typical conflict would arise after the corporate comptroller had just completed a decade of modernizing his operations. His massive investments were funded by removing whatever information capabilities were available to the local operators. This is similar to situations where heavily armed palace guards eliminate the local militia after confiscating their rifles under the pretext of making the community more peaceful.

Such conflicts escalated further when local managers got pounded by queries from the information-rich central staffs. Financial analysts now learned about problems before on-site supervisors understood what was going on. True to its theocratic prototypes, this led to a steady accumulation of additional power by headquarters staffs. I have worked for organizations where local managers responsible for tens and sometimes hundreds of millions of dollars of revenue had very little discretionary power over adding one clerk to their staff. Decisions over budgets, personnel levels, travel expenses and salaries were made by central planners who claimed superior efficiency and intelligence, largely because they possessed most of the businesses' information assets.[108]

The Rise of the Barons

When the local operators discovered that they were getting ambushed from corporate headquarters without adequate information defenses, they began to reconstitute their weakened information capabilities. Increased demands for explanations called for countermeasures in the form of voluminous and well-informed replies. Retaliation also required

---

108. In the early 1970s the per capita expenditures for information technology per financial analyst in Xerox were in excess of $27,000 per annum. That amount was more than the total annual budget for automating customer service support in a good-sized sales branch.

retaining local information for local processing before passing it on to headquarters in summary form.

Meanwhile, the need for market segmentation and faster response to competitive threats forced partitioning of the functionally organized corporations into separate kingdoms, now called "strategic business units." The expansive marketing and product management charters for these operations were devised by marketing people as the monolithic corporate empire was divided into many kingdoms. In that process, they usually neglected to preserve a slice of information independence. The new masters had no love for computer people who could have counseled them in how to acquire information defenses. Throughout the pushing and pulling for greater decentralization, computer people remained loyal to the centralist point of view because that is what they knew and where the careers were to be found.

What business unit management could not achieve on their own, they got by default. The central information establishment, still reporting to the chief financial officer, usually made the mistake of learning about information technologies from only one source, typically their sole computer vendor. It is a testimony to the power of the traditionally close bond between IBM marketers and the corporate financial and computer establishment that whenever someone tried to divide the information technology empire, cost calculations were invariably produced that proved that breaking up the mainframe and programming centers was uneconomical.

This period also gave rise to the unsound practice of making financial evaluations primarily in terms of short-term hardware and software expenses instead of including the full information handling costs of the users.

The Working of the Invisible Hand

The way computer systems were put together over the years made computer operations practically indivisible. The vendors' doctrine, technology, marketing tactics, pricing and dominance of their customers' personnel training assured that all decisions resulted in the perpetuation of the previously successful patterns of computing monopoly. Therein lies the flaw which in due course inflicted irreparable damage, principally to IBM, and led to the permanent loss of legitimacy of everyone associated with centralized operations after about 1985.

The best the barons possessing newly acquired information autonomy could get under these circumstances was to negotiate agreements that required the central information services department to charge for services. Some companies called that chargeouts, others allocations. A few organizations imitated commercial pricing practices.[109]

The effects of this policy on the central information processing monopoly were devastating. Business units now conveniently discovered that they could buy low cost computing power by shifting the most cost-ineffective workload from the central mainframe to newly available minicomputers. The economic performance of the mainframes in supporting on-line terminals was pathetic. The communications costs and response times from the central processors to the factory, branch warehouses or engineering support were expensive and poor. In addition to ineffective technologies, the services now demanded by the operating personnel carried enormous overheads. The traditional data center cost accounting methods loaded most of the overhead costs onto volume production runs, such as those generated by mature financial applications like payroll, billing and inventory accounting. This sort of cost accounting made the justification of frequent hardware upgrades to the central establishment easier to do.

Under such conditions, it was easy for an autonomous business unit to show enormous savings whenever it cannibalized the most overpriced applications from central data processing. The game was a simple one. You got a bargain priced minicomputer from DEC. You used it for those computer services that were the most uneconomical from the central organization. You then compared the two. It was clear that giving birth to a new mini-data center ought to be very advantageous.

Everybody concentrated on comparing hardware costs and made decentralization decisions mostly on that basis. However, the econom-

---

109. See Paul A. Strassmann, "Managing the Costs of Information," *Harvard Business Review*, September 1976 for the description of pricing practices of the Information Services Division, Xerox Corporation.

ics of those decisions should not have concentrated on the relatively trivial hardware costs but examined what would happen to everybody's overhead expenses after splitting the workload. Because of this lack of analytic perspective by the centralists and the concentration on variable costs by the decentralists, the outcome of the gradual disassembly of the central computer shop tended to increase overall cash costs for information technologies to the corporation. A less charitable interpretation would suggest that the centralists did not wish to disclose their misallocations of overheads, while the decentralists had every reason to hide their real start-up costs while pursuing their ambition to build up an independent technological capability.

The Expense of Baronial Possessions

The business units gradually acquired their own computers complexes only to discover that, like in marriage, the cost of the wedding does not adequately predict the total cash expense of keeping a family. After purchasing inexpensive hardware, the business units started building up their own expensive systems staffs.

While this was going on, there were no total cost reductions from decreasing workload at central operations. The corporate staffs absorbed displaced resources by engaging in expensive conversion projects to keep their obsolescent mainframe software alive and coming up with new applications. Overhead costs that were allocated to a reduced volume of transactions also increased. Clever business units found it profitable to remove only those applications from central operations that carried a disproportionate share of the overhead burden. Whenever central operations responded with selective underpricing to business units that were about to defect, their economic condition further deteriorated because they now had to spread large fixed overheads over a diminishing volume of business.

Much of the overhead of central processing was for supporting corporate staff and keeping up obsolete technologies in the absence of adequate central funding for modernization. The decentralists' cost comparisons took advantage of the latest technologies. Instead of building up staff, they relied on consultants who could deliver the desired results for a fixed fee. In the absence of a due process for re-balancing information resources in concert with rapidly shifting economics of computing and software, computer acquisition decisions became political acts in which the newly empowered business units were settling long standing grudges.

The Monopoly Crumbles

The introduction of minicomputers broke the monopoly of IBM in the same way that gunpowder broke up the power of the mounted knights. Vendor diversity became a generally acceptable hardware and software acquisition policy after 1975. Companies learned how to integrate systems supplied by whoever was best. Minicomputers also brought to systems management a completely new collection of computer talent. Much of it came from the scientific and engineering community that previously did not even talk with the types from the finance shop, whose origins were in punch card accounting instead of mathematics and science. The Digital Equipment Corporation, which became the prime supplier of high performance minicomputers, asserted a powerful influence on how to think about operating systems and communications capabilities that were independent of hardware and could talk to any other vendor.

The age of the minicomputer, the liberation of computing from the dominance of financial management, as well as the disappearance of reliance on a single vendor created an instability from which many large corporations have still not recovered.

The minicomputer dealt the death blow to the sound idea that was first pursued in the 1960s of managing data as an enterprise resource. After the disintegration of the mainframe empire began, it was no longer possible to get anyone to participate in a corporate-wide data administration effort, regardless of the merits of such an undertaking. Whenever anybody brought up the obvious advantages of easier horizontal flows of data across the various divisions or departments, the wounds acquired during the minicomputer liberation wars would start to ache. Agreements to appoint a low level technical task force to study the opportunity were the usual solutions.[110] After disposing of the matter in that way, it would not be addressed for a few years, until the issue would be brought up again by some naive newcomer.

We also can observe in the age of the minicomputer the trend to abandon orderly information habits such as information security, protection of software integrity, cost accounting and professionally managed development of computer specialists. Any infrastructure will deteriorate if special interests place higher importance on taking care of their immediate needs at the expense of services that are best shared in common. However, the confrontations between the central staffs and the decentralists had become sufficiently antagonistic that a viable balance of power could not be negotiated and then sustained as conditions changed. The politics of moving to minicomputers was carried out by abstract rhetoric instead of reasoned compromise.

Was a different conclusion possible in these confrontations? This is like asking if Louis XVI could have negotiated peacefully with Mirabeau. With an early agreement on governance[111] the French parliament could have avoided some of the worst tragedies of the revolution.[112] The excesses in breaking up database integrity and reducing security that accompanied the introduction of minicomputers are regrettable because they increased the overall costs of computing for most corporations at the price of defeating the power of the central computer establishment.

Minicomputers stimulated the spread of computerization throughout the corporation. They made it possible to bring about the

---

110. In 1968, the Deputy Secretary of Defense signed a data administrative directive ordering immediate implementation of a Department-wide data administration program. When I investigated what happened, I received a series of voluminous task force reports that had been published in five year intervals. There was still no action on a Department-wide basis as of 1990. Similarly, one of the largest corporations in the world got its Chairman of the Board to sign a data administration policy. The policy directed corporate-wide implementation of data standards. After five years and two excellent task force reports later, there was no trace of anyone doing anything about it.
111. Such an agreement was drafted by Thomas Jefferson, then American ambassador to the court of Louis XVI, and respected by both the king and parliament.
112. For the development of this theme see Simon Schama's monumental *Citizens, A Chronicle of the French Revolution,* Knopf, New York 1989

direct participation of operating people with systems design where previously this required making requests to the central staff. That the minicomputer operations were unconstrained by procedure, audit and control made experimentation and innovation much easier. Most importantly, they did not require a large initial expense.

None of these lessons in coping with the benefits and liabilities of minicomputers were good enough to prepare organizations, and DEC particularly, for the microcomputer revolution that came ten years later. Perhaps that is the worst we can say about the minicomputer chapter in the history of corporate information management. Executives failed to learn what happens when political motives and technology trends line up against economic realities. Ultimately, economics prevailed. The reign of the central computer staff lasted only while there were sufficiently fat profit margins to support the rising overheads. When these profits disappeared, the hunting season on overhead was open. Where the migration from the central mainframe to distributed processing was planned, overhead costs remained under control. Elsewhere, the information overhead spilled into every organizational unit and became hard to capture.

Me, Myself and I

There is a sizeable collection of books that explores the driving forces that shaped the new wave of computing that appeared in the early 1980s. Microcomputer chips, floppy disks, low cost video displays and Visicalc got the credit for this explosion which has few precedents in the history of technology. Other than the railroads and the automobile, there is little else that compares to microcomputers in their sudden appearance, rate of growth, cultural effects and consistent underestimation of their influence by even their most optimistic supporters.

I do not wish to dwell on what is a matter of record about this outburst of technology. The driving forces behind the microcomputer revolution were the social and political reactions to the unsatisfactory conditions that prevailed in information management. Minicomputers had already paved the way by giving individuals a good taste of independence from the monopolists.

The development, culture, software and penetration rate of personal computing started as a truly U.S. phenomenon. No other nation has devoted as much attention, money and energy to the acceptance of microcomputers. In the beginning of the computer age, the investment for getting started in manufacturing this technology was sufficiently small that just about anybody could aspire to leadership in this business.However, only U.S. entrepreneurs initially seized the opportunity to evolve the technology at a rate that left conventional engineering organizations accustomed to the discipline of mainframe and mini-computer designs quickly behind.

The ease of entry into the early microcomputer market also explains the rapid rate of product innovation and consequent rapid disappearance of outdated products from the marketplace. For example, there was a point of time in 1981 when the British could claim that they had more devices with microcomputer capabilities in the hands of consumers than anybody else in the world. However, shortly afterwards this potential advantage vanished because the British rate of innovation could not keep up with the competition that offered new and more useful capabilities because they had no government subsidies to rely on.

Because of the low cost of entry into microcomputer manufacturing and microcomputer software, a number of governments began heavily subsidized projects to accelerate modernization of their economies, such as in France, Brazil and the U.S.S.R. These projects failed because they could not keep up with the U.S. pace of innovation that was set by small entrepreneurial firms. In the cases of Brazil and the U.S.S.R., and in some respects also in France, conditions in the workplace reflected the persistence of elitist approaches to information management. These countries could not cope with the essential concept of the microcomputer which was the cultivation of independence from hierarchical organizations. These ventures vanished despite the ambitions of the technocrats in government ministries to use a native microcomputer industry to leap ahead of the Americans.

The Reformers

The individuals who gave birth to microcomputer-based computing shared many common characteristics.[113] They possessed a highly developed sense of individualism that was closely linked to the experiments of the "me" generation of the 1960s that rejected the established authorities. Every one of them was a social outsider in terms of background, behavior and habit. Without exception, they saw IBM and what it represented as the enemy.[114] The ideologues of personal computing also flaunted a commitment to environmental ecology. They preferred bicycles to autos, sought employment in small enterprises instead of large corporations, accepted employee ownership in the form of stock-options rather then competitive salaries, resisted conventional norms of behavior and appearance by dressing in distinctive clothing and detested of every hierarchy that did not recognize technical merit when making managerial appointments. In terms of education, they represented an exceptional collection of highly diverse talents, with broad interests in the most arcane collection of topics you can possibly imagine. These were not narrow technical specialists. Their aspirations were those of renaissance artists, although later when many became very wealthy, they became as conventional as most other Silicon Valley entrepreneurs who had set out merely to make money.

The quintessential rhetoric of the microcomputer era can be found in the pronouncements from Apple Computer and later Macintosh developers. They professed to cater to children and artists before serving the needs of accountants. They offered devices for intuitive communication instead of imposing a structured discipline. They favored graphics quality over calculation speed. They gave customers a device for personal expression, not a calculating machine.

---

113. These remarks are based on personal acquaintance with a number of the leading protagonists.
114. A televised advertising campaign by Apple Computer upon the introduction of the Macintosh made that clear. This series of TV commercials attacking totalitarian caricatures of IBM is a classic example of how a new technology can be also promoted an ideological statement to a customer segment that is ready to accept that.

The Counter Reformation

Whenever the fervor of the reformers dims after their initial break-through, the establishment finally wakes up to the loss of their followers. At that point, an adventurous establishment figure co-opts some of the reformers and uses them as a front for marketing the old ways in a more acceptable form. Thus reinvigorated, the old regime takes over and wins the next round in a never ending cycle of innovators versus conservators.

In a metaphoric sense, that is the history of microcomputers. The original concepts about microcomputing had their origins in fundamentally different values than those of mainframe computing. These ideas came to fruition between 1972 and 1980 in Xerox Corporation's Palo Alto Research Center [PARC] in the form of high resolution screens, microcomputing, low cost memory and autonomous communication methods that made these ideas workable.[115]

Most corporate laboratories of computer vendors, including the mammoth complexes in IBM's Yorktown Heights and AT&T's Holmdell, had at their disposal far greater resources and many more scientists than the handful of PARC researchers who have accounted for most of the innovations. What made the difference was not technology, but a revolutionary point of view. The IBM and the AT&T laboratories were working mostly for the glory of perfecting central control. The ethics and beliefs of the researchers on Coyote Hill in Palo Alto represented the essence of the unique Californian cultural type that put individual gratification ahead of all other values. The politics of the self met the politics of the hierarchy, and the result begot a device that forever altered not only the structure of computing, but how individuals in a democratic society will communicate in the future.

---

115. The major contribution of PARC was the development and low cost licensing of Ethernet to everyone starting in 1976. Ethernet is a communication method that does not require a central switch to keep track of the coming and going of individual messages. From an intellectual standpoint I consider the development of Ethernet-based communications as one of the most important innovations of the 20th century. It offers a technical implementation of the free market ideology that autonomous self interest and negotiated conflict, according to established rules, eventually will result in the greatest common good.

The counter reformation is now fully back in control of the means of production that support microcomputers, except in software. Software may be the next frontier where innovators will most likely take over and start a new cycle of obsoleting what is old. Meanwhile, the executives in charge of the microcomputer manufacturing divisions of Dell, Compaq, Apple, DEC, IBM, Hewlett-Packard, Novell, Microsoft and Lotus do not emulate revolutionaries but much the same methods as those who run Procter & Gamble, Nabisco, Ford and Pepsi. They have commenced their metamorphosis into disciplined executives who care about market share, distribution channels and price/earnings ratios instead of gambling on another major technology breakthrough.

As the pendulum keeps swinging away from the revolutionaries it appears to make perfectly good sense to appoint someone without any computer experience to become the head of the largest information technology firm in the world. As personal computers become network peripherals, the politics of computing shifts from the missionary to the institutional point of view. In that arena the establishment always wins, because it possesses superior means for sustaining a community of shared interests, until the next major innovation cycle starts again.

Working at Home

When future historians and anthropologists try to appraise the effects of microcomputing, they will most likely find the shift of information work from offices to the home to be the most remarkable social consequence. Personal computers and inexpensive local connections to nationwide networks make commuting unattractive, part time work at home profitable and self-employment of professionals feasible.

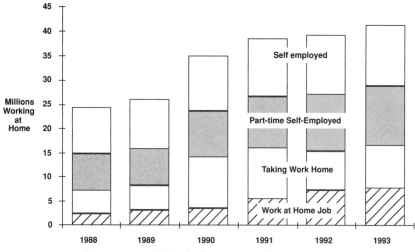

Figure 16.6 U.S. Information Cottages[116]

Alvin Toffler, who is perhaps the most prominent contemporary futurist, first discussed the arrival of the electronic cottage in 1980.[117] By the end of that decade, it had become a reality for a fifth of the U.S. workforce. A was an ambitious futuristic projection fourteen years become accepted practice before the Toffler's prophetic publication is out of print. With U.S. work life expectancies for information workers rising to fifty years of useful employment, it now takes a stretch of the imagination to forecast what the successors to the personal computer will bring in terms of social changes in the next fourteen years.

The history of the microcomputer is an excellent exercise in retrospective analysis for anyone who wishes to anticipate the social and economic consequences of a new technology before the revolution sweeps away the old and familiar. For that reason, I like to remember the mistaken views of IBM, Xerox and DEC executives who consistently disregarded the signs of what was coming, despite having access to the best expertise available in the industry.

---

116. "The Information Age in Charts," *Fortune*, April 4, 1994
117. see Alvin Toffler, *The Third Wave*, William Morrow and Company, 1980, Chapter 16.

For a number of years, IBM executives maintained that micro-computers would generate enormous demands for mainframe comput-ing because these new devices would depend entirely on central support to get any work done. As result IBM embarked on a huge expansion program to build more mainframe computers.

DEC executives could not understand why a person would wish to have one computer all to himself. Their entry into the microcom-puter business was not decisive and never recovered to gain any signifi-cant market share in that business.

Xerox executives rejected using their *Star* workstation and laser printers as an early entry into desktop publishing because the market was not seen as big enough to challenge IBM's position, which was the only target that Xerox leadership found worthwhile. Despite the best technology available, the conventional thinking of Xerox management made them pull back from making decisive commitments to innova-tion. After a few years of aimless ventures and acquisitions they aban-doned the microcomputer business in the same way as they dumped the mainframe business in 1974 when they tried to convert a successful scientific computer company into a poor imitation of IBM. The Xerox experience offers a sobering lesson to every general who plans his cam-paign based on what enemies did in the last war.

If industry experts could so grossly misjudge the impact of micro-computing, how can a customer plan for the future applications of information technologies? The following may help:

- Do not ask anyone with a vested interest in the status quo to forecast the future.

- Set aside a budget that encourages experimentation with innovative uses of information technologies out-side of established rules and policies.

- Organize an independent intelligence gathering orga-nization to identify unconventional threats or oppor-tunities.

- Use mistakes as an opportunity to learn, not to search for culprits.[118]
- Retain the services of an independent advisory board from diverse disciplines to critique your technology plans.

---

118. The misjudgments about microcomputers by DEC and Xerox originate in the inability of these organizations to examine and evaluate the lessons learned from their initial failures.

17

PRIVACY

Personal privacy is the foundation of all freedom.

Personal Privacy

One cannot manage information systems without recognizing that passion permeates everything that becomes politically acceptable. Around the world, a large share of the information workforce has a deep emotional attachment to their personal computers. If one tries to tamper with this relationship, one will be attacked with the fury of a homeowner defending his home.

Figure 17.1 Perfect Privacy

Some of this love is not selfless. The personal computer allows office workers to work for themselves. Perhaps their most frequent activity of this type is the composition of resumes, correspondence to enhance one's public image, personal mail and self-education to acquire new marketable skills.

Next in the order of importance are actions to protect the person's job. This includes memoranda to prove and explain arguments, lists of contacts that may someday be useful, and files that make others dependent on you.

Perhaps the greatest value in having a personal computer of your own is the opportunity to play around with software without much interference from anyone else. Playing with software is a popular activity of information workers who are eager to use company time to compensate for the generally woeful absence of adequate training. It provides the privacy and time to acquire new skills that everyone acknowledges to be the key to further advancement.

It is important to note that neither resumes nor self-serving memoranda were easy to hide under the regime in which the record of every keystroke was in the central computer. The mainframe mentality of central data processing departments, and by guilt of association the IBM corporation, received the same distrust as King George III by the American colonists or the Soviets by most Eastern Europeans. Initially, any move towards linking standalone computers by means of centrally managed networks would appear as an attack on personal privileges and privacy.[119]

Protecting and preserving the privacy of computer files is one of the most painful issues any information executive must address. It will not go away, even if you decide to overlook it. If you neglect it, it will

---

119. By 1993 approximately 40% of over 150 million microcomputers installed worldwide for business purposes were connected to some sort of a network.

come back someday. It will bite you or your successors, with potentially enormous costs for getting your digital archives reorganized.[120]

Currently the only practical solution to personal privacy dictates the imposition of tight technical rules on how to enter, retrieve and store information. A physically separate erasable device, or a partition of data storage space dedicated to an individual on a server should be the only places where an individual may be allowed to store private data.[121] Only that individual should be able to initiate the copying of private data. Access to a person's private memory should be password protected and encrypted. An individual should force replacement with zeros all such information whenever leaving employment.

Property Rights

If you explicitly allow private uses of company property you may not impose standards on every detail of what people do with the computers that have been allotted for their personal use. Private uses of company property requires permission, as a matter of corporate policy. Personal files or personal applications should be able to receive exemption from conformity to corporate standards. There are circumstances in which individuals should be able to manage their allocated computer capacity, especially when they have on their desktops the power of a super computer. However, private uses of personal computers must not be allowed to become an implied right.

With strictly personal use of computers also comes the responsibility for not abusing such privileges. Individuals should pay their own money for strictly personal software. Most of the software for personal use, such as games, text editors, mailing lists, databases of social organizations, and checkbook managers, are copies passed around among casual friends. Copyright infringement liability for such uses should be

---

120. As an example, your digital files may be subject to search either by government or lawyers looking for scraps of damaging information under prevailing disclosure rules. If you have not separated what is personal from business transactions, you will expose your employees to encroachment on their privacy.

121. Allow the removal of a personal disk only from a disk drive located on the local server device. Such acts require compliance with security and privacy rules, possibly including verification by a third party.

the individual's and not the corporation's, though litigating lawyers will be always on the lookout for sloppily managed computer networks of organizations with deep pockets.

If an individual receives the privilege of using some corporate computing assets for private use, he must consent to the organization's security and property protection standards. At the time when a person identifies himself while gaining access to a computer, such as entering a password, the screen should display a notice explaining under what conditions such access becomes an agreement.

Copying corporate information into personal files and then treating it as a personal possession deserves especially strict notice, because this practice can result in removing valuable assets without leaving any trace when the employee leaves. This is especially problematic when employees do company work at home on their own equipment. Company and family records become intermingled on the same physical storage device. In the absence of explicit rules, attempts to seek damages for theft of information may not stand up in court.

Figure 17.2 A New Method for an Old Trade

When I talk with chief information officers of large organizations, I find they avoid publishing policies which define personal information rights and obligations. Such policies are controversial and impossible to implement unless they become an accepted way of doing business over a long period of time. In this book I planned to include examples of the rules of governance that concern protection of personal privacy on a corporate network. However, I had to back off because finding myself involved with issues such as intellectual property rights, copyright and interpretations of the meaning of what is "work for hire." As I explored these topics, I discovered they have as yet untested legal implications waiting for court decisions to establish applicable precedents. What are the legal rights of a corporation when employees share ideas through e-mail or when it engages specialists who telecommute are matters requiring new interpretations which may take many years to settle.

Until legal doctrine catches up with the reality of personal computing, I favor absolute prohibition of any use of corporate property for personal purposes. Microcomputers are now sufficiently inexpensive that individuals can purchase their own devices or receive separate equipment on loan. Such arrangements would establish a clear separation between corporate and private information and allow for a clearcut compartmentalization of personal information.[122]

Organizational Privacy

No enterprise can operate by communicating electronically only within itself. Every enterprise architecture must provide direct electronic links to suppliers, contractors and customers. Whenever that involves direct access to databases there is an exposure to legal conflicts. The most glaring example of such a situation is the recent antitrust action in which airline companies were accused of engaging in price-fixing because they

---

122. Compartmentalization is a term used in all intelligence work. It calls for physical isolation of networks, computers and even memory space so that information cannot be passed or even copied from one compartment to another without authorization.

performed early updates to their reservation systems informing competitors and travel agents about pending changes in air fares.

Cases are now appearing where a manufacturer provides computer-aided models of complex parts, along with manufacturing instructions, to potential suppliers for preparing bids. There are instances in the automobile business where small shops have acquired such digital copies from suppliers by covert means. The computer codes contain instructions for guiding automatic metal-working machines in producing perfect copies of the original parts. In the automobile parts replacement business, selling copies is highly profitable. The practically untraceable theft of engineering data is less risky than stealing the physical parts.

One of the most successful examples of linking a customer with a supplier by means of a secure, value-added service is the FedEx Tracking software, available at no charge. A customer may inquire, via a modem connected to an ordinary telephone line, about the status of his shipment. This is accomplished by dialing into a computer dedicated to customer support, and connected to the operational data base though a one-way link. A typical screen is shown Figure 17.3:

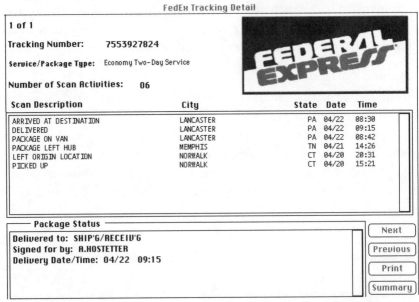

Figure 17.3 Direct Connection from Customer to Supplier

Isolating inquiries from operational databases creates the desirable compartmentalization of information. Creating compartmented databases that permit access only through prescribed procedures and through guarded electronic gateways are essential conditions for all electronic security. As far as I can tell, the FedEx tracking systems meets these requirements.

Arranging for secure connections between suppliers and customers becomes much more difficult when computer applications become directly linked for operational control. Consider the case of Wal-Mart involving thousands of personal computers:[123]

- 3,400 Wal-Mart suppliers have links to the point-of-sale information.

- 1,000 Wal-Mart suppliers have full on-line access to their own product sales and inventory data in the Wal-Mart's internal database.

- Point-of-sale computers automatically trigger orders to suppliers.

- Fast moving items are monitored directly by suppliers.

- Supplier payments are triggered automatically when products are sold.

- Inventory-replenishment information is connected with trucking fleets for continuous monitoring of the flow of goods.

A system of such complexity suffers from a large exposure to security violations, especially in the handling of payments, availability of competitive pricing data, and intelligence about a competitor's production capacity. In the next few years we shall see many firms following the enormously profitable example of Wal-Mart. When such systems extend their scope on an international scale, the opportunities for electronically enabled information piracy and fraud will proliferate.[124]

---

123. *Indications*, CSC Consulting, Volume II, I, 1994

Direct electronic contact with external organizations maximizes the exposure to fraud and espionage. The technical architecture and politics of information management will have to react in the coming years to the pressure to deal with personal privacy, property rights and security issues. Abdication characterizes the handling of these matters right now. Privacy and security responsibilities are placed in the hands of local management who do not have the resources, expertise or technology to deal with sophisticated technological infothreats. In many corporations, the current headlong rush to proliferate distributed client/server operations will come to a halt when it becomes clear that centrally administered network control technology is essential for information security.

Information Intrusion

Digitally encoded archives offer something no government has ever been able to achieve in order to assert effective control over its citizens, at a reasonable cost. Electronic files can potentially last forever. Digital archives are inexpensive because both the cost of storage and the ease of information retrieval make them superior to paper archives.

An example of what computerized information retrieval can do is the case of a drug dealer who was caught while unsuccessfully trying to swallow a slip of paper with only a phone number and the name "John." In less than 45 minutes, the U.S. Financial Crimes Enforcement Network retrieved enough evidence of money laundering and undeclared income to support a criminal indictment. First, they located the physical address of the phone number. Next, they matched the names of the occupants with the Currency and Banking database as well as an Internal Revenue database. Previously recorded money transfers were attributable to the same address and to a person whose name was also "John." After selecting several of the matching transactions for inspection, it was possible to identify the full name and home address

---

124. Paul Strassmann is on the Board of Directors of the EDI World Institute and visiting professor of Information Warfare at the National Defense University. His forthcoming text, *Executive Guide to Information Warfare,* will cover matters related to information security.

of the suspect, including Social Security number, date of birth and bank account numbers. The bank statements gave away the required evidence.[125]

The above situation is one that George Orwell could have used when he described a surveillance-based totalitarian regime in his book, "1984." Orwell never would have succeeded as a security officer in charge of surveillance. His technology depended on video cameras, microphones and taped transcripts of police interrogations that are too labor-intensive to be of practical use. To implement what George Orwell described in his book you would need about one operator per 20 to 40 persons under surveillance. For the full coverage of the U.S., this would require about 15 million trusted operators, not counting the electronic maintenance technicians taking care of the sensors. In case you do not trust your operators, you would need another three to five million guards to watch the watchers. Without computers, Orwell's police would never have been able to find the information that they were looking for.

Multimedia personal computers and point-of-sale recording devices now offer a practical means by which a government authority could perfect a relatively low-cost Orwellian order. Under the guise of equitable tax collection and tracking of illegal money transfers, the government could convince the citizenry that recording every transaction is politically expedient. All this would take is the enforcement of mandatory standards for all data, graphics, audio and video messages, starting with electronic commerce and ultimately covering all transactions in the society, including the replacement of credit cards for cash. All other communications would have to be made criminal acts.[126]

Apart from political considerations, file management is the primary technical difficulty in implementing such a nightmare. The problem in all intelligence work is screening out masses of irrelevant

125. Anthony L. Kimery, "The Government Wants to Look Into Your Bank Account," *Wired*, December 1993
126. Voice-activated text generation and voice-print identification will provide this capability very soon. Fully automated cataloguing of text and data is already available.

information to find items that are useful.[127] Whenever we contemplate the future of an information-based society, the intrusive government scenario will always arise. Current speculations about the intent of the U.S. government in pursuing a national information infrastructure policy agitates a paranoia that had never been put to rest among those concerned with the preservation of civil rights. The current proposals for a government-controlled, universal health insurance system include an electronically readable national identification card containing encoded personal information. Since every Orwellian scenario of computerized surveillance calls for such a card, no wonder the simultaneous launching of national health insurance and the national information infrastructure initiatives by the U.S. government have raised the alarm of encroachment on civil liberties.

Corporate Implications

Until constitutional guarantees of personal privacy are reconciled with security and welfare for a society that is increasingly dependent on computer systems, the politics of privacy will continue to interfere with the needs of comprehensive information management. Meanwhile, corporate information management executives will not get much guidance from legislative or Supreme Court decisions as to how to protect the personal privacy of individuals, suppliers or customers. They will have to deal with this issue by declaring that the corporation, not individuals, retains the full legal rights, accountability and responsibility for all information that resides, enters or exits its networks. The full implications of such a policy are far reaching. It will shape decisions on how to organize, manage and design information systems perhaps more than any other influence.

---

127. Enormous advances are being made using artificial intelligence and especially neural nets to automatically index and classify information for rapid retrieval from million gigabyte files of raw data. See H. Chen, "A Machine Learning Approach to Document Retrieval," and J.Favela, J.J.Connor, "Accessing Memory in Networked Organizations," *Proceedings of the 27th International Conference on Systems Sciences,* IEEE, 1994.

Encryption

The most significant roadblock to an all-knowing police regime is encryption. Because electronic information is easy to steal or corrupt, encrypting data stored in files or being transmitted offers the only practical protection. Defense agencies, banks, insurance companies, private individuals and criminals resort to encryption for safeguarding their most valuable information. Encryption options are now in commercially available software, at no extra charge. <u>Without encryption and authentication of the keys with which to de-encrypt data, the existing financial networks could not operate.</u>

I find it curious that most people who talk about encryption have never seen it in action. To illustrate what this is all about, the following is the encrypted version of the underlined sentence printed above. The encryption is a feature of the Symantec Utilities™ software:

```
ÊØ&ª:Íÿö¯Ê-EÎï,6e₃fiÖ≥Ù›ËhàRÖ Æ      Ó      £    ¸    -
WΩX»t:TÊ'œVfit:TÊ'œVfit:TÊ'œVfi∏,8èΩƒÑK]É®Â¸7Øñ白É'Ωā'
ôƒãàÙX«g:√ü$'6[∑'2;ccf_4"Gfiäzúóóß8Q|_ó˙¬CªÿÏ\ò§◊ ɾ√'@"-ñï
–  … r ® w H ë 🍎 å ] O à ' ° < ÿ „ ñ É Ï é ¨ Ω ã ' ò -
¸ìè¹Ô–)®¿?öc£éÙ»X°â_ÓgÏp „Ùg±]Àc£éÙ»X°âè9Æ¸oŸsp „Ùg±]Àc£
é      Ù    »     X      °     â      _      f      G      -
ö°ú®"OΔ}*-ZøoÒıútßé˘¨âëXFÄ©Íu#\Í\ ƒ*ca¨Δ·®` <8#'ofiF<™√$(
N            *              ◊                 r                  -
≈Åj¹l≥U§`KbMÙq+ä¯Ÿ$±BΔô🍎;»ßÆ")Êöuæ‡¶œÄΔÒjG,™'ÕÀyçI-
iöõÖÃÕ\9k"_D
```

This gibberish suggests how difficult it would be to decode what it means. The encrypted passage contains more characters than the source text. The composition of the lines does not suggest where individual words begin or end. The characters do not use only the standard alphabet, but also the full set of symbols that are available to computers. Although just about every encryption code ultimately can be broken if analyzed by sophisticated software that runs on a powerful supercomputer, it provides a high measure of protection against intrusions on privacy. Only specially trained security experts can be expected to decipher an encrypted message.

The Faustian Bargain

Encryption is a two-edged sword. It protects you, but it also protects any bad guys that the government may wish to catch. This is why the current debates about whether the government should, or even could if it wanted to, dictate an encryption standard is such an important matter. No government-mandated secure encryption scheme will ever receive an unlimited level of trust needed to fully protect the privacy of a person's communications.[128] There may be no such thing as a practical secure encryption code that is unbreakable. Nevertheless, there are some scientists who have taken up the challenge of finding an unbreakable scheme. The latest idea is to exploit nature's uncertainty principle and to use, as the encryption key, the positions of electrons in an atom.

There is enough encryption software readily available from a wide range of sources so that whoever wants it can cook up a unique encryption arrangement.[129] Drug lords, terrorists and insurgency leaders will make sure that they acquire their own encryption/de-encryption routines from widely available sources, that will be hard to break as long as they use e-mail to communicate. However, encryption of telephone conversations is an entirely different matter. Encrypted phones are expensive, unless they are manufactured in large quantities because much of the encryption and de-encryption is done through hardware that is specially protected against tampering. For widespread use, this equipment would have to be standardized. This is why the current discussions about the "Clipper Chip," which sets a standard for encryption and for the government's potential access to de-encryption keys from

---

128. I define "secure" encryption as one that requires considerable expertise, much expense and super-computers to crack. For instance the R.S.A. 129-digit encryption key code, now widely used in banking transactions, took seventeen years and over 100 quadrillion calculations to decode. See Gina Kolata, "100 Quadrillion Calculations Later," *The New York Times*, April 27, 1994, p.A13. Recent advances in decoding method have vastly improved the capability to decypher encrypted messages.

129. The KGB employed thousands of extremely capable mathematicians to develop encryption codes. A large segment of this expertise has now emigrated. Many are now employed in small entrepreneurial software firms in Australia, Canada, Israel, France and the U.S. The 1992 software catalogue from the Rescrypt Corporation, in Moscow features ten virus protection programs, twenty-six access limitation programs and twenty three cryptographic methods, including a 256 character key generator.

"escrow agents" who are supposed to hold the keys in trust until court-authorized wire-taps order their release.

I find much of the debate about the government's authorization of the "Clipper Chip" an example where too many unrelated issues, including the possibly faulty technical design, became jumbled up into arguments where it is difficult to sort out what is essential and what is just incompetent politics. From the standpoint of lawful protection of privacy while preventing criminal abuses, I find the "Clipper Chip" approach of split keys held in escrow, by a trusted party, an elegant compromise. However, information security is not achieved only through encryption. For instance, secure digital signatures are far more important. They do away with the necessity of having to protect password and identity codes through encryption.

Encryption is the Faustian bargain of the information age. On one hand, encryption is the best means of protection against an Orwellian state. One the other hand, encryption makes it very difficult for the state security apparatus to apprehend criminals and terrorists. I just came across an advertisement on the Internet that is a precursor of what will be appearing on the electronic highways with increased frequency:[130]

> Your name has come to our attention. We have reason to believe you may be interested in the products and services our new organization, BlackNet, has to offer.
>
> BlackNet is in the business of buying, selling, trading, and otherwise dealing with *information* in all its many forms. We buy and sell information using public key cryptosystems with essentially perfect security for our customers.
>
> Our location in physical space is unimportant. Our location in cyberspace is all that matters. Our primary address is the PGP key location: "BlackNet<nowhere@cyberspace.nil>" and we can be contacted (preferably through a chain of anonymous remailers) by encrypting a message to our public key (contained below) and depositing this mes-

---

130. This message caused a great stir because it offered a plausible way of perpetuating untraceable infocrime. The message ultimately turned out to be a clever hoax demonstrating how the Internet could become a pathway for undetectable information smuggling.

sage in one of the several locations in the cyberspace we monitor. Currently, we monitor the following locations: alt.extropians, alt.fan.david-sternlight, and the "Cypherpunks" mailing list.

BlackNet is currently building its information inventory. We are interested in information in the following areas, though any other juicy stuff is always welcome. "If you think it's valuable, offer it to us first." Trade secrets, processes, production methods (esp. in semiconductors). Nanotechnology and related techniques (esp. the Merkle sleeve bearing). Chemical manufacturing and rational drug design (esp. fullerines and protein folding). BlackNet can make anonymous deposits to the bank account of your choice, where local banking laws permit, can mail cash directly (you assume the risk of theft or seizure), or can credit you in "CryptoCredits," the internal currency of BlackNet (which you then might use to buy other information and have it encrypted to your special public key and posted in public place).

I wonder what Thomas Jefferson would have decided if he were confronted with such a communication. My guess is that he would have had no choice but to include the freedom to encrypt as an extension to the Bill of Rights for the electronic age, but also make it feasible for security guardians to apprehend criminals by clever means. So far, every society has seen fit to regulate and inspect naval, rail, air and road traffic because unsupervised transportation may cause damage. I do not sympathize with advocates of totally unrestricted freedom for electronic communications to traverse global circuits without any limitations whatsoever.

18

SECURITY

Without security all other privileges lapse.

Even if you choose to avoid dealing with matters of personal privacy, you cannot escape dealing with the protection of organizational memory. National security operatives, regulatory agencies, the FBI, criminal prosecutors and defense lawyers know that most information of any value in a modern organization passes through computers at one time or another. Trapping information as it passes from one electronic medium to another, or from electronic to paper or vice versa, offers the best opportunity to steal it or tamper with it.

The need to protect the privacy of information is directly related to the need to preserve the intellectual capital of an organization. Engineering drawings, experimental results, customer history, market research statistics and research memoranda are often more valuable to a high technology corporation than its buildings or equipment. In a global consulting firm, the accumulation of client data, analytic worksheets, memoranda, software and reports represents the collective organizational memory that gives it a competitive advantage. In an investment management firm it is the right information at the right time that generates all of the profits.

This accumulation of data is currently in filing cabinets, on thousands of miles of magnetic tape and in the memories of long-term employees. Making this treasure of accumulated experience readily available for re-use or for learning is a challenge that many organizations have just begun to address.

Many organizations have started ambitious projects to make information available anywhere, anytime and to everyone by electronic means. Business magazines, academics and quite recently even politicians have found the idea of universal sharing of information by electronic means an attractive topic to discuss as a way to project the image of a forward looking leadership. After all of the visionary pronouncements are made, the responsibility for designing and implementing an organizational memory goes to the people in charge of information systems. They begin with a search for a technical solution.

Creating, and then protecting knowledge assets is primarily an organizational and security issue rather than a question of the technical means to get the job done economically. In this respect, the experience of intelligence organizations involved with national security is more relevant than the expertise of someone who has been designing payroll or materials databases.

Figure 18.1 Organizing for Security

To build a universally accessible organizational memory one has to first choose the rules for the compartmentalization of information.[131]

That defines how to establish the rules of who can access what and how to administer the retrieval of information in specific instances. That will engage you in disputes about the ownership of data. It will bring to the surface the need for declaring under what conditions one part of the organization will yield access privileges to others. You must realize that much of the power and status of middle management and experts derives not so much from what they do for customers but what they do for their peers or superiors.

The model I use for dealing with governance equally applies to security. You must follow the same rules in security matters as you do for governance because the granting of a franchise to knowledge is the same as admitting someone to the privileges of power.

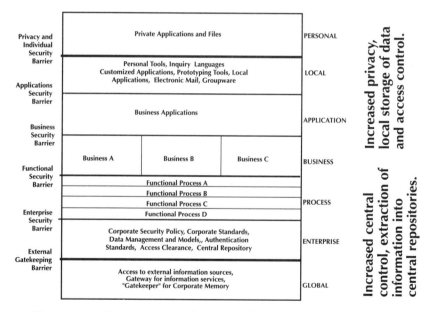

Figure 18.2 Compartmentalization of Organizational Memory

---

131. All information is placed into well defined compartments which specify the accountability and custody for this information. Information can be added or extracted from these compartments only if one follows prescribed security rules. These include practices such as the tagging of individual records by their level of security, and assigning to individuals access privileges to individual file folders.

The role of security barriers, sometimes called *firewalls* by information security people, is to keep track of who gets what information and when. This is how organizations have traditionally kept control over work anyway. However, there are important differences because computer networks make organizations more vulnerable to abuse. Efficiency calls for easier electronic access. Potential misuses argue against it. Compartmentalization along the lines of governance offers the safeguards that authority, responsibility and security will be consistent.

Global Barriers

The External Gate-Keeping Barrier pictured in Figure 18.2 offers an assurance that communications to and from external sources will pass through a uniformly controlled channel. Many people need access to various network services, such as Internet, Compuserve, Dow Jones, Reuters and so forth. In the case of electronic commerce (EDI, Electronic Data Interchange) this is a business necessity. Channeling all such traffic through one or perhaps very few guarded gateways also offers the advantage of consolidating the purchase of network services.[132] It removes the need to equip each personal computer with individual dial-out modems. Dial-in and dial-out connections to the public network are holes in any security fence surrounding your information assets. The fewer openings in the fence, the better. A guarded gate will be always superior to allowing people to enter wherever there may be a convenient gap.

The greatest security exposure arises from traveling employees and people with work-at-home privileges. Improvised local area networks make it possible for people to dial in with a minimum of precautions, such as entering only the right password. After somebody gets inside the network, he or she can traverse it with little interference from anyone or anything except for obstacles that are inherent flaws in systems design.[133] Hostile strangers and particularly employees contemplating fraud will always look for the pathways that are easy for your trusted

---

132. This is especially true of global organizations.

employees to use. By observing such traffic, it will take very little effort for an unauthorized person to learn how to masquerade as an acceptable visitor.

Every modern organization must be able to permit dial-in connections from salespeople, customers, part-time employees and suppliers. The only question is how and where. Creating a global barrier makes it possible to locate those few entry points where someone can watch break-in attempts effectively and inexpensively.

Enterprise Barriers
The Enterprise Security Barrier should contain the master keys for unlocking organizational memory. It contains the data model which identifies and catalogues the location of all databases, the security classification of these databases and copies of the keys that show by what process one can unlock all files. Behind this barrier are also copies of all security access clearances granted to the process, business, application and local level gatekeepers. This is why this barrier must be designed with the greatest care and may require simultaneous authentication from two independent sources before anyone is admitted for entry.

Prevailing security arrangements are typically very poor because they do not separate what is truly critical, such as access to a master copy of data models, from what is optional, such as retrieving programs from the application library to make maintenance changes for local use only. I find that most systems combine small amounts of extremely sensitive information with masses of data that are of no consequence. That happens partially out of habit, largely because nobody has ever designed it otherwise and most often because that makes a number of people indispensable.

---

133. One executive explained to me that "...our chaotic conditions are our best security protection."

Figure 18.3 Security Barriers

The safeguards at the enterprise barrier could be automatic, such as when an authenticated person makes changes where specifically authorized. Until an organization has in place a secure corporate-wide network, many gate keeping actions at this level will require human intervention.

The protection of enterprise level assets also raises the question of how to handle multilevel security. That applies when an authorized person may retrieve confidential information, copies it illegally and then passes it on for general use. How to protect against such abuse is a highly technical matter. It is important to realize that without multilevel security you will have to isolate each network that handles protected corporate information. You will end up with many separate networks, each with built-in barriers against cross-overs from one to another environment. That is an expensive way of obtaining security, because it will force the placement of several personal computers on the desk of anyone who must consult multiple sources of information. You will find that practice often in financial services firms that may have up to five separate computers surrounding one trader. The corporate adoption of multilevel security methods, especially at the enterprise level, will become an attractive solution in due course.

Centralizing accountability for keeping track of information assets at the enterprise level is equivalent to the chief financial officer's responsibility for recording the location of the physical assets of a firm. Every personal computer potentially offers the capacity to cart away a truck full of files containing the most valuable corporate knowledge. The personal computer can accomplish that at a fraction of the cost of the truck, without a trace, unless security barriers are in place. This is why the enterprise barrier must dictate permanently recording any act that copies a confidential data base into any medium that is portable. Therefore, the recording of all transactions that could be the source of possible compromise to the organizational memory should be on non-alterable optical media.

Process Barriers

The purpose of the Process Security Barrier is to decentralize the management of access to enterprise-wide functions, such as legal, payroll, personnel, planning and marketing. Accordingly, the General Counsel, and the Vice Presidents of finance, personnel, planning and marketing would set up gatekeepers to authorize access to their functional files.

Business Barriers

The Business Security Barrier recognizes that global organizations possess an enormous diversity of information needs. They accumulate large amounts of information that can be properly understood and interpreted only in their context. The security fence that must surround the information assets at the business level could vary in strength depending on the value of what is protected. Therefore, the scope and the amount of resources to be devoted to this rampart could be different even within the same enterprise. For instance, a distribution subsidiary in Spain could adopt different practices than a high-tech subsidiary in Canada that includes critical manufacturing capabilities.

Application Barriers

Applications create files. Therefore, the design of databases must include rules for data entry and report extraction. Applications that allow the widespread automatic replication of databases to several locations at the same time warrant special care.[134] I am particularly concerned about the relaxed way some application designers handle error corrections and adjustments to financial entries, where the most fraud takes place. All such occurrences should not be handled within that application but at the next higher level of security, such as at the business or functional levels.

Local Barriers

Defining how to manage the boundaries between the private and local security thresholds likely will be the most difficult of security tasks. To protect against contamination by damaging viruses and realize savings from central management of software licenses calls for the control of updating software for each personal computer from a higher level.[135] It calls for centralized configuration management of both hardware and software.

How can you reconcile respecting the privacy of personal computers with the intrusion of network control for software management? The solution lies in the physical separation of personal files from those that belong to the enterprise. All business applications are owned by the enterprise. The privilege of access to the network can be granted only by the enterprise. Therefore, individuals must comply with the rules essential for assuring security. Once a transaction created within your personal computer leaves the personal layer of governance, enterprise rules take over.

This leaves unanswered the question of what happens to information you extract from higher levels for insertion within your personal space for further copying, and possibly for extracting through removable media. As I see it, the only safe way to prevent losses of confidential information is to prevent employees from creating personal

---

134. Lotus Notes are the most widespread example of such a practice. Replication of databases is essential for assuring their physical survivability. Without adequate safeguards, uncontrolled replication becomes an invitation for the theft of information. In the information age, you do not carry away your loot. You replicate it without a trace.

135. "Viruses" can take many forms. For instance, *Working Woman* magazine proposes a novel way to fight sex harassment. Install X-rated (pornographic) software on the computer of the alleged offender and then turn the monitor so that anyone passing the empty office can notice it (*Wall Street Journal*, January 18, 1994, p.1).

files from any source other than from software installed exclusively for personal use. There are a number of feasible technical solutions to achieve this result. Whatever the solution, it will be controversial. The possessors of the personal computers will be highly averse to any measure which limits their previously unrestricted means for taking advantage of corporate information.

As unpalatable and restrictive as tight security may be for the management of corporate information assets, in due course individuals will discover that it will be to their benefit to place an unscalable wall between their personal privacy and corporate files used in conducting business. For an organization to gain unqualified trust in its electronic community, it must make sure that it is secure against abuse from within and subversion from without.

19

REENGINEERING

You cannot reengineer something that was not engineered to begin with.

In political form, the practitioners of reengineering apply methods much more akin to what you get in a *coup d'état* than what you find in the negotiated processes of constitutional government.[136] Reengineering is always the method of choice whenever there is a *coup de main*.[137] In the last two years, every new CEO for a major U.S. corporation who was not brought up from the ranks announced the initiation of a reengineering program. It offers an acceptable public relations cover for mopping up lingering opposition and placing new lieutenants in positions of power.

Origins of Reengineering

Early in 1993, an epochal event took place in the U.S. For the first time in history, white-collar unemployment exceeded blue-collar unemployment. In the experience of older generations, a college education enti-

---

136. An overthrow of the current government by radical means. For strong parallels see Gregor Ferguson, *Coup d'Etat - A Practical Manual*, Arms and Armour Press, 1987, Dorset, England. The role of mercenaries is analogous to the use of consultants in takeovers. Both mercenaries and consultants get to know too much to be kept around in positions of power after the coup succeeds.
137. Takeover by assassination of the top leadership.

tled one to a job with an excellent earning potential, long-term job security and opportunity to climb a career ladder. If there was an economic downturn, unemployment was something that happened to others.

Large-scale white collar unemployment should not have come as a surprise. Since 1979, the U.S. information workforce has kept climbing, and in 1993 stood at 54% of total employment. Forty million new information workers had appeared since 1960.

What do these people do? They are very busy. They are mostly corporate overhead in business, or social overhead if they work in the public sector. They are lawyers, consultants, coordinators, clerks, administrators, managers, executives and experts of all sorts.

The expansion in computer-literate jobs greatly increased the amount of information these people could process and therefore demand from others. It is the dominant characteristic of information work that it breeds more information work. It does that at a rate that is faster than the growth in number of people added to the information payroll. Computers turned out to be multipliers of information labor, as contrasted with machinery that reduced the amount of agricultural and factory labor.

The greatest growth in information labor has been in the government, which now employs more people than the manufacturing sector. Government workers are predominantly engaged in information activities, such as passing applications back and forth in some agencies, and then distributing money. This requires compliance with complex regulations, which in turn creates the need for more information processing.

Who pays for the costs of all this information work? Everybody does, either in higher prices or as increased taxes. As long as U.S. firms could raise prices, there was always room for more overhead. Starting in the early 1980s, international economic competition started seriously eroding U.S. market share in key industries, making it imperative for corporations to reduce staff costs. Blue collar labor essential to manufacture goods was either outsourced to foreign lands, or automated using proven industrial engineering methods to substitute capital for labor. After the mid 1980s further major cost cuts could come only from reductions in overhead. Could you substitute capital, in the form of computers for information labor to recover competitive strength? By 1985, it was clear this would not work. Regardless of how much capital was plowed into the service and government sectors, apparently productivity got worse. Something else had to be done to reduce overhead expenses.

Overhead Cost Reduction

Early attempts to reduce overhead by announcing twenty percent or more across-the board layoffs in major corporations misfired. The most valuable experts left first to start up business ventures, most often with the knowledge they gained while the large firms lingered in bringing innovations into the marketplace. Much of the dynamic growth of Silicon Valley in California and the complexes surrounding Boston, Massachusetts have their origins in the entrepreneurial exploitation of huge research and development investments by large corporations.

For instance, Dr. George Pake, the head of Xerox Corporation's Palo Alto Research Center [PARC] received the coveted Presidential Medal for the advancement of U.S. science. PARC was perhaps the most prolific source of novel technologies subsequently brought into the marketplace by over twenty successful start-up ventures. The President cited Dr. Pake for "...making the Xerox laboratories a national asset."

The next wave of overhead cost reduction taking place from 1985 through 1990 was even more wasteful. Across-the-board targets to cut overhead, without the benefit of improving any of the business processes, showed up in bulletins to the financial press. Companies that resorted to these crude methods did not know how to measure the value-added of information workers. Therefore, they applied methods that had been somewhat effective in controlling blue collar employee costs. However, that was not successful. The same kind of treatment that removed factory workers who did not have much power made the remaining management staff react in counterproductive ways. They exercised their power to block much needed reforms. In the resulting turmoil, much of the corporate leadership became demoralized. This hurt the companies, especially when the disorientation happened in managing customer service or product quality.

Figure 19.1 Business Process Analysis

Total Quality Movement

The TQM (total quality management) movement responded to the rapid deterioration of morale in the workplace and gained enthusiastic acceptance. TQM offered improved approaches to the business process by emphasis on quality circles, worker motivation, participation in decisions, employee training and self-directed work. Much of the TQM movement depended on driving innovations and improvements from the bottom of the organization upwards.

TQM became extremely popular where people could see visible results, such as in factories, service organizations and customer support. TQM accomplished marvels in boosting the productivity of direct labor, although that was not where the greatest losses occurred. Corporations, especially large ones, suffered from having excess management. Labor productivity increased as work migrated to contractors, while overhead staffs remained in place and coordinated that which required less management than before. TQM did not do much to improve the productivity of managers. The managers' jobs were primarily to coordinate with each other, instead of serving customers. TQM was the most effective in those areas where customers were served.

Whenever quality circle meetings ran into managerial pathologies, they could not do much about it. There was no way to apply the bottom-up TQM process to managerial coalitions. Politically, such rearrangement could come only from the top of the organization.

When competitive conditions kept shrinking profit margins further, the costs of management were the only place where major savings were available. It was time to break the long standing management tradition of never treating managers as disposable. The situation was ripe to turn management against management. In political terms, starting an intraorganizational civil war offered an attractive solution to an economic problem.

Industrial Engineering

This is where reengineering came in. It proposed to apply traditional industrial engineering methods of process analysis, activity costing and value-added measurement to cut overhead and eliminating redundant managerial work.

Industrial engineering was never a bottom-up process. Its practitioners have traditionally been professional change agents and emissaries of top management. Industrial engineers, especially when hired as consultants, are trained to sniff out excess costs more precisely than comptrollers. When the finance establishment wishes to make major cuts, they find a third party to initiate the surgery. It is a testimonial to their sublime political skills that the smart comptrollers never directly attack their potential competitors in marketing, manufacturing, personnel or legal services. That would incur the permanent animosity of those who someday may have to work with them or for them. That is why comptrollers like to hire industrial engineering consultants.

Application of Reengineering

The essence of reengineering is to make the purging of past excess staffing binges more palatable to senior executives. Over the years, these executives became accustomed to increasing their own staffs as a way to gain greater organizational clout. It is an unspoken convention that staff positions in a hierarchy exist independently of whether or not they affect anything that the customer needs. The primary purpose of much of middle management and staff is to act as guardians of a bureaucracy's budget, prerogatives and influence. Reengineering thus offers a welcome explanation to cover up for past mismanagement when hiring thousands of now dispensable employees.

If you want to perform surgery on management overhead, do not do it in a dark room with a machine. First, you must gain acceptance from those who know how to make the organization work well. Second, you must elicit their cooperation in telling you where the cutting will do the least damage. Third, employees must be willing to share with you insights about where the removal of an existing business process will improve customer service.

Budget cutters who do little else than seek out politically unprotected components of an organization cannot possibly know the full consequences of their actions. Reengineering offers to the reengineering consultants, hired for quick results, an easy way to cut costs without thinking too hard. In its most popular present form, reengineering calls for throwing out everything that exists and recommends reconstituting a workable organization on the basis of completely fresh ideas. The new business model is supposed to somehow spring forth from the inspired insight of a new leadership team.

Reengineering is a contemporary repackaging of industrial engineering methods from the past, except that it has none of its analytic rigor. It has been adopted by business enterprises that must instantly show improved profits to survive. However, reengineering of management differs from the incremental and carefully analytic methods that were used by industrial engineers for streamlining physical labor.

Dictatorial Characteristics

Reengineering is a business improvement method that dictates change primarily from the top of the organization. It places heavy reliance on outsiders to lead it. It assumes that you cannot trust your own people to fix whatever ails your company. Reengineering accepts what the experts, preferably newcomers to the scene, have to offer. Experienced old-timers are usually not asked or expected to correct conditions they have been collectively tainted with and which now need improving.

In reengineering, it is the role of most consultants to recommend what the "to be" conditions ought to look like, without spending much time understanding the reasons for the "as-is" conditions. The stated credo of reengineering is to forget what you know about your business and start with a clean slate to "reinvent" what you would like to become.[138] These consultants advocate using the clean slate or clean sheet of paper design as a way of applying deductive reasoning that revives a practice that had fallen into disrespect over three hundred years ago. It provides the rationale for reinventing government, even though the U.S. government has been around for over two hundred years. It provides justification for reinventing the corporation by outsiders, who have no prior experience or understanding how to produce and deliver existing products and services to current customers.

Deductive vs. Inductive Reasoning

To comprehend fully the philosophical roots of contemporary reengineering, we have to examine its approach to reasoning and problem resolution.

Mankind has been experimenting with two forms of dealing with problems: deductive and inductive. The deductive form has prevailed over most of history and was the only form of logic allowed by the medieval church and the marxist regimes. Deduction defines a group of facts or ideas that are already accepted, as a known principle, and then makes a statement, called inference, about the sameness of something new with what is therefore believed to be true and universal. Deduction always proceeds to reason from the general to the specific. For instance, medieval views about the universe were developed by deductive reasoning from Aristotelian assertions about nature. As an example, Aristotelian views about what happens to objects when they fell was derived from the principle that a cannon ball made of iron would fall to earth faster than a cannon ball of the identical size made of wood because it was heavier. For almost two thousand years that view prevailed because nobody found it advisable to take two cannon balls and drop them from a tower. Most of the medieval political order, medicine, astron-

---

138. A half page advertisement from Arthur Andersen in the March 1, 1994, *Wall Street Journal* proclaims: "You are committed to dramatically changing your company. You have gone back to a blank canvas." Those who propose a blank canvas approach should remember an old scout saying: "If you don't know where you are a map won't help."

omy and law were based on deductive logic derived from unquestionable dogma that came from a generally acknowledged authority. Because it claims its origins from an authoritative source, such as a professor or consultant, deductive reasoning is always certain in its findings by claiming a derivation of its facts from established axioms.

In contrast with the deductive form or reasoning, the inductive approach progresses from facts and observations to provable conclusions. Inductive reasoning arrives at its generalizations only after having examined evidence that is supported by observation of specific instances. Modern science is based on inductive methods. It does not permit arguments by correspondence, logical derivation or analogy but only on the basis of verifiable facts and experimental evidence that leads to reproducible results. The uniquely American school of philosophy, pragmatism, follows inductive reasoning in every respect. The practice of industrial engineering has its origins in the application of the concepts of pragmatism in the workplace. Inductive reasoning is always uncertain about its conclusions because there may always be some additional variables or evidence that may reveal additional insights. Besides, inductive conclusions are much harder to establish than deductive assertions.

The Deduction of Best Practices

Making deductive arguments is much easier than coming up with an inductive collection of evidence. Typically, a consultant will parade an exhaustive catalogue of what are, in his opinion, the "best practices," which he is now ready to prescribe as a cure for the client's problems. How a consultant concludes that his particular list of best practices fits a particular situation is rarely, if ever, open to discussion. As one of the editors of a journal on information management and as frequent referee of research papers, I have now a sufficiently large collection of papers where consultants and university professors have set out to collect a list of "best practices." Invariably, they use survey questionnaires to come up with a list what people think is important. Apart from having the survey questionnaires filled out by a statistically uncontrolled sample of individuals, and findings that are not reproducible, the fundamental flaw with this approach is that none of the "best practices" lists of have been ever openly related for verification to an objective measure of performance, such as profitability.

Deductive reengineering calls for changing a client's behavior to what fits on the approved list as the "best" approach. The only problem is that every reengineering consultant subscribes to a different list of what is important. Nevertheless, deductive reasoning is widely applied in evaluations based on comprehensive audit checklists or in selecting CIOs for awards. The Arthur Andersen advertisement declares its inductive preferences by stating that "... our professionals will start by sharing...what works best for others."[139]

There was a time when owning IBM stock, smoking Lucky Strikes, driving a Cadillac, depositing your money in a Savings & Loan Association and owning an assault rifle were the "best" on somebody's list. If you suspect having acne or AIDS, emulating somebody's list of "best" practices will not do you much good. You better find someone with sufficient inductive knowledge to first correctly diagnose what is wrong and then help you.

To arrive at a conclusion by inductive reasoning requires collecting evidence and learning that is based on experimental verification. Inductive logic relies on finding what works, regardless whether it fits into a generally accepted pattern or not. A consultant who relies on the inductive discipline would spend much time studying why an organization malfunctions and what are some of its unique characteristics. An inductive consultant would recommend not necessarily what matches others, but has been shown to work in a particular situation, under similar circumstances. Inductive reasoning does not convey the glib assurances of deductive prescriptions. Recommendations based on inductive reasoning are specific, actionable and incremental.

Recommendations based on deductive reasoning are likely to be generic and drastic. Deductive findings will have a great appeal to those who have only a generic understanding of the facts and who wish to

---

139. Arthur Andersen, *ibid.* Identical advertisements appeared in *Forbes* and *Fortune* magazines.

get quick answers. Inductive conclusions are unglamorous and usually take a long time to implement.

Deduction allows you to prescribe what to do based on somebody's authoritative concept of what ought to be ideal conduct. Therefore, deductive consulting is relatively easy and can be accomplished with rhetoric that can bypass having to deal with the details. Induction is difficult, requires patience and calls for a great deal of substantive knowledge about conditions in the workplace and in the marketplace. This is why I believe the current popularity of deductive reasoning is only a temporary setback to the sounder traditions of industrial management that are based on pragmatism.

Disregarding Experience

You can never totally disregard your people, your relationships with customers, your assets, the accumulated knowledge and your reputation. You will find versions of the phrase "...throw history into the dustbin and start anew" associated with every failed radical movement in the last two hundred years.

Most reengineering proponents do not worry much about formal methods. They practice techniques of emergency surgery, most often by amputation. If amputation is not feasible, they resort to tourniquet-like remedies to stop the flow of red ink. Radical reengineering may apply, however, under emergency conditions of imminent danger as long as somebody remembers this may leave an enterprise in a crippled condition. There are drastic cures from which a patient may never fully recover because of demoralization. Reengineering is swifter than a more deliberate approach. No wonder the simple and quick methods are preferred by the impatient and those who may not be around to cope with the unforeseen long term consequences.

In the most radical forms of reengineering, participation by most of the existing management is superfluous, because the new regime wants to junk their methods anyway. Under such conditions, bringing in an executive to run a computer company who was good at managing a cookie company makes perfect sense.

During reengineering, debates receive little encouragement since the goal is to produce a masterful move that suddenly will turn everything around. Autocratic managers thrive on an opportunity to preside over a reengineering effort. Reengineering also offers a new lease on the careers of chief information officers who prefer to forge ahead behind the shield of technology to induce revolutionary changes in management practices.[140] A number of spokesmen in recent meetings of computer executives offered reengineering as the antidote to the slur that CIO stands for "Career Is Over" because it offers a new mission.

Haste and Reengineering

Reengineering conveys a sense of urgency that does not require financial analysis and certainly not on formal risk assessment. Managers who tend to rely on bold strokes rebel against such analytic constraints.[141] When it comes to business case analysis, we find the traditional confrontation of the tortoise and the hare. The plodders insist on analysis while the hip-shooters laugh at it and prefer the bold strokes inspired by their deductive visions. Sometimes the hip-shooters win, but the odds are against them in any endurance contest.

Reengineering does not allow sufficient time for the much needed adaptation to changing conditions. It imposes changes swiftly by fiat, usually from a collection of new managers imported to make long overdue changes. Even if this approach may be good for shocking an organization out of its bad habits, the changes will be hard to implement for fear of job loss. Anyone expected to act differently will have second thoughts before committing to supporting the transition from the old to the new.

Reengineering has the advantage of being the choice of last resort when there is no time left to accomplish business process improvement. In this sense, it is akin to saying that sometimes dictatorship is more effective than democratic participation. Without probing why the lead-

---

140. A 1993 survey by the Computer Sciences Corporation – a leading reengineering consultant – showed that 63% of 556 corporations were engaged in major reengineering projects. About 40% of these efforts were led by information technology executives.
141. The widely known management guru, Tom Peters, says "Weird is good. Crazy times call for crazy organizations. CIOs ought to collect weirdos. There is nothing more stupid than narrow-minded discussion of information technology benefits." See *Computerworld*, March 28, 1994, p.71 for details.

ership of an enterprise allowed conditions to deteriorate to require surgery by chain saw, I am starting to see indications that the many of the radical reengineering cures may end up causing chronic damage instead of dealing with a curable disease by more clinical means.[142]

Constitutional democracies, despite occasional reversal in fortune, have never willingly accepted dictatorship as the way out of their troubles. The record of attempts to deal with the crises in governance by radical solutions is dismal. Though occasionally you may find remarkable short term gains, extreme solutions that destroy human capital have always resulted in an era of violence and troubled times of social retrogression.

Public Sector Reengineering

Despite admirable pronouncements about reengineering by the U.S. government, it will be a long time before anyone finds out if that is just a smoke screen for more spending. As long as the federal government continues to increase taxes – the easiest way out of any cost pressures – the prospects of reinventing government as a way of reducing costs will remain dim.

Reinventing government does not deliver savings if, throughout the process, you keep expanding the scope of government. You can have less bureaucracy only if you streamline functions that have accumulated enormous administrative overhead, such as loan guarantees, public housing, education and health care. Prior public sector attempts at rationalization of administrative costs have never delivered what was originally promised.

The latest Washington reengineering campaign may turn out to be a retrogression instead of an improvement. You do not enhance a stagnating economy by claiming to save a probable hundred billion so

---

142. Beware of giant reengineering projects. The cancellation rate for software projects is directly proportional to the overall size of the system and is acute above 10,000 function points, or one million source statements. For large systems in excess of 10,000 function points, the probability of cancellation is greater than 65%. Caspers Jones, *Assessment and Control of Software Risks*, Prentice Hall, 1994.

you can bring over a trillion additional dollars under public sector controls.

An emetic will be always an emetic, regardless of the color and shape of the bottle in which it is packaged. It does not do much for those who maintain a healthy diet by eating only what their body can use. A cure claiming to be an emetic but which nevertheless encourages gluttony will increase obesity.

The Extremist Strain

Reengineering is a great idea and a clever new buzzword. Any manager would support the idea of taking a defective business process and fixing it. Industrial engineers, methods analysts and efficiency experts have been doing that for a long time.

However, efficiency through reengineering introduces a radical means to achieve corrective actions. This extremism offers what appears to be instant relief from the pressure to show immediate improvements. Reengineering, as recently promoted, is a new label that covers some consultants' extraordinary claims. To fully understand the intellectual roots of reengineering, let the most vocal and generally acknowledged guru of reengineering speak for himself.[143]

- "American managers ...must abandon the organizational and operational principles and procedures they are now using and create entirely new ones."

- "Business reengineering means starting all over, starting from scratch."

- "It means forgetting how work was done...old titles and old organizational arrangements...cease to matter. How people and companies did things yesterday doesn't matter to the business reengineer."

- "Reengineering...can't be carried out in small and cautious steps. It is an all-or-nothing proposition that produces dramatically impressive results."

---

143. Michael Hammer and James Champy, *Reengineering the Corporation - A Manifesto for Business Revolution*, Harper Business, 1993.

The Extremist Point of View

When Hammer was asked "How do managers contemplating a big reengineering effort get everyone inside their company to join up?" he answered in terms that reflect the violent way how to promote progress:[144]

- "...On this journey we...shoot the dissenters."

The theme of turning destruction on your own people remains a persistent motive:

- "...It's basically taking an ax and a machine gun to your existing organization."[145]

In view of the widespread popularity of Hammer, I wonder how executives can subscribe to such ferocious views while preaching about individual empowerment, teamwork, partnership, participative management, knowledge-driven enterprise, learning corporation, employee gain sharing, fellow-worker trust, common bond, shared values, people-oriented leadership, cooperation and long-term career commitment.

The anxiety of the survivors of reengineering is perhaps the principal reason why companies do not realize the gains for which they originally planned. Employees who pull through endless waves of cuts become so distrustful, overworked, insecure and traumatized that their productivity drops and morale is permanently injured .[146]

---

144. "ASAP Interview with Mike Hammer," *Forbes Magazine ASAP*, Summer 1993, p.71
145. J. Maglitta, "Interview with Michael Hammer," *Computerworld*, January 24, 1994, p. 85
146. Joann S. Lublin, "The Walking Wounded - Survivors of Layoffs Battle Angst, Anger, Hurting Productivity," *The Wall Street Journal*, December 6, 1993.

Figure 19.2 Some Reenginering Choices

I usually match the ideas of the new prophets with past patterns. It helps me to understand if what I hear now follows methods tried before. I find Hammer's sentence structure as well as his dogmatic pronouncements as something that resonates with the radical views put forth by political hijackers. Just replace some of the nouns, and you can produce slogans attributed to those who gained power by overthrowing the existing order. Here are a few samples:

- "Reengineering...will require a personality transplant...a lobotomy."[147]

- "I want to purge from the business vocabulary: CEO, manager, worker, job."[148]

- "What you do with the existing structure is nuke it!"[149]

---

147. "Back to the Future," *Computerworld*, June 1, 1987. [Note: Lobotomy is surgery in which nerves in the brain are cut to disable some of their functions.]
148. "Interview with Mike Hammer," *Forbes*, ASAP, Summer 1993.
149. "Mike Hammer, the High Priest," *Site Selection*, February 1993, p.55

- "...reengineering must be initiated...by someone who has...enough status to break legs."[150]

- "...the way you deal with resistance [to reengineering] is ...a bloody ax. Al Capone once said, you get further with a gun and a kind word than with a kind word alone."[151]

- "...you either get on the train or we'll run over you with the train....The last thing that reengineering does is to enhance the manager's sense of importance. Managing isn't important."[152]

- "...Don't try to forestall reengineering. If senior management is serious...they'll shoot you."[153]

It may be a coincidence that the most widely read book on reengineering carries the provocative subtitle *A Manifesto for Business Revolution* and claims to be a seminal book comparable to Adam Smith's *The Wealth of Nations*, which is the intellectual underpinning of the free enterprise system. All you have to remember is there is another book, also bearing the title *Manifesto*, that successfully spread the premise that the only way to improve capitalism is to obliterate it.[154]

Morality in Warfare and Commerce

What is at issue here is much more than reengineering, which has many worthwhile elements. The question is one of morality. The morality of warfare, vengeance, violent destruction and the use of might over right has been with us ever since primitive tribes competed for hunting grounds. Societies have recognized the importance of warfare by sanctioning a class allowed to kill enemies, while adhering to a code of loyalty and self sacrifice for the good of the tribe.

---

150. R. M. Randall, "The Reengineer," *Planning Review*, May/June 1993, p.20.
151. "The Age Of Reengineering," *Across the Board*, June 1993, p.31
152. "The Age Of Reengineering," *Across the Board*, June 1993, p.33
153. "The Future of Middle Managers," *Management Review*, September 1993, p.53
154. Another term popularized by Mike Hammer in the popular "Reengineering Work: Don't Automate, Obliterate," *Harvard Business Review*, July-August 1990

The morality of commerce has been with us at least since the advent of the Athenian democracy starting about 600 B.C, that was based on commerce . In its ideal form, that has remained the foundation of our western civilization, it was based on shunning force, coming up with voluntary agreements, collaborating with strangers and aliens, respecting contracts and promoting bargaining that would benefit both the buyer and the seller.

Just about every major national tragedy in the last few centuries is traceable to the substitution of the morality of warfare for the morality of commerce, under the guise that this would lead to greater overall prosperity. Hammer's adoption of the non-redeeming expressions of military violence crossed the line of what is culturally acceptable by our heritage. Reengineering is and should remain an activity concerned with commerce and follow that morality. One should leave the military morality to those who have to deal with the likelihood of having to defend their community against tyranny.

There is no doubt that U.S. industry is under competitive attack and under pressure to increase earnings. That does not justify declaring war on your most educated and experienced cadres. Competition and profits are a contest that takes place in the arena of commerce where the winners, in the long run, prevail by being superior in using human talent, initiative and knowledge.

Revolutionary Changes

I have listened carefully to the extremists who are the most prominent promoters of the proven old ideas now selectively repackaged as a managerial innovation. Their well financed promotional efforts have succeeded in gaining at least temporary respectability for reengineering. I have found they have successfully translated the radicalism of the 1960s, with its slogan "Do not reform, obliterate!" into a fashionable, money-making proposition. The clarion call for overthrowing the status quo is similar to that trumpeted by the radical students who occupied the dean's office. Now the same arguments can be transformed into lucrative consulting services. If you ask many of the radical proponents of reengineering what they did while they were attending college during the 1960s, you will find a surprising number of erstwhile anti-establishment advocates.[155]

If you look at political revolutionary movements back to the times of the French Revolution, you will find their leaders fixed upon seizing power from the Establishment under whatever slogan they could sell. Most of the extremist leaders over the past 200 years have been intellectuals who rarely produced anything other than pamphlets and speeches, and have been consistent in making conditions worse after they took power into their hands. There is one thing that all past revolutionary movements have in common with the current extremist views of reengineering: in each case, the leaders call for complete and uncompromising destruction of existing institutions. It is only through this kind of attack on customs, habits and relationships that newcomers can gain influence against an opposition disabled into inaction. The common characteristic of an elite that agitates for positions of leadership is arrogance. They are the only ones who claim a superior insight into the future and therefore expect unquestionable trust from followers.

I am in favor of making evolutionary improvements in the way people work. If you want to call that "reengineering," that's fine, though I prefer to call it "business process improvement." You cannot reengineer something that has never been engineered to begin with. Organizations have evolved instead of being engineered, because it is impossible to put together complex human relationships as if they were machine parts.

What matters is not the label, but by what means you help organizations to improve. The long record of miscarriages of centrally planned radical reforms and the dismal record of reengineering as acknowledged by Hammer, suggest that an evolutionary approach is likely to deliver better improvements.[156] No wonder that eighty-five percent of the 350 top executives who have tried reengineering in their

---

155. This includes a number of prominent politicians who are now clamoring for "reinventing the government."
156. Jeff Moad, "Does Reengineering Really Work?" *Datamation*, August 1, 1993, p.22

operations are dissatisfied with the results of their efforts.[157] Six out of every ten executives in this survey said they encountered unanticipated problems or unintended side effects from reengineering. These findings are echoed in another study by the Computer Sciences Corporation, the firm with the reputation of having the largest and most prosperous reengineering practice. In a study of 500 corporations with experience in reengineering they found a dissatisfaction rate of close to 50%.[158]

157. Julia King, "Re-engineering Slammed," *Computerworld*, June 13, 1994, p.1
158. Julia King, *ibid.* p. 14

20

PROCESS IMPROVEMENT

*If you do what you have always done, you will get
what you always got.*

Lasting improvements in business processes require the support of those who know your business and who will see to it the changes become effective in the workplace. This requires creating conditions for continuous, incremental and adaptive changes. Cutbacks in employment that respond abruptly to a steadily deteriorating financial situation are a sure sign management has been either incompetent or asleep, or both. It is always good to ask the CEO who just dismissed 20,000 people: who put them on the payroll to begin with?

I am deliberately avoiding here the popular synonyms, reengineering and business process redesign. Those expressions convey an obsolete metaphor in which someone who has superior knowledge "designs" and "engineers" something and then passes the blueprints to operators who had little say about the content and methods. I do not believe organizations can attain lasting progress through "redesign" for just about the same reasons why reengineering will not work if imposed as a drastic and sudden solution. Evolutionary change stimulates the imagination and the morale of the workforce. It creates conditions for personal learning and discovery of innovative ways to cope with challenges and adversity.

Wholesale dismissals of employees, accompanied by a push for long-time employees to resign voluntarily, will traumatize the survivors with fear and the avoidance of any initiative. It first will get rid of those who are the most qualified because they can find employment elsewhere. You will end up with an organization with self-inflicted wounds while the competition is gaining on you. If you lose your best people, you will have stripped yourself of your most valuable assets. The presumption that a person is obsolete or redundant is not a reflection on the intrinsic usefulness of that individual. It testifies to the neglect of top executives to innovate and grow an enterprise. Human beings are never a surplus. What you have is a shortage of value-creating jobs that were not created by competent management.

Figure 20.1 Downsizing

Liquidating a company is easy and can be quite profitable. Selling off accumulated assets can, for a while, give the appearance of prosperity just as exiled French and Russian nobles did when they were auctioning off their jewelry. Eventually somebody ought to also start thinking about how to rebuild the enterprise for permanent growth. The challenge of all business process improvement is to lead today's losers to be tomorrow's winners by opening new opportunities for talent that otherwise will disappear.

How do you achieve business process improvements under adverse conditions? How do you motivate your people to give you their best efforts so they may prosper again, even though some positions of privilege will change or cease to exist?

Improvement Through Cooperation

To be successful, business process improvements depend on the commitment and imaginative cooperation of everyone. To improve business processes, the leadership must convince all parties that only through working together can there be a gain in their long-term prospects. Business process improvement should rely primarily on the accumulated knowledge of existing employees to find circumstances that will support creating new jobs. That does not mean everyone will continue whatever was done before. Many jobs will cease to exist. It is the role of competent management to create jobs for their people by offering new products and services.[159]

In business process improvement projects, the people directly affected by the potential changes should study the "as-is" conditions and propose "to be" alternatives to achieve the desired gains. Everybody with an understanding of the business should participate. External help should be hired only for expertise that does not exist internally.

Node Trees

Business process improvement calls for applying rigorous methods to charting, pricing and process flow analysis of "as-is" conditions. You can construct thousand– and even ten-thousand element diagrams out of standard components and combine them to run as a simulation. Adopting a standard way to chart workflows greatly simplifies communications. Individual departments may start building their own workflow descriptions. They should make whatever simplifications are advantageous that do not involve others. When external communications inhibit further gains, node "tree" diagrams that reveal how various pieces fit together are of great help.

---

159. The foremost exponent of this point of view is Tom Davenport. His *Process Innovation: Reengineering Work through Information Technology*, Harvard Business School Press, Boston, 1992, is an incisive and practical treatise of great value to all who wish to improve their business processes.

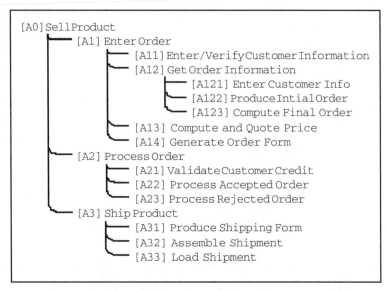

Figure 20.2 Top Branches of a Node Tree Diagram

Node tree diagrams must be consistent in identifying every element of a system so that conversations about reorganizing people or restructuring software are unambiguous. They are extremely helpful in discussions whenever someone diverts attention from matters of substance, usually at the top branches of the node tree, to minutiae buried under the sixths or even tenths layer of detail. Node trees make it possible to keep the agenda topics at their appropriate level without disconcerting diversions into details that should be talked about only after the fundamentals have been sorted out and accepted. Politically, node trees are very valuable. They make it possible to pull conversational provocateurs back to the agenda.

Process Flow Simulation

By adopting a formal business process flow diagramming method and following a consistent technique for tracking costs and elapsed time, as illustrated in Figure 20.3, it is possible to understand how extremely complex processes fit together. This eliminates the need to carve up business processes for no better reason than to make them manageable.

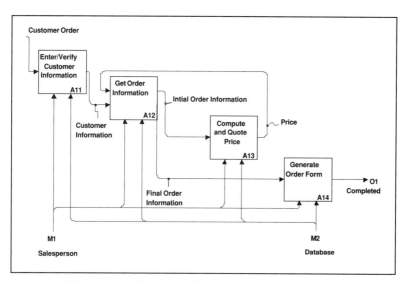

Figure 20.3 Sample of a Workflow Diagram[160]

You are never finished with business process improvement. New payoff opportunities will always emerge as people learn and have new insights into operations. The primary objective of business process improvement is to create a learning environment in which renewal and gain will be an ongoing process instead of one time shock therapy.

People learn best by experimentation and by having access to methods that enable visualization of alternative solutions. That is why I favor workflow methods that can simulate understandable results. Consider five hotly debated scenarios in a billing department where there is an honest disagreement as to what is best:

- #1: Keep things as they are. This sustains the "as-is" condition;

- #2: Change procedures and check customer credit before taking orders;

- #3: Reallocate staff from credit to billing;

160. Courtesy of Meta Software Corporation of Cambridge, Massachusetts.

- #4: Reorganize from functional organization to "customer teams;" and,

- #5: Apply "expert" systems to do all routine clerical work.

No debate can settle these questions without modeling the proposed rearrangement of work elements, people and computers. A workflow simulator can produce a model to test the viability of each scenario.

After you have constructed an "as-is" picture, it is relatively easy to run and rerun it and see the consequences under different assumptions. You can then show the simulated outcomes of alternative solutions to management. In Figure 20.4, scenarios are compared using cost as the outcome.

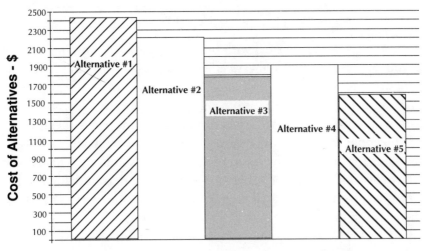

Figure 20.4 Cost Comparison of Alternatives[161]

Costs should never be the only measure of performance. Superior customer service is what makes businesses grow and earn above average profits. Business process improvement decisions are often sub-

---

161. Output from workflow simulator. All fixed and variable costs for the entire process were added up automatically. Courtesy of Meta Software Corporation of Cambridge, Massachusetts.

ject to "paralysis by analysis" because nobody can agree on which course is best. That is usually the result of difference in biases found in different departments. Finance would always favor lower costs, and marketing would argue for faster response time to customers. How do you reconcile these different points of view? This is where workflow simulation can be of help. It can show how various options compare from the standpoint of timing to complete critical transactions, as demonstrated in Figure 20.5:

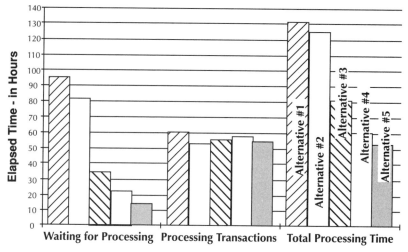

Figure 20.5 Simulating Processing Time

Workflow diagram simulations tried out as "what if" cases are of unlimited use. You can use them as a statement of systems specifications, since they are much more precise than any text description. They are very useful in negotiations about organizational responsibilities, which occur during mergers, restructuring or outsourcing services.[162] As a political device for arriving at inter-organizational peace treaties, especially after a period of protracted animosity, dynamic workflow diagrams are superb. For example, they are ideal in displaying the utilization of personnel:

---

162. I would never outsource any critical information service without first agreeing on the workflow diagram for both parties to the new arrangement.

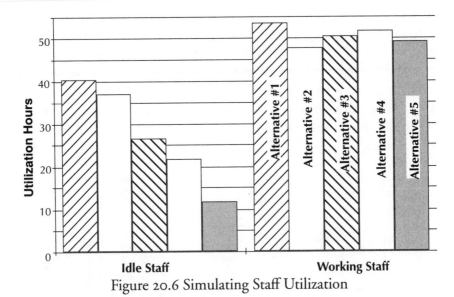

Figure 20.6 Simulating Staff Utilization

Figure 20.6 reveals that gains in efficiency come from reducing idle staff time rather than working harder. Such an argument may be useful in reducing resistance to change.

Organizing Business Process Improvement

Successful business process improvement balances the involvement of information managers, operating managers and subject matter experts. Cooperative teams can assemble under non-threatening circumstances. They should be encouraged to spend as much time as possible discussing different points of view. Unanimity is not what business process improvement is all about. Differences of opinion should be noted because the greatest value in making a decision is not in the agreement, but in views that reveal what could possibly go wrong. A workflow diagram that illustrates each viewpoint could be of enormous value in preparing for contingencies. If the debates remain unresolved, higher management can be then consulted.

I have participated in a number of meetings held to negotiate terms of co-existence with the aid of workflow diagrams in anticipation of major systems changes. The participants were able to see the consequences of different workflow configurations immediately projected on presentation screens as the issues were raised. After these people became accustomed to the new approach, progress toward workable agreements was remarkably rapid. The clearly visible results of the simulation models left little room for the usual obfuscation of issues by those who were seeking to obtain counterproductive gains for themselves at the negotiating table.

Business process improvement requires that you perform a business case analysis, which not only calculates payoffs but also reveals the risks of each proposed alternative. This approach is sound but, unfortunately, most current methods for performing business case analysis of computerization projects do not have sufficient integrity to be acceptable to financial executives. Better methods include formal risk analysis in all calculations.

The overwhelming advantage of business process improvement is in its attitude toward organizational change. The relatively slow and deliberate effort is more consistent with the way people adjust to major changes in their personal lives. Every day should be a process improvement day, because that is how organizational learning takes place and that is how you gain the commitment of your people. At each stage of process evolution, your people can keep the pace with their leaders because they learn to share the same understanding of what is happening to the business. They have the opportunity to think about what they are doing. Precipitous layoffs discourage their willingness to use their own time and talent to improve the workplace.

Emerging Trends

The traditional approach to improving economic performance relied on reorganization or the imposition of new leadership as a solution. The usual outcome was to favor functional specialization and functional consolidation using the assumption that similar functions, under the control of highly trained professionals, would yield to economies of expertise. This sort of thinking justified consolidating of legal, accounting, market research, pricing, product development and computer departments into huge functional organizations which could achieve great efficiency as long as their tasks were standard and sequential. The bias favoring centralization of knowledge is founded on ideas of running industrial mass production operations.

Top management has come to realize that a very large share of information management work is neither standard nor sequential. As the costs and delays in coordinating vertical functional organizations exceed the alleged benefits of specialization, the idea of horizontal organization based on business processes has gained acceptance. Both reengineering and business process redesign favor improving horizontal process flows irrespective of any organizational hierarchy. In many respects, the new process-driven orientation reflects the frustrations of operating people when restrained by rules imposed by the central, functional guardians. This gave to reengineering and business process redesign their anti-establishment color.

If enterprise management abdicates the role of countering the excesses of vertical functional expertise to the initiatives of process-driven enthusiasts, they may find themselves supporting a counter-revolutionary movement in the hope of re-establishing a workable balance between the extremes of both functional and process thinking. Swinging from one extreme to another may accomplish little and will disorient the employees.

A more balanced approach offers many advantages. Functional obstacles to a more streamlined business process (such as legal, financial and personnel rules) should be identified before everything is handed over to process-driven autonomy. That is precisely why I emphasize the importance of the political process. The purpose of defining governance is to place safeguards so that neither monarchic extremes of "functionalism," nor anarchic tendencies favoring local "process" solutions will prevail without first checking on the economic viability of either approach.

Reengineering, like all management novelties, will start losing popularity soon as a premier consulting activity. What will replace them? If you accept that new management fashions arise to correct the excesses of the prior fad, then it is likely that the next consulting theme will carry labels such as reintegration, reunification, coherence, fusion or whatever word suddenly would resonate with the spirit of the times. If the clever concept artists prevail, the next consulting fad may be labeled organic harmony, information ecology or systems integration synthesis.

To build truly integrated, yet highly adaptable systems that will support the rapidly changing environment of the future will require the adoption of the concept of *information building blocks* allowing the constructing large systems aggregations for information management of inter-related enterprises. Living organism are constructed from such aggregations which make it possible for changes in ecology to take place without interfering with the elemental *building blocks* from which they are assembled, such as atoms, protein molecules, DNA and organs of living things. A rough outline of a future vocabulary for managing *information building blocks* seems to be emerging. These are:

• Entities. Data is the raw material for all information systems. Entity relationships are becoming the basis for defining and organizing data independently of applications.

• Objects. Software logic is the means for transforming data into information. Object oriented programming is becoming the encapsulated know-how for organizing applications.

• Agents. Intelligence is the means for converting information into knowledge. Agents, the software equivalents of robots, are likely to grow into an extension of human capabilities in completing complex tasks.

• Processes. Workflow is the organizing principle of all information work. To manage the use and deployment of software agents, the definition and management of information processes will become the means for extracting productivity and value-added out of information work.

• *Open Configuration Management.* Sometimes just called *Open Systems*, offers the electronic environment for making it possible for entities, objects, agents and processes to co-exists in a continually evolving progression towards greater capabilities. *Open Configuration Management* does not require organizational or technological upheavals to happen that would require simultaneous changes in all of the building blocks. *Open configuration management* is the key to allowing a steady accumulation of learning taking place without imposing uniformity on every building block.

21

SOFTWARE

Software is a new form of immortality.

Software Process Improvement

If your software organization is not delivering on its promises, someone will surely recommend that you ought to follow the Software Engineering Institute's software process improvement (PI) methodology.[163] Establishing and then following a consistently controlled software development process has great merit. I find the PI method to be more in tune with defense acquisition procedures than with the creative development practices of successful commercial vendors of software. My skepticism concerning the PI model will persist until someone conclusively demonstrates that there is a positive correlation between someone's PI rating, with quality and costs.[164] I would also like to see proof that successful commercial software companies have consistently qualified for a high PI rating.

---

163. Watts S. Humphrey, *Managing the Software Process*, Addison Wesley, 1993.
164. The PI method assigns numerical grades to levels of accomplishment. Your grade depends on complying with the checklist compiled by experts. This technique is widely used in judging ice-skating, beauty contests and awarding the Baldrige Prize for Quality. A rating of four is supposed to be twice as good as a rating of two. This reminds me of Aristotle and his followers who for almost 2,000 years maintained that a ten-pound ball falls ten times faster that a one-pound ball without ever trying to verify that proposition.

I support the idea that a formal software improvement process is desirable and have spent large amounts of time and money in promoting structured software methodologies and tools. Like cleanliness, clear thinking, and healthy habits, improving an existing software process will always have merit. However, poor performance of a software organization is not something you can fix by passing exhaustive check-lists in order to receive a higher PI certification.[165] Before you begin working on the software process, you must first establish the economic and political basis for making people more productive.[166] If the programming staff does not trust their business leaders and if they worry about their jobs, even a PI Level 4 team will deliver only marginal results.

Software Independence

It is not the elements of logic that change in the structure of an upgraded information system, but the way they work together. In a typical business application more than 85% of the basic routines deal with information retrieval, management and display. This applies particularly to accounting, medical, materiel, marketing and inventory systems, which represent the bulk of current computer applications.

Aside from political reasons, we throw out old applications when existing hardware platforms have become too expensive to operate, even though much of the logic of the original software remains identical to its replacement. We can no longer afford to do this because there is just too much accumulated code around to pay for a complete rewrite.

---

165. Lee E. Cobb, "A CASE for Maintenance," *American Programmer*, March 1994. Cobb concludes that CASE tools are very helpful, but the management approach, customer support and organizational culture is likely to have a much larger impact.
166. For an excellent discussion of how downsizing saps the morale of a software organization, see Pat Loy, "Downsizing - The Threat to Process Improvement & Software Excellence," *American Programmer*, December 1993

Figure 21.1 Ready for Reincarnation

Keeping the original applications is becoming much easier because of the increasing acceptance of *open* systems standards. These call for hardware independence from software, which means that technological obsolescence of computers should no longer dictate discarding software. Hardware independence makes it feasible to transfer an application from an obsolete machine to one that has superior performance for less money.

Software as Inheritance

After three to four decades of adding new applications to a business, this accumulation of software represents an enormous collection of knowledge that defines how the organization operates. Not all of it is old junk to be discarded so you can start anew. Besides, that hoard is just too large to be replaceable in a short time period. Software functions that reflect how you conduct you business are valuable assets, even if they are shabby. They are held in a trust that requires maintenance and improvement through continued rejuvenation and replenishment. Every new system and enhancement provide a means to exploit and increase the value of the amassed software by having as little discarded as possible.[167]

Legacy Software

The retention of "legacy" code is politically unpopular.[168] "Legacy" systems have become identified with the unresponsive, costly, non-interoperable, arrogant mainframe regime of yesteryear. Local operators who aspire to information independence by acquiring their own mini-data centers have embraced with enthusiasm the idea that nothing short of total replacement of software will gain them their information sovereignty.

When the bills for the operation and maintenance of local information networks come in for the cottage software shops, there will be a backlash against letting costs get out of control. By that time, the local operators will have lost interest in pursuing complete independence. They will be in no position to attract the talent and justify the budget that is necessary for software engineering commitments that span decades. Amateur programmers weaned on spreadsheets and libraries of software routines have a simplistic view of what it takes to make thousands of lines of computer code work successfully.

The most likely outcome of the collapse of decentralized software management will be the reinstatement of some central expertise to manage knowledge repositories, promote software reuse and propagate standard systems engineering methods. Central staffs will also take over the technical responsibility for software salvage and object recycling. That

---

167. Ed Yourdon, one of the foremost experts on software and editor of the *American Programmer* journal, maintains that 20% of the maintenance budget is typically spent fixing faults that crept in during the original development of corporate systems. Fixing such mistakes will extend the useful life of software.

168. "Legacy" is a recent term applied to the software you already own and maintain. "Legacy" is also a bequest of property given by testament from someone who is deceased. This usage of the term about software conveniently implies that a legacy system is something for which neither you nor anybody else can be held accountable.

requires much patience, a high level of expertise and long term funding that local operators cannot sustain.

In the future, information political contests will be fought over issues that concern managing software assets. That change in emphasis will be difficult for those information executives, who over the last thirty years, were constantly embroiled in conflicts about the control of hardware. Whoever accepts that conservation of software assets is now the key to all information politics will end up as a leader.

The autonomous local operators will be allowed to make local modifications to standard software packages. However, technology decisions with long term consequences will come from technical experts who will not necessarily be company employees. Assembling and testing application software from standard, reusable and function-specific components lends itself to enormous economies of scale.

The most likely outcome of the shift from software as an artistic craft to a commercial commodity will be the transfer of software management from corporate ownership to commercial competition. This will remove software policy debates from the province of corporate information politics to decisions that are subject to economic competition.

Legacy Systems

Legacy systems are systems that you already have. They represent an accumulation of several decades of continually patched, procedural code, in languages that are not compatible, running under operating systems that are hostile to each other and requiring enormous amounts of maintenance hours because both the affected business procedures as well as the underlying software have become increasingly incomprehensible.

Legacy systems have the advantage that they accomplish the expected job. Customers have become accustomed to cope with what they get. The prospect of replacing these fragile processes while supporting sensitive business operations gives nightmares to every information executive.

Contrasting legacy (e.i., bad) systems against new integrated, distributed, object-oriented, modular and *open* systems (e.i., good) is legitimate only if you also project the cash flow showing which small investments will get you most of what your customers demand. There is not enough money around to do everything that will satisfy everybody. When setting the objectives for conversion of legacy systems it should be clear you will never have sufficient resources to safely discard what you already have in favor of something completely new.

Introducing a more controlled system design methodology than we have had available in the past, information executives will end up tending to keep legacy systems in their inventories. Innovation will consist of adding to what you already have, discarding pieces that are not salvageable and rebuilding only that for which you absolutely cannot find a replacement in any other way.

The formulation of objectives when and how to migrate legacy systems by means of planned evolution must take the highest priority on the agenda of the information management policy board. Evolutionary migration requires large investments in systems engineering tools, modernization of equipment and networks, and training of not only programming staffs, but also point-of-use operators. The choices of how to proceed with migration are numerous to make the decision an easy one. In each case you will get pressure from suppliers, contractors and consultants who want you to travel on the path that they control. This is why migration cannot be left as totally unconstrained choice for each operating manager to make opportunistically. Otherwise the organization will drift away from its architectural, interoperability and software conservation principles.

For an enterprise with a large accumulation of legacy systems – which includes all established organizations – there are no technical strategies other than evolutionary migration strategies. Defining the path of such migration requires placing limited objectives along the way. The managerial skill in coming up with such a plan and then making it happen will be the ultimate test which only superior information management teams will pass.

Migrating Legacy Systems

Most of our legacy information systems resemble shanty towns. Incinerating all shanties as a way to improve living conditions is not a good model for any city plan. I consider total systems reengineering, especially when it advocates abandonment prior to reconstruction, a violation of the principle that all growth is evolutionary rather than an original, instant, and perfect creation.[169]

The primary goal of responsible systems managers is to manage software wealth so that it evolves and adapts gradually at a low maintenance cost, instead of being discarded and repeatedly reconstructed anew. Perpetually upgrading accumulated software assets instead of launching major new software conversion projects ought to be the ideal state for an organization, unless it enters a completely new business.[170]

Systems managers have a bias favoring people engaged in development. They consider people who perform software maintenance as having a lesser status. That is one of the reasons why computer executives concentrate on getting funds for brand new projects and   modernizing and the upkeep of what they already own. You should treat resumes that boast only of new ventures with caution. A record of successfully planting saplings does not prove the ability to tend a profitable orchard.

The Flight From Mainframes

In the last five years, the balancing between those favoring gradual renovation as compared with those seeking instant dramatic changes has become a matter of information politics rather than economics. Information revolutionaries are seeking independence from the heavy hand of the central computer organizations. One way to achieve this is to declare everything that is on the mainframe to be completely worthless. Consequently, moving applications from large computers to small computers has demanded the making of substantial new investments without much proof as to value. The prevailing bias is to discard mainframe legacy systems and replace them with brand new applications running on "client/servers" that offer lower hardware costs. It is usually

---

169. If you follow the Bible, you know that happened only once.
170. Upgrading includes adding off-the shelf software objects as well as packaged applications to the existing software collection.

presumed that the client/server will make it possible for small autonomous units to set up their own data processing shop. The distribution and downsizing of computing power has merit in many instances. However, recklessly discarding the accumulated software and forcing employee retraining is too costly to be the preferred alternative in all cases.

It takes much longer to prove economic rationality than political expediency. The evidence is emerging only slowly that client/server environments may not be less expensive. The following observations deserve attention:[171]

- "The costs of running a large network of personal computers are 300% higher than supporting a like number of users in a mainframe environment."

- "The support costs per personal computer in a large scale operation is about $24,000 over five years, or about four times greater than the costs of acquiring the inexpensive hardware."

- "Even after projecting further declines in costs of personal computers and increased economies in support, the projected 1998 costs per personal computer user will be still 50% higher than per mainframe user."

- "Moving applications from mainframes to workstations is expensive. The support costs per user increased from $4,000 to $15,000 per year while many important jobs, such as backup of files could not be done well."

- "PacifiCare Health Systems spent more than half of its 200% conversion cost overrun in training, because the migration from mainframes to client/servers was much more difficult than expected."

---

171. Bill Laberis, "Pull the Plug on Computer Hype," *The Wall Street Journal,* April 25, 1994, p.A14

- "In 1991, the managers at the Microsoft Corporation, the apostles of client/server computing, announced they would remove all mainframe computers from their organization by 1993. Somehow that schedule has now moved to 1996. If Microsoft could pull the plug on mainframe computers, they certainly would have done it."

Unfortunately, much of the debate between those who are trying to preserve continuity and those who find central coordination a burden leaves top management unable to decide what is a workable balance between these extreme positions. These arguments must be restated in financial terms that reveal the long term consequences of each proposition. Credible financial analyses are necessary before top management can act with an understanding of the consequences of any decision. Client/servers represent the seventh round of investments in software.[172] Before you spend a huge amount of money on modernization, you must assure yourself that the next investment round will provide systems with a much longer useful life than those from the prior cycles.

The distribution of computing power to local operations should not require you to destroy what you have and force everyone start anew. It requires building coalitions and agreements supporting a negotiated compromise between computing power retained centrally and computing capacity available locally. It calls for distributing what is locally unique and keeping together what is common, as defined by rules of political governance.

---

172. The first round was the conversion from tabulating machines to card-driven computers. The second round was conversion from card computers to machines with tapes and disk drives. The third round was conversion of files to databases. The fourth round was the conversion to applications for on-line access from terminal. The fifth round was the conversion of systems to on-line access from smart machines, also called "clients." The sixth round was buying packaged software for local use on local microcomputers.

22

Reuse

Wealth grows from a steady accumulation of useful knowledge.

Reusable software components ("objects") offer the single largest cost-reduction opportunity in your information systems budget. Hardware expenses have shrunk to less than 15% of a typical corporation's total information systems expense. From now on, what matters is software. By far the most decisive influence in managing the costs of systems and extracting from them the greatest business value is the competence with which you manage your software. Despite the compulsive fascination of comptrollers and customers alike with the minutiae of hardware price differences, you cannot make much of an impact on your budget with bargain hardware. If you try to minimize your hardware costs overzealously, you will surely increase your software expenses far more than they should.

To be economically superior, new systems must have substantially lower maintenance costs than their earlier versions. Lifetime software maintenance and software conversion expenses to another computer could easily exceed 1,000% of the initial investment.

Software Portability

To sustain a long and useful life, software code must be easily portable from one computer to another. An acceptable level of portability exists when over 90% of all application code can relocate, without a major investment or headache, to a new computing environment. The need for such high levels of portability comes from the imperative of preserving organizational knowledge in software. If you consider that software logic is indestructible and does not wear out, then thinking in terms of at least 20 years is a reasonable life expectancy for individual software modules, assuming that normal maintenance keeps the business utility of the software up-to-date.

Unfortunately, today's software managers do not think in such farsighted terms because they do not expect to be around when the benefits from reuse arise. That explains why application software elements are not constructed using tools that would make the software reusable. "Scrap and patch" is easier than "build and recycle." It all depends on whether you think of software logic as a disposable paper plate instead of a piece of the family dinner service. There is a place and time for paper plates as well as for porcelain. I consider the use of corporate knowledge more like a family occasion than a quick roadside snack.

Figure 22.1 Software Portability

Technology Recycling

As of 1993, desktop hardware is on a two to three year major innovation cycle. Soon, many computing functions will migrate from desktops to palmtops, and surely to wrist-tops. "Finger-tops" cannot be far away. These devices will have the natural life span of all electronic novelties. Your firm cannot possibly afford to reprogram applications every time your hardware changes.

Plastic, glass and metal from computers for which there is no further use are becoming an ecological problem, as hundreds of millions of discarded electronic appliances now clutter up our garbage. The currently projected sales of personal computers in the U.S. for 1996 is 46 million units.[173] In less than seven years, all of it will end up as rubbish. That is about a million tons per year. The economic value of reclamation from such trash is only a small fraction of what society can gain by making sure that the intangible innards of this debris – the software that populates it – is amenable to salvage.

Figure 22.2 Computer Progress as Cause of Computer Trash

---

173. *Business Week,* September 6, 1993, p.80

Every six years – that is when the ratio of price to performance of new information technologies improves by a multiple of at least 100 – you are likely to have a convincing economic case to relocate most of your applications to whatever machine will do the task better and cheaper. The functions performed by the applications that have relocated also should be amenable to easy restructuring to new uses. For instance, home banking services running on a simple microcomputer could be enhanced to include a shopping service with video interaction capability. What is entertainment becomes business, and vice versa. Telephones become computers, as computers become multimedia receivers.

Most of the features involved in banking transactions should remain the same, regardless of whether you link the customer to the bank by phone, TV or a satellite-beamed antenna from a moving car. The hardware looks different in each case, but most of the software functions should stay untouched if you want to avoid the horrendous costs of reprogramming and retraining every time a device is replaced.

Software that today is as hard to modify in a major way as if it were a statue made of stone. In the future software should be constructed from reusable elements that can be rearranged to continue offering old services, as well as to be readily receptive to performing new functions, without first having to scrap everything. The reusability and flexibility to integrate both the old as well as the new functions defines whether you have an open systems software architecture or not.

Software and Business Reorganization

The ability to subject software to continual transplantation is essential to economically support frequent major reorganizations. It is mostly the constant reshuffling of relationships that generates what appears to be a totally new system requirement. *What* companies do does not change as much as *how* they do it.

If you ship boxes of cheese from a warehouse, you need to complete only a small number of business functions. Your information system reflects your definition of the respective roles of the clerk on the loading dock, the warehouse manager, the transportation coordinator and the accountant. Cheese will always ship in similar boxes, load on similar trucks and invoice in similar ways irrespective of how the company swings from centralization to decentralization to conglomeration to divestment and then back around. Your job as the information executive is to make sure that the essential business tasks will function, no matter who does it. Your software should be easily portable and reusable wherever and whenever management decides to make changes in how people relate to each other.

When software is not reusable, there is a precipitous discarding of old applications and proposals to launch brand new applications. Anguished pleading for new systems often turns out to be simply a request to repackage existing procedures. The proposal to build a new system is nothing more than a re-arrangement to fit whatever a new fiefdom wishes to use in establishing its new prerogatives. You can easily detect such moves if the proposed new applications does not have an effect on the economics of the business.

Disruption as Rationale for Change

It is the rate of change in the relationships among organizations that governs the rate of replacement of most computer applications. It is not software that wears out. Depreciated hardware is always cheaper to operate, as long as it does the job and has the benefit of fully automated support. It is the organizations and their leadership that wears out faster than any technology.

Millions of lines of code become obsolete because the accumulation of decades of undocumented maintenance has made them indecipherable. Millions of lines of code containing an enormous amount of intelligence about a business cease to have any value because the original applications developers viewed software development as hand-crafted art. What wore out were the systems managers, not the technology.

Obsolete inventories have always ranked high in attracting management's attention. Write-offs of obsolete goods or factories frequently appear on financial statements. Yet the continuous discarding of software through re-programming forces the discarding of perhaps the most valuable intellectual capital of a service-based organization, instead of just refurbishing it. Such destruction of assets hardly gets any notice because the idea of salvageable and reusable software has not as yet become a generally accepted principle of conservation and recycling.

Figure 22.3 Hardware Obsoletes Faster Than Knowledge to Use It

The U.S. tax code encourages such waste, since it allows most software development and all maintenance expense as immediate write-offs. The tax code has not as yet recognized that the total accumulated costs of U.S. software already exceeds the book value of all of our steel mills, automobile factories and railroad equipment by a large margin. The tax code should encourage the preservation of reusable software "objects" by recognizing them as a replenishable resource that deserves more favorable tax treatment.

Reuse as a Political Agenda

Currently, computer applications are like buildings whose architecture does not allow much room for extensions, additions or re-decoration. They tend to lock into the information processing logic that every client bureaucracy wishes to preserve. Computer software that follows such traditions is a cocoon that envelopes ill-defined territorial claims of a power structure that dictates the systems specifications. No egyptian pharaoh, chinese mandarin nor soviet commissar ever possessed the means to replicate their will as perfectly as is possible through software. An application that prohibits entry of any exceptions to established controls is the perfect policeman.

Established middle managers will exert influence to make sure that computer people do not come up with systems that are flexible enough to allow for easy rearrangement of the status quo. When newcomers take over, the opposite happens. All major reorganizations, especially disturbances such as mergers or acquisitions, invariably lead to ready approval of requests for bigger computer budgets. This pays for applications that re-program the rules of how people will operate under the new regime. New management, with new ideas that vindicate their takeover, will readily consent to proposals to junk the old and build new applications without any financial justification whatsoever. The "new" systems are endorsed as innovation so that the new chieftains do not have to reveal their real purpose of imposing their will upon their subjects.

Reusable and readily transportable software – what we presently call "software objects" – is a powerful idea. This assumes that all business functions and processes evolve while retaining many of the useful elements of existing business functions from one stage of evolution to another. Software elements should be like a toy village made out of LEGO™ blocks that can be easily re-arranged upon short notice and with little effort. The economic value of such software lies in its adaptability to evolutionary changes in relationships. Reusable and *open* systems software has the capacity to fine-tune information systems to new conditions without major disruptions. That flexibility is one of the many ways of demonstrating the important contribution of *open* systems to the economic value of information technologies.

23

LEARNING

The capacity to learn is the basis for all future gains.

Over the life of a computer application the largest single expense is not software or hardware but the time spent in training and supporting those who make use of it. All software expenses are people costs charged two ways, once during creation and the second time during its use. The costs of using software can easily exceed the cost of creating it a hundred-fold or even a thousand-fold over its useful life.

The greatest contribution to the usefulness of applications is the ease with which people learn to make them work. Applications are likely to be discarded when the cost of human errors exceeds benefits. Applications are redesigned when customers find they do not understand them.

In most environments, the costs of learning and using software are excessive because technology-driven computer specialists do not have the expertise or motivation to reduce training and learning expenses. With rare exceptions, training and start-up costs are not recognized as information technology expenses and therefore receive little attention from the designers whose performance is mostly evaluated in terms of meeting development schedules and budgets.

Cost of Errors

In a typical business setting, the people who use computers are under continuing stress. Unless their jobs call for dealing with only one application, they must wade through displays that have dissimilar graphic displays, inconsistent commands and different solutions whenever errors occur. Whatever they learn can be disrupted by vacations, holidays, absenteeism and meetings. This is why it takes much effort to figure out the meaning of a computerized procedure when the time comes to do actual work. One sure sign of the lack of proper training, or poor application design, is the presence of cue cards and hand-written instructions that operators paste to their desks and terminals.

Systems designers should pay attention when computer operators fumble because of an unforeseen procedure or error condition. That is when undocumented work-arounds appear. Observations by anthropologists confirm that the way an organization adapts to computers is slow, incremental and comes from informal procedures people develop mostly for themselves. An application becomes useful when people acquire habits making software workable in personally acceptable terms, rather than as envisioned by the original designers. A good design makes acquiring new habits intuitively easy and therefore has low training costs. You can measure bad design by the incidence of frustrating experiences, high training costs, idle time, processing delays and frequent calls for assistance.

Dissipation of Knowledge

When your plans assume a build-and-junk cycle involving heavy maintenance expenses and frequent investment in new applications, most of the accumulated informal learning among your people will disappear. You will lose the expertise that makes your applications do the work of which the original designers were not aware. When you make such knowledge obsolete, you will pay dearly for its replacement. External consultants and reengineering experts usually do not have the incentive to respect the informal learning processes as essential for gaining acceptance of any new computer application. When under pressure to make the installation of a new system as quickly as promised, the allowance for adaptive learning will be sacrificed. Although the project budget may look good, your company will see a rise in administrative overhead, a decline in employee morale and a loss of customer satisfaction.

Radical methods of computer-based business process reengineering suffer from the fundamental flaw of treating training and learning as an instant event. They are not. Learning is a social and evolutionary phenomenon in which anything new connects to whatever is already existing knowledge. If the premise of reengineering is to obliterate everything people accepted as customary, then training for the replacement will be stressful and wasteful.

Collective Knowledge

Data and software provide the most reliable intelligence about how an enterprise performs its essential business functions. There is an enormous accumulation of informal knowledge about the enterprise in paper files, myths, customs and speeches. These informal sources are the most relevant in dealing with changes, opportunities and future prospects. However, when attempting to find out what is going on, it is the computerized record that is the most comprehensive source of all information. The logic with which you manipulate information is the link between raw data and the actions taking place.

No firm now can exist without easily retrievable memory about customers, products and competitors. There are many profitable companies that view their files as the basis of their customer franchise. They get to know more about some of their customers' business practices than the customers' own managers.

Over the last ten to fifteen years, as organizational volatility increased and managerial tenure became shorter, the preservation of historical information increasingly fell on the guardians of the computer files. Paper records have become not only expensive to maintain, but also difficult to find. The new custodians of data are information systems executives.

If reengineering efforts dictate the junking of existing systems and replacing them with totally new applications, the chief information executives may find it impossible to preserve the accumulated data. Completely redesigned applications will sever the links to the past. Even if the raw data is available, they will not be able to maintain the logic with which to retrieve whatever is in the files. Total redesign makes archives useless. An organization that does not preserve its memory may be at a disadvantage by having to compete as if it were a start-up venture without any of the benefits of established relationships.

Organizational Learning

Every organization possesses traditions. That is the result of the gradual learning that ultimately accumulates into something we call an "organizational culture." It is the accretion of all the experiences, customs and conventions that make human cooperation possible because it makes reactions more predictable. It provides stability that allows people to keep agreements and fulfill expectations.

The source of all legitimacy for political leadership is found in the privileged position to create conditions that make it possible for people to work together for a common purpose. Followers expect from their leaders the rules and the resources enabling them to collaborate and share information. Making it possible for organizations to function is the only justifiable basis for the power held by executives.

When conditions favoring a free flow of information do not receive reinforcement, bureaucratic ossification will set in. The power over information dissemination will be consolidated in the hands of a few autocrats so that everyone must come to them for approval in running the business. That happens frequently in large corporations and often in government.

Failures by the executives who temporarily hold decision-making powers does not automatically call for dramatically excising everything old from the organization. You do not need to dig up the roots of a mature tree and transplant it to a more fertile ground. For mature trees, fertilization and pruning may offer a better, faster and cheaper solution. You do not have to throw out all systems to get rid of information stagnation at the top of the organization. You can fix that by removing those obstacles that slow down responsiveness. Organizational learning is the equivalent of fertilization and pruning. The organization receives encouragement; excesses get trimmed back and not uprooted.

Profitability of Employee Development

An examination of the best financially performing firms in the U.S. from 1972 to 1992 shows they share:

- Enlightened relationships with people;
- Emphasis on the development of employees;

• Preservation of human capital.[174]

The top leaders in financial performance during this time were Southwest Airlines (+21,775% return to shareholders), Wal-Mart (+19,807%), Tyson Foods (+18,118%), Circuit City (+16,410%) and Plenum Publishing (+15,689%). None of these firms had any proprietary technology. They operated in industries with intense competition, widespread bankruptcy, no barriers to entry and many substitute products or services. In 1972, none of them were market leaders. They did not enjoy any economic advantages when they began.

Each of these winners adopted widespread employee stock ownership, transformed the entire workforce into manager-associates, granted a high degree of job security, provided aggressive employee education programs, sponsored job rotation for skill development and promotion from within.

People-oriented management is necessary in an age when your principal assets walk out of the offices every night and return only if you keep investing in them.

"Achieving competitive success through people involves fundamentally altering how we think about the workforce and employment relationships. It means achieving success by working with people, not by replacing them or limiting the scope of their activities. It entails seeing employees as a source of strategic advantage, not just as a cost to be minimized or avoided."[175] Whatever that says about people is equally applicable to software. After all, software logic is a capitalized human mind.

Organizational Memory

One way to look at software is to see it as communication among people in an organization. Software represents the agreements, reached after negotiation, on how users communicate with programmers, how programmers communicate with machines, and how machines respond to users. To increase the residual value of software, there must be recogni-

---

174. J. Pfeffer, *Competitive Advantage through People: Unleashing the Power of the Workforce,* Harvard Business School Press, 1993.
175. Pfeffer, *Ibid.*

tion of how people can best develop and use it. The process of software-mediated communication has to be flexible and fast. Programmers, testers, analysts and users must be able to express their needs effectively in order to achieve lasting cooperation.

What we currently call software expenses mostly reflect the costs of meetings, head scratching and shouting matches.[176] If you want interoperable as well as long-lasting systems, the human dimensions of software creation and maintenance must be *open*, transparent and more graceful than has traditionally been the case.

Figure 23.1 Preservation of Knowledge

---

176. Caspers Jones estimates that 65% of software expenditures are a waste of effort on nonproductive activities. See Caspers Jones, *Sick Software*, *Assessment and Control of Software Risks*, Prentice-Hall, 1994.

How do you preserve the understanding gained during your systems development and system maintenance efforts after they become embodied in software? As computers take over most of the information handling functions of your enterprise, you will have to look at software as a way to codify how you conduct business. Software and the record of all communications involved in the development and maintenance of information systems represents the collective memory of each person who participated in deciding on how that business should operate.

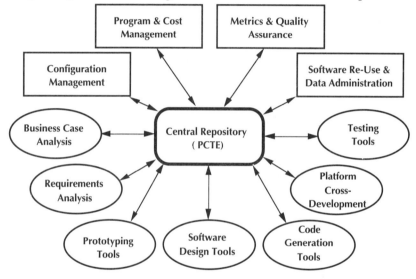

Figure 23.2 A Knowledge Repository

You can view the knowledge repository as the means to document how members of the organization negotiate cooperation. It contains the accumulation of what a firm has formally learned. It should contain a complete set of all of the building blocks that make up the structure of information management. The knowledge repository also becomes the equivalent of a library of legal decisions handed down by judges and regulatory agencies, since it will keep track of all amendments, changes and corrections to the original intent. It is one of an organization's most valuable assets, because it permits the reconstitution of the firm in the event of a disaster or its cloning in case of acquisition and diversification.

A history of software changes records the evolution of cooperation as it becomes refined and improved. While software is born in pain, it is not something you abandon when your technology vendors declare it a burden they do not wish to maintain any longer. The accumulation of what you have learned over many years deserves to be conserved because you will never have enough money to completely replace it.

Learning as a Continuum

If an organization wishes to preserve its accumulated knowledge, it must be able to transfer its culture along with new improvements from generation to generation as new employees join. Software is a form of accumulated organizational experience and therefore need not require complete reinvention every time new management, or a new political administration, shows up. In fact, a large number of organizations today have software assets which are worth more than the tangible assets recorded on their balance sheets. It would be as irresponsible to discard all of these assets as to burn down a village just because you want to put in some new roads and sewers.

All innovation carries a penalty. However, it is easier to make changes successfully if there is a design that is flexible enough to accommodate them. There are organizations that have structured themselves around institutions and attitudes favoring an easy acceptance of new situations. The early American settlements in the western lands were fortunate to have leaders with sufficiently good foresight to lay out city plans that allowed for replacing temporary shelters when prosperity made that possible. Preserving organizational knowledge involves designing organizations for learning. If a company has lost that capacity, expunging all that is old and replacing it suddenly with a comparably small layer that is new is not a sure cure.

Education for Information Systems

Education and training are critical ingredients in realizing the benefits from information systems. Untrained people will use only a fraction of what a system can potentially deliver. That means a system must be sensitive to the capabilities of the operator. One of the reasons for the astounding acceptance of Apple's Hypercard software is in its menu in which you can identify yourself as a "novice," "expert," or "teacher". I also like computer applications that have a "Preferences" line on their menu which allows you to set the repertoire of features at "Simple" or "Full," with optional gradations in-between.

Discourage applications that dictate only one level of competence. Office workers should be able to start on their jobs by first doing only essential work that requires minimum training. After an employee starts to function, learning can be as rapid as responsibilities develop. Remember, the really worthwhile gains in productivity come from completing increasingly complex tasks requiring progressive learning. Teaching everyone the identical routine will limit productivity gains to the lowest common level of achievement.

I usually gain more useful information about the utility of a computer application from its training manual than from its technical description. Do not let systems analysts write your training instructions. Never let a programmer touch them. These folks are not only too expensive, but are likely to treat their subjects as machines. Find some retired English teachers to design and write your training aids, preferably the ones who got discouraged by ten-year old pupils and need to earn a decent living as part-time workers-at-home.

By all means favor "on-line" tutorials. In its most primitive form this consists of designating one key as the source of "Help." If you push it, you will get a message in a window, such as "INSERT NAME OF FILE." That would cover all cases where you do not know the meaning of a box in which there is a blinking cursor. Unfortunately, most of these automated messages are only reprints of pre-selected passages from a three-inch manual which nobody reads anyway. Your problem may, however, have nothing to do with the name of a file, or, even if it does, you do not know what FILE the computer is talking about. For "on-line" learning to be useful, the computer should have sufficient logic to understand the context of requests for assistance or the incidence of errors. Intelligent assistance, in the form of expert logic that is integrated into the application, will increasingly be demanded from software vendors.[177]

Learning Assistance

If you wander through a typical office you will find a good number of people who are supposed to be working are conversing with the local computer expert who dispenses advice to everyone needing assistance in getting their computer to function properly. For continuous learning you need to give everyone access to a personal "wizard." Companies that have sold you a software package for $149.95 usually tell you that all you have to do is to call an 800— number and you will get help that way. If you have held on to a busy 800— line or listened to a recorded message as often as most people, you will conclude that you cannot expect to get much help for the small price you paid for your software. Besides, most anguished cries for help are specific to the situation in your company. Setting up "on-line" help staff to guide people through the frustrations of their workplace learning experiences should be an inseparable feature of every application.

Keeping track of the kind of questions people ask will allow your organization to realize total quality goals. Fix what troubles people most and you will have taken much of the frustration out of using computers. I continue to be amazed how few organizations have linked educational support to overcoming sources of chronic problems. The prevailing practice of sending memos to the programming shop to fix a consistent error is equivalent to complaining about crime to overworked jail keepers. Make your educators an integral element of your efforts to make information systems not only technically but also personally responsive.

---

177. Tax preparation software is a good example of the application of intelligent help. For instance, the package I used in filing my taxes kept reminding me about missing information and warned me about inconsistencies in data entry. It also suggested where the forms were incomplete and where I may have forgotten to claim deductions.

Distance Tutoring

Bringing your educators into immediate and direct contact with the workplace, where people need help, will not be always welcome. Teachers prefer the classroom approach of batch-processing students through a standard sequence of instructions. Teachers like classrooms, where everybody sits attentively and follows a prescribed tutorial sequence. Education executives also favor the classroom because it gives them a discernible product to sell, whereas providing on-line help is much more like consulting. Answering questions, which is the Socratic approach to learning, is not only more work but it's harder to control by an educational bureaucracy.

Figure 23.3 Computer-Assisted Training

Middle managers doe not like on-line tutoring in the workplace either. It involves a third party providing guidance on how work should be done, something that middle management considers their privilege. When students are enrolled in a course, managers often feel somebody is taking over their duties. Learning while working also introduces an element of unpredictability into a person's work pattern which is often difficult to monitor.

Teaching should be done at the student's point of need instead of at points of convenience for the teacher. Despite the current bias against remote-assist tutoring, I find an enormous cost reduction potential in providing customized support to people at work instead of processing them through conventional course work. Whenever you approve a new computer project you should demand a detailed plan and full budget for training and education. Remember, over the life of a computer application the cost of training, retraining and tutorial assistance will always exceed the original development costs by a large multiple. As your costs of machine cycles and acquiring software come down, training, education and support becomes the single largest information systems expense.

The Costs of Ignorance

Consider a typical spreadsheet software package costing only $200. It takes at least $1,000 for a two day course telling a person how to use it. That includes the person's salary plus tuition. Afterwards, the student may lose anywhere from ten to fifty unproductive hours, or anywhere from $500 to $2,000, to experiment before you can assume you will get some productivity. How much of this expense can you save by providing on-line help where the tutor and worker can look simultaneously at the same display? Most likely an amount that is worth the multiple of the purchase cost of the software.

How much can you save if you are not dealing with a simple software package, but with a typical business application, such as order entry or inventory management? Over the life of the application we are talking about even greater gains. Considering administrative and clerical personnel on-the-job turnover plus absenteeism to be well in excess of 25% means saving over half of a person's training and support costs every four years. As business applications become more complex, 15 to 25 hours of training are not uncommon. That is $500 to $1,000. With a typical person having to learn at least four computer applications, on-line tutoring offers a substantial gain in addition to improving the reliability of what gets done. For complex applications, such as an airline reservation system or a currency transfer authorization, investing in on-line tutoring, coaching, and assistance can make an enormous difference in whether the benefit of a system will flow to the business or be consumed as unproductive time.

Education as a Business

Shifting responsibility for one-time classroom training from its traditional source, the systems development shop, to on-line support converts education from a local monopoly to a network service that has potential for global reach. It transforms this activity from a high-cost batch processing operation to something having the potential of becoming a competitive business. I expect that when education, training and tutorial support moves from the classroom to the electronic delivery medium, it will become one of the growth industries of the 21st century.

Since the late 1960s an enormous amount has been written about the inefficiencies of our educational delivery methods. The prolific writing by academics in this field has not been followed by noteworthy successes. All we have are the remnants of well-funded but ill-conceived government and private ventures that expected to generate huge profits by introducing networked information technologies into public schools. The public schools, even with generous subsidies, cannot deliver cash savings that would pay for the expensive networked teaching. The proof that on-line learning is profitable will have to come from commercial applications. This will not arise if it is conceived as a clever afterthought to planning a computer application. Education must become an integral element of an overall strategy that supports a whole family of computer applications covering the entire enterprise.

Training, education, and support should become a key ingredient in any business strategy that depends on information management for success. People learn after they start acting differently rather than act differently after they learn. That means most job-related learning belongs where it can do the most good, which is in the workplace and not in the classroom. Distributed and low cost computer networks will make this not only feasible but also profitable.

A Knowledge Based Theory of Labor

Indiscriminate discarding of knowledge, as an enterprise asset, whether in the form of employee training or software, has origins in ideas proposed over a century ago about the value of capital and labor. These theories claim that only capital assets increased the productivity of labor. Consequently, the productivity of an enterprise is measured only in terms of the productivity of its capital, such as return-on-assets or return-on-investment. The providers of capital are then entitled to the surplus, called profit or rent. If knowledge happens to be necessary for labor to make better uses of capital, that becomes the justification for a higher wage rate for labor. By this reasoning, those performing the actual labor are not entitled to collect rent from the knowledge they have accumulated. Labor can receive only fair compensation for the time worked. The most they are allowed to do is to be paid premium wages.

The above reasoning is not only misleading, but results in judging the value of employees on the basis of their wages, rather than how fast they accumulate knowledge capital. The productivity of labor is not only a matter of wages. Productivity comes from knowledge capital aggregated in the form of useful training and experience.

Let me illustrate this by an example. You hire an untrained person who meets entry level requirements, such as literacy, a work ethic and socially acceptable behavior traits. His or her wage will be based on prevailing wage rates for entry level skills. Ten years later, that person becomes a valuable manager, earning three times the entry level wages. How does a firm justify spending three times more on the same person?

The accumulation of company-specific knowledge explains the difference. During those ten years, the organization invested anywhere from a year's salary to several years of salary in helping the employee to function more effectively. Hardly any of that expense shows up as a direct cost. Most of it is in the form of attending meetings, having phone conversations, keeping up with company gossip and making errors that get corrected. None of that contributes to anything the customer is willing to pay for. Industrial engineers call such expense "overhead." I call it money spent on company-specific knowledge capital. If organizations spend their money well, employees with ten years of accumulated knowledge will be worth more than what the company pays them. In that way, the company will be recovering the investment on its knowledge capital as incremental profit.

Let us look at the same situation from the standpoint of the employee. To increase his earning capacity, the employee counts on the company investing in developing his skills beyond whatever investments he makes on his own, such as reading books, attending courses and involvement in professional activities. However, working for the company consumes most of the time available to do this. Therefore the best hope for raising one's earning potential is what shows up on the resume as work experience that is not company-specific. It is the hope of every employee to acquire marketable knowledge of greater value than his wages. If that happens, the employee will be able to recover his investment in knowledge-gaining by getting a promotion. If that does not happen, he can find better paying employment elsewhere. He will collect incremental profit on knowledge assets in the form of the difference in the wage rate he could not get from the current employer.

If you replace the word "software" wherever the word "knowledge" was used above, you will find the statements to hold true except that *open* systems software will increase the capacity for knowledge accumulation at a faster rate, whether seen from the standpoint of the firm or the employee. If a corporation's investment in people increases the value of people faster than their salaries, everybody gains. The corporation creates employee value added. The employee acquires knowledge capital on which he can collect added income. Tragedy occurs when none of the above works out. This occurs when the corporation practices and teaches obsolete skills. Then the employee is not marketable, except at depressed wages.

The cost to develop information workers, which I define as an overhead expense for acquiring company-specific knowledge, is very often much greater than the depreciation of fixed assets and greater than profits for most corporations.[178] The time has come for enterprises to manage knowledge capital as perhaps their most significant asset.

The marketable knowledge an information worker acquires during his lifetime is the only means to increase his earnings. The potential lifetime earning capacity of a recently graduated engineer, with a starting salary of $40,000 and real income growing at 4% per annum, is $6 million.[179] Without the added value from continually acquired knowledge, his lifetime earnings would be 67% less.[180] This explains why it is necessary for individual information workers to start managing their own knowledge capital for maximum returns to themselves as well as to their employers.

---

178. My study of a random sample of twenty two 1994 Fortune industrial corporations showed the following totals: Overhead costs (Sales, General & Administrative expense) = $33.1 billion; Depreciation and Amortization costs = $11.7 billion; Profits = $1.3 billion.
179. Calculation assumes the capacity to pursue a career over a period of forty eight years. With current advances in health care that is a reasonable projection for the 21st century.
180. Calculation assumes that compensation will keep up with only inflation.

24

TOOLS

Tools are a measure of all human progress.

A value-based approach to analyzing information systems investments demonstrates why the conservation of viable long-lived assets is profitable. As shown in Figure 24.1, long-term benefits arise from retaining:
- Your trained workforce;
- Preserving reusable software components; and
- Custody of data.

Retaining training and software investments requires a planning horizon spanning more than ten years. In the case of data, one has to look ahead more than twenty years because making major changes in the organization and database definitions is too expensive.

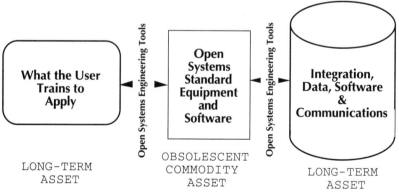

Figure 24.1 Long-Term and Obsolescent Assets

Everything that is not a long-term asset is ultimately obsolete. Whatever loses value rapidly should be replaceable without having any effect on what is conserved. Therefore, hardware, customized software and operating systems should be disposable without affecting employee training, the structure of databases, communications networks and reusable software "objects."

Technology Obsolescence

Microcomputers, which will continue to consume the largest share of all hardware expenditures, are becoming antiques at a prodigious rate. The current measure of depreciation of microcomputers is the monthly decline in the prices of Intel 486-based microcomputers, now averaging 6.5% per month. Nothing in the history of mankind has ever improved cost over performance at the rate of 6.5% per month. Over the next decade, given the rate at which new technology will arrive, the rate of obsolescence of microcomputers may increase further. If that happens, point-of-use devices will become more like consumer appliances, except they will have a technology life span of less than two years. This will make computer hardware a disposable commodity with some of the market characteristics of toys whose acceptance comes and goes with fashions and fads.

Figure 24.2 Signs of Obsolescence

The prospect for reduction of software costs is even greater than that of hardware. The marginal cost for making and electronically distributing a copy of application software is only a few cents. It is a basic economic reality that the price of a commodity reaches an equilibrium when it reaches its marginal cost. What matters is not the cost for hardware and software, but the costs of keeping these assets integrated, supported and understood by people who use the output delivered by computers.

Protecting Long Term Assets

To protect training, data, and software, you will need systems engineering tools that sustain the long-term elements through short-term disturbances. This is a "snap-in, snap-out" approach to keep what is disposable from what you do not wish to change. This solution requires, however, a high level of standardization so that when an obsolete workstation is uncoupled from the network, the new one can immediately take over. One way to estimate the value of an *open* systems architecture is to compute the difference between the costs of disengaging only the economically obsolete equipment and software, as compared with the costs of having to replace the entire setup.

To achieve this "snap-in, snap-out" world requires an integrated computer-aided system engineering environment.[181] Open system solutions are not feasible without appropriate systems tools to make them work. Such tools enable the relatively painless attachment of the potentially obsolete hardware, operating systems, compilers and applications to the long-term superstructure consisting of accumulated knowledge.

Prolonging Software Life

The desired goal is to have a systems development and maintenance environment having a useful economic life span of several decades. This should influence how organizations divide responsibilities. Decisions having long-term consequences should be made by people with differ-

---

181. Also known as I-CASE.

ent missions and skills than those who engage in delivering immediate results.

The fundamental culture of an organization takes a long time to develop and even longer to change. As computerization gradually integrates how people cooperate and communicate, managing information technologies must involve ways to match design methods with the manner in which an organization functions. People should not be forced to keep pace with computerization; computerization must adapt to the pace of organizations.

None of this implies that adopting advanced information processing means should be slow. On the contrary, this calls for accelerating the rate of learning by which people can assimilate innovation. Software tools must make it possible to add new functions without disrupting what people already have accepted. The most important tool in an integrated systems engineering environment will be the capacity to make adjustments to computer-managed workflows without overhauling computer applications or changing what people see on their screens.

Responsibility and Accountability for Software Assets

Decisions that prolong the lifespan of technology should be at the level appropriate to making decisions to build factories, entering into new markets and choosing who will take over senior management posts. The master technical configuration of systems should be decided at the level where an organization determines what research to pursue and which new business investments to make. In this respect I continue to be dismayed by the absence of well articulated discussions regarding the role of the CIO as executives with the responsibility to conserve of corporate information systems assets.

The CIO's frequently voiced ambitions to be like the CFOs (Chief Financial Officers) miss the point that the CFO, by regulatory and fiduciary practice, is recognized as being responsible for the recording and reporting about the custody of corporate assets. The CFO accounts for assets listed in the financial reports. However, the published accounting statements rarely, if ever, include the value of accumulated information assets such as software and data, which now exceed the reported assets of service sector companies which now generate most of the gross national product in the U.S.

The decision to commit to an integrated systems engineering environment therefore mandates direct involvement by top management and the designation of the CIO to monitor and account for all efforts that safeguard information technology assets. It calls for allocating funds, talent and attention to something that may take years before the benefits are readily apparent. Regretfully, I do not see that happening. With the current instability and confusion as to the proper roles and qualifications of a CIO, it will most likely take an astute CFO to alert top management executives that some of the most valuable assets are not being properly conserved. The political consequences of such a move are predictable. The CFO will re-assert powers, under a different guise, that were temporarily passed on to the CIO years before.

The Development Environment

Statements of business requirements that do not depend on specific hardware or software require a development and testing environment from which change can be managed. Before you put into effect anything that could disturb what your people, customers or suppliers do, you must have assurance that you will get only the desired result and not some unforeseen effect, such as interference with another application or increased vulnerability to failure. Money you saved from using *open* systems should be used to improve the quality of information services, reinvestment in enhanced capabilities or passed on to shareholders.

If you are managing your software with integrated computer-aided systems engineering tools, the retention of any particular machine code becomes unimportant. As illustrated in Figure 24.3, code that actually executes on a particular computer should not receive maintenance at the procedural level (such as COBOL, Ada or C), because it would become dependent on a particular hardware and software environment. Even more significantly, procedural level maintenance requires expertise that calls for years of professional training.

With a powerful set of software design tools you can now define business procedures at the requirement level, where they are illustrated in process flow diagrams that are understandable to a general manager. Some of these requirement level languages are sufficiently intelligent to allow a person with only a few hours of training to specify how to improve an application.

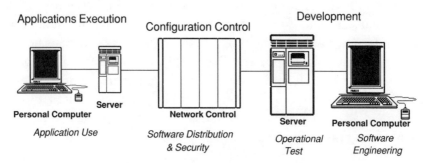

Figure 24.3 Separating Development from Execution

For example, if you wish to move a microcomputer-based desktop application to a pocket computer with a custom operating system and unique microprocessor electronics, you could do so. Your development environment would acquire a software tool that works with the pocket computer. The tool would receive the original requirement level specifications that describe how the application ran on the desktop. Next, the tool would convert the high level "requirement" definitions directly into instructions that can work in the pocket computer. Whenever the pocket computer gets new features, you can discard its software and generate a new set of instructions. The relocation of an application from the desktop to the pocket computer involves "portability"[182] as well as "scaleability."[183]

It all sounds easy and you may wonder why nobody has done that before. Portability and scaleability are possible only if there is a disciplined set of standards for a family of toolsets to communicate with a

---

182. "Portability" is defined as the ability to move an application, with a minimum of cost or delay, from an existing technology to any other open systems technology.
183. "Scaleability" is defined as the ability to move an application, with a minimum of cost or delay, to any other *open* systems technology that has the capacity to increase or decrease the transaction-handling capacity in multiples of hundreds to thousands.

wide range of devices and a variety of operating systems. In technical terms, that is what *open* systems interfaces and *open* systems portability standards are all about. Only in the last few years has it been possible to convince groups of competing computer vendors to adopt common standards to make portability and scaleability technically feasible.

Integrated computer-aided systems engineering tools are the key to attaching and detaching temporary and obsolete assets from valuable long-term assets. Such tool sets enable organizations to obtain the full economic value of an *open* systems environment.

Problems with Software Maintenance

The current wide gap between business processes and the software they use is unquestionably the primary reason why software degrades to uselessness or requires a great deal of maintenance to keep it from becoming irrelevant. I consider most of the costs classified as "maintenance" to be part of "development." There is always a small of amount of true maintenance expense, like fixing technical defects. Whenever a programmer changes the logic of a program, or engages in conversions or integration with other software, I consider that activity to be deferred software development. If the original design was poor or had no consistent architecture, what masquerades as maintenance is really an effort to patch over fundamental design errors. You can uncover evidence for this if you determine the share of total development costs spent on the negotiating systems requirements between business managers and systems people. That can easily consume up to a third of the total hours expended on the initial development and well over half of the hours used in completing the maintenance action.

The fault lies in the language used by the business people, which is concerned with workflow and organizational relationships, as compared with the language of the systems people, which focuses on procedures and machine-controlled communications. You would have to search a long time to find another group of people who depend on each other as closely but have fundamentally different ways of seeing the purpose of their common endeavors.

Articulating Systems Requirements

You will never reach the desired high level of residual worth of software unless your systems engineering process encompasses both the workflow descriptions as well as specifications for generating software code.[184] The fundamental flaw of just about every existing computer-aided systems engineering methodology is they cater primarily to improving efficiency of the least important software activity which is code generation. The language of existing tools was originated by programmers, addresses matters of concern only to programmers, and solely for programmers to make their jobs easier. That is an inadequate approach to making organizations preserve their information systems for everyone.

We need a more reliable yet easier way to facilitate communications between business managers and technicians. Such tools must encompass more goals than what is offered now by programmers' tools. Changes in business conditions must be shared among all participants. Most importantly, descriptions of workflows and relationships must be maintained in terms that are independent of any hardware or software. The purpose here is not to convey the logic of the business in the arcane language of programmers, but in ways that managers can understand and express. Managers must be enabled to comfortably define the business rules for subsequent computer programming by the experts, and preferably by intelligent software translators. A number of firms are already offering the capability to generate reasonably efficient procedural code directly from workflow diagrams, thus by-passing the laborious and error-prone coding work.

The increased residual value of the software that originates from high levels of business process descriptions, preferably from managers themselves, comes from automatically regenerating specific software code. The regenerated code then embeds itself into whatever new technical environment becomes available. In this way you never write brand new software code that fits only a particular machine. When the time

---

184. Trying to achieve a minimum 90% residual value of software elements is a reasonable objective. That implies that portability or scaleability will incur only a maximum 10% penalty in conversion expenses, as compared with the original development costs.

comes to change equipment or operating systems, the code in the old machine is recreated from its high-level description of the business.

Manufactured Software

A great deal of attention is being currently given to the low-wage advantages of non-American programmers who may displace U.S. software leadership in a few years.[185] Accordingly, Indian programmers, who are now available for $10 per hour ought to have a decisive competitive advantage over programmers costing $60 to $75 per hour. You can also hire an Indian Ph.D. for the same price as a graduate from a community college in the U.S.

These comparisons miss the point that program coding now occupies less than ten percent of total development expense, and a much smaller proportion of the total software acquisition cost. Much of the expense for application development is from coordination, which is always difficult when communication needs to take place over distance and across different cultures. For most advanced technologies, the competitiveness of any organization, regardless of national origins, will come from its tooling and not its wage rates. For instance, an optical character recognition machine can now compete for the data entry business even if wage rates for off-shore keypunching would be less than thirty cents an hour. Labor cost differences are not the deciding factor for competitiveness whenever management effectively organizes the use of advanced technologies.

Are these tools sufficient in themselves to preserve the long-term residual value of software investments? No, they are not. In the same way that operating systems standards, interoperability standards and communications standards are necessary but not sufficient to preserve software investments, tools alone will not deliver the desired economic performance. We have to examine additional ways to ensure that an organization takes advantage of every available opportunity for manag-

185. Ed Yourdon, *Decline and Fall of the American Programmer*, Englewood Cliffs, N.J.: Yourdon Press, 1992

ing information technology with expertise and the benefits of specialization.

Openness

The open and evolutionary approach to systems management has a
political dimension that has not yet been adequately discussed in professional publications. Talking in terms of organizational politics is
essential because it demonstrates a willingness to be realistic about the
use of information as the means to distribute power and allow people to
negotiate workable compromises.

Open and evolving systems provide the infrastructure that adjusts
gracefully to changing administrative processes and relations with vendors and customers. Open systems are desirable not only because they
enable the purchase of competitively priced standard hardware, but they
shorten the period of adjustment to major business changes. It is essential to create an environment where change is safely incremental, rather
than drastic, with its risks of costly failure.

You should avoid the precipitous and complete replacement of
people, training, software, networks and software, especially as proposed
by the most rabid advocates of revolutionary changes. You may increase
the value of your information systems by salvaging the most useful elements of what you already have before you consider making any
improvements.

Dimensions of Open Systems

Preserve the value of your information with incremental business
process improvements that are supported by information systems which
are not affected by major changes in transaction volume. Save money
through software you can transport, no matter what operating system
controls the hardware. Reuse logic that will work independently of the
choice of the coding language.

Technical openness, although necessary, is not sufficient. The
increased volatility in how institutions conduct their affairs calls for systems designs that can absorb the shocks of mergers, acquisitions, divest-
ments, centralization, decentralization, reorganization, restructuring,
realignment, reengineering, and redeployment. If information man-

agement indeed reflects information politics, then the design of information systems must be sufficiently robust to avoid expending large sums every time the power structure changes. A resilience in coping with changed conditions defines a system as being politically as well as technically *open*.

How does one plan to attain both technical and political *openness?* That comes from what some call a technical architecture, and what I call adaptive governance. Flexibility is something for which one plans and trains. It will not arise by itself. It must be an act of purposeful leadership.

Significance of *Open* Systems

Pursuing *open* systems solutions is applicable to much more than computers. It is one of the most important policies for guiding all information management practices, especially as it applies to training and developing people. *Open* systems offer a way to conserve the value of the knowledge assets employees acquire. The payoffs from preserving and diversifying this knowledge capital are enormous. Not only does it extend the life of hardware and software, but it also makes individuals more adaptable and responsive.

The immediate rationale for pursuing *open* systems, which is the preservation of assets, extends beyond adopting technical standards. It affects how we structure the coordination of information resources, particularly the accumulation of organizational knowledge. *Open* systems convey an important message that complements concepts such as free trade, freedom of the press, human rights, and civic liberties. *Open* systems make it possible to break many of the proprietary barriers to universal communication. *Open* communications allow knowledge embodied in the diversity of cultural heritage to be shared globally, irrespective of the technological conditions found locally. *Open* systems will make computer-mediated sharing of knowledge the basis for global cooperation, no matter what the language, culture or level of technological sophistication.

PART III

LEADERSHIP

Ill-defined directions lead to confused
implementation.

25

OBJECTIVES

Without purpose doing anything well is a waste.

Information superiority can be one of the principal means to achieve competitive superiority. The value of the assets, the number of employees or the customer franchise can quickly disappear if information systems do not supply management with intelligence about threats and opportunities. A company's information objectives should be therefore defined in terms of how customers will differentiate it from competitors and how your management will be able to react to changing conditions with greater effectiveness. This should guide the selection of the measures used to judge the effectiveness of information services.

For example, if you are in the package delivery business, ask yourself the following questions: do you offer customers the lowest cost, the fastest or the most reliable service? Depending on how your organization aspires to excellence, your approach to information management will be different. The accurate articulation of goals is therefore of paramount importance. When there are no clear goals, no information system can compensate for their absence. You can readily drown in bureaucratic busy work if your computers have no other purpose than to produce more information more efficiently.

Goals vs. Objectives

"Goals" and "objectives" are confused with each other in most presentations to top management. As I see it, "goals" are hopes and aspirations for the distant future which are not necessarily attainable. Goals are lofty ideals, such as the U.S. Declaration of Independence, or what some speech writer produces as an inspirational message from a Chairman of the Board. One should not trifle with statements of goals. They are the bonds that bring together all the constituencies within organizations. Leaders must declare goals to continually affirm and refresh shared beliefs. Shared beliefs are essential for all cooperation to take place. Without goals that can elicit the allegiance of its members, organizations will regress to making only opportunistic moves. Frequent improvisation or reinterpretation of goals uses up valuable resources by making the organization plunge into and then back out of dead-end directions.

Figure 25.1 What is a Realistic Goal?

Objectives must be explicitly measurable performance commitments. Objectives must be measured to determine how near you are to where you want to be. If you do not have a calculable test of performance, you cannot claim to have an accountable objective. Goals are expectations, prospects, possibilities and ambitions. Objectives are reality, schedules, benchmarks, cost targets, and what you can afford. Goals are what dreams are made of.

In a typical presentation where someone proposes spending money on computers, the discussion of goals is likely to overwhelm statements that pin down objectives.[186] Embarking on information systems projects on the basis of wishful expectation is a step towards a likely disaster.

Objectives and Customer Satisfaction

How do you come up with useful objectives for information services? The best way is to pay close attention to what customers say about the value you deliver, as compared with what competitors offer. In-depth customer interviews instead of mass-mailed questionnaires are essential in understanding how customers feel. Conversations with previous customers are especially valuable if you probe for the reasons why they switched to the competition. In intelligence work, the interrogation of defectors is more productive than eavesdropping on those who remain loyal.

When you conduct a customer survey that receives a 50 percent response to your mail-in questionnaire and shows 85 percent satisfaction levels with your service, you should not be complacent. The 50 percent responses you did not get could be all from unhappy clients who have no incentive to tell you about it. Your statistics also do not include people who have already left you, and do not count any more as a customer. If the turnover of customers is high, you may have too few customers in your sample to tell you much that is conclusive. Data center customer satisfaction surveys are particularly untrustworthy without special precautions to include people who have already shifted workload to their own microcomputers. There are available excellent market research methodologies that produce statistically valid results.

---

186. In large bureaucracies, overdoing the "goals" and starving the "objectives" is understandable misdirection. If everyone can interfere with getting something accomplished, your best bet is to concentrate on generalities instead of the deliverables.

Therefore, all customer satisfaction surveys should include measures as to their reliability as well as a proof of the validity of conclusions.

Unhappy comments about slow staff responsiveness requires you to make speeding up services a new objective. Repeated failures to meet commitments will give you another item to include in your list of objectives. If reports from defecting customers uncover an information-related deficiency, this is an additional objective for your list.

The easiest and fastest way of improving anything is to first fix what has fallen into disrepair. If that does not provide a complete cure, you may start searching for new objectives that emulate the best practices of others in those areas where you are deficient. You do not achieve much by following indiscriminately somebody's list of recommended best practices, even though that is the favorite approach of most consultants, auditors and prize award committees. Mimicking somebody's abstract virtues can lead you into wasting scarce resources in pursuit of capabilities that will not do much to solve your current problems. I object to the fixed criteria of the national Baldrige Prize for Quality because it rates corporations on their compliance with procedures and practices that do not necessarily have anything to do with their competitive performance in the marketplace, which is the only reliable measure that tells you have customers vote with their purchase decisions. Specific measures for inducing customers lost to competition to return offer better insights than somebody's generic textbook prescriptions.

The prime objective for any systems organization should be to deliver superbly what had been promised. Only after you accomplish that should you reach for new horizons to conquer. Do not buy a new product from a vendor whose old product does not work yet. Do not trust a team to deliver brand new, advanced technology if they have not mastered what others have installed long ago.

Cost Reduction Objectives

An effective information systems chief should set tough financial objectives to cut the unit costs of information services. Regardless of how visionary or popular the chief may be, out-of-control costs and schedule slippage will ultimately ruin everything else.

Because mainframe prices are falling about 45% per year and microcomputer prices are dropping 6% per month, your executives should expect computer processing savings of at least 25% per year, at least every year over the next decade.[187] I also expect at least 30% compound reductions in the cost of software development and maintenance from software re-use and increased availability of standard applications packages. Considering that information technology expenses account for only about 25-35% of most transaction expenses, overall productivity targets of about 10% are therefore a reasonable target. Therefore, you should be able to show your executive committee a chart like Figure 25.2 which shows administrative expenses per transaction declining from $235 to $145, for cumulative savings of 57% over a four year period:

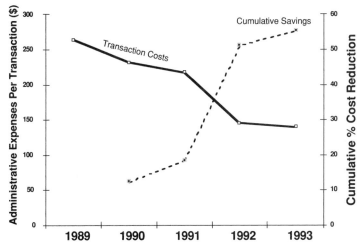

Figure 25.2 Example of Unit Cost Reduction Indicators[188]

---

187. Every major cost-reduction in hardware technology for the next ten years is already in the laboratory or in pilot tests somewhere. Forecasting the costs of information technologies is not difficult because estimates are readily available. However, the bulk of the savings will not come from less costly devices, but from elimination of labor cost that presently surrounds these devices. For instance, tape handling, console operations and attending to printers will disappear. 188. Maryfan Johnson, "Fannie Mae, Cashing in on Client/Server," *Computerworld Client/Server Journal,* February 1994, p.39

The information technology establishment must deliver demonstrably low cost information services. To prove to its customers that this has been done, the information chief should engage systems evaluation services for competitive "benchmarking." There are a number of firms that would calculate your ratios, such as unit costs, and compare them against those of others in your industry. Benchmarking is a complex business. You should be wary of selective evaluations that show only those ratios where you excel.

Benchmarking consultants perfectly fit the old saying about professionals who borrow your watch, tell you the time, keep the watch and charge you for time keeping. The most important asset of benchmarking consultants is the size, statistical validity and robustness of the ratios against which they evaluate you.

When you are benchmarked, you provide your consultant with valuable data that will be reused in all subsequent consulting engagements. The consultant needs you as much as you need him. Therefore, make sure the scores revealed to you include details consultants usually like to keep to themselves, such as measures of reliability, sample size and evidence that your comparisons reflect companies with similar characteristics. Before you share the benchmarking results with your top management, make sure there is documentation showing how and why the evaluations apply to your case.

It is not enough to prove that you are experiencing steadily declining information processing unit costs. You must also prove these benefits are not merely expenses shifted from where they are under careful examination to where they are overlooked by headquarters. There are CIOs who have boasted about reducing their information technology budget by conveniently ignoring the shifting of expenses to business units where they become "operating expenses."[189]

To support the claim that lower information technology costs indeed translate into declines in total expenses, it would be useful to

---

189. This is one of many plausible explanations why, in most corporations, the introduction of microcomputers did not get much attention from the keepers of the central establishment.

show what happens to total administrative expenses that correspond to Figure 25.3:

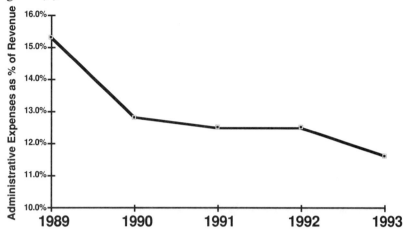

Figure 25.3 Example of Declining Administrative Costs[190]

Figure 25.3 corroborates that the organization has realized substantial reductions in overall administrative expenses, of which information technology represents over a third of costs.

Setting Objectives

Failures arising from missing well thought out and clearly defined objectives are relatively rare. Organizations usually do not perish because they did not reach objectives closely related to their experience and to their record of past accomplishments. Books are full of stories about small bands with inferior resources and powerful adversaries that nevertheless achieve what they set out to accomplish because their training and morale prepared them for the ordeal ahead.

Failures arise from choosing objectives whose ambitions do not match the will and expertise to achieve them. You will fail if you pick objectives inspired by rhetoric instead of commitment and capability.

Bankruptcy and collapse come from overlooking external threats. These originate by neglect of opportunities that are picked up instead

---

190. Maryfan Johnson, ibid.

by a competent adversary. You will also fail if you pick a too easy target. You will limit your commitments to a comfortable purpose while you overlook either a deadly risk or miss a once-of-a-lifetime opportunity.[191]

It is the primary role of leaders to identify goals and then define objectives. Good leadership has the ability to pick and gain acceptance from the followers of the objectives that may score large gains while containing exposure to losses. Understanding the rewards and risks justifies the elevated status and the high income of leadership. Everyone who aspires to command must competently influence and ultimately take on this role.

Once it was the royal seal that was the sign of sovereign authority to issue decrees. The modern equivalent of this is the formal announcement of the objectives of the enterprise. Such acts do receive the attention they deserve. The President of the United States must give a State of the Union address. The ability to influence such declarations is a sure sign of political ascendancy.

The act of announcing information objectives should be more than a rhetorical exercise. It should be the product of well-considered arguments concerning the balance between ambition and reality. Formulating a statement of information objectives must be a deliberately structured policy-making process. Otherwise, maneuvering for political position will detract attention from drawing up a realistic declaration. Improvised statements give muddled directions, a sure setup for failure in the near future. You must refrain from deriving your organization's new information objectives from presentations that sell an otherwise unpalatable project.[192] Under no circumstances should you ever first announce your objectives as a public relations campaign to cover up recent failures. Advertising and press conferences are the worst of all

---

191. You do not light a match to see if a spilled liquid is gasoline. It is the enemy whom you neglected to engage early enough who ultimately kills you.

192. For example, the current administration in Washington would like to increase tax collections by requiring that taxes be paid whenever a taxable transaction takes place. That would involve a highly unpopular intrusion on personal privacy. Instead, systems experts have cleverly announced that their objective is to eliminate labor-intensive tax filings for the majority of taxpayers.

possible forums for launching new objectives. The appropriate time and place for declaring new objectives is to share them with people who will have to implement them and who should be given every opportunity to discuss them before they become public.

Figure 25.4 Leadership by Press Release

Setting and updating of objectives, at every level of the organization, must gather diverse critical views. This process should have safeguards to fill gaps among the interests represented. It may also be useful to involve outsiders who hold controversial but sound opinions.

Example of Poorly Targeted Objectives

A classic case of poorly targeted objectives occurred in Xerox over twenty years ago. Xerox's stated goal was to become the "architects of information" in the document-intensive computerized office. To finance this dream, Xerox defined its top objective as maintaining a high return-on-assets. The bonuses and profit sharing plans for executives reflected how well they achieved their return-on-assets objectives.

The consequence of concentrating on an objective that was constructed around a financial measure was to overlook the loss of customers in copying, a business Xerox already owned and came to neglect. This ultimately led to a sale of assets, a disastrous drop in market position, deteriorating profits and distraction of management from pursuing major innovations when the time came to exploit them. The return-on-asset objective ultimately lead Xerox to seek salvation in the finance and insurance business. That move incurred such high losses that exploitation of impressive innovations was not feasible for a long time afterwards.

It may be of interest that the "architecture of information" objective for the Xerox Corporation, that haunted its employees for decades, was the result of a speech writer's clever catch-phrase for a talk by the Chairman to financial analysts who were becoming displeased with profit trends. Nobody expected this speech ornament would stick as a declaration of both goals and objectives.

Basic Beliefs

Goals and objectives answer questions such as "what business are we in?" and "how do we excel in that business?" Often, top management is reluctant to make such declarations because someday someone could compare actual accomplishments against promises. A convenient way of avoiding a potential embarrassment is to limit any public pronouncements to stating a set of beliefs. That has the advantage of announcing generalities which leave little room for any arguments. Consider the following statements by the new CEO of the IBM Corporation, announcing revised fundamental beliefs to guide all employees in the future:[193]

- "The marketplace is the driving force behind everything we do.

- At our core, we are a technology company with an overriding commitment to quality.

---

193. Laurie Hays, "Gerstner is Struggling As He Tries to Change Ingrained IBM Culture," *The Wall Street Journal*, May 13, 1994, p.1

- Our primary measures of success are customer satis-faction and shareholder value.

- We operate as an entrepreneurial organization with a minimum of bureaucracy, and a never-ending focus on productivity.

- We never lose sight of our strategic vision.

- We think and act with a sense of urgency.

- Outstanding, dedicated people make it all happen, particularly when they work together as a team.

- We are sensitive to the needs of all employees and to the communities in which we operate."

There is nothing in the above statements that would not equally apply to a large number of corporations. One cannot possibly object to such generic assertions. Organizations should use every opportunity to affirm their faith. However, beliefs without goals and objectives are sterile. Without commitments to deliver specific results, professions of managerial philosophy are more suitable for the pulpit than for a gathering to inspire employees seeking specific guidance from their leaders anyway.

Too Many Objectives

Many organizations currently are plagued by too many unrealizable interests chasing each other. I have sat through lengthy presentations in which the first twenty slides consisted of a shopping list with every fashionable idea put forth in the latest books or magazine articles. The number of objectives seem to rise in order to tranquilize opposition by promising something for everyone, which most likely means that hardly anyone will get anything.

Overabundance of objectives is sometimes rationalized as diver-sification. That was popular for a while, until companies had to refocus on their inherent competencies. Adding to the Xerox's troubles more than twenty years ago was the pursuit of over thirty-five separate busi-nesses, of which only two or three possessed world class capabilities to compete with adversaries.

Having only a limited number of sharply defined objectives results in delivering what is promised, within budget, on schedule. That does not mean that once you succeed, you cannot add to what is already working. If you are a policy maker, your greatest value will be to assure that your project managers receive the appropriate number of consistent objectives.

Focus

Focus, focus and focus are the three most important criteria for sifting through a long list of objectives. Appointing representative steering committees and systems review boards does not necessarily help. Large review groups become parliaments that tend to expand wish lists until systems managers are overwhelmed by demands unsupported by budget, consistency and persistence. If you need a jury to narrow down choices about options, it better be a small number of decision makers who will have to live with the results and pay for them.

It is a natural tendency of all systems managers to acquiesce to customer wishes as a way to make peace with those who vote during the next project review checkpoint. If systems projects are continually adding objectives, they must ultimately fail because of inconsistent priorities for spending limited funds.

I do not think it is possible to follow more than three to five objectives in any major systems undertaking. During biblical times Moses got into much trouble on the first attempt to present a list of too many from the ultimate source of authority. Typical systems plans start with an impressive preamble that hardly ever lists fewer than twenty goals. I would rather see a few well-articulated objectives that can unify an organization to concentrate on delivering measurable results, than a mass of well-intentioned directives that are infeasible to put into effect.

Every business textbook will tell you that the key to successful systems is the management of expectations, except that nobody tells you exactly how to do it. I once worked for someone who said that if you do not expect too much, you will not be disappointed. That wisdom does not seem to prevail among computer people. The practice of prudently understating expected results loses to the compulsion to covet the most sophisticated and thereby the most risky solutions. Systems professionals must learn to manage the setting of objectives. It requires a disciplined approach to concentrate management's attention on only a few critical measures that also lend themselves to tracking interim results. If you state objectives in terms that anyone can verify for accomplishment, the reconciliation between expectation and reality should become much easier.

Examples of Information Systems Objectives

To illustrate specific, measurable and understandable objectives, here is a sample of what I consider as acceptable declarations:

• By June 199X, the unit cost of operations for data centers, software development and software maintenance shall be in the lowest quartile of companies, using the benchmarks of the XXXX Corporation.

• By December 199X, we shall have a detailed implementation plan how to put into effect a new customer pricing program in less than XX hours.

• By 199X, we shall be able to set up a new district branch office, equipped with a full complement of standard information services, in less than XX days.

• By 199X, we shall have a standard and consistent system connecting all employees and company dealerships with e-mail, facsimile, telephones and video conferencing.

¶ By 199X, all applications in the corporation shall run beneath a standard corporate graphic interface to which every employee has received basic training at the beginning of employment.

26

ROLES

Uncertain leaders have perplexed followers.

Computer people have good reason to be insecure. When IBM or DEC dismiss 60,000 employees, it is just another sign that all is not well in cyberland. *Business Week* recently told your CEO, COO and CFO that COBOL programmers will be obsolete by 1998 because of automatic code generators. If you happen to make a living maintaining COBOL, that will hardly increase your confidence in your future career. The rumor that your CIO is looking for another position will not improve your outlook. How can you maintain your reputation as a guardian of computer mysteries if *The New York Times* reports that mainframe performance will be available at the local toy store for less than $500?[194]

So, you embark on a search of models of successes to emulate. You think to yourself that if you can find a model of excellence, then surely you can learn to improve your prospects. Happily, there are institutions that thrive on publishing, celebrating and awarding eminence. There are Miss America contests, Academy Awards, and then there are

---

194. John Markoff, "Toys Now, Computers Tomorrow?," *The New York Times*, April 20. 1994, p. D6. The article compares a 1975 IBM mainframe costing $10 million capable of processing 10 million instructions per second with a 1995 Sony PCX video game costing $500, capable of processing 500 million instructions per second.

magazine contests, such as "whose information systems are tops at giving customers great service?"

Identifying Excellence

Improving customer service is definitely an idea to which every computer person could hitch a career. Quality is "in." Customer care through computers should be the right ticket to promotions and an increased budget. One would think that all you have to know is what the top rated companies do to merit their ratings. Then, study what the prominently profiled computer people have to say. After that, all of your doubts about your career prospects ought to vanish and you can take that expensive vacation you cannot afford. Or can you?

What do you learn from stories about 3M, AMP, Caterpillar, Corning, Dow Chemical, Ford, GE, IBM, Motorola, Procter & Gamble and Xerox — the industrial corporations that came out at the top of one of these contests in 1993? What the computer people and marketing executives of these companies have to say is common sense: "Ruthlessly track down and wipe out every element of customer dissatisfaction through excellent service." On a more practical level, one of the winners noted that "Customer-focus groups kept telling us how often they were disappointed...when we assigned a single service engineer. To avoid these problems... we assigned teams of about eight engineers." Obviously, you now could use a computer system to sort out whom to send where and when. There is an opportunity for you if you can seize it.

IBM, DEC, Phillips, Bull and Apple are laying off computer people regardless of how enthusiastic their executives are in telling journalists about superior customer service. Knowing a great deal about two of these wounded companies, I can attest that they subscribe to every measure declared as the "secret of success" for the use of information technologies. Every computer executive seeking employment will also endorse such secrets. Who would dare to say otherwise? Trade journal reports about great customer service ideas are helpful but certainly not sufficient guides to achieving excellence.

The problem is that what you read is what the winners' executives say without telling much that is of any use to the competition. Generalities from the mouths of those being judged are not evidence.

Privately held opinions of a self-selected jury have a built-in bias. What then is helpful? What about the customers' views?

Beyond the subjective ratings of "great customer service," there is one much better measure: How did customers vote with their checkbooks? This is profit, and is defined by *Fortune* as the "total return to shareholders." *Fortune* publishes this data for 500 U.S. corporations every spring. Trends in the "total return to shareholders" are one of the most important indicators that signals the board of directors, stock market and executive management whether a company is gaining or losing. The sinking "total returns to shareholders" ratings for IBM, DEC, Phillips, Bull and Apple prompted these firms to let go a large number of excellent people, regardless of what they thought or did about quality.

I checked on the *Fortune* financial performance rankings of the companies rated for their high quality of information systems in 1993. I looked at the 1993 as well as the 1983-1993 results, just to make sure that a short term blip did not distort my conclusions.

The *Fortune* rankings (the numbers in brackets indicate the company's standing among the *Fortune* 500. These numbers are in the order of decreasing financial performance) of the contest winners were: 3M [213], AMP [276], Caterpillar [122], Corning [289], Dow Chemical [205], Ford [38], GE [173], IBM [412], Motorola [33], Procter & Gamble [159] and Xerox [136].

Only Ford and Motorola were in the top ten percent of companies. The rest averaged an uninspired ranking of 220 out of 500. The ten year average rankings were consistent with 1993 standings except for Xerox, featured as the "...model worth copying..." whose long-term profit ranking of 186 approached only average performance.[195]

---

195. The Xerox case is particularly instructive in how facts and opinions often diverge. Xerox has consistently been cited for excellence in information management and has won numerous recognition awards from computer magazines. Academic journals frequently cite Xerox as a case of effective information management. Yet, when you look at its record of economic value added since 1982, it has been negative each year as reported by Stern Stewart Management Services, New York, 1993 (Millions of dollars, 1982-1992: $-433; $-449; $-947; $-1,054; $-493; $-310; $-238; $-305; $-573; $-788; $-1,877). The first test any company must pass in claiming excellence is the customer vote. The best way to identify that is to show consistently positive economic results.

If you are not sure what defines excellence in the use of information systems, I recommend studying what Ford and Motorola practice. Then examine how forty-eight other companies in the top 10 per cent of *Fortune* profit rankings manage their information systems.

If you want to achieve unquestionable excellence, then work on understanding what pitfalls to avoid. The fifty companies at the bottom of the *Fortune* list are experiencing those. Remember that solid information about the causes of failure conveys more useful insight than any assertions about superiority. The road towards excellence has signs that point to the continuous elimination of defects. You can improve faster by overcoming disabilities than by attempting to surpass somebody else's virtues.

The financial performance of the top firms is the most important piece of evidence, but certainly not the only one, that demonstrates how customers recognize quality in the only terms that matter: cash in the till. Use the *Fortune* profit rankings to explore why certain corporations consistently deliver shareholder gains while others do not. You may find better ways to learn about patterns of excellence than relying exclusively on professionally retouched beauty contest snapshots. Most opinion-based surveys and excellence ratings are popularity contests because they provide the easiest way to collect information that needs no further proof of its validity.[196]

Outsourcing as a Loss of Identity

An organization that has adopted a layered approach to the governance of information management will find ways to contract out easily detachable functions to someone with greater efficiency. Under those circumstances, outsourcing is healthy and profitable. Contracting out a part of the information systems function will not diminish the importance of that function, provided that the outsourced mission can be brought back as a core competency whenever that becomes necessary.

---

196. Opinion surveys that rate financially poorly performing companies highly are a better measure of the excellence of the public relations department than the systems department.

With outsourcing there should be no loss in identity or understanding what is important for sound information management.

Those who have intertwined their business and technology functions within self-sufficient information systems departments may find it difficult to choose which pieces can be contracted out. They may solve their inability to balance centralization and decentralization by transferring all systems work to a single contractor.[197] If this happens, it would be a mistake to expect the supplier to eliminate conflicts between business units and the corporate support organization by offering services that are presumed to avoid internal political disputes. The contractor would get the job of dealing with internal squabbles about allocation of shared costs and try to resolve claims about priorities in making software changes. The reliance on commercial pricing practices assumes that traditional commercial relationship between customers and providers of information services will finally bring peace to the fractious relationships within the information systems function. I do not believe this to be the case.

Companies that have suffered internal conflicts in the absence of clear governance policies will not resolve these matters by bringing in an outside party. Contracting out information services is not like outsourcing the manufacture of circuit boards or axles. Information systems will always remain an integral element of a business. Therefore, the winning outsourcing contractor will inherit unresolved disputes unless the contract forces order and governance in information management on parties that previously resisted less drastic means to accomplish the identical purpose. Otherwise, outsourcing is primarily a political solution and only secondarily an economic move. Politically motivated outsourcing brings larger profits to the contractor because the company doing such outsourcing will not gain the greatest economic advantages from such a deal.

---

197. It was the internal structure of information systems management in the General Motors Corporation that made the outsourcing of all information technologies to EDS the preferred option, as seen from the standpoint of top management. Today, many key executives acknowledge that GM should have retained a number of critical functions.

Figure 26.1 A View of Outsourcing

There are instances where upgrading and modernizing software and hardware have been outsourced to a commercial provider because top executives simply gave up trying to learn to manage their own information systems. Bringing in an outside vendor only makes the internal conflicts between central coordination and distributed autonomy worse because it is in the best financial interest of the contractor not to intrude on unresolved internal disputes. Outsourcing under such conditions is unhealthy and costly to the client.

Managing and preserving accumulated organizational knowledge is primarily a political and only secondarily a technical matter. Persistent internal conflicts do not get any better by passing the custody of managing knowledge to someone else. Outsourcing information systems as a way to solve internal mismanagement does not accomplish much. Organizations that contract out for that reason will lose one of the most critical opportunities for learning about themselves because now this learning will take place for the benefit of the contractor at the company's expense. The systems people who remain in the company will suffer from a loss of identity because they will never learn which career path is the right one toward which to commit their energies.

Outsourcing makes a great deal of sense if an organization has already resolved most of the issues of governance and has clearly separated the enterprise roles from business and application functions. The chances are an experienced operator of data centers, telecommunications, network control or transaction services can deliver more efficient capabilities than any home-grown effort. If the layers of governance are in clearly defined modules, then contracting them to another organization for a much lower price would be advantageous.

Identity

Over many years I have studied the careers of chief information officers (CIOs). Surveys show that the average tenure of CIOs is only two and a half years. Their time-in-job survival is quite low. The turnover rate of U.S. CIOs in 1992 was 17.5%. This ranged from 7.5% among companies with less than $100 million revenue, to 25% among companies with more than $5 billion in revenue. The reasons current CIOs indicated why their predecessors left were: 33% dismissed or demoted; 20% resigned; 9% lateral move; 9% promoted and 8.6% retired.[198]

The professional background of those appointed to CIO position is changing. In 1993, individuals with business and no technical background became CIOs twice as often as technologists.[199] The selection of a trusted amateur instead of an expert to be in charge of technology is an indication of the frustration of chief executives. I take this to be an early signal that a large number of corporate heads have decided to take their organizations out of the technical race. This is a step in the direction of ultimately outsourcing all information technologies to professional specialists. It relieves top management from distractions and allows them to concentrate on building those few competencies that are unique to their business.

---

198. Survey of 534 North American CIOs by Deloitte & Touche, *Computerworld*, August 9, 1993, p.86
199. Joseph Maglitta, "Meet the New Boss," *Computerworld*, March 14, 1994, p. 82

In the turmoil of swapping technology experts for business loyal-ists, and vice versa, the heroes of yesterday become the rejects of today. This is a particularly common occurrence in New York City, where there are more reject-to-hero and hero-to-reject stories than anywhere else in the world. The irony of the highly regarded *InformationWeek* magazine awards to the "Best CIOs of the Year" is that too often the winners leave their jobs shortly afterwards.

Since my retirement from Xerox in 1985, I have had the opportu-nity to examine information management organizations in many com-panies. Some of these are very large, with multi-billion dollar budgets. Other information management departments are quite small, with chief executives reaching out to computers as the way to gain a "competitive edge" on a tiny budget. With few exceptions, I found a surprisingly large number of CIOs were failing in their jobs. They forgot to take care of the basics in the business of information management: mod-ernization and cost reduction. The failing CIOs were spending too much time chasing corporate visions, strategic uses of technology and business reengineering, while their computer shops continued to be too expensive, unpredictable and unresponsive in the delivering what was expected and needed to support business operations.

Signs of Failure

What are the clues that a CIO is failing? You could hear rumors the Chairman, President or the Deputy Secretary is searching for a candi-date to replace the current CIO or "information resources management executive."[200] You will hear that another reorganization is pending. You will get phone calls from recruiters checking up on qualifications claimed in resumes. The CEO appoints an information policy steering committee chaired by the comptroller. Consultants are engaged to study

---

200. The Information Resources Management (IRM) executive is the title of a CIO in the public sector. It is a more accurate description of the job than "chief information executive," as the scope of the position excludes important information functions such as public relations and advertising. Despite its exalted title, the IRM job is just another label for managing com-puters. In practice it does not include what I have defined in this book as "information man-agement." You may not necessarily know what people do from their titles.

whether information systems should be centralized, decentralized or outsourced altogether.[201]

What happens to information technology budgets is also revealing about the impending demise of the current CIO. If expenses reported as "computer costs" grow faster than revenue in the private business, or agency appropriations in the public sector, there is likely to be a backlash. Corporate management will notice that users are setting up their own computer shops because the organization managed by the CIO does not deliver workable solutions. Sales people, production planners, engineers and designers will become part-time systems managers instead of taking care of customers. They will gladly engage in such job diversification, while blaming the existing computer organization for forcing them to do it. Here are a few additional symptoms of a likely CIO fatality:

- Applications are not compatible and interoperable. It takes days before customer returns become reflected in inventories or billing credits.

- Improvised databases and unconnected local area networks proliferate like weeds. Local branch offices set up their own customer prospect tracking files that are inconsistent with accounting, shipping and market research data.

- Bootleg applications conceived by enthusiastic amateurs spring up everywhere. Local managers request additional personnel for systems maintenance.

- Executives engage in disputes because their local data bases give them contradictory information. During a meeting of the corporate executive committee, the chief financial officer and the executive vice-president of mar-

---

201. Computer people looking for jobs are the best source for acquiring detailed competitive information. It is easy to find out who is available from a target organization. Job seekers usually do not refrain from talking about confidential data. Your biggest problem would be to detect exaggerations that give your competitors credit for greater accomplishments than warranted.

keting clash about the number of items sold that month. The local army commander and the headquarters differ about the number of troops on a military base. The Air Force and the Defense Logistic Agency engage in acrimonious exchanges about the amount of fuel actually available to fly combat missions.

The downfall of the CIO will finally take place when a magazine article reveals that competitors already offer their customers options the present CIO only proposes in the latest budget request. The General in charge of command and control retires when a critical satellite picture becomes available to everyone except to the commander who could do something about it.

Patterns of Failure and Success

What happened to failed CIOs? When I talk to involuntarily retired CIOs, most of them blame their misfortunes on the microcomputer. They say it entered into their organizations too fast and without appropriate controls. They also blame IBM and DEC for not delivering an "architecture" that would bottle the escaped genie of personal computing into some sort of controllable scheme. This kind of thinking is like blaming the rain for water in the living room. Why not examine the possibility that the roof leaked because somebody did not replace missing tiles while the sun was shining? Why not consider that the failed CIOs had consistently underestimated the growing gap between their own performance and the rising expectations of an increasingly literate workforce? Why not admit to failure due to self-inflicted neglect, rather than something that came from the outside and overpowered the unsuspecting CIO?

I spoke once at the Carnegie-Mellon University awards ceremony for distinguished achievement in managing information technology. That year, the winners were Salomon Brothers, Boston College, the Chase Manhattan Bank, McGraw-Hill, Wal-Mart Stores, the U.S. Department of Defense, Allianz Insurance Corporation (Germany) and the Tucson Unified School District. Using first hand knowledge of some of these winners and reviewing the citations for their accomplishments, it was apparent the winners managed to channel the microcomputer "disorder" into constructive channels. They managed costs. They aggressively modernized. The winners were hands-on operating managers who delivered to their organizations reliable, operationally viable, low-cost and rapidly reacting systems. There was little theoretical jargon or high technology terminology in what these executives said about what they did. No fluff, no utopian extrapolations into the 21st century. Just facts that concerned the here and now, and projections of greater successes tomorrow built on top of what was success today. I liked the character of these CIO winners. They are the sort of people who fix their roofs before it rains.[202]

The Roots of Failure

Where, why and when did the losing CIOs drift away from their conservative attitudes to manage computers as a high quality service?

History teaches us that some people, as well as nations, fail when they accept unrealistic ideas about their environment. New ideas spread from preachers and publicists who pander to the dreams of those who nurse ambitious hopes. The prevailing malaise about the effectiveness of information management is directly traceable to a few persuasive thinkers whose ideas were first disseminated in the late 1970s and early 1980s. Most of these people were academics who subsequently became consultants, although none had ever managed any sizable business operation.[203]

The model set before an ambitious CIO was simple: Forget mundane details such as the integration of *Local Area Networks* and *Wide Area Networks*, delegate data administration to "techies," let the vendors take care of migration to new technologies and do not worry about

---

202. None of the Carnegie-Mellon winners matched the profile advocated by the widely followed opinion shaper of the role of CIOs, Michael Hammer. He described the qualifications for leadership in information technology as requiring the skills of "witch doctors," "magicians" and "wizards." Accordingly, the ideal candidate would be a Ph.D. in computer science, with a background in systems development, technology architecture and technology development. *Computerworld*, March 20, 1989.

203. A typical expression of which sentiment is that "... Information systems executives possess a problem-solving, multidimensional way of thinking that makes them the strongest candidates of the role of the corporate reengineer. In fact, he /the professor/ predicts that at some future time CIO will come to stand for Chief Innovation Officer." P. Krass, "Building a Better Mousetrap, What Role do MIS Executives Play?" *Information Week*, March 25, 1991, p.24

software assets, because "open systems" will take care of that.[204] Instead, become an "information visionary," set aside for yourself a key role in laying out the strategic directions of the business, start the reengineering of the entire company and use your position to campaign for the top jobs. Anointing computer executives with such aspirations was welcomed, because it gave legitimacy to shedding the image of a dead-end technologist career. What you got now was a new path with unlimited possibilities.

Harking back to the radical spirit of the 1960s, the same academics coincidentally preached the obliteration of the existing organizations through computer-propelled "reengineering." The unfortunate association in the minds of operating executives between the leadership aspirations of the CIO and the destructive aspects of reengineering would subsequently assure an enduring enmity for any CIO crusader.[205] Some professors influenced scores of MIS executives in this heroic view: "...the chief MIS executive must lead the reorganization of their companies, creating new corporate structures and innovative ways of doing business."[206]

---

204. An example of this sort of thinking comes from Les Ball, a principal at CSC Index: "Forget about technical expertise and long-range platform planning. The primary job of the future CIO is to be guarding and controlling the process of acquiring knowledge. He or she may have no technical experience. In their new role, the CIOs will be charged with duties that sound more like alternate titles for monarchs such as guardian of the knowledge base, architect of the learning organization, ambassador to the business units. The new breed of CIO will need to know little about the technology they manage." John P. McPartlin, "Meet the 21st Century CIO," *Information Week*, May 24, 1993.

205. Niccolo Machiavelli advised that an ambitious prince should always avoid from being tainted by fratricide.

206. Quoted in the July 3, 1989 issues of *Information Week*, p.37

Figure 26.2 A Potentially Fatal Misunderstanding

Accordingly, information chiefs had unique qualifications to lead the reformation of corporations because "...information systems people know intuitively how to structure and solve large, complex problems. M.I.S. executives can realign a world-wide corporation because of their ability to think about systems. The information systems executives' mission is to transform and redeem stagnant businesses and in this way become agents of corporate innovation."[207] The attendance of CIOs at conferences that advocated these views has exceeded capacity for many years.

The CIO's Image

Subordinating computer executives to the unpopular dictatorship of the comptroller, or chief financial officer, goes back to the 1950s and 1960s when computers were a finance department monopoly. Starting in the 1970s, the CIO gradually emerged from under the control of the

---

207. *Information Week, ibid.*

finance establishment and began seeking an independent role as a peer in the hierarchy, on a par with marketing, manufacturing, personnel and operations. Equality in status was achieved when the budget under the CIO's control was sufficiently large to place him as one of the top ten spenders in the organization.

Over the next ten years, CIOs gradually shed the tainted image acquired during their days as the comptrollers' henchmen and dispensers of monopoly-priced services. The successful CIOs earned the trust of their peers whenever they became responsive to customer needs. They became respected members of the management team when they offered competitively priced services that did not take advantage of their monopolistic position to extract funds from captive customers for extravagant ventures.

However, only a few CIOs successfully converted from a monopoly to a market-driven posture. Their predisposition towards monopoly was influenced by enormous fixed costs for software maintenance and six to eight year depreciation schedules for mainframes. Any introductory economics text will say that if variable costs tend to be close to zero and the fixed costs are overwhelming, then price fixing and eliminating competition offers the easiest solution. Nobody told CIOs that short term enjoyment of monopoly economics leads to a long-term disaster whenever customers find an alternative source of supply.

By the 1980s, the untenable economics of most of the CIOs' empires, combined with the long political history of untrustworthiness, made it easy for operating executives to break the back of any CIO who aspired to more than a subservient role. Information technology was now too important to remain safely in the hands of the computer establishment, with its long track record of monopoly, delay in modernization, non-competitive pricing and frequent exhibitions of arrogance of power. Just to be on the safe side, the functional barons saw to it that central computer establishments was dismantled as soon as the minicomputer, microcomputer and a rapidly growing computer services industry made that economically attractive. It is during this period that high turnover among CIOs first came to everyone's attention.

The CIO Disorientation

Executives often ask me why nobody prevented the current chaos and proliferation of non-interoperable computing, data and software. Why did most CIOs avoid co-opting threatening innovations, such as local area networks, and offering them to their clients on more attractive terms? That is like asking why the European lords did not co-opt the Mongolian hordes that invaded their realms for a century. From a political standpoint, that was not feasible because the agriculturally-based feudal lords of Europe did not have much in common with the invading nomadic tribes from the eastern steppe. There were no institutions that could form the basis for reaching agreement on common goals or shared principles of governance.

When the microcomputer invasion occurred, neither the academics nor the vendors offered a way to balance the traditional integration and asset conservation roles of the CIO with the users' insistence on local autonomy at just about any price.[208] The suddenness of the microcomputer onslaught does not offer a good excuse for this conceptual paralysis. The proliferation of minicomputers in the 1970s offered enough warning to anticipate massive attacks on the mainframe fortresses not later than by the mid-1980s.

Instead of dealing with this matter as a question of political "governance," the conflicts involved posturing, image projections, publicity, preferred practice sermons and popularized versions of academic sociology. The solutions offered were closer to psychotherapy than to the practice of pragmatic politics. Instead of negotiating and experimenting with new institutional forms for coping with the problems of everyday operations involving hundreds or thousands of computers, the academics and vendors explored how to redefine the character of information

---

208. It was an accepted hypothesis at IBM corporate headquarters in the early 1980s that personal computers were good for mainframes, because they would generate demand for centralized machine services. On the basis of this assumption, IBM expanded its manufacturing capacity for large computers enormously. Exactly the opposite development took place. Whenever it was feasible, the trend was to move machine cycles to the local computers. Most of the large layoffs from IBM involve shedding the immense plant capacity investments of the early 1980s.

management. They adopted the language of psychology, suggesting that changing one's personality is perhaps the most desirable way to adjust to external challenges. The problem with this approach was there were as many opinions about suitable personality adjustments as there were consultants and academics.

The early 1980s were the turning point for changing the characteristics of information management from pragmatism to ideology. The change produced a shift from an orientation toward operating results to a focus on *preferred practices* for managing information systems. According to this view, you ought to follow a prescribed set of processes enumerated by the experts. If you can score well on someone's authoritative checklist, superior operating results should appear. In the absence of verifiable results, all you had to do is accumulate the right number of points for the right kind of attributes, according to weighting factors assigned by experts.

Recently, I reviewed the results of a comprehensive effort to define excellence in information management.[209] It was a 156 page questionnaire detailing over 200 desirable information management practices, with points and relative weights of importance assigned to each factor. Most of the points were rewarded for following practices declared as *politically correct* processes, such as having the right documents, holding the right meetings, getting the right approval signatures, and following the prescribed systems development cycle. The checklist paid no attention to making a thorough assessment of existing problems, evaluating potential threats from competitors or checking out the economic fundamentals for affordability. The checklist neglected assessing the quality of personnel to innovate, modernize and experiment.

This reminded me of the culture of the mandarins, the Chinese emperor's administrators, who destroyed the once economically and culturally superior Chinese civilization by forcing everyone to follow the *correct* process without paying much attention to the substance of what needs to be improved. I blame this intrusion of mandarin-like

---

209. Conceived by one of the largest consulting firms in the world, with an international reputation for innovative leadership.

conduct on much of the disorientation in current business and political thinking.

Pragmatic vs. Mandarin CIO

CIOs who are pragmatic politicians shed their vulnerable cost structures, make it easy for managers to acquire microcomputers without much headache, and offer innovative application solutions quickly and at low cost. They take a practical view of who is their constituency – their customers – and take care of them. They stay close to everyday operating problems. Most importantly, they care about motivating and the well-being of people who build and use their information systems.

CIOs who view themselves as the mandarins in charge of the correct information management processes instead of performance choose to avoid turmoil by lifting themselves above it. In their opinion, the proper role of the CIO is to shift from the oversight of the organization's technological infrastructure to following the shortest path that leads to the seat of power. Instead of managing information, the mandarin CIO would shape business strategy for the "information age."

Somewhere along the way, the process-oriented CIOs lost sight of their primary purpose which is the delivery of reliable and low cost information services. Driven by ambition and prompted by preaching visionaries, they have become infatuated with new roles in which they cannot succeed unless they can simultaneously sustain technical excellence for which they are already responsible.

This drifting away from the basics received encouragement from an increasing propensity to appoint executives with hardly any information services experience as CIOs. Whatever the cause, this leads the CIOs away from their primary mission. The process-oriented CIO will engage in enthusiastic bidding for leadership roles to promote whatever new idea becomes fashionable, such as total quality management, groupware, electronic commerce or multimedia.

CIOs in Charge of Reengineering

The current tendency of the process-oriented CIOs to take over the leadership of reengineering programs makes them extremely vulnerable in their relationship with their peers, on whose support they depend. Reengineering focuses on eliminating unnecessary management positions and reorganization of traditional functional roles. It has had a devastating effect on management morale, especially when this is done in an unthinking and insensitive manner to institute large-scale layoffs. The CIO who uses his position to become a contract mercenary will be remembered as a destructive and potentially alien agent.[210] Reengineering, if driven primarily by the CIO, will negate the capacity of the CIO to negotiate a governance covenant on how to manage information.

There is nothing wrong with a talented CIO gaining responsibility for an innovative program that will make him a leader among his peers. There is nothing wrong with a CIO becoming a COO or CEO. However, a review of actual promotions does not bear out that this occurs in real life. COO and CEO jobs almost always go to those individuals who have shown a steady record of earning revenues from customers or who have earned the trust of the Board of Directors as guardians of shareholder interests.

CIOs who have succumbed to the simplistic view that they should be strategists instead of tending to their shop usually decrease their probable job tenure expectancy to a half life of less than 15 months. The only ones who have gained from promoting ideas that extend the CIO's ambitions beyond realistic limits are consultants, who have been earning $25,000 for lectures and $500 per hour for "strategic consulting" in reorganizing the CIO function after the next failure.[211]

The position of CIO is not and cannot be a proximate stepping stone into the executive suite. The CIO will have to become an accepted operating executive of a major business before his peers will ever give him the political support so essential for such advancement. The time has come for the CIOs of this world to get back to basics and clean up their non-interoperable, redundant, obsolete, over-priced, error-prone, schedule-lagging and credibility-lacking systems. Whoever

---

210. *He who lives by the sword, dies by the sword.*
211. The topic of reengineering now earns up to $50,000 per speech. See *The Wall Street Journal,* May 19, 1994, p.1

can deliver the best systems will survive to compete for a job as an operating manager earning revenue from paying customers instead of living off the allocations of administrative overhead. The CIO who presides over a modern equivalent of a "constitutional convention," during which a viable balance between central coordination and local initiatives leads to harmony, will become the godfather of information governance.

Loss of Power

- A recent survey of 236 large companies revealed that nearly half of the top information technology posts are held by individuals with primarily business and not computer backgrounds.

- A recent survey showed that CIO turnover has increased for the sixth straight year.

- Over the past year, top technology positions were filled with people with business backgrounds twice as often as they were filled with people with computer backgrounds.

- A mere 5% of the 350 firms polled by the Institute of Management Accountants had their information systems groups reporting to a chief information officer.[212]

What you are witnessing is a trend that points to consequences we can now foresee. Corporations are in the process of giving up managing their computer technologies as a local cottage industry. The next round of modernization investments will be under the management of large commercial companies that can show a lower cost and lower risk in providing MIPS, kilopackets and gigabytes.

Regardless of aspirations to a different status, information systems managers are only brokers between the consumers of information products and the information technologies delivered by vendors. As infor-

---

212. These statistics are from an editorial in *Computerworld*, March 21, 1994, p.42

mation technologies become a commodity purchased from competing vendors, the capacity to make purchasing decisions shifts to the consumers. Expensive brokers will disappear under such conditions. They are disintermediated in the same way as small local retail establishments became displaced by supermarkets and superstores, leaving room only for specialized establishments.

Within the next twenty years, you will see over half of the information technology assets moving into the hands of commercially run service utilities. "Outsourcing" is just a name that masks a profound change in the way technology may support the majority of customers in the future. What you see is the end of the craft guild mode and the beginning of the industrialization of information processing. Corporations will be able to take their information technology budget out of overhead and make it a variable cost, just as labor and materials are now a cost of production. For that they will not need a CIO, but a chief technical officer who will assure enterprise-wide systems integration of information systems, because every executive will be a chief information management officer. In this way, CIOs will have succeeded beyond their dreams, though not exactly in the form they originally visualized.

27

CHARTER FOR THE CIO

Sound directions will make even mediocrity look better.

What should be the charter for a chief information officer? The following is a description that may make sense for large and autonomous multibusiness organizations:

A Functional Summary

The chief information officer (CIO) is the senior officer responsible for the development and administration of information management policies. This individual assists top management in formulating organization-wide information service goals and objectives, fosters a shared commitment to their fulfillment, and provides oversight to assure implementation.

Figure 27.1 A Map Is Useful Only If You Know Where You Are

Responsibilities also include developing and controlling an organization-wide information systems budget, strategic information services planning, information systems architecture, standards for data management, assurance of the interoperability of applications, and information security. To whom the CIO reports is less important than the effective support he receives in getting the missions accomplished.

There is a great deal of disagreement as to what are the appropriate roles for a CIO. At least one glossy monthly business magazine each month explores different ways to deal with this issue. The views featured in these magazines are ambivalent on whether the CIO's skills should be primarily technical or business related. The usual answer that they should be both is too simplistic, since it avoids the question of what are the tasks, organizational role, responsibilities and expected objectives of a CIO. Until one defines the rules of governance which in turn define the responsibilities of a CIO's peers and customers, no single answer is valid.

It is interesting to note how CIOs from very large firms view their roles. In a recent interview, one CIO asserted a narrowly technical point of view about the scope of his job: "My vision is for information systems to act as consultants in bringing technology to the table. This is becoming a reality as we outsource our mainframe and implement an RS/6000 with an Oracle server database." Another CIO was moving in the opposite direction, striving for as much detachment as possible: "I need to figure out how to get away from PC acquisition and PC installation, operations, and telephones. I want to get out of the standards game."[213] Whether or not these assertions were appropriate is not clear without knowing much more about the circumstances under which these officers operate.

Some readers of this book may wish to have a checklist of some of the tasks that may occupy a CIO of a major corporation.

---

213. Both quotes are from Susan Cohen, "The Client/Server CIO," *Forrester Research*, September, 1993

Duties and Authorities

- Establish overall strategies and policies for managing corporate information that increases shareholder value-added.

- Assist in the formulation of information management principles and ensure that there is a process in place to implement information strategies and policies comply with the business plan of the organization.

- Establish information security policies and standards for all information, including safeguards for protecting the accumulation and preservation of information.

- Define and manage the information system configuration management processes.

- Establish consultative committees and boards as necessary to implement the approved information principles.

- Oversee the development of the technical and managerial talent of all personnel engaged in managing and implementing of information systems, including training and educational advancement.

- Chair the information management policy board, composed of senior business managers who will provide guidance for the development of information standards and review information planning objectives.

- Establish budgetary procedures and assist in determining expenditure levels for carrying out information management activities. This budgetary procedure will require concurrence with all proposed expenditures on information management related activities.

- Establish periodic mission-focused reviews of the allocation of information resources within the organization. The CIO shall have access to all financial information regarding information resources to validate activity-based charges for all information services.

- Establish a records and data management program while ensuring compliance with legal requirements for maintaining records.

- Control funds necessary to encourage innovation and entrepreneurship. A significant percentage of the information systems development budget ought to be set aside for this purpose.

- Serve as a leader in promoting business process improvement methods in order to implement more effective information processes, whether computerized or not.

Principles for Guiding CIO Actions

- The principal task of the CIO shall be formulating and disseminating information policies for meeting business needs.

- The CIO shall ensure that processes and organizations are in place for information systems to adhere to approved networking, security, data definition and data compatibility standards in order to facilitate access to organization-wide networks and data.

- Local business managers will remain fully accountable for the financial benefits of their directly controllable information resources. They will also be responsible for the costs of developing and operating their information systems.

- Operating costs of information services shall be reported as transaction costs so that managers can gauge the total costs needed to accomplish their missions.[214]

- Information service costs shall be budgeted as integral to business costs.

- The costs of services shall be compared with fair market prices to identify potential cost savings.

- The CIO shall review all major investment proposals for information systems on the basis of risk-adjusted discounted cash flow methods that will apply over the entire life cycle of a program.[215]

- The CIO shall be expected to evaluate any proposed investments that rely exclusively on internal development. The best available commercial products shall be used whenever possible to achieve early benefits, reduce costs of development and allow for ease of replacement in the future.

- The CIO shall ensure that programs and procedures are in place to reduce or eliminate the vulnerability of communications networks and computers to dis-

---

214. I do not know of any organization where the captive customers do not vigorously express their desire to control their information technology costs. In reality, billing practices for data center services show that only about half of the internal customers actually pay for most of the services they receive:

Billed to Customers	Companies Surveyed
100%	34.9
80% to 99%	11.1
60% to 79%	3.2
40% to 59%	6.3
20% to 39%	3.2
1% to 19%	7.9
No charges	33.4
Total	100.0

Source: 1992 *DP Budget Yearbook*, Computer Economics, Inc. , Carlsbad, CA.

215. Cash flow analysis does not distinguish between capital and expenses. It only recognizes benefits that show up as gains in cash. Discounted cash flow places higher value on cash today than on cash tomorrow. Risk adjustment reveals not only the expected payoff, but also the worst as well as the best potential outcomes.

ruption and damage. Risk analysis and contingency plans shall be developed for rapid recovery of essential services in the event of a disaster. Insurance costs based on replacement value shall be used to establish the risk-adjusted justification for investments in safeguarding information assets.

- The ability to store and retrieve data quickly, accurately and comprehensively shall be an essential requirement for all applications in fulfilling their mission to provide superior customer service. The CIO shall be the advocate in favor of providing customer contact personnel with the capability to make complex inquiries, generate local applications, and construct experimental systems solutions.

- All data that is transported beyond the local area network shall be considered part of the enterprise level assets. Accountability for the custody of data shall be delegated by the CIO to a designated functional executive, who will control data standardization, data format certification and access to the data repositories.

- The CIO shall oversee continual improvements of the organization's business systems to better serve newly emerging needs. Advantage must be taken of the benefits of information technology's rapidly lowering unit costs.

- Prior to any systems development or enhancement of existing systems, changes in business practices shall be evaluated and approved by operating management. The CIO shall not assume responsibility for business process redesign. Only operating managers with direct responsibility for costs and benefits shall act in that role.

- The CIO shall be the advocate for evolutionary introduction of information technologies. Rapid incremental deployment shall be the preferred method.

- The CIO shall establish yearly productivity objectives that are verifiable and measurable for system services and report to corporate management on their progress.
- The CIO shall be solely responsible for engaging independent sources of benchmarking data which compare the company's results against the best industry practices.
- Common business practices shall be promoted and implemented across similar decentralized units. Standard industry software shall be adopted unless unique conditions are established, documented and approved by the CIO.
- A corporate-wide information infrastructure shall allow all personnel to rapidly and readily communicate electronically with each other and facilitate the ready availability of data regardless of geographic location or organizational authority.[216] The infrastructure shall be managed centrally, but preferably not under the immediate direction of the CIO, except in smaller organizations.

Ownership of Infrastructure Assets
One of the most persistent controversies about the powers of the CIO concerns his direct control of infrastructure operations, such as data centers, programming staffs and network control operations. There are no standard answers because they will largely depend on the size of the organization. In a small business unit, you cannot justify paying for

---

216. Infrastructure is defined as the worldwide telecommunications network, data centers, services and applications of common concern (e.g. electronic mail and media processing, including audio, graphics, data and video). The infrastructure includes the corporate-wide information systems architecture, policies and standards for the development of all commonly shared software and systems engineering tools.

expensive talent unless you enlarge the job to include both the staff and operating responsibilities under the same person.

Viewing the CIO as an expert whose skills are too narrow to qualify for any other job in the organization could be a mistake. I view the position of the CIO as one of the best executive development and training opportunities for diversifying the skills of high-potential general executives. If layered "governance" is already in place, it becomes much easier to appoint to the CIO post someone who will rotate out of that position after three to four years to further career advancement within the firm.[217] Under such an arrangement, the CIO should be supported by a very senior and long-term tenure Chief Technical Officer.

Should the CIO own corporate information technology assets, especially data centers and communication networks? There are conditions where such ownership would inhibit the CIO from operating as a policy setter and arbitrator of disputes. He would always be suspected of having a bias that favors what he is managing.

If outsourcing technical services is even a remote possibility, it would be prudent to assign management of central infrastructure services to some other executive. I favor moving corporate data center operations and central programming pools to a separate "utility" organization that could report to an operating unit where the operation of information systems is already an established business function. If the operation is sufficiently large, it could be run as a separate business unit. Oversight of internal pricing, budgets and project priorities would place the CIO in an uncomfortable position in the event that his decision would enlarge the scope of his operations. You cannot be judge, jury and defendant at the same time.

---

217. Making the CIO's job a political appointment, as is presently under consideration in Washington, D.C., demonstrates a misunderstanding of the role of this position. The role of the CIO should be focused on internal excellence, which involves a thorough understanding of how an agency functions. If governance is in place, that CIO role is best filled from the career Senior Executive Service. You will not be able to recruit and retain information management talent into government if the top job is only a transient appointment of the politically faithful.

Is the CIO Like a CFO?

The title "CIO" first emerged in the late 1970s. Prior to that, those who managed large information systems complexes carried the simple titles of Directors or Vice Presidents of Information Systems. The CIO title was an attempt by those who had just become liberated from the finance organization to seek parity with the Chief Financial Officer, the CFO. By analogy, information was everywhere, just like money, and therefore the CIO could claim comparable status to someone who presided over accounting and finance. This sort of thinking diverted an entire generation of systems executives into an unrealistic search for status and a position on the board of directors.

CIOs are not like CFOs, despite the similarity of the acronym that implies similar status. The CFO has a fiduciary responsibility not only to the chief executive, but also to the shareholders and the public for maintaining proper records of assets and liabilities. The work of the CFO must be certified for integrity by an independent auditor. For this reason, the CFO must exercise tight control over accounting and finance operations, including direct control over the appointment and qualification of all finance and accounting personnel. Managers can obtain accounting and finance information from only one source. The CFO controls and manages an incontestable 100% monopoly. There is nobody who can challenge that except an outside authority, and even then with great difficulty.

None of the above applies to the CIO. There is no fiduciary responsibility, no absolute control over information management and certainly no monopoly over the means or uses of information. Whatever monopoly power the CIO ever enjoyed in controlling computer technology no longer exists. The evolving role of the CIO is more like that of the chief personnel executive. Managing people is every manager's job in the same way as information management is every manager's inescapable responsibility. The personnel function is a policy, quality and long range guidance function that employs a relatively small number of specialists performing critical tasks such as recruiting, training, compensation planning, pensions, medical affairs and career development.

The typical personnel department exercises policy control over approximately eighty percent of the value added of any enterprise. They spend less than one percent of the overall budget to manage that function, with all other expenses under the direct control of operating managers.

If information management, by rules of governance, is vested entirely in the hands of operating managers, the typical information systems department will exercise policy control over approximately five percent of the value added of any enterprise. With ninety percent of that amount becoming a readily purchased commodity, the power base of the CIO is not only small and shrinking, but insufficient to sustain the overly ambitious hopes of recent years.

None of the above discussion is intended to deflate the critical importance of information management, information systems and information technologies as a catalyst for achieving competitive advantages. The importance of body part does not depend on their weight. The failure of any one of them can cause disability or death. A healthy body is the result of a balanced interaction in which every part performs well. I wish to place exaggerated CIO claims into a proper perspective to make sure this critical organ does not become the source of an unbalanced and possibly cancerous growth.

Managing

The task of managing includes examining a company's power structure and evaluating how well information policies line up with actions by top management. The alignment of information policy with corporate politics is one of the ways to assure a company's prosperity. In the absence of an alignment among actions and policies, the organization will suffer from the corporate equivalent of mental disorders such as schizophrenia. When that happens, most of the energies of management are absorbed by internal negotiation instead of paying attention to external reality. Here is an example of contradiction between policy and reality:

The new chairman of one of the largest banks in the world promoted a vision to provide uniform nationwide banking services, regardless of geographic location. While the chairman enjoyed the widespread publicity given to his pronouncements, the bank continued to give most discretionary decision-making powers to branch managers. This included control of adapting basic business processes to fit local conditions. Operating management also encouraged the geographic regions and the global product business units to build unique marketing, financial, credit, personnel and product management capabilities. Each region and business unit was investing in separate and unique computer applications.

While the chairman was talking about universal service, his new CIO was busily constructing, at an enormous expense, an all-inclusive centralized database intended to drive new and completely uniform applications. These applications would rapidly replace all local systems already in place. What the center was planning as well as implementing and what the operating units were doing was inconsistent. Such organization schizophrenia could not continue for long.

When profits took a precipitous dive for five quarters in a row, not because of excess computer costs but because of bad loans, the new CIO left several days after the chairman's resignation. The new management, looking for ways to fix the damage, authorized enormous cuts in the information technology budget.[218] That had great emotional appeal to managers and employees, who readily identified the computer people and not the loan officers as the cause of the losses.

The moral of this story is that information technology can make a useful contribution only if it is compatible with the way a company operates, rather than how it matches the chairman's public relations campaign.

Claims

Whenever you wish the public to find out about your company's computer accomplishments, have your paying customers boast about them. If they prefer to remain quiet, let them demonstrate your organization's

---

218. This inflicted permanent damage to the bank's competitive position. The ultimate cost of rebuilding a competitive information processing capacity was much greater than the budget cuts. The delays cost even more in terms of loss of market share.

excellence by granting your company a superior market share as well as exceptional profitability. Excellence in information management is an achievement that can be endorsed only by satisfied customers in the form of market share and premium prices, not by publicity or experts who judge your reputation by what they read in magazines.

It is good politics, in commercial competition, to disguise the sources of your competitive advantage. Corporate boasting reduces the competitor's expense for intelligence-gathering, attracts imitators and makes the corporation a preferred target for talent raids. This advice does not apply to systems development in government, to consultants and to corporate employees, where precisely the opposite tactics offer the greatest gains.

Unless you have a unique computer solution that would be of interest to readers of a technical publication, what is really worth talking about to the general public is implementation that paying customers recognize as value-added. What matters in your resume is only what you have actually done to increase the economic value-added of the organization.

Political Astuteness

Always make sure that your top management's decisions endorse every major change in information management practices. Here is a case of why this is important:

Branch managers used to have large administrative staffs for order entry, credit checking, expediting of shipments, billing adjustments and handling of customer complaints. To save costs, top management ordered the consolidation of the administrative staffs into ten regional centers. What used to receive local resolution by informal means now required elaborate computer applications. The computer budget increased three-fold to pay for reprogramming all of the major applications and to set up ten regional processing centers.

While the new applications were still under development, the regional consolidations of administrative personnel took place in a hurry, without adequate training or systems support. Customer complaints instantly soared and billing writeoffs increased. The marketing organization reacted to this disorder by giving sales people additional administrative duties to do work previously performed by local clerical personnel.

When sales productivity plummeted and sales personnel turnover skyrocketed, top management approved hiring additional personnel to handle work that never left the branches. They also authorized purchases of minicomputers to support local paperwork. This was opposed by the systems people as bypassing the approved corporate systems architecture and counter to the regionalization program.

For a period of two years, the systems organization continued working on the regional systems that would be run from computers under their control. The money came from the regional budget and therefore they built the system according to the wishes of the regional administrators. When the regional consolidation project terminated precipitously and top management announced they favored decentralization back to the branches, the systems department was severely criticized for its inability to adapt to changing conditions. The CIO was dismissed.

For a period of two years it was apparent that regional consolidation would not proceed as originally planned. The systems department should not have been blind to that. It should have stayed close to all customers, not only to the regional bureaucracy that favored centralized systems management.

Technology Adventurism

Do not indulge in self-initiated sorties into hostile political arenas using brand new technology as an enticement. You can never crawl out of a policy swamp by continuing to promise spectacular technological gains. Even if you happen to succeed technically against considerable odds, you will fail politically and will never get anything accepted. Small unit parachute drops behind enemy lines, well in advance of an organized full campaign, have high odds of being wiped out.

During the 1960s and 1970s, it was perfectly acceptable for computer people to use the most recent information technology as a means for personal advancement. After failing, these explorers could realistically hope to be rehired by another firm that was glad to capitalize on their competitors' mistakes. The new employer also got the advantage of a competitor paying for the training of new staff members. That approach no longer works. We are living in a different era. Now when you fail in a major post as a senior information executive, you remain a failure.

Technology adventures pay only if they receive top management's prior endorsement that initial losses will be acceptable as a learning investment in how to use unproved technologies.

Building Support

Minimize cultural risks. Good politics involves not damaging the organization that surrounds you. You serve the organization of which you are a part. Organizations have a culture, and you cannot go against that culture without consequences that will haunt you. You cannot use information technology to counteract the mental set of the people who will have to live with it. You can influence it somewhat, but you cannot overcome it. The surest way to successfully reform an organization is to build constructive innovations on top of the best that already exist.

I learned that resolving technical questions is a matter of much lower priority than the need to settle who decides, who controls, and who has the power of the purse. Two recent runaway projects will illustrate what can happen when the drive to implement sound technological plans becomes alienated from the objectives of its sponsors.

In 1982, a consortium of banks led by Bank of America started a leading-edge system for trust reporting. Two years later, after generating more than 3.5 million lines of code, the project was not implemented because it ceased to reflect rapidly changing operating needs. Despite every indication that the project would be a failure, it continued. In 1988, only when the actual expenditures became a large multiple of the original budget, the banks abandoned the project. The most anybody is willing to admit is that an $80 million investment is not worth anything.[219]

---

219. P.G. Neumann, R. Hoffman, "Risks to the Public in Computers and Related Systems: Details of BofA's Costly Computer Foul-up," *Software Engineering Notes*, Vol..13, No.2, 1988, pp.6-7

The Bank of America case is not an isolated incident. There are others like that, except they do not get reported because there is no advantage for anyone to admit failure except in situations where the press finds out about it. In my judgment, the failure in this case was not technical but political, because the stakeholders in the project could never agree either on the scope or the schedule for this ambitious effort.

Political failure can happen even to an organization that boasts of its technological prowess, and to executives who have earned international prominence as leaders in information management. The next case involves the collapse of a widely promoted information system conceived and managed by AMR Information Systems (AMRIS).

In 1988, AMRIS began developing a technologically advanced reservation system that would integrate airline, car rental and hotel information. The $125 million project, known as *Confirm*, was to be a joint effort with substantial funding supplied by partners Hilton, Marriott, and Budget Rent-A-Car. Immediately after the project started with great fanfare, a host of problems began to emerge involving project management disputes that manifested themselves as technical problems. Instead of halting development to resolve the conflicting priorities of the partners, the project continued its costly effort. In 1992, the project came to a halt because of irreconcilable political differences among the partners. This friction resulted in an escalation of costs, which gave the minority partners a good excuse for abandoning the joint effort. AMRIS is currently suing its partners over the failed venture, claiming they withheld funds and failed to complete specifications. Marriott is seeking $64 million in damages, claiming that project managers from the American Airlines concealed problems.[220]

The failure of the *Confirm* project is a classic example in which the compulsion to make advances in computer technology gets ahead of the realities of sponsor relationships. The lesson here is that every major computer project should get the attention of a trusted senior executive who is not the project's sponsor, who acts as the project manager's men-

---

220. J.P. McPartlin, "The Collapse of Confirm," *InformationWeek*, October 19, 1992, pp.12-19

tor, helps in overcoming political problems, and kills it if unresolved differences persist for too long.

Governance Before Action

Information technology is now so pervasive that it is starting to influence the lines of authority that traditionally follow the vertical flow of information from the top to the bottom of the hierarchy. In the new reality rapid and low cost coordination allows information to move horizontally. Information processes are common across hierarchical layers regardless of how the organization chart happens to look at any particular moment.

Until you resolve the inherent conflicts between the "operators," who require unambiguous vertical authority, and the "functionals," who try to impose coordination and unity horizontally across disparate organizational units, you will be placing information technology smack in the middle of an intraorganizational brawl. This is why a balanced concept of operations must be accepted before you can ever hope to implant a computer system into the body of an organization that will not reject it.

28

INNOVATION

A little rebellion now and then is a good thing
/Thomas Jefferson, 1787/.

Every organization, regardless of how inept, has somewhere within itself a source of excellence. Every organization nurtures a few isolated pockets of homegrown excellence. They are usually found where the central bureaucracy does not reach easily. For instance, in the U.S. Department of Defense, I discovered such a pocket in Central Alaska, where I found a fount of imaginative system innovations.

Home Grown Innovation

A skillful executive will nurture those seeds of excellence, because they are a genuine source of future success. They are precious because they flourish despite many obstacles. The rogue system that everybody loves but which does not get official endorsement demonstrates that excellence, as rare as it may be, can grow from a minuscule budget if you have a few talented and persistent innovators.

Continually pump modest funds into supporting small-scale home-grown initiatives. Do not try to import all major new technology developments from outside of your organization. Do not depend on consultants as the primary source of your innovation. If you outsource all imagination, you will find that there is nobody left in your organization to manage the absorption of technological advances when they are finally ready for operational use.

Let the Professionals Manage

Let go of the compulsion to have your own computers do everything your company needs. Computer executives still cling to an obsession with control that goes back to the era when possession of computer hardware really mattered. Once upon a time, ownership of a glass-enclosed computer room was a potent symbol of power. Tending a computing center is no longer synonymous with control over "information." Centrally managed computing utilities don't have much say about the transactions that pass through their data processing machines. Computing networks now are available for rent, where you can acquire all the computing services your organization will ever need. Somebody always will be ready to sell you all the MIPS (million instructions per second) you want at the end of a communications pipe, provided that you are ready to accept that as a matter of policy rather than expediency.

Control Only What Matters

Today, in many centralized organizations, I see computer executives obsessively making sure that every personal computer expenditure in excess of $999 receives up to six signatures for approval.[221] This is an obsolete way of looking at the environment.

The central assets of an enterprise that matter are policy, organization, software, personal intelligence, training and data. Who owns the computers is becoming increasingly irrelevant, provided this occurs by choice and not by casual improvisation. There is no longer a political gain for a computer executive to seize computing centers as a power base. Control of computing centers makes sense only if they are technologically obsolete and if they are fat with excess costs. If that is the case, data center consolidation, downsizing and modernization justify seizing computing centers to generate cash savings for more productive reinvestment. Several times in my career, I have taken over computing

---

221. There are mail order houses specializing in selling computers as assemble-it-yourself components to the agencies of the Department of Defense. When you examine their catalogue you will find no item priced over $999.

centers as the "cash cow" to finance badly needed improvements that otherwise had no funding.

If you do not have the managerial capabilities or the up-front investment resources to manage your own consolidation program, you can always find an experienced computer services company ready to take over. Arguments against letting others manage your confidential applications are no longer valid, though I would always worry about the security aspects. For example, Inland Revenue, the British government's tax collection agency, recently signed a twenty-year $1.5 billion deal with Electronic Data Systems. This involves the transfer of approximately 1,500 data center employees from the British Civil Service, consolidation of most of the thirteen data centers and the sale of the mainframes. EDS is then free to process British taxpayer data on any computer it chooses.[222] The chances are that a contractor may end up protecting data processing sites far better than the original custodians, especially if there are penalties for lapses in security.

Direct physical control of mainframe, mini and microcomputer budgets no longer holds the key to unlocking the business value of computers. Control is useful only if it makes demonstrable economic sense. Don't reach for it as a way of accumulating assets to aggrandize your influence.

Take Unoccupied Territories First

Make sure you retain the freedom to manage the introduction of major innovations. It is better strategy to fill unoccupied territory than to break down fortress walls. Attacking an existing bastion surrounded by bureaucratic procedures that has its budget protected and depends on hard to maintain software for its exclusivity, is usually an invitation for a newcomer to commit technological suicide. First, try to do what has not been done before. Many of the winners in information management distinguish themselves by doing the unusual and filling vacuums. Remember the first principle of all maneuver warfare is to land forces

---

222. See Bruce Caldwell, "EDS Provides Tax Relief," *InformationWeek*, November 29, 1993.

where they can score a big success prior to moving out after the main objective that may be harder to crack.

Figure 28.1 Innovation is Not Always the Most Timely Answer

Alliances and Benefits

Give to everyone a stake in accepting the policies you are advocating. Making an alliance with you should be easy. It should not involve additional costs or political penalties. For example, if adopting of standard data definitions calls for a costly conversion that a small unit cannot afford, it is good information politics to subsidize the cost from a central fund, provided that it will also benefit others.

Successful systems implementation should never be publicized as being exclusively an information technology accomplishment. The business value of computers is in their use, not in the technology itself. People who apply the application are the ones who earn any gains. Technologists may only claim they found a way to get the job done fast and economically. All output belongs to the customer. Information technology is just a clever way to reduce costs.

Innovation Is Experimentation

Always remember that the single largest cost element of any information system is not hardware or software, but the "brainware" of the people using the systems. People learn only by adding new information to what is already familiar. Every individual's experience with new uses of computers is unique. It cannot be a standard classroom exercise, unless you are willing to indulge in much wasted time. Like children, adults learn by experimentation. What finally secured popular acceptance of microcomputers was the spreadsheet. It offered to every person the opportunity to learn incrementally, by allowing them to continually revise and upgrade their understanding of relationships between rows and columns of calculations.

Figure 28.2 Innovations is Experimentation

It is politically imprudent to present to your management detailed plans as to how and precisely when a major new application will become fully operational. That will depend to a large extent on the learning ease and acceptance of the new application in the workplace. The best you can do is to promise that your initial delivery of systems will be so overwhelmingly successful that the customers will beg you to give them additional capabilities. The next best thing is to offer an estimate of the expected ranges of expenditures and schedules, where exceeding the pessimistic estimate will be recognized as failure.

Entrepreneurship

A CIO should have some venture capital available for exploiting high risk and high payoff opportunities. It is the characteristic of a good multiple venture portfolio that you can afford a ninety percent failure rate and still come out ahead with enormous gains on the one or two projects that deliver well beyond initial expectations. It has always been my policy to spend up to five percent of my information management budget, depending on affordability, on innovations that have the potential of great leaps in performance.

Small venture investments should not require elaborate justification, except for risk analysis that would establish how much you can afford to lose before you cut the venture off. Once the venture is on its way, you also must perform risk analysis to find out how much more money you may have to spend to deliver an enormous success. Venture investments should be diversified, placing wagers on more than ten projects to make the odds work for you. All venture funding should be given in small increments so that it does not subsidize failure.

Entrepreneurs

Your most talented people should be encouraged to take on venture projects. Rotating your most promising talent into ventures should become a way to develop your future leaders. For this reason, individual failure should not be penalized as long as everyone has been honest about what happened and costs do not overrun original commitments. What matters most, however, is what your people will learn. All great advances, whether they were in steam engines, pharmaceuticals, xerography or rocketry, began as failures converted into success by applying what was learned from mistakes.

Should you disown your failures and then let some other organization benefit from what you should have learned? The better way is to leverage the lessons learned to get ahead faster than the others. Failure can be considered either a total write-off or a down payment for doing better next time. How you handle failure also will influence the ethical behavior adopted by your people. Executives who cover up bad news can expect their subordinates to act in the same way.

Funding Innovation

Every information systems organization should have some funds set aside for exploration and innovation. Some of the best new applications come from imaginative people who do not fit readily into the established computing order. Instead of restraining them, give them some money because they don't need much. Often these software artists use resources borrowed from otherwise unproductive sources. Inspired in-house entrepreneurs are the cheapest resource for innovation you can get.

Unless you are in the computer business, you should not do original software research and development. The exploratory development projects should cover only experimentation with innovative commercial applications. These are now appearing in great profusion due to the enormous creativity readily available as result of the low cost of entry into the software business.

For exploratory projects seek out bright, irreverent people and treat them with affection and respect. In due course, the successful ones will become responsible adults, good managers, vote conservatively and become pillars of the establishment.

Diversifying Innovation

Keep your experimentation outside of the big central organizations that are sufficiently busy keeping the old systems going and therefore cannot give appropriate attention to innovation. They usually waste whatever resources you give them for modernization and rarely admit to fallibility. To prevent your main body of technologists from becoming obsolete, frequently rotate them into small leading-edge pilot projects. When there is enough evidence that experiments have succeeded, you can move the pilots back into the main stream.

Figure 28.3 Innovation Needs Incentives

Pilot programs are also ideal for taking advantage of the enormous talent that is now readily available from consultants. The computer services market is filled with small and highly focused consulting firms who offer an enormous accumulation of specialized expertise. They can be engaged with a relatively minimum amount of time spent on proposals, contracts and administrative reviews. It is good business for an organization to maintain relationships with a wide circle of experts in every conceivable computing discipline. The availability of display-sharing electronic communications makes it advantageous to set up long-term relationships with dozens of the top specialists. Specialists in small consulting firms are available on an hourly basis, without the time consuming expenses of travel and at low rates because their overhead is minimal.[223] The judgment of a seasoned professional in a few minutes can save you months of wasted effort from an enthusiastic but amateur staff.

The politics of running an internal venture portfolio requires complete and candid disclosure of the status of the projects to top management, and to whoever funds them. Under no circumstances should you attempt to burden your overhead with experiments that could fail. Risky explorations should be funded out of profits or by an appropriation from a corporate research and development fund, not by what customers perceive as taxation to pay for the technologists' mistakes. It is also good politics to keep everyone informed about the progress of the experiments. If they are expensive and remain hidden for too long somebody will surely pick up a scandalous example as a pretext for engineering a takeover.

A *coup d'etat* based on exposing isolated cases of failure to innovate is deeply destructive of employee morale. It may permanently injure the capacity of the organization to adapt to rapidly changing conditions.

Suppression and Stimulation

Successful information management depends on trust and the willingness of employees to initiate improvements in how information systems are put into effect. Of all of the explanations I have read so far about the loss of IBM's position of leadership, the one that is most plausible describes how IBM's corporate management isolated itself from the marketplace by intimidating its own loyal innovators.

Government agencies and the military are replete with stories of organizational paralysis induced by short-term appointees who dictate their own agenda without consulting people with a great deal of experience. Political heads can wield their power to drive out everyone but the most compliant followers. It takes much less time to poison a well than to make it safe for drinking afterwards. Similarly, it takes a long time before people in an organization trust and confide in a new exec-

---

223. The overhead expenses for large consulting firms exceed 200%.

utive to receive suggestions for improvements that are essential for his success.

It is one of the primary responsibilities of the CIO to see to it that the spirit of experimentation and innovation remains strong, while nurturing it under controlled conditions. A flame can serve as a pilot light or it can burn down a house. It is an act of sublime managerial skill to sustain the spirit of permanent and low cost innovations.

29

SURVIVAL

Every long-term plan starts with today's actions.

I have by now coached a sufficient number of newly appointed CIOs to suggest an approach that some of them may find useful in most business situations. Because of the high turnover rates, a new CIO normally comes into power not through peaceful succession but through a management-initiated overthrow. The chances are that the prior CIO failed because top management was never clear about the roles of the information managers. The chances are that there are no rules of governance except for some perfunctory procedures about required approval signatures. Most likely, the new CIO is inheriting a territory without much order.

During the first day on the job, the new CIO will meet his peers, most of whom have been occupying key positions for decades. They are the ones who helped getting rid of the predecessor and are likely to do the same again unless the new CIO figures out how to change the rules for managing information. If the CIO sticks with the status quo, his fate is predictable and his demise is only a matter of how long it will take.

The fate of most contemporary CIOs reminds me of the gunslingers hired by desperate citizens to bring law and order into the Northwestern Territories. Hardly any of them died of old age. None of them lived long enough to retire from the job. If the newly appointed sheriffs were lucky enough to live at a time when statehood would soon arrive and if they survived enough gunfights, they ended up as good mayors. The introduction of constitutional law made all the difference in their life expectancy.

Similarly, very few CIOs retire these days from that position unless they get enough time to help their organizations put into place generally accepted rules of governance. First, however, they have to survive the first fifteen months.[224]

Figure 29.1 CIO Succession Planning

All Short-Term Decisions Become Long-Term

If a CIO aspires to longevity in his job, or even better, to an eventual promotion into a revenue-generating executive position, he will have to understand that he is initially judged only on his short-term accomplishments. However, all short-term ventures become long-term commitments. If the CIO survives the initial trials, his subsequent

---

224. Fifteen months is the statistical half-life of recently appointed CIOs.

recognition will primarily depend on what he does to enhance the long-term viability of information management to support business plans. The capacity to cope with immediate emergencies already will be taken for granted. Therefore, the CIO cannot wait. Even during the initial probation period, he must start setting the stage for moves that would pay off in two to three years.

The investments into programs that align information systems with the business plan take precedence over all other actions. However, the CIO also must see to it that the technology base of the organization is sound and efficient. In choosing opportunities for long-term infrastructure investments, my first choice is to concentrate on acquiring the capacity to produce and maintain software at substantially lower costs than was the case under the previous CIO. My second choice would be to modernize the telecommunications infrastructure to deliver unit costs of perhaps one tenth of what the organization currently pays.

There are immediate savings to be gained by reviewing the economics of entrenched institutions, such as local data centers. By all means extract from them all the available cost reductions. However, the fundamental economics of data center operations ultimately depends on the choice of software systems, on ensuring the acceptance of systems engineering methods and on selecting network capabilities to cope with the proliferation of local area networks, leased lines, cellular phones, facsimile machines, answering devices, servers, gateways and routers.

Chances are the new CIO's predecessor did not pay attention to what initially needs little cash, but enormous amounts of talent and long lead times to get anything accomplished. With new software and telecommunications technology breakthroughs, the new CIO should search out investment opportunities where nobody in the company has ventured before.

Remember, the greatest long-term opportunities are in exploiting innovations that fundamentally alter the economics of information processing. Creating conditions for the introduction of such major innovations is where the CIO must make a mark in due course. Executives do not get much credit for bailing water out of a leaking boat, although if they fail in that they will drown with the crew. The hero is the one who bails just long enough to get everyone aboard a safe ship. Here are a few practical suggestions:

Establish Credibility[225]
Within the first three to six months, the new CIO should:

- Initiate a process for shrinking the overhead costs of the existing organization. Do this by reassigning personnel to value-creating projects that involve delivering services to paying customers. If that does not generate sufficient improvements, divest personnel and assets to decentralized business units that need to improve their information systems to remain competitive. If that still does not cut overhead sufficiently, transfer the remaining central assets to commercial organizations that are good in converting somebody's fixed overhead to their own variable revenue. Currently, everybody calls that old trick by a new name: outsourcing.

- Identify high potential information systems executive and managerial personnel in your company and launch a program to deploy them wherever they can best support your efforts. The message will quickly get around that good talent has a future with the new CIO.

- As much as possible, avoid bringing in old cronies from the former place of employment. That destroys morale and tags the new CIO as an alien who does not associate readily with the natives. If cronyism is excessive, the new management team will get a suitable epithet, such as the *Mafia*.

- Resist the temptation to have recruiters raid other companies for executive talent to fill most of the key

---

225. A 3-6 month Plan for action.

positions. Talent raids are extremely costly. They wreck the compensation structure and alienate the majority of the people on whose support the new CIO depends to survive. Besides, nobody ever performs as well as presented in the resume or during the interviews. Many of your own people have resumes as good looking as the ones your recruiters are passing on for serious consideration.

- Avoid belittling the capabilities of the people the company already has on payroll. One can learn much more about their faults than about the people one considers to recruit. People previously considered as below average can perform superbly if the morale is high and the leadership is good. Therefore, the new CIO must re-energize people who had the reputation as under-performers and make them into heroes.

- Appoint people from the existing resource pool, even if that means taking the risk to jump a few exceptional people one or two ranks up. In this way, the CIO will gain the loyalty and knowledge of those who know the layout of the minefields. The newly promoted crew will have an interest in assuring survival by warning the new CIO before he steps on an unlatched trap door.

- Launch at least three major programs with immediate payoffs, regardless of how small. Management does not expect too much, at least initially. They have greater interest in the new CIO not fouling things up, instead of scoring remarkable gains. Even better, complete something that had been in limbo while waiting for the new CIO to show up.

- Draft policies and guidelines that define the principles for the conduct of the information systems practice. Make sure top corporate management signs off on an early draft of a "constitution," and especially on the budget authority. The peers of the new CIO will judge him by how quickly he seized control of the purse strings.

Solve Critical Problems[226]

Within the first six to fifteen months, the new CIO should:

- Select about three applications that depress current earnings projections, or, in the case of a public agency, represent a major liability and which you can turn into an asset. Put into place tightly managed remedial programs that will demonstrate the capacity of the new team to solve a small number of generally recognized difficult problems.

- Get top management to commit unqualified support and adequate funds for the priority programs, especially if they require unswerving determination to get them done. Do not start programs that lack total support from top management. Make sure that top management reviews progress frequently. If there is an unfavorable development, the new CIO should be the first one to bring it to top management's attention.

- Use the next business planning cycle to identify high potential cost reduction opportunities, including migration to systems that meet immediate competitive needs.

- Put in place a program for recognizing hidden examples of systems excellence, regardless of where they come from or if they follow approved procedures. After validating the potential value of such examples, provide the initiators with material rewards and publicity. Provide ample funds for such home-grown initiatives so that they become accepted for general use.

---

226. A 6-15 month Plan for action.

- Form alliances with the corporate planners, and with the financial budget and analysis organizations. Usually they accurately reflect the top management concerns and biases about the level of expenditures for computers, and the alignment of information systems investments with business plans.

- Add a seasoned financial comptroller to the CIO staff, who will protect the systems budget and make sure that the numbers presented to top management are consistent with what the financial organization is reporting. Finance can undermine the credibility of any executive, any time they wish to do so.

- Form a close alliance with the chief auditor. Transfer systems analysis personnel to the audit organization to increase their technical competence in performing audits on compliance with corporate information policies. The new CIO must obtain cooperation and support from systems managers who report to divisional or agency executives. Therefore, the CIO staff must not check on the veracity of claims by people who work for others. A strong and independent systems audit organization can be a valuable resource for balancing cooperative and supportive roles with the need to safeguard corporate interests, information integrity and information security.

- Bring together individuals with extensive experience within the company, from diverse specialties and with different levels of authority, for frequent "focus group" sessions. The purpose of such meetings would be to identify threats and opportunities to the information management function. Be discreet in making use of sensitive disclosures, and be readily accessible to those who claim that they have discovered a potential system disaster for which the new CIO will now be responsible.

- Start consolidating redundant applications and data-bases in functions that are already organized around a corporate-wide "horizontal integration" process, such as finance, personnel and logistics.

- Assert technology leadership in data administration, software reuse and systems engineering. It is very important that technical personnel identify the new CIO as someone who has a competent and independent understanding of the risks inherent in all systems related decisions. Demonstrate the new regime will take technical advice from any competent source, regardless of where it may be in the organization.

- Create one or more centers of technical excellence that will become the conduit for innovation and modernization. Give high visibility and provide frequent recognition to individuals who make a contribution to advancing excellence. Specially reward and acknowledge the contributions of individuals who have persisted in the face of opposition and ultimately were proven to be correct.

- Appoint an experienced personnel executive to the CIO staff to guide a comprehensive resource assessment effort and manage the training and professional development efforts.

- Deliver a standard business process improvement methodology for use in all future systems development projects.

CIO Prospects

I hope that some of the new CIOs in the next decade will have the benefit of walking into a job that is well understood, constitutionally defined and has a due governance process already in place. The rules of governance would make it possible to concentrate on building up systems capabilities instead of devoting energy to quelling internal disputes.

Would I change anything in the survival checklist for these CIOs? If I had a choice, I would start investing in the long-term ventures much sooner and with greater determination than was possible in the past, because many technologies and services will be more readily available in the future. Truly large gains from management information systems usually take a decade to gestate before superior returns can be realized. The ability to extract enormous gains does not come from rapid progress in computer technologies. The pace of change is slowed down by hesitation, when uncertain managers push reluctant people to accept new ways of working. What often slows down progress in information management is not only intra-organizational conflict, but also the lack of trust by employees that computerization will increase their value and enhance their careers.

Chief executive officers of corporations who hire CIOs as if they were mercenaries will get exactly what they have bargained for. They will get quick action and temporary improvements at the price of an exodus of home grown talent and the demoralization of local occupants. There are now itinerant, "gun-for-hire" CIOs. They leave their posts to become temporary executives, who travel from organization to organization, staying only long enough to put a new system in place, manage a specific project or revamp the systems department.[227]

Creating information management capabilities for a 21st century enterprise has many of the characteristics of nation-building. It requires long-term political commitments to preserving common bonds, strengthening shared beliefs, relying on negotiated agreements, having the assurance of a due process in all disputes, safeguarding the rights of individuals and keeping faith in long-term rewards. You do not get these in frontier settlements where the occupants never stay long enough to build a community, and where safety, law and order may rest only with hired guns.

---

227. The idea of a CIO as a mercenary is no longer unthinkable. Melanie Menagh concludes that "...many companies no longer feel the need for a permanent chief information officer; and many CIOs are longing for challenging work with a minimum of political hassles. Temporary CIOs can be a win-win solution."(*CIO for Hire*, Computerworld, June 6, 1994, p.83). I vehemently disagree with this point of view. You do not rent a wife to raise a stable family.

PART IV

RECOLLECTIONS

There are more useful lessons in understanding mistakes than in analyzing successes.

30

INDUSTRY

*Listen to your enemies. They are the only ones who
will tell you everything you did wrong.*

General Foods

My joys and disappointments as a chief corporate computer executive
varied according to the environment in which I served. My first corporate information executive job with a large and complex organization
was with General Foods in 1961. It involved managing the classic battle
between corporate centralization and divisional ownership of computer
centers. At that time, the divisions were going to buy fifty mainframe
computers and run them as separate operations for each plant, warehouse and headquarters.

I thought that General Foods ought to consolidate much of this
equipment, so that when the next generation of larger mainframe computers arrived there would be greater savings not only in operating
expense, but in minimizing conversion costs when replacing fewer
machines. With the exception of the comptroller, no one wanted to listen to arguments about the benefits of taking a corporate view of computing. Top corporate managers, who were mostly legal and marketing
executives, remained uninvolved spectators. Meanwhile, the divisional
executives tried to carry on with a lesser number of computers, but only
within the boundaries of their own operating division, ending up with
only token savings. Nobody could tell much about efficiency, because

any savings were instantly absorbed by computer budgets rising at the rate of more than twenty percent per year.

Data center consolidation was technically and economically the right thing to do, since skilled computer personnel were an extremely scarce resource in 1962. Early in 1962, I installed on the largest IBM mainframe then available a corporate-wide system which brought together inventory management, production scheduling and logistic dispatching into a single integrated application.[228] We rented the large mainframe from a major New York chemical corporation, for whom it was a glass-house showpiece of their scientific prowess even though they had only a few applications to run on it. They had enormous amounts of machine time available over weekends which they offered at a marginal price. During a few hours on Saturday mornings, this machine could process more data than all of General Foods' computers laboring for a month.

The new application was enormously successful. It made possible for a production scheduler to evaluate inventory positions, for every product, at every location in the U.S. It made all production plans, transportation routing and promotional actions visible simultaneously. Instead of trickling this data through several departments over a period of up to forty weeks, as was the normal procedure, the central planning staff had all of this information available Monday mornings, reflecting conditions as they were on the prior Thursday. The effects of this enormous shortening in the reaction times were spectacular. For example, nationwide inventories of Jell-O decreased by thirty percent within a year. That was easy, because the old system of sequential scheduling of all decisions produced excesses such as a forty year supply of three ounce lime Jell-O packages in the Atlanta warehouse. In addition to inventory reductions, the system made it possible to schedule marketing promotions faster, cut cross-warehouse trucking expenditures by fifty percent and ultimately make it possible to consolidate most production from eight factories into one.

---

228. This was on an IBM 7090 computer.

The new integrated computer application did not achieve the gains by applying clever mathematical formulae, even though the computer program contained quite a bit of mathematical analysis. It demonstrated that integrating information from diverse and previously incompatible sources made it possible to make decisions simultaneously that previously could be done only sequentially. It was this experience that convinced me that the benefits of computers arose more from their communications links than from their calculating capabilities. The fundamental flaw with the General Foods approach to information management was a lack of understanding that rigid separation of telecommunications from computer services, production planning from distribution, and packaging procurement from plant scheduling. This left too many sovereign potentates running their own independent local fiefdoms the best they could do without adequate information, which damaged overall business performance.[229]

Data center consolidation that would maximize communications across functions did not occur during my tenure at General Foods, only many years subsequently. It became a pawn in a contest for asserting divisional independence from corporate staff domination.[230] Corporate management was not sure what they needed or wanted from information management, and therefore did not wish to move to an unfamiliar battlefield. They chose to contest divisional autonomy on more familiar grounds which involved much larger sums of money, such as control over advertising expenditures. In the absence of a commitment to manage information systems as something that warranted corporate attention, top management watched from the sidelines as key computer managers left for better opportunities elsewhere.

---

229. This allowed each division to manage their sales statistics in creative ways to maximize marketing bonuses.
230. In one case, the divisional comptroller chose to purchase equipment from the soon to be defunct RCA corporation to make certain that he would be totally incompatible in hardware and software with everybody else. That decision cost the company an expensive conversion later on.

Amid the political disorder at General Foods, I got an offer to become the chief corporate information executive of Kraft, in 1964.[231] They wanted to consolidate their diverse and increasingly uneconomic data centers.

Opportunities, such as at Kraft, at the time were readily available to anyone with a few years of experience in managing a corporate information systems department. If you were a "centralist" in one organization and your views ceased to be in favor, you could always move to another firm where the pendulum was swinging that way. Careers improved by moving every several years as companies started experimenting with organizational redesign as a way to keep up profits.[232]

Kraft

After we began consolidating local computing facilities at Kraft into regional centers, a new set of top marketing executives realized they did not want to centralize data processing after all. They only wanted to centralize marketing operations. It took four years to make that clear as a matter of policy. In the interim, direction remained ambiguous because there was no established process for aligning information plans with business plans. Most of the computer staff that originally supported decentralization were displaced by the centralists, only to see that reversed shortly thereafter. The centralists received demotions and came under the control of a new wave of experts who were more in tune with the wishes of the marketing staff. After surveying the swings in direction, I finally figured out that the design of information systems had become a substitute for resolving who was responsible for managing the sales administrative functions.

---

231. Then called the National Dairy Products Corporation.
232. The association of mobility with risk has not changed much. In 1992, CIOs have averaged 22% increase in compensation. This is in contrast with an average 4.6% increase in all information systems salaries. High turnover at the top is pushing salaries up and creating a demand for top IT executives who can quickly produce results. In 1988, a VP of IS made 2.8 times the compensation of a junior programmer. The gap has widened every year since then. Today, CIOs and VPs make 4.6 time the salary of their juniors. Although the top job is well paid, it is not secure. It has the highest turnover rate of any IS category. See "Top Salaries Soar, Ranks Remain Flat," *Datamation*, August 15, 1993, p.28.

The cause of Kraft's problems in computing was substituting marketing politics for information policy. That was not an isolated occurrence. Whenever I talked with fellow information technology executives, they also noticed the same phenomenon at their companies. They tried to operate complex systems despite contests that were in reality proxies for larger intramural disputes. Computer executives were rarely, if ever, at the table when the negotiations over corporate policy decisions took place. Therefore, technical experts were always participating in a game without knowing all of its rules. This explains why a computer executive unwittingly could become either a hero or a reject, regardless of intentions or results.

One of my major accomplishments as the chief information officer of the Kraft holding company was to initiate the replacement of the company's IBM computers with Honeywell machines. In 1964, at the time of the introduction of the "360" generation of computers, IBM could not deliver adequate computer capacity for a reasonable price. IBM experienced delays in delivering the promised new software to run this equipment. The not-so delicate methods used by IBM to forestall the displacement of their equipment offered a good lesson of how dependent one can become on one's technology supplier. My long-standing commitment to the cause of *open* systems goes back to the day when I expected to lose my job for making the right decisions.

To the credit of the top management of Kraft, they backed me fully in the then novel view that computing was becoming a commodity that was only as good as its management, not its vendor. The Honeywell computers provided many Kraft locations with reliable and low cost computing capacity. In due course, IBM recovered its traditional advantage, and many of the new computer installations throughout the world again bore the IBM brand name. However, there always remained with some Kraft executives a lingering question whether having ever left the fold of IBM was an excessively risky move. In those days, no chief computer executive would ever be fired on technical grounds as long as he rented IBM equipment.

I have fond memories of my time with Kraft. I found their top executives honest, hardworking and dedicated to the prosperity of the firm, but took too long to learn how to harness computers. However, they never compromised integrity. They admitted their mistakes and took any losses as learning experience, which they used to the benefit of the company. They made headway slowly and cautiously, but enjoyed some of the most efficient computing services I have seen anywhere.

Xerox

Early in 1969, Xerox had acquired a specialty computer company (Scientific Data Systems) for an unheard of multiple of its worth. To demonstrate the new acquisition's capacity to produce commercially viable equipment, Xerox was seeking someone who would eliminate all IBM computers at Xerox in short order and replace them with computers carrying the Xerox brand name. There was hardly any chief computer executive of a major corporation who could or would claim the displacement of IBM business applications as a major professional achievement. The recruiter located me very quickly.

My appointment to be the Xerox chief information officer shows that making a fundamentally sound bet can play an important role in someone's career. I would have never guessed that installing Honeywell computers would be the primary qualification for advancement. The moral of this story is that in politics you can never outguess who ultimately will end up as the winner. You might as well do what is right and take the consequences, rather than what is expedient and expect a lasting reward.

When I got to Xerox, they had just made a commitment to centralize control over administrative support of marketing. In the early 1970s, Xerox was a sophisticated and highly profitable company. If they wished to centralize marketing systems, I was happy to oblige. As I had learned at Kraft, there was a more fundamental contest hidden beneath the simplistic presentation slides that announced that intention. At Xerox there was contention between the financial comptrollers and the marketing managers. This is a traditional battle, as ancient as the confrontations between nomads and farmers, between local autonomy and absolute monarchy.

As a matter of tradition, the Xerox corporate computer managers always sided with the head comptroller, since they worked for him. Much of the current resentment against the mainframe establishment is traceable to the rancor formed twenty to thirty years ago by the marketing people against comptrollers, and Xerox was a prime example of that. These classic ideological battles fought by the information technologists, usually for the losing side, do not as yet have a chronicle that would convey the emotional dimensions of these conflicts.[233]

When I arrived at Xerox early in 1969, the line operating personnel were beginning to free themselves from the bondage of finance by setting up their own regional data centers. All that happened afterwards reflected the drive to achieve information processing independence.

The most dedicated sponsor for introducing information technologies into businesses, from 1950 up to the mid 1970s, was the comptroller. Information technology was the comptroller's possession and was amply funded to empower the financial establishment to know in fine detail what everyone did at all times. For instance, in 1973, each financial analyst had at their command over $30,000 of computing expenses per year.[234] The service organization which was the principal point of contact with the customer was supported with only $295 of computing power per capita per year. Such an unbalance is, of course, a perfect solution for anyone who strives to keep control over all decisions.[235] Xerox had just imported a new cadre of comptrollers from Ford and IBM, and these executives had the habit of checking on every penny spent by anyone except themselves.

---

233. There are many colorful stories on this topic worthy of an enthusiastic chronicler of corporate mythology. I hope that someone will take up the challenge.
234. Using expensive time-sharing services that utilized the APL language to prepare elaborate financial models.
235. The growth of information technology personnel to 3 to 4% of total employment for manufacturing firms has been widely noted. I have never managed to get comparable numbers for accountants and finance analysts. Robert W. Gunn, who specializes in downsizing comptroller departments, has been quoted in the March 14, 1994 issue of *Business Week*, that finance staffs in large companies average 5% of total employment, and in some cases account for more than 10% of the company's payroll. I find the last number hard to believe, although I should not be surprised, based on the number of financial analysts always present whenever decisions were made.

Figure 30.1 Corporate Contests, 1970s Style

By that time, operating managers began to chafe loudly under that style of management. The issue of who ran information management at Xerox unfolded as a monumental struggle that nobody wanted to discuss openly. It took over fifteen years before a new chief executive acknowledged the nature of these contests. That required the departure of two chief financial executives who competed for positions of power and the separation of another financial executive from the presidency.

Meanwhile, each side was arguing principles and general concepts so well that no independent observer could have picked which side was right. A procession of consultants delivered alternate recommendations about every two years that only confused the matter further while the conflict lingered.

Both sides in this contention were wrong because they argued their case in terms of short-term advantages, rather than in terms of governance, federation objectives and cooperation opportunities that would be in line with the corporation's strategic goals. Top management tried to alleviate this conflict by rearranging the names and boxes on organization charts at least every eighteen months. That never solved anything, since changing organization charts without changing business processes is like transplanting a growing orchard from one corner of a rocky field to another. Much of the energy that should have gone during all of those decades into learning how to use computer technology ended up in often spiteful contests between contending factions.

I am not suggesting that comptrollers are wicked people. They are well-intentioned professionals who have deep convictions regarding their role as the guardians of who spends what money where. In fact, organizations are now paying a penalty for the dethroning of that disciplined management structure. Currently, chaos prevails where distributed processing and personal computers proliferate without any of the data discipline or standards established under the comptroller regime. The alternative to a stultifying finance-dominated absolutist regime is not necessarily a lively, creative and productive anarchy.[236]

The Xerox Information Services Division

It was only in the early 1970s, at the beginning of the minicomputer liberation movement, when information technology started coming out of the hands of the comptrollers altogether. Early in 1970 I proposed and received approval to form, as profit center, a Xerox Information Services Division to deliver to U.S. operating units computing, telecommunications, administrative, management consulting, systems development and programming services at commercial rates.[237] As General Manger, I adopted commercial practices for pricing, controlling and customer relations that nowadays would favorably compare with "outsourcing" vendors. Large savings were realized in the consolidation of voice and data networks through purchasing of some of the most advanced corporate telecommunication capabilities available anywhere

---

236. It is interesting that Xerox has just decided to outsource most of its information processing capacity in the U.S. on a long-term contract to EDS, the archetype of order and control. I do not doubt that in the case of the EDS bid there was a substantial financial advantage to Xerox. However, the politics of the situation also suggests that imposing a tighter order on information systems must have been a strong motive for divesting data centers, communications and local area networks.
237. From 1971 through 1975, Xerox's Information Systems Division reported to the chief computer executive, who reported directly to the president of U.S. operations.

in the world. Data center operations started on an annual twenty percent unit cost reduction track, that has continued to this day.

The Information Services Division successfully installed and operated one of the largest time-sharing service businesses using Xerox Data Services computers, which were well suited for that purpose. We never converted payroll, invoicing and manufacturing systems from the IBM environment, despite much prodding. When Xerox finally decided to exit from the computer business early in 1975, the major software assets of the corporation were conserved because they were sheltered from political interference. The moral of that story is that even through information management is an intensely political matter, you cannot use political means to dictate technical solutions that do not work.

With the creation of the Information Services Division, the comptroller became just another information customer, rather than the dominant purveyor and sole custodian of information. It is a testimonial to the robustness and soundness of the principles behind the formation of the Xerox Information Services Division that it remained intact and growing for another twenty years after I left for posts in corporate strategic planning. The basic soundness of offering information technologies as an integrated "utility" service, abstaining from the politics of systems design, has held up for two decades, while every other department and operating unit of Xerox went through frequent changes in organization structure and business strategy.

31

THE ROAD TO CIM

Hardship is one of the prerequisites for all advancement.

This chapter will explain why and how the Corporate Information Management (CIM) program of the U.S. Department of Defense (DoD) became an established doctrine by 1992, and is now independent of individuals, political appointments or Administration. In confirmation hearings for the post of Assistant Secretary for Command, Control, Communications and Intelligence and Pentagon's Information Resources Chief the nominee said: "I plan to reinforce and accelerate migration toward CIM systems to eliminate duplicate legacy systems....There is nothing more important to the Department of Defense than corporate-wide business and management systems. CIM is the vehicle to get us there." (June 1993 Hearings, Senate Armed Services Committee).

The Deputy Secretary of Defense in October, 1993, confirmed the original CIM goals and directed that the following to be achieved:

1. Select standard "migration systems" by March 1994.

2. Complete transition to standard systems in less than three years.

3. Cease funding non-standard systems.

4. Implement data element standardization program.

5. Proceed with "functional improvement" processes, including software engineering modernization, establishing a corporate functional integration board and cross-functional databases.

Thousands of DoD officials are currently acting on CIM principles. However, CIM is not completely new or alien to the U.S. government. CIM is a revival of the original intent of the Federal government to institute Information Resources Management (IRM) as a way to streamline all administrative, control and managerial processes.

As had occurred in the business community two decades before, the IRM responsibilities were taken on by those in control of computers. After they received their appointment, IRM managers proceeded to redefine their missions so as to make information management subordinate to computer systems. That left most of the information management costs without the benefit of any systematic design and in the hands of local administrators. As executives holding IRM titles kept losing influence, and their scope narrowed to controlling only large central data processing operations and large development programs, the flow of information in DoD became more disorderly and costly. The IRM function drifted away from the fundamental purpose of Defense, which is to fight wars. The purpose of CIM was to put management of the U.S. defense information capabilities back into the IRM job.

CIM is not a solution to conditions that are unique to DoD. It is equally applicable to all public sector organizations as well as large multinational corporations. Because of its enormous scope, CIM is still in development at the present time, with many tasks waiting to go into operation.

CIM principles, policies, guidelines and practices offer a managerially sound and technologically advanced process for organizing information management functions for any diversified enterprise. This is particularly true for organizations open to public scrutiny, whether from Congress, a regulatory agency or a corporate supervisory body, such as Board of Directors' committees and auditors. It therefore should be useful to report on the lessons learned so far from this experience. Executives involved in managing information technology will find it interesting to see how this largest of all information management projects came into existence. Its methods deserve further examination because it offers an excellent case study of the practice of information politics on a scale never before experienced. Those who have an opportunity to learn from what works will not need to waste resources repeating what others have already learned.

The Origin of CIM

Without the late Donald Atwood, then Deputy Secretary of Defense, there would be no CIM. Deputy Secretary Atwood arrived in the DoD in 1989 with a thorough understanding of how information management is inseparable from general management. From his recent experience as vice-chairman and senior operating group executive of General Motors, he realized that information management is powerful in stimulating major business process improvements.

Deputy Secretary Atwood was the key negotiator during and after the acquisition of Electronic Data Systems (EDS) by General Motors. That merger deserves a special chapter in the history of U.S. computing as an example of how organizational conflict can damage the practice of information management. On short notice, General Motors transferred all of its information systems personnel to EDS. The chairman of General Motors, Roger Smith, believed he could solve his information management problems by divesting his company of all information systems personnel and computer technologists. For a number of years afterwards General Motors was unable to improve the responsiveness of its business to competition. The outsourcing of all information systems to EDS coincided with a rapidly dropping market share, severely deteriorating profits and acrimonious disputes about the fairness of EDS processing charges to General Motors. I became involved in these contentions by providing General Motors corporate staff with benchmark indicators about what could be expected as a reasonable level of spending for information technology. My strictly confidential findings were compromised when somebody leaked my memorandum to the already highly irritated plant managers, who proceeded to use this data to vent their displeasure with anything else that EDS attempted to do.

This exposure to the political and economic aspects of information management sharpened Deputy Secretary Atwood's appreciation of why information management could be one of the best tools for achieving cost reductions in information handling, provided that it was done through a process that had legitimacy and acceptance. He understood how clearly defined information management charters are a prerequisite for modernizing and cost reduction through computerization. He also appreciated the importance of sound, deliberate, well planned, participatory and non-destructive approaches when making organizational changes to realize the enormous potential of information technologies. CIM was conceived as a seven year program to be executed under the same management in order to assure coherent implementation based on fundamental changes in the methods of information management in DoD. The Deputy Secretary's direct involvement in steering CIM was thoughtful, consistent and unwavering. Despite the demands of the Gulf War and military actions that followed it, Deputy Secretary Atwood always made ample time available to discuss CIM progress. He considered CIM as one of his major accomplishments during his term in office.

Most importantly, Deputy Secretary Atwood had the necessary executive powers to reallocate budgets and change how organizations reported in the DoD civilian hierarchy. Without inspired leadership, understanding, and power to do something about there is no reform. At the inception of CIM, all of those attributes were present. That explains, perhaps more than any other influence, why CIM made a mark in the Pentagon where previously heralded programs had left no trace at all.

In July 1989, Deputy Secretary Atwood and Dick Cheney, the Secretary of Defense, launched the Defense Management Review Decisions (DMRD) process that influenced the subsequent development of CIM. The DMRD process was responding to the direction from President Bush to "realize substantial improvements...in defense management overall." The DMRDs established policies and directions to improve defense capabilities while overall DoD budgets were being cut. The DMRD process was an administrative innovation that worked around the cumbersome program, planning and budgeting process that had reigned supreme as the mechanism for making long-term weapons and force acquisition commitments. In scope, detail, administrative complexity and computational efforts the DoD planning process was comparable only to the centralized approach to managing the Soviet economy.[238]

The initial DMRDs clearly stated that improvements in information management would maintain defense strength while the President and Secretary of Defense achieved cost reductions through cutting overhead, not fighting capabilities. All DMRDs were subordinated to this central concept. To give this program a distinct doctrinal identity, it received the culturally unprecedented label of "Corporate Information Management."[239]

Early in 1989, the DoD comptroller had identified $6.9 billion of cost reduction opportunities to come from cuts in information systems, over the subsequent seven year period. These savings would come from consolidating data centers and merging redundant applications. However, the comptroller simultaneously launched far-reaching plans to cut budgets for every conceivable aspect of Defense. These cuts added up to $71.1 billion and required substantial improvements in information management practices if they were to succeed. The problem was there was no explicit process to link the $71.1 billion in functional efficiencies, such as in materials, logistics, personnel, health and financial management, to the cost reduction goals placed on the information resource managers.

All of these committed efficiency enhancement targets became part of President Bush's 1990-1997 DoD budget forecast that called for a total of $411 billion in budget cuts from projections made prior to the

---

238. Until recently, the U.S. Department of Defense rightfully earned its claim as "the second largest planned economy in the world." DMRDs adopted corporate planning practices to cope with increasingly volatile global political and economic circumstances after the disintegration of the Soviet Union began.

239. The introduction of the Corporate label into Defense, which has neither a profit nor a business structure, was predicted by most Washington observers to guarantee its short life. When the new administration came to town in January 1993, bets were placed on CIM not surviving through the summer. It is a testimony to the vitality of the CIM approach that it has survived and continues to receive accolades.

disintegration of the Soviet Union as the major military threat to U.S. national security interests. To grasp the meaning of these astronomical numbers, one has to understand that the $411 billion budget cut originated from a rapidly changing political climate in the U.S. Congress. The DMRDs were needed to lessen the damage to national security after the sudden euphoria about the possibility of universal peace wore off. The purpose of the DMRDs was to mitigate the impact from the coming Congressional appropriation cuts in tanks, ships, airplanes and fighting capacity by increasing efficiency in managing the non-combat functions of the DoD.

Most of the $411 billion savings demanded by President Bush's plan would come from cutting back on military bases, ships, airplanes, tanks and military personnel. Even with the projected severe cuts in military strength, there was still a $71.1 billion gap remaining between the projected costs of DoD operations and what was affordable according to budget forecasts. Secretary Cheney and Deputy Secretary Atwood announced that they would bridge this gap by improved management and that CIM would deliver a major share of that improvement. Figure 31.1 shows how CIM tasks were related to the overall cost reduction effort and Figure 31.4 shows the share of the CIM effort:

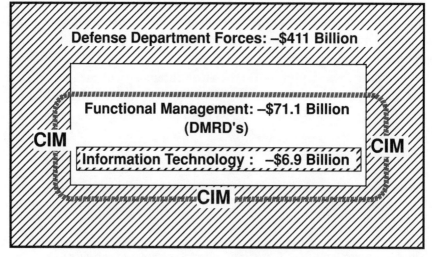

Figure 31.1 Defense Cost Reductions and CIM

The intent of the DMRDs to safeguard increased war fighting capabilities did not impress the thousands of managers, administrators and clerks who over the years had spun perhaps one of the most costly webs in the world of unnecessary paperwork and meetings. Since World War II, the DoD continued to expand its numbers of non-combatant personnel despite highly critical Presidential Commissions, Government Accounting Office complaints and unceasing Congressional investigations.

The DMRDs signaled that business as usual in the DoD would have to change. Cash came out of budgets. Tasks were assigned. The Deputy Secretary repeated publicly that CIM would lead the charge for a more efficient and modern Defense support infrastructure. On October 4, 1989, he formally introduced the CIM program stressing the need for effective standardization, quality and consistency of data to support sound management decisions throughout the DoD. The objectives for CIM became central to enhancing defense effectiveness while achieving cost reductions in non-combat operations. The target savings, by function and service were as follows:

Functional Category	Target Savings ($ billions)	% of Total Savings
Materials and Logistics	46.7	66
General Administration	9.8	14
Automated Support & Systems	6.9	9
Finance, Procurement & Contracts	5.6	8
Base Operations, Facilities	2.1	3
Total Savings ($ billions)	71.1	100

Figure 31.2 Functional Cost Reduction Tasks for 1990-1997

Armed Service	Target Savings ($ billions)	% of Total Savings
Army	21.0	29
Navy	21.5	30
Air Force	22.5	32
Other Defense Agencies	6.1	9
Total Savings ($ billions)	71.1	100

Figure 31.3 Services Cost Reduction Tasks for 1990-1997

Throughout its history, CIM withstood attempts to limit its scope to only the $6.9 billion reduction in information technology expenses. It took repeated efforts to convince Congressional staff, comptrollers, inspectors and Assistant Secretaries that CIM is one of the most potent means available for achieving major operating efficiencies.[240]

About half of the $71.1 billion cost reductions throughout the DoD could come from changing long standing policies and practices. For example, most of the savings in materials were achievable by ending the stockpiling of unneeded strategic materials. That left about half of the DMRD savings dependent on CIM methods that called for business process improvement, rationalization of information handling and elimination of redundant paperwork:

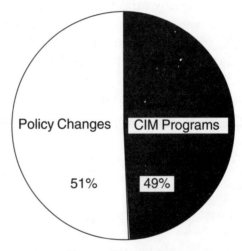

Figure 31.4 CIM Share of DoD Cost Reduction Tasks

What remained was an unspecified $35 billion cost reduction task, that would have to be filled through improving every business process, preferably through information technology. In the case of the Department of Defense that objective was to support the most effective fight-

---

240. At a recent Senate Governmental Affairs Committee, the Defense Department comptroller was accused of accounting ineptitude. In responding, the comptroller said "...CIM would be the answer. He indicated that he would make CIM top priority." *Government Computer News*, April 18, 1994, p.1.

ing force that would be affordable for $411 billion less than had been previously planned.

Lessons from the origins of CIM are applicable to most situations where information management suddenly becomes one of the principal means for realizing critical enterprise ambitions. It requires inspired leadership. It calls for top executive involvement. It must rely on financial targets. It calls for executive power to direct implementation. Without these ingredients, even desirable and feasible information management initiatives suffer miscarriage or grow up with severe defects.

Early CIM Efforts

The responsibility for implementing the information technology DMRDs was in the hands of the comptroller's chain of command. The DoD comptroller was the designated IRM (Information Resource Management) official. A relatively small IRM oversight staff had always reported to the comptroller as far back as anyone could remember. The key positions were occupied by executives who wished to use the consolidating of data centers and merging of redundant applications for accelerating all other DMRD projects. They subscribed to the typical view of most financial establishments that information technology should be the bludgeon for forcing management reforms.[241] They violated one of the canons of what not to do in information management. You cannot begin the overhaul of an organization by first altering its computer systems.

---

241. This view persists in many forms. The plans of the current Government Information Technology Services (GITS) Working Group of the Office of Management and Budget (OMB) pursues "Reengineering of Government Through Information Technology." The proposed approach reflects the attitude prevalent when CIM began. You do not reengineer through a computer-led initiative. Information technology should follow the decisions of executives who have operating responsibilities.

Figure 31.5 Paying Too Much Attention to Computer Problems

To simplify the CIM effort, two task forces went to work. One task force recommended paring down the burdens from the proliferation of more than 10,000 mainframe computers at more than 1,000 locations by moving the mainframes to a handful of central sites. The entire scheme was inspired by the need to achieve quick operating cost reductions in computer expenses. The proposal looked to rapid physical consolidation as the source of savings. The proposal did not offer a network design, it neglected to consider the role of distributed computing, it did not have a credible concept of operations, it did not show how to organize and manage a $2 billion per year operation and it did not show how corralling obsolete mainframes into a few megacenters would avoid the likelihood of a monumental collapse.

The second task force had the ambitious goal of coming up with a single software application for every business function. New software was to replace an enormous collection of technically old computer programs that were delivering similar results. The problem was that although the outputs from these diverse applications were similar, each of the old programs were constructed to the customer specifications of different business processes. The old processes were all different because they grew to fit the bureaucracies that conceived them.

One of the acknowledged principles of systems management is that computer programs reflect the behavior of the organizations that pay for them. Each defense organization function is somewhat different from another because the origin and funding source for each organization were indeed unique. For example, the Air Force Reserve Officer Training Corps (ROTC) had its own personnel and payroll computers because they considered themselves inherently distinct from the Army ROTC. If you accumulate such differences in process but not in substance over more than a thousand similar situations in the DoD, you could understand why the consolidation of redundant applications would make sense. If you further compound the differences in procedural details by awarding the responsibility for implementation to different contractors, you will get an infinite variety for intrinsically similar tasks.

The leaders of the second task force were technical experts, who reported four levels below the comptroller. When confronted with the enormous scope of their work, the task force split itself into ten teams.[242] At one point in 1990, there were over two hundred DoD systems people working on this project on travel status, plus innumerable consultants. These people occupied most of the available commercial conference rooms in the vicinity of the Pentagon, making conceptual outlines of the new applications on flip-charts. There was not enough wall space in all of the conference rooms on which to tack on all the conceptual outlines of systems that would address the complexity of DoD. To overcome this limitation, the teams had to follow a popular low cost, off-the-shelf CASE (Computer Aided Software Engineering) tool.[243] That was not much help, since the primary mission of the representatives of each bureaucracy in the task force was to assure their organizations' control over information management would remain

---

242. The teams had to investigate more than 40,000 applications running with approximately 1.6 billion lines of legacy code having an average age of fifteen years.
243. This tool was not sufficiently powerful to support the work of the tasks forces because it was designed to handle the generation of software code. The scope of the problems at hand called first for reaching agreement about common business processes, which required more advanced tools.

unchallenged and unchanged. The new systems would end up a conglomerate of every conceivable feature dreamed up by anybody. From a large collection of old disorderly applications, DoD was headed for a single large new disorderly monster for every business process.

Figure 31.6 Early CIM Efforts

Dozens of subcommittees sat in conference rooms trying to do conceptual designs of "open-systems, integrated database, client-server, machine independent, portable, fourth generation" applications based on standards for which there was little commercial support. All of this would be programmed in the mandatory Ada language, in which DoD personnel had only limited experience. The new, consolidated computer programs were supposed to replace the existing accumulation of mostly undocumented code, running on just about every kind of hardware ever sold by anybody.[244]

The application task forces did not use any method for evaluating the benefits of their various proposals. They relied exclusively on subjective valuations obtained by group consensus of "critical success factors." They did not support any of the proposed investments with an economic rationale that would commit to net cash savings. Such a ratio-

---

244. This included equipment purchased in the late 1960s that still emulated 80 column card tabulating programs inherited from the 1950s.

nale would be essential as Congress kept removing cash from the DoD spending authorization at an accelerating rate.

The methodologies, processes and attitudes expressed during these early efforts reflected the traditional "grand design" approach to computer systems. It was of the IRM people, by the IRMs and largely for satisfying IRM specialists' problems. The entire effort was responsive to the comptroller's decree to find ways to cut computer expenses. Since CIM was given considerable start-up funding to achieve the desired savings, the IRM establishment saw in it an opportunity to launch much needed modernization of computer technologies, not the modernization of DoD business practices.

Figure 31.7 A Comptroller's Systems Concept

By concentrating on the comptroller's dictate to cut $6.9 billion of computer expense, they did not address the $71.1 billion target for increased effectiveness. The IRM practitioners did not have much experience in business process improvement. They did not operate in an organizational structure that would allow them to execute an improved business process, except in the comptroller's department. There was no policy, no technology framework, no business process model, no concept of operations. It was an attempt to impose systems uniformity by relying primarily on central IRM staff to become agents of change at a time when the power of the central computing establishment was already losing control to local, autonomous systems based on mini- and microcomputers.

The final task force presentations to top DoD executives concerned computer applications, not Defense issues and solutions. The orientation of the presenters was indistinguishable from what I had seen in the 1970s from computer specialists at Sears, American Express, Shell Oil, Xerox and AT&T. The ideas were vintage 1960s mainframe jargon re-bottled in 1990s buzzwords.

In view of the widely acknowledged presence of duplication, redundancy, proliferation and general chaos in information systems management, the initial consolidation ideas received the support from the Congress and the comptroller. The politicians were eager to realize short-term cost savings, and the computer establishment had less political clout in resisting cuts than anyone else.[245] From the standpoint of the DoD outsiders such as congressional staff, eliminating duplicate applications and consolidating redundant data centers was something that was simple and understandable. The inefficiencies of existing operations had been already thoroughly documented in numerous reports from the General Accounting Office, which kept calling for radical improvements. Congress obliged; it cut the military departments' systems development budgets severely and transferred about a quarter of what remained, over $1 billion, to the comptroller for use as a lever in forcing consolidations.

The Executive Level Group

Sometime in September 1989, mounting concerns were expressed by a number of respected observers about the direction of the CIM teams. Deputy Secretary Atwood decided to create a Department of Defense Federal Advisory committee for Information Management to review

---

245. The allocation of cost cuts is largely a matter of political popularity. Opinion surveys consistently single out the computer department as one of the most difficult to deal with, and least effective corporate functions.

and comment on how to implement CIM. The committee, designated as the Executive Level Group (ELG), reported directly to Mr. Atwood.[246] Appointing an outside committee made sense. If you want to make major changes in an organization that has deeply entrenched habits and conventions, it is politically prudent to bring in outsiders for an independent assessment. These outsiders must have a broad perspective. They must have prior experience in doing organizational surgery. The ELG group had these qualifications.

The ELG met regularly for six months. They examined the elements of the $9.2 billion annual IRM budget. What they found was neither sensible nor economical. There was a leadership, policy and technological planning vacuum at the top. The world's largest information processing organization looked more like a circus than a coherent enterprise.

In September 1990, the ELG delivered to the Secretary of Defense a plan for CIM directions. The basic idea was that if you want to have an integrated war-support capability, you need an integrated information strategy. The report explained which policies were necessary to obtain coordination. The military departments grudgingly endorsed the ELG recommendations.[247] The proposed policies were sufficiently general so that the recommendations would not immediately upset the zealously guarded established order.

The Joint Chiefs of Staff voted in favor of CIM as long as it would keep out of command, control and intelligence systems which accounted for the overwhelming share of DoD information technol-

---

246. The ELG committee consisted of: David Hill, CIO of General Motors, Chairman; Duane Andrews, Assistant Secretary of Defense for Command, Control, Communications and Intelligence; David Chu, Assistant Secretary of Defense for Program Analysis and Evaluation; Gary Garrett, Partner, Andersen Consulting; Jack Hancock, Executive Vice President, Pacific Bell; George Lundy, Dean of Faculties, Loyola University; David Norton, President, Nolan, Norton, Inc.; Sean O'Keefe, Comptroller of the Department of Defense; Paul Strassmann, retired Vice President, Xerox Corporation.
247. The political leadership of the military departments, guided by Deputy Secretary Atwood, reluctantly signed up over the objections of the uniformed services. The services saw in the consolidations, to be executed by the Office of the Secretary of Defense, a major disruption in the balance of power which until then heavily favored their insulation from the inherent instability in direction coming from short-term political appointees and Congressional staff. I have a great deal of sympathy for these apprehensions.

ogy expenditures. During the negotiations for securing the endorsement of CIM, the military departments extracted an agreement that any further efforts towards corporate-level data center consolidation, as proposed by the comptroller and the Congress, would stop. In the place of DoD-wide consolidations, each military service would manage its own mergers independently. In return, the military departments and the Defense Logistics Agency agreed to deliver large savings that would meet the DMRD goals.

An uninitiated observer would not have grasped any of the circumlocutions made by the Generals, the comptroller and the senior civilian executives who attended the summit meeting about the future of CIM. The merits of proceeding with CIM were secondary to the politics of preserving of the status quo. Resistance by the military services collapsed when it became apparent that Mr. Atwood was firmly committed to proceeding with the CIM plans. The only question remaining was how to negotiate the least amount of damage to the real or perceived autonomy of the military services. Despite excellent work by computer experts in fashioning CIM principles, the birth of CIM in the Department of Defense was of political origin. As the story of CIM unfolded, it illustrated the reality of all information management as being primarily a political phenomenon and only secondarily a matter of economics or technology.

CIM Principles

The principles of the ELG are as good today as they were first written. They are common sense, generic and may apply to any large organization that depends on operational interdependency to carry out its missions:

- Information will be managed through centralized control with decentralized implementation.

- Simplification by elimination and consolidation is to be preferred to automation whether developing new or enhancing existing information systems.

- Proposed and existing business methods will be subject routinely to cost-benefit analysis which includes benchmarking against the best public and private sector achievement.

- New business methods shall be proven or validated before implementation.
- Information systems performing the same function must be common unless specific analysis determines they should be unique.
- Functional management shall be held accountable for all benefits and all directly controllable costs of developing and operating their information systems.
- Information systems shall be developed and enhanced according to a Department-wide methodology and accomplished in a compressed time frame in order to minimize the cost of development and achieve early realization of benefits.
- Information systems shall be developed and enhanced in the context of process models that document business methods.
- The computing and communications infrastructure shall be transparent to the information systems that rely upon it.
- Common definitions and standards for data shall exist Department-wide.[248]
- Wherever practicable, information services shall be acquired through competitive bidding, considering internal and external sources.
- Data must be entered only once.

---

248. The ELG group was treated to many tales of information incompatibilities. There were at least seventeen known ways to identify a geographic location. In some instances the same set of numbers designated a different spot on the ground. Universal Transverse Mercator Coordinates were not the same as Geographic Coordinates. Marines asking for Air Force bomber support could not be sure that they were marking the identical spot. Similar disparities were known about many other critical data, such as identifying dates, time and names of military units.

- Access to information shall be facilitated, controlled and limited as required. Information also must be safeguarded against unintentional or unauthorized alteration, destruction or disclosure.

- The presentation by the system to the user shall be friendly and consistent.

What subsequently become known as the "CIM model" was summarized in the following diagram:

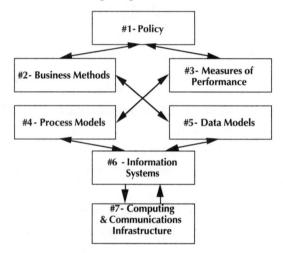

Figure 31.8 The CIM Model, in Order of Priority of Decisions[249]

This model defined a new point of view and the priorities of CIM:

- Policy ahead of everything else;

- Business methods and performance measurement ahead of modeling; and

- Information systems and technology decisions take place only after all the conditions for its success are in place .

---

249. This diagram was first drawn by Mr. David Hill, the ELG chairman.

Many DoD people who saw the CIM model for the first time observed that it reflected a common sense approach that was neither noteworthy nor new. They did not appreciate that in reality, systems managers followed precisely the opposite sequence. DoD systems managers usually first focused on the technology and only then looked for its justification.[250] Hardly anyone had a comprehensive set of information management policies. When such policies were available, measurements concerned technical details. Typically, business models were incomprehensible to everyone except to their originators.

The CIM approach called for a shift from a technology acquisition point of view to a managerial and operational orientation. Given prevailing practices, the CIM approach was novel in that it called for changes in organizing the management of all information resources.

Role of Command, Control, Communications and Intelligence

Most ELG members became concerned about the limited responsiveness of the $9.2 billion per year IRM establishment to the rapidly changing defense situation. The IRM bias, buttressed by OMB (Office of Management and Budget, Executive Office of the President), GAO (General Accounting Office, an investigation arm of the Congress), and GSA (General Services Administration, an independent office management agency), regulations, focused entirely on "back office" automation such as finance, personnel, medical, materials and logistics. These were highly structured operations, layered between walls of procedure, paperwork and regulatory minutiae.

The "customer end" of Defense, which is in Command, Control, Communications and Intelligence (C^{3}I), operated as a collection of separate and disjoint enterprises. C^{3}I was estimated to be at least three times larger than IRM systems and was a conglomerate of thousands of systems arising from a patchwork of contracts over several decades. Command did not necessarily tie in with Control, even within the same military service. Command or Control did not communicate well, if

---

250. "If client/server architecture is the answer, what is the question?" is one way to describe a large number of contemporary corporate systems plans.

at all, with Intelligence. The Intelligence systems were not integrated and maintained security by making it hard for battlefield commanders to find out what was going on.

There were stakeholders who made sure the situation remained unchanged this way, although there was a notable exception. The Army had already started a modest transition that would conceptually, organizationally and technically unify many of the administrative support functions for battlefield support. That was not easy because Congress interfered by dictating, for political reasons, that any information systems that affected the Army Reserves could not be connected to the Army's peacetime or battlefield deployment systems.

Every textbook on information management asserts that unless you start with system design from the "customer end" inward to the "back office," you will end up with something that may be elegant but irrelevant. The mandate to the ELG was clear because of the insistence of the armed services. CIM would concentrate on the "back office," would not touch C3I and would assure that finance and accounting remain the priority for systems investment and reform. The comptroller and Congress kept advancing that point of view as auditors kept producing new reports about discrepancies and malfeasance in DoD's financial affairs.

The organizational structure of DoD also inhibited any consideration of C3I as an element of defense information management. The Assistant Secretary of Defense for C3I reported to the Under Secretary of Acquisition. This biased the C3I office to view information technology primarily as a procurement matter. Integration and inter-service interoperability were not a priority because information management was of little concern to an organization focused on acquisition. In a few cases, attempts were made to achieve interoperability through inter service procurement of an identical system. I do not know of a single case where that succeeded, which demonstrated the futility of attempting to achieve systems integration by means of acquisition policy instead of governance and systems architecture.

To reassert the financial management priorities and grasp control over CIM funding in 1990, the comptroller launched a massive consolidation of finance and accounting operations into a newly created agency, Defense Finance and Accounting Services. This was supposed to demonstrate the application of CIM principles. With the comptroller and his staff in leadership positions, the ELG could not realistically advise how DoD could focus CIM to improve war fighting capabilities.

Creating the Corporate Information Function

Events overtook ELG concerns about the untenable barriers erected within the DoD between administrative and C^{3}I systems. To start much needed reforms, in November 1990, Deputy Secretary Atwood moved the C^{3}I responsibility from the Undersecretary of Acquisition and had it report directly to himself. A few days afterwards, he moved the IRM function from the comptroller and assigned it to the Assistant Secretary for C^{3}I.

I view these organizational changes as being of greater consequence than the formation of CIM. By placing combat support systems as well as administrative systems under the same executive, it was now possible to acknowledge that all defense information is a seamless continuum that is not divisible by organizational arrangements favoring only one point of view. The unification of oversight over all defense information created conditions for linking all defense information into an interoperable web. A full understanding of this revolutionary change has yet to become recognized by military organizations as an operational doctrine.[251]

By February 1991, the new IRM chief of the DoD put in place all of the fundamental elements that would henceforth shape CIM.[252] He:

---

251. When that finally takes place, this will not be done by computer and telecommunications specialists, but by operational commanders who will finally come to recognize that joint information-based warfare must be an essential element of all U.S. defenses. One of the least publicized accomplishments of the new C^{3}I organization was to issue a policy directive on information warfare in December 1992. It represents a major milestone in the development of military doctrine for coping with new threats to national security.

252. Duane Andrews, Assistant Secretary of Defense. Reporting to Mr. Andrews were also the Defense Intelligence Agency, the Defense Mapping Agency, the Defense Investigative Service and the Defense Information Systems Agency, plus a collection of information-related departments and directorates. Mr. Ronald Knecht, the Special Assistant to Mr. Andrews, managed the drafting of policy statements that passed through a tortuous route of staff reviews.

- Enlarged the charter of the Defense Communications Agency to cover all information services, becoming the Defense Information Systems Agency (DISA).
- Created within DISA a well-funded CIM support organization, dedicated exclusively to supporting CIM objectives and providing a large pool of manpower from which to execute CIM-funded projects.
- Appointed a Director of Defense Information, at the level of Principal Deputy Assistant Secretary, and delegated to him the responsibility for CIM program management.[253]
- Delegated the authority for guiding functional information systems to Office of Secretary of Defense Principal Staff Assistants (Undersecretaries and Assistant Secretaries).
- Directed ongoing CIM programs to comply with the principles outlined by the ELG.

Innovation Calls for Unconventional Thinking

The role of the ELG offers useful lessons in how to use consultants constructively:

- Get help from trustworthy and experienced professionals who do not have any direct political or financial stake in the outcome of their findings.
- If you want to innovate, do not accept conventional organizational boundaries.
- To get anything important done, give to the consultants the essential prestige, intraorganizational visibility and frequent access to top management.
- Pick leaders who had already done what you aspire to do. Make sure that in the group there is at least some-

---

253. The author remained DDI until the change in administration, in January, 1993.

one who is not necessarily an expert, but whose job is to ask pertinent questions outside the scope of the given task.[254]

- Do not get the outsiders involved in decisions that only inside management can carry out.
- Use advisory groups for setting new directions and counseling on fundamental policy issues. They should not be henchmen for the management's otherwise unpopular decisions.

---

254. This was the role of Father George Lundy, S.J. The "odd man" theory of having someone with a different background serve on a task force was successfully applied by the British for WWII operations research. You always need someone who thinks "outside the box" to guard against the tightly circumscribed thinking of even the best technical experts.

32

Implementing CIM

Progress is the addition of what is new to what already works.

As the new Director of Defense Information, I arrived early in 1991. In any organization, a new manager has only a few weeks to demonstrate how his approach differs from the one of the previous order. I had to pick where to make the first stand. The first move had to be strategic. The move had to assert a key ELG principle. The first action had to direct people away from marching towards failure. The decision had to deal with an unfilled need.

Prior to 1991, the CIM efforts violated just about every ELG principle. The proposals of the data center and applications consolidation task forces were not executable. Even the most optimistic delivery dates for totally new replacement systems extended into the 21st century. How to deliver the committed cost reductions by 1997 was unknown. Most importantly, the projected effects of the proposed application consolidations on achieving the $71.1 billion committed savings in inventory, materials, financial accounting, health maintenance expenses and general administration were not available. So far, only the Department of Defense systems people were talking to the Department of Defense computer experts. There had been no process in place to bring the functional and operational leadership to the table to alter the business processes that would generate the expected savings.

My first task was to stop spending money on task forces that could not deliver promised results. The second priority was to salvage as much value as possible from the work done within the past eighteen months. Work on the "grand design" stopped and the task force personnel returned to their units.

The concept of "evolutionary migration" replaced the "grand design" direction. The "migration" idea was simple: build upon the best systems you already have and ultimately merge everything into the applications that survived a tough screening process. Evolution would be more effective and efficient than original creation.

Whatever good ideas came forward during the first two years of CIM would be of good use when the new CIM teams assembled under new direction. Although the official birth of CIM dated back to October 1989, the ensuing turmoil of moving money and people around meant the CIM program was not truly started on its current course until the beginning of the next fiscal year, in October 1991.

To survive increasingly impatient Congressional staffs, CIM had to show that it could cut costs. CIM became the custodian as well as manager of about a billion dollars per year that Congress had allocated to it for two years in succession. CIM had to demonstrate that it was profitable. The problem was that after two years of promises, CIM was running out of Congressional patience.

The ELG principles dictated that without effective measures of performance CIM could not succeed. However, CIM had been marching to the wrong music. Its orientation had been to cut information technology costs which were reported to OMB as IRM expenses, as required by legislation and regulations. The numbers reported to OMB measured information systems expenditures consistently, but without much relevance, since they did not capture the bulk of DoD's information management expenditures. The chief culprit in these reports was the bias conveyed by the Brooks Act, which was solidly based on concepts prevailing in the late 1960s and early 1970s. The central assumption of this legislation was that one could control information costs by tightly managing the acquisition of computer equipment used for administrative purposes.

Figure 32.1 After Policy Comes Implementation

Information Resource Management could not achieve its purpose by making the acquisition of computer systems as onerous as possible. IRM, as defined by its original intent, was meant to address the total cost of information origination, information manipulation, and information storage, which are mostly personnel expenses. Falling semiconductor prices had brought the costs of computer hardware to less than five percent of life-cycle costs for information management. Therefore, the focus on acquisition, what the DoD IRM organizations concentrated on, needed changing from computer hardware procurement to a concern about total costs for all information handling. Instead of spending an overwhelming amount of attention on the approximately two billion per year spent on purchasing computers, the proper scope of IRM should have been the estimated hundred billion annual expense for all information-related activities.

The first step toward measuring information effectiveness was the adoption by CIM of the *Functional Economic Analysis* (FEA) method for evaluating IRM investments. In a matter of weeks, the office of the Director of Defense Information released the first version of the FEA software. FEA remains now one of the pillars on which all CIM projects must be justified. The basic premise of FEA is that the success of a business can be ascertained by its risk-adjusted discounted cash flow, regardless of its organizational structure.[255] FEA looks at the overall functional costs of a business process, in which information technology is usually only a minor cost component. The DoD has now completed hundreds of FEAs. They found the overwhelming source of savings was in functional costs such as administrative personnel, inventories and transportation. In one DoD operation the information technology cost was less than 4% of the discounted cash flow of the project, although the early delivery of new application software was critical to timely realization of the other 96% of net cash benefits.

The introduction of FEA was traumatic and in many respects shattering to the IRM traditional views because it forced an examination of user costs and benefits to an extent never attempted before. Managers who were starting CIM projects had to take a business view and maximize cash benefits that would directly support the much needed improvements in operating effectiveness.

While the FEA was being established, a collection of Congressional staff, auditors, inspectors and magazine reporters engaged in discussions of whether or not CIM was already a failure. To measure CIM accomplishments, they looked for year-to-year reductions in DoD expenditures for computers, as reported to the Office of Management

---

255. Risk-adjusted discounted cash flow [RADCF] is a term used by investment analysts. "Cash flow" is the projected amount of cash generated minus cash consumed by a project. "Discounted" means that the cash expected today is worth more than cash expected tomorrow. "Risk-adjusted" means that uncertainty about the estimated benefits and costs to be experienced will devalue the cash flow estimates more than estimates known with precision. The RADCF is calculated by a computer program that runs a standard spread-sheet package several hundred times to simulate the effects of risk. The RADCF software was developed by the Institute for Defense Analysis according to the precepts found in Chapters 9 and 10 of *The Business Value of Computers*. The *Functional Economic Analysis Model*, including program diskettes and *Guidebook*, are available from the Defense Technical Information Center, Cameron Station, Alexandria, VA, 22304, as report AD M200225, 1993. Over one hundred publications documenting the progress of the CIM program are available from this source.

and Budget. I maintained that the value of CIM was better determined by how well it supported efficiency gains tracked by DMRDs and not simply by what happened to computer expenditures. The gains from DMRDs were reported to Congress by Secretary Cheney semi-annually.

The FEA point of view eventually prevailed because the projected savings from reduced computer expenses were insufficient to generate the cash needed to meet Congressional expectations. Doubts about the financial viability of CIM by Congressional staffs, OMB, GAO, the press, industry associations, onlookers from the military services and the Inspector General were eased, at least temporarily.

Information Policy Board

Information management is as much a matter of style as of substance. With the move from the comptroller's department to C^3I, questions abounded: Will I adopt dictatorial, conspirational, participative or impulsive approaches to managing change? Shall I use the considerable budgetary clout to force, cajole or entice the entrenched office holders to adopt new methods? Will I staff my office with hand-picked confidants who previously worked with me in private industry, or will I rely on the existing civil service functionaries to assist in the transformation of systems practices? Early actions were closely scrutinized by the approximately 80,000 systems people for clues of developments to come, as well as by a similar number of contractors for indications of what to expect from the new regime.

The standard approach for most appointees to a new senior position is to form a council, board or steering committee. Such bodies usually start with the best intentions. However, their wide ranging charters and expansive pronouncements about expected reforms often are overtaken by the pressure of events. Thus participative councils become transformed into occasional forums in which members are asked to endorse decisions that had been already concluded by the new leader and a few hand-picked confidants. CIM could not afford either a dictatorial nor a conspirational style because the inertia of the existing establishment required making changes not only from the top down, but also from initiatives within the organization. The formation of an effective advisory board was essential, but the rules had to be set so that the board truly worked as a decision-making body.

Within two weeks after arriving, I announced the formation of a fifteen person policy board representing major departments and agencies of the DoD. The board would meet every Wednesday from 10 to 12 a.m., and arrive at policy-execution and standards formulation decisions by majority vote. The Board would vote on admitting agenda items, assign the responsibility for completing staff work and set the schedule when a decision would come up for a vote. Before a decision could finally come up for a vote, the completed staff work would be shared with all parties so that nobody could ask for a postponement of a decision. All decisions of the Board became effective immediately.

The Information Policy Board turned out to be a good way to gain the cooperation of highly independent military services on joint projects by consensus instead of fiat.[256] The legitimacy of the board as a rule-abiding body became affirmed on the day when a proposal that I strongly favored lost to a majority vote opposing it.

From "Grand Design" to Migration Systems

FEA had a profound effect on how people started viewing systems development. Almost in every case, constructing a brand new system that would supersede many similar old applications was the least desirable choice.[257] The preferable alternative was to select the best one of many redundant applications as the "migration application" of choice. This application would survive as the other systems were gradually phased out, gaining the redundant systems' resources as well as their functions. This approach did not rule out getting rid of accumulated legacy systems and starting afresh on a new solution. However, each such costly and risky venture would be subjected to the tough discipline of having to prove its case.

---

256. Much of the credit for the effectiveness of the Board goes to its first executive secretary, Col. Gilbert Hawk, U.S.Air Force. His successor was Col. David Schottel, U.S. Army. In the first year of operation the board completed work on over seventy new processes and standards.
257. The number of cases examined was over 1,000 applications out of a total population estimated to be well over 10,000.

To popularize the CIM approach to migration instead of building new systems, an enterprising organization actually made up bumper stickers with catchy phrases. Aggressive marketing should not be limited only to consumer products. One of the CIM bumper stickers says *Reuse or Buy Before You Fabricate.* Reuse combined with selecting the best that is already available leads to an immediate generation of cash instead of suffering through a prolonged negative cash flow until a project breaks even. Merging redundant applications into migration systems also reduces maintenance and operating expenses. The greatest benefits are experienced by the business function. Picking the best migration application and then enhancing it for universal use simplifies training, reduces data errors and begins the journey towards ultimate improvement of business processes.

It takes less effort to simplify a consolidated application than to chase after dozens of legacy systems which are fundamentally similar in what they try to accomplish. Figure 32.2 illustrates the CIM migration concepts which emphasize eliminating redundant systems prior to engaging in business process redesign. The introduction of new and advanced technologies would follow only after the number as well as the scope of computer applications are trimmed down to represent a much simpler set of business processes.

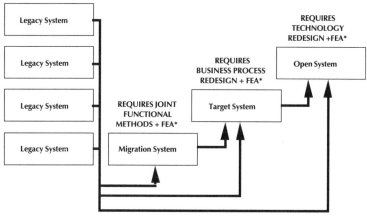

*FEA= FUNCTIONAL ECONOMIC ANALYSIS™

Figure 32.2 An Evolutionary Migration Schema

The adoption of "applications triage" which was to eliminate over nine thousand existing legacy applications in the DoD is now a generally accepted view of how to modernize information systems. A new CIM systems integration organization now maintains a directory and diagrams of how and when various legacy applications shall march to extinction.

Migration tree diagrams like the one for financial applications illustrated in Figure 32.3, turned out to be an effective way to communicate the overall CIM direction. Each migration of applications within a function involved consolidating databases into a surviving application. For example, the migration tree for the finance function illustrated the plan for how over ninety major financial applications were to be merged ultimately into only seven in less than five years, with payroll consolidations leading the way. The acronyms on the chart describe the individual applications.

In this respect, the DoD followed managed improvement precedents set by the private industry, such as Xerox, which consolidated seven general ledger systems into one. This allowed Xerox to centralize work from four data centers into one and eliminate more than one hundred positions. Another example was the General Electric Corporation, which consolidated thirty-four different payroll systems into only one, while reducing financial processing centers from five to one. In that process GE eliminated four hundred positions.

No function stands alone within an organization. In the DoD the vertically organized finance, accounting, personnel and medical systems all had horizontal connections to other departments. For example, authorizing medical disability pay required extensive information exchanges between the payroll, personnel and medical applications. The biggest gains in business process improvement arose from horizontally linking applications that previously were isolated from each other and therefore required considerable clerical labor to overcome the gaps in the information flows. The display of the individual functional trees served as a powerful means to explain how the various applications and data would ultimately converge. This is important, since the bureaucratic clout of any DoD department rested on its self-sufficiency in controlling its sources of information.

Large organizations grow redundant information handling capabilities because each office unit prefers to be independent of somebody else's information sources and computer applications. Such quests for independence are instinctively protective acts of every office-holder. Depending on somebody else's actions is not only risky but reduces the opportunity to justify additional staff. The DoD migration trees helped to clarify the interdependencies between isolated branches and the core applications that supported separate organizational units.[258]

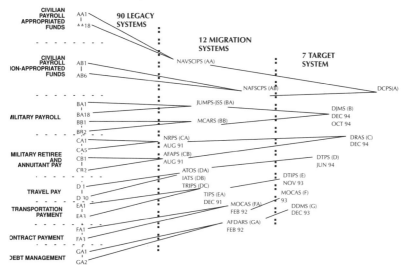

Figure 32.3 Migration Tree for Selected Financial Applications

After a cluster of legacy applications are merged into one or two successor applications, there was still work to be done. At that point, the CIM policies called for introducing business process improvement (BPI) methods that involved simplification, simplification and simplification before any major automation investments would be allowed to take place. It was only after completing BPI that we encouraged dis-

---

258. Migration trees were developed by Dr. Michael Mestrovich, director of the Defense Information Systems Agency's Center for Integration and Interoperability, a CIM initiated and funded organization.

cussions about technical issues such as client servers, integrated data-bases and distributed systems.

Gold Nuggets

To motivate DoD organizations to participate in CIM, the "Gold Nugget Award" emerged as the symbol that CIM was receptive to rec-ognizing the best practices, regardless of where they were situated. It is good politics to honor the accomplishments of the organization that surrounds you. Organizations have a culture, and you cannot be per-ceived as attacking that culture without adverse consequences. The mil-itary, perhaps more than any other organization, except those with tribal or religious roots, depends on loyalty and personal commitment to sus-tain itself in its service to the nation.

Perhaps the most significant and proudest contribution of CIM was in seeking out Gold Nugget managers and placing them into new CIM positions of considerable scope and responsibility. You qualified as a Gold Nugget person if you had a long-established track record in the Department of Defense, earned great respect from your associates, and your current position was a dead end.[259] In my first eight months as Director of Defense Information, I spent much time talking to people and making a list of potential CIM executives. The objective was to reach out for talent wherever it was, which was not necessarily only in the Pentagon or the established IRM community. The most reliable sources of information about potential talent were contractors and con-sultants with long standing experience in doing business with the DoD.[260] If two or more competing suppliers respected the talents of a systems manager, I could be fairly certain about that person's qualifica-tions.

---

259. Of more than thirty Gold Nugget CIM senior executives, only one was hired from out-side DoD and that was for a highly specialized technical assignment.
260. Contractors and suppliers were glad to come and brief the Director of Defense Informa-tion on any topic. Many of these executives were retired defense officials with seasoned judg-ment. I remain immensely grateful for the generous counsel and advice offered freely, without prejudice or expectation of favors.

You cannot use information technology to attack the beliefs, habits and customs of the people who have to depend on it. You can influence attitudes and expectations to some extent, but you cannot overcome the dedication of any organization, especially the military, to take care of its own. The best and surest way to change the direction of an organization is to build innovations on top of the best that already exists. It became one of the CIM practices to nurture sources of experience that were the best of their kind in the desired direction of progress. CIM funded a number of small ventures as a way to reward talent and demonstrate that innovation was welcome. Here are some of the guidelines used by the DoD for promoting home grown business process improvements:

- Demonstrate your leadership by first solving a significant problem.
- Link new programs to recognized targets and objectives.
- Broaden the scope and definition of what system work is all about to include all information management and not just computerized solutions.
- Win commitment by helping people to learn how to apply new tools and discover new opportunities for themselves.
- Communicate effectively the complexity of what you are trying to accomplish so that project plans are realistic. Obtain adequate resources to deliver expected results.
- Recognize and reward excellence.

Creating Policies
CIM would be always running against a deadline of when it would cease to be an initiative with a code name and become a viable perma-

nent institution.[261] CIM would become a success only if its innovations became accepted tradition. This meant producing directives, instructions and guidelines that would endure the change in political administrations. Most importantly, it called for a massive educational program that would make innovation a permanent part of life for the DoD. Better skills and understanding were needed to cope with the increasingly complex technology essential to modernizing the defense information infrastructure.

Formulating these policies called for drafts, debates, coordination, approvals, releases and interpretation. An apt analogy to DoD policy work is surgery to fix broken bones. It is necessary for continued good health, requires expertise, takes too long, is too expensive, is unpleasant and once done is hard to undo. Without established policies and training in how to apply them, even well funded systems innovations will not survive beyond their birth.

When done properly, policies can last longer than the tenure of those who make them. Making a practice into a policy is the only means for assuring the institutionalization of innovation in a large organization, especially in the public sector. The highest level of authority must issue such policies in order to legitimize the implementation tactics used. Policy to an innovator is like tank support for the infantry. Bravery is necessary but is not sufficient to get the work done.

The CIM program has produced an exemplary array of information management policy innovations that are now the foundation for managing defense information. The text of most of these policies was written in understandable high-school level English. Most of these policies have generic applicability to many large enterprises. They deserve to be imitated, since good policy writing is rare. Here are some of the key policies that are shaping the future of CIM:[262]

---

261. From its inception, I managed CIM as if I were to run it for an extended time. That turned out to be a flawed assumption. My apartment lease in Arlington, Viriginia had a longer term than my appointment in the Pentagon.
262. The policy branch of CIM was directed by Mr. Harry Pontius.

- **The Defense Information Management Program Policy.** Defines scope, principles and organizational relationships. The grand charter of everything CIM stands for. Many of the ideas in the first part of this book dealing with "Governance" reflect the discussions of how to articulate the relationship between information management and general management tasks.

- **Defense Information Management Policies and Procedures.** Defines the "due process" for communicating about how to plan and implement information systems. The idea that information management is a political process practiced by other means arose out of the difficulties in articulating roles and responsibilities. The adoption of the constitutional model for describing layers of governance was the result of attempts to express complex ideas about information structures in a simple form.

- **Life-Cycle Management of Automated Information Systems Policy.** Defines the control and oversight process, while it emphasizes evolutionary and incremental development.

- **Business Process Improvement Policy.** Includes a manual of how to analyze business processes and recommend improvements in information flow.

- **Data Administration Policy.** Includes a manual how to manage the standardization of data elements. The charter for the most ambitious data administration program ever conceived. The key to systems integration and interoperability. Without data administration there is chaos.

- **Functional Economic Analysis.** The policy that links the economic evaluation of alternative information management solutions to the delivery of business results.

- **Technical Architecture Framework.** A five volume compilation to guide standard systems development. Includes an important Technical Reference Model that specifies approved standards for development and acquisition.

- **Graphic Interface Style Guide.** Offers instructions about what computer screens should look like to minimize training costs and errors.

- **Activity and Data Modeling.** CIM has institutionalized the IDEF (ICAM Definition Method, where ICAM stands for Integrated Computer Aided Manufacturing) method as the standard language for business process description. This method originated in the late 1960s in the Air Force, but gained prominence only after adoption by the commercial manufacturing sector in the early 1980s. There are other proprietary methods that perform a similar function, but IDEF stands unique as the only method on which a number of vendors standardize their software modeling tools.[263]

  The CIM program was instrumental in getting IDEF launched as a Federal Information Processing Standard. CIM also funded a large scale expansion in the use of this standard.[264] The adoption of IDEF as a CIM standard became the single most successful

---

263. For the stimulus to proceed with the adoption of IDEF tools I am particularly indebted to Mr. Dan Appleton and Mr. Dennis Wisnosky.

264. CIM also pioneered the enhancement of this technique by adopting Electronic Meeting Systems (EMS) for group decision-making. In a study of twenty three cases of activity and data modeling, researchers found that business process models were completed on average about ten times faster using EMS than by traditional discussion-and-flip-chart means, while consuming five times fewer person-hours. For details see Dennis, Hayes, Daniels, "Reengineering Business Process Modeling," *Proceeding of the 27th International Conference*, IEEE, 1994.

CIM venture investment. It was acquired as a Golden Nugget from the U.S. Army Corps of Engineers.[265]

- **Activity Based Costing.** Although this enormously effective tool was suspected of poaching on the comptroller's privileges, it was necessary to make an investment in this method as a way to start the automation of the systems planning and business improvement processes. To make it acceptable to the finance people guarding their prerogatives, activity based costing became an adjunct to the activity and data modeling program.

Technology Improvement Programs[266]

- **Data Administration.** Development and operation of the DoD data repository. A key CIM strategic asset. Acquired as a Golden Nugget.[267]

- **Technical Integration Management.** Instituted the development of an overall technical architecture, configuration control and the management of cross-functional interfaces. This effort is an absolute requirement for assuring enterprise-wide interoperability of systems and data.

- **Technical Reference Architecture.** Guides the evolution of applications toward *open* systems.

---

265. Mr. Mike Yoemans, subsequently the Deputy Director of Defense for Business Process Improvement came to CIM from the Corps of Engineers and provided the leadership for spreading these methods throughout the DoD.
For additional details see Bui, Duvall, Elliott and Emery, "Business Re-engineering: Lessons Learned From the U.S. Army Corps of Engineers Modernization Program," *Naval Postgraduate School Report NPS-AS-93-007*, October 1992.
266. Most of the technology improvement programs were under the direction of Brigadier General (Ret.) Denis Brown.
267. See Bui, Dolk, Donohue and Hayes, "Data Management: Implementation Lessons Learned From the Army Data Management Program," *Naval Postgraduate School Report NPS-AS-93-004*, September 1992

- **Enterprise Architecture.** This is the Holy Grail of all systems people. Advanced systems textbooks tell you that every organization must have one. Several CIM program directors attempted to come up with this abstraction, only to fail. Only someone with a depth of understanding about how the Pentagon really works could come up with anything of use. Several drafts of this document are still circulating in the Pentagon, because under the cover of "architecture" everybody now understands that it is a profoundly political document about who really controls what information.

- **Software Reuse Program**. Development and operation of the DoD software repository. Another CIM strategic asset. Acquired as a Golden Nugget.[268]

- **Software Assessment and Improvement Program**. Adopts and administers the software maturity evaluation program.

- **Integrated Computer-Aided Software Engineering.** Provides all development organizations with standard software engineering tools and related training and technical services. Essential for achieving massive reductions in software costs. A key CIM strategic asset. Has far reaching consequence on the future of the DoD systems workforce. Promoted the adoption of the European Community standard as the basis for DoD's "systems knowledge repository" and is in the process of becoming a Federal Information Processing standard. Co-opted as a Gold Nugget from the Air Force.

---

268. See Bui, Emery, Harms, VanHook and Suh, "A Clearinghouse for Software Reuse: Lessons Learned from the RAPID/DSRS Initiatives," *Naval Postgraduate School Report NPS-AS-93-006*, October 1992. This program was under the direction of Dr. Kurt Fischer.

- **Information Technology Reuse Services.** Offers a streamlined hardware acquisition process and should extend the useful technology life of equipment. Another CIM strategic asset. Acquired as a Golden Nugget.
- **Defense Information Technology Services Organization.**[269] This organization provided the cadre of people to test, evaluate and build a world-class information management organization within the Defense Information Systems Agency. This organization is gradually becoming a cost-competitive operation and a showplace to demonstrate that the public sector can operate information services entrepreneurially.

Implementing Business Process Improvement

In terms of the scope and long range impact of CIM, business process improvement became one of its most important contribution. It established a formal process for describing information flows using standard notation and standard costing principles. This made it possible to start working on several process improvements simultaneously. Separating the work flow into smaller groups made it possible to achieve partial gains in local applications. Work could begin on an especially profitable element of the overall process without waiting for the resolution of all of the questions that would certainly come up while several organizations were negotiating agreement on how to make changes in their relationships. Achieving local gains also made it possible for people to gain confidence in working together so that they could later perform more complex tasks as a cohesive team for even greater gains.

Figure 32.3 represents the fundamental relationships of all DoD business process improvement projects, regardless of how small or complex. This should be seen as an example of the definition of relationships that can be shared and understood by a large and diverse group of

---

269. The first director of this organization was Mr. Clyde Jeffcoat.

people. As long as everyone has access to the definition and design of the goals, each can see where his own participation fits in. This method proved to be a powerful communications tool.

Figure 32.5, in standard CIM format, was used to illustrate how the master objectives could be split into subordinate tasks for assignment to committees, consultants, or task forces:

This kind of format was set as a standard in CIM, and was very useful in tracking the hierarchy and progress of each task. By establishing and maintaining maps of process improvement tasks it was possible for people to work in parallel. This saved time and coordination as compared with the traditionally sequential DoD practice that followed principles of phased project management.

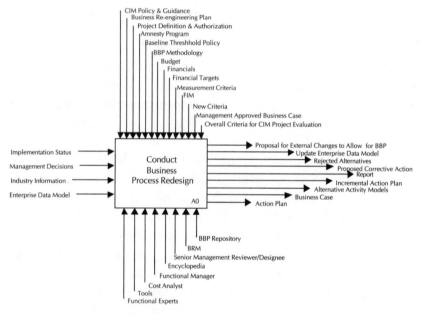

Figure 32.4 Master Diagram for Business Process Improvement[270]

---

270. The abbreviations on this diagram are as follows: "FIM" stands for functional information manager, a senior executive responsible for a business process. "BBP" stands for budgeting and business planning. "BRM" stands for business resource management.

Opportunities for improvement were everywhere around the DoD, yet the existing processes of approvals, reviews, concurrence, evaluations and coordination were so cumbersome that even the most competent, dedicated and hardworking talent could produce only minimal results.[271]

During my inspection of one of the large DoD supply warehouses, I randomly picked up one package from the conveyor belt to learn about the paperwork involved for that item. Inside was an eighteen inch piece of thin copper wire. The shipping papers valued the wire at thirty-six cents. It had been returned to the warehouse for restocking into inventory. Further investigation showed that the wire originally came from a 5,000 foot spool and that a computer kept track of the spool's use for each repair incident. If the actual consumption of wire was less than the inventory on hand, the computerized monitoring procedure called for returning all unused wire for reuse. The intent of this procedure for keeping track of valuable items represented a misapplication of sound controls where it did not matter. The cost of the paperwork alone was a large multiple of the value of the wire. Besides, nobody would ever order an eighteen inch piece of wire.

In the same warehouse, I happened to see on the loading dock a huge object ready for shipment to Dhahran, Saudi Arabia. In May 1991, the Gulf war had been long over and it was peculiar to see something being shipped there, since we were loading every available ship with materiel for return to the U.S. The object was a replacement undercarriage assembly for a heavy tank transport. The order date was early December 1990 for repairing one of most important vehicles in the campaign against Iraq. The shipment had never been cancelled.

In another case, the automatic inventory replenishment system ordered transshipment of a standard, commercially available transistor worth thirty-nine cents from one warehouse to another that was forty

---

271. Mr. Deane Erwin, assisted by Mrs. Mary Howard, helped to steer CIM through the procedural quagmire of the Pentagon. Mrs. Cindy Kendall, Deputy Assistant Secretary of Defense, made sure that we learned how to communicate with the various Congressional staffs, the General Accounting Office, the Office of Management and Budget and the Inspector General.

miles away. The estimated packaging and transportation costs for this transaction were forty-four dollars.

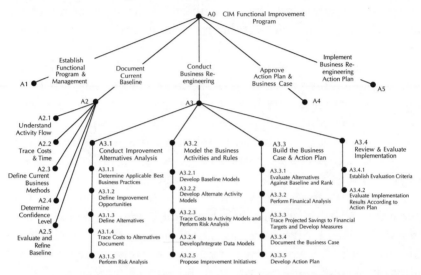

Figure 32.5 Map of Process Improvement Tasks

In another instance, a bid solicitation for $25,000 worth of ant bait was twenty-nine pages long. It took two-hundred and twenty-seven days to award the contract. During that time a large number of administrators, clerks and officials were busy handling that bid. The paperwork for non-competitive procurement of a helicopter spare part took two-hundred seventy three days. A prolonged fabrication, delivery, inspection and testing schedule took place in addition to that. No wonder DoD inventories were huge.

On the basis of many similar observations, I concluded the existing information systems supported inflexible and monolithic bureaucratic procedures that tolerated no deviations, even though the prescribed acts violated common sense. The individuals who operated the systems were perfectly aware of the foolishness of what they had to do sometimes, but were unable to do anything about it. They followed rules, not results. Making any change in the logic of the computer systems was not only extremely difficult and time-consuming, but often made the irrationality of the system worse by adding further complexities. Operators viewed the computer systems not much differently than the sorcerer's apprentice who could not stop a magic spell from growing into a disaster.

A typical example while implementing the CIM approach to business process improvement is the Fort Sill Directorate of Engineering project, which is one of over a five hundred of such analyses conducted since 1992.[272] The approach always called for first drawing up an "as-is" view of the target's information processes, such as illustrated in Figure 32.6:

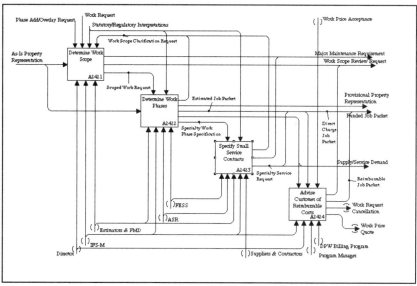

Figure 32.6 Ft. Sill Engineering Management Processes

By assigning costs to each of the work flow elements in Figure 32.6, it was possible to calculate the unit transaction costs for every business activity as shown in the following table:

---

272. This is an example of diagrams that illustrated business process improvement methods. These were prepared by a number of consultants under direct guidance by Mr. Michael Yoemans.

Business Process	Transactions/Year	Unit Cost
Prepare a Service Order	51,000	$2.40/order
Approve/Disapprove Work Order Request	4,100	$58 /request
Develop Work Order Estimate	860	$336 /estimate
Support In-house Work Order Activities	2,400	$197 /order
Specify Supply/Service Request	31,000	$11.50/request
Receive Depot/Purchase Delivery	66,000	$14.10/receipt
Issue Supply Item	167,000	$7.30/issue
Issue Work Order Supply Items/order	15 items	$109 /order
Process In-house Work Order	1,900	$364 /order
Process In-house Work Order with Estimate	500	$700 /order
Process Contracted Job Order	240	$788 /order
Provide Construction Order Engineering	250	$7490 /order

Figure 32.7 Ft. Sill Business Process Activity Costs

With a good understanding of the process costs, it was then possible to start running simulations of the financial consequences of altering the flow of information. Intuitive estimates of the greatest possible
gains were not always reliable. The availability of an information work
flow model for every business process made it possible for a group of
managers to analyze and recommend a large number of possible
changes and negotiate compromises about which activities to delete. A
proposal for eliminating non-value added work from the Ft.Sill
processes would appear in Table 32.8:

Activity/Process	Reference	Module	Actual Cost	Unit Cost
Validate Property Requirements	A2415	Non Value	$128,890.44	$16.74
Submit Requirements	A2411		$79,868.17	$10.37
Determine Special Interests	A2412		$42,813.33	$5.56
Prioritize Requirements	A2414		$10,439.42	$1.36
Classify Accounts	A2416	Non Value	$659.18	$0.09
Total Cost			$262,670.55	$34.11
Total Non-Value Added Cost Content			$129,549.62	$16.83
Total Potential Cost			$133,120.93	$17.28

Figure 32.8 Cost Reduction Potential in Business Process Analysis

In the Ft. Sill project, the elimination of activities that involved
processes A2415 and A2416 showed an average unit cost improvement

potential from \$34.11 to \$17.28 for activities that have approximately 7,700 transactions per year. The potential saving would be then \$129,550, without impairing defense support.

An Information Management Doctrine for Defense

A doctrine is a set of shared values that makes it possible for individuals to independently make decisions with the full confidence that their acts will be consistent with the goals and expectations of their associates. A coherent defense information management doctrine emerged as result of CIM activities. I consider doctrine to be of paramount importance to any successful social or business endeavor, because it greatly simplifies managerial tasks and creates a sense of commitment that unleashes the enormous human potential that exists in every government organization.[273] The following is a list of some of the CIM doctrinal concepts:

- All information management strategies must correspond to defense plans. All peacetime applications must be capable of operating under war conditions.

- Technical systems integration will become a core defense capability and cannot be outsourced. The Defense Information Systems Agency becomes the integrator of all contractors performing integration tasks for individual systems programs.

- The current overemphasis on technology acquisition shall be replaced by planning for total functional life-cycle costs that include the costs of operating and using an application.

- Business process improvement will be applied as a continuous, incremental and evolutionary productivity enhancement process.

---

273. Military services have detailed doctrine manuals covering every conceivable activity, such as the Air/Land doctrine, the tank maneuver doctrine, special operations doctrine, mine-sweeping doctrine, air superiority doctrine and so forth. An information management doctrine was long overdue.

- Charges for information technology shall be based on activity-based costing.
- Fiscal controls will shift to the customer. Compensation for transaction services will be on a fee-for-service basis.
- Transaction costs shall be benchmarked against commercial services and must carry fully allocated overhead costs for making any comparisons.
- Systems management will shift from vertical hierarchies that are location- and organization-specific, to horizontal functions that cut across the entire DoD. The goal is to follow and support entire business processes.
- Most of the locally developed applications shall migrate to standard systems. Standard applications shall concern primarily data management and will offer tools for developing local options for output presentation.
- All data shall become a defense asset which must be centrally controlled for integrity and security.
- Security and survivability controls shall be centralized.
- Systems integration and interoperabilty testing will be mandatory for all applications and networks.
- Business process improvement shall take place prior to any major investment in information technology.

CIM Rules

Every doctrine evolves a set of rules which in due course become shared beliefs. CIM developed these rules from the above set of doctrines:

- Require DoD certification of all data definitions.
- Assure single source data origination stewardship.
- Issue data definitions to contractors as government furnished material.

- Dictate the maintenance of data models for all applications.

- Initiate database backup and archive functions from the next higher organizational level.

- Pursue electronic data interchange agreements with other agencies, suppliers and contractors.

- Pursue evolutionary and incremental systems deployment. Do not attempt all-encompassing major systems replacements.

- Train as you fight and design (prototype) as you train. Rely on military exercises to come up with suggestions about how to improve systems.

- Give the commanders capacity and facilities for making complex inquiries at points of use. Do not encumber the central development organization with the job of changing report formats or making minor changes in screen displays.

- Construct variety from software elements and not hardware.

- Do not chase every conceivable technology development. Concentrate on major cost reduction opportunities.

- Hardware, software and communications capabilities should be provided from proven commercial sources and not developed internally.

- Establish core competencies by creating a small number of specialized organizations with expertise to support DoD-wide needs.

- Seek out and develop skilled managers of information technology innovations.

- Acquire a cadre of experts for areas that form the core of unique DoD information competencies.

- Make sure that the technology programs share a unified strategic direction with measurable goals instead of standing as isolated explorations.

- Make communication networks designs inseparable from computer systems. Do not separate the telecommunications management organization from the computer services organization. Communication is more than establishing a circuit connection. It must also assure that the contents of a message becomes integrated with the recipient's computing environment.[274]

- View the computer network as an extended workstation. The network is the computer, and everything attached to it are peripherals.

- Recognize the inherent vulnerability of all networks in war and therefore place the maximum amount of computing capacity at points of use.

- Integrate data, voice, graphics and video into a single shared network.

- Establish a structure of network monitoring and control for all communication networks to assure single point resolution of all failures.

- Provide value-added communications functions, such as directory, security, information interchange and software distribution, as an infrastructure "utility" service.

---

274. Many of the current problems in information management in DoD had their origin in the limited views of what is communication as seen by the Army Signal Corps. Assuring the passage of an analog or digital pulse between two points is necessary but certainly not sufficient. Most DoD communications now involve programmed computer-to-computer sharing of software applications. Arranging for person-to-person communication, the principal preoccupation of the Signal Corps, is much simpler because all information processing is done in a person's head.

- Expect that information systems will be choice war targets and therefore test survivability against attacks by adversaries specially trained in information warfare methods.

Figure 32.9 Information Warfare

- Validate each systems design for worst case scenarios for survivability, especially for attacks involving terrorists, other-than-war actions and espionage.
- Achieve survivability primarily through redundancy and not by complete dependence on physical protection means.
- Support critical databases from low-risk sites such as off-shore floating platforms or U.S. based centers.

- Subject the network to hostile tests, conducted by third party experts to identify security and survivability risks.

- Control access to network entry points, especially for software management and maintenance.

- Design security into hardware configuration, with particular attention paid to authenticating network access privileges.

- Maintain central monitoring over all actions initiated from mission-critical terminals.

- Lengthen technology life by continually upgrading modular software and hardware instead of following a "discard-and-construct" approach to acquisition.

- Distribute software from re-use "warehouses." Define, store and distribute software objects for use in all development. Require contractors to use previously developed objects and application templates.

- Require technical designs that allow a single workstation to serve all individual information needs from diverse sources.

- Establish standard display interface styles to minimize training expenses and errors in use.

- Favor designs that allow the use of scaleable computing capacity using standard commercial microprocessors.

- Follow international commercial standards primarily and Federal standards only if industry standards are not available. Military standards may be used only if none of the former standards apply.

- Adopt a standard software development toolset and software repository for all application planning, development, implementation, testing and maintenance. Require contractors to deliver their software in a format that is compatible with the software repository.

- Reduce security risks from on-site maintenance of microcomputers and servers by relying on backup spare units for immediate replacement of failed units. Carry out maintenance at secure service centers.

- Purchase hardware and software separately to avoid the constraints imposed by the vendors' preference for proprietary solutions.

- Install new software or upgrade it through network managed services. Do not allow unauthorized insertion of software at the local level.

- Provide protection against software intrusion through global configuration management of hardware and software from network control points.

33

THE POLITICS OF CIM

Conflicting directions lead to hesitant action.

All innovation should begin with studying the failures of those who have tried the idea before. There is more useful information for guiding business process improvement in credible stories about failed information systems than from any other source. The corollary to this observation is that fancy executive presentations selling a new computer application has limited value because they usually avoid an assessment of what can go wrong.

Government Accounting Office (GAO) reports are some of the most extensive sources of horror stories about DoD failures in acquiring, managing and using computers. This public documentation, although biased in favor of fault-finding, forms a comprehensive collection of good ideas gone wrong, and bad ideas turning into disaster. In private industry, reporting about systems failures is unusual. Mistakes are hastily buried to avoid embarrassment. The computer trade press differs from newspapers and magazines that thrive on exposés. The computer trade press is reluctant to print calamity stories that would offend someone, especially vendors who are advertisers. Computer debacles are hardly ever written up in scholarly journals because academic discipline calls for an uncompromising identification of the causes of failure. Such diagnosis is extremely difficult to do by verifiable means.

The GAO is in the business of uncovering failures because that is what Congress wishes it to do. Thousands of pages reveal a litany of aborts, overruns, breakdowns and contradictions. Such unique reporting conveys a hard-to-believe record of persistent ineptitude. For CIM to fix any of that would require changing practices that were systemic and common to most of the reported incidents. CIM could not try to stamp out hundreds of potential fires. A CIM staff of only fifty in the Pentagon would certainly worsen the situation by attempting to check on the doings of about eighty-thousand DoD systems people, and many more contractors. There is no way the CIM staff could prevent a malfeasance that the GAO could easily discover afterwards. The best a small corporate staff can do is to dramatize examples of excellence and to identify the common elements for most of the mishaps. A good corporate staff sees to it that excellence is recognized and rewarded. It also makes sure that pervasive and chronic causes of failure are remedied. Developing policies that lead to the prevention of consistent failures is the sole justification for central staffs, especially if the source of the trouble is at the top of the organization.

The Flawed Acquisition Process

The fundamental flaw shared by all DoD systems and mentioned in almost every unfavorable GAO report originates in the DoD acquisition process. The acquisition laws, regulations and practices enforce an approach that views each major new computer system as a separate, discrete and independent program.

This acquisition bias has its origins in concepts of financial controls originated at the DuPont Company around 1910, and subsequently perfected by Alfred P. Sloan at the General Motors Corporation in the 1920s. According to these concepts, what matters is the budgeting and control of capital expenditures, since the measure of industrial performance is the return on capital. This view may have been appropriate during the era of rapidly expanding industrialization.

Controlling capital instead of understanding operational problems also has the advantage of offering to a small number of managers, and to Congress, a politically manageable capacity to exercise control. We are now in an era in which human resources, motivation, morale and information determine the superiority of all organizations, and particularly the military. The capital-rationing view that is manifested through overemphasis on acquisition controls is not only obsolete but actually damaging to organizational effectiveness.

As consequence of tightly controlled policies that insisted on breaking up all information systems into tightly isolated individual systems development programs, the DoD ended up with an inventory of tens of thousands of computer applications. Every year it had added thousands of new ones. With recent minor exceptions, each system was designed and built with a unique technological approach, under a unique contract, mostly with unique data formats, often with unique communications networks, and little or no integration with past or current applications.

Every contract officer and contractor found it advantageous to apply unique methods in designing and implementing their systems. To accelerate the implementation schedule after lengthy delays in the acquisition process, contract officers and contractors found it necessary to fit their project into a technical environment that was limited in budget, time, and local resources. The DoD acquisition system then forced the construction of the lowest cost self-contained system that fit local conditions. It was like constructing a house with only locally crafted materials, with no benefit from in-place roads, sewers, electricity, water supply, telephones and lumber from a building supply warehouse.[275]

The traditional systems acquisition process shown in Figure 33.1 appears to be simple. One of the systems research centers in DoD completed a detailed business activity flow diagram that described every step in the systems acquisition process. That was easy, because the process was clearly defined by well over ten thousand pages of procedures and regulations that told a program manager exactly which forms to fill out to secure permission to progress from one project check point to

---

275. During the years of the "cultural revolution," each Chinese village was encouraged to build its own steel mill so that the local party officials could learn about industrialization by supervising it. That set back the economy for many decades. The DoD acquisition process reminds me somewhat of the Chinese backyard steel industry of the 1960s. The only difference is that the Chinese stopped doing it.

another. The systems acquisition diagram called for completing over five-thousand steps in a rigidly prescribed sequence. No wonder it took five to ten years and many hundreds of millions of dollars to deliver any major new information system. Only a small part of the process attended to customer needs.[276] Much of the effort and elapsed time was spent on those steps preceding systems design that involved the planning, advocating and securing funds for the proposed program. Most of the schedule delays were due to the tribulations of hardware acquisition. An exceedingly large portion of the process dealt with making sure that a unique technology solution was subject to validation, measurement, testing and reporting for an assortment of auditors, inspectors, regulators and comptrollers.

My examination of the acquisition process found that the number of days devoted to developing the concept and delivering a working system was much less than the days spent meeting, reporting, supervising, answering auditors, making presentations and weaving through the procurement maze. This squandering of time and personnel was still not as injurious as the delays and errors caused by micromanagement of the enormous number of officials involved acquiring instead of making the technology work.

---

276. Perhaps one of the most ornate monuments to excessive control and the stagnating effect of bureaucracy is something called the Major Automated Information Systems Review Council (MAISRC). The Army, Navy and Air Force have their own versions of this process, which further compounds the complexity of reviews. Each project may have anywhere from three to five milestones. Each milestone requires upwards of forty separate documents to certify what has been done. These are not simple documents, however. The operational testing stage alone consisted of forty seven separate certifications. No wonder that prudent project managers allocated up to 40% of project staff to getting their package through committees, hearings and audits. There is a consulting industry that thrives on the generation of the required documents for each acquisition ordeal. The going rate is about $800,000 per milestone.

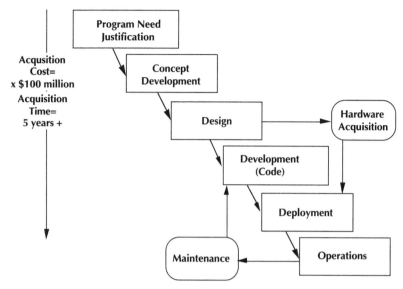

Figure 33.1 The Traditional DoD Systems Acquisition Process

Cutting Down the Scope of Acquisition Programs

The Executive Level Group originally chartered by the Deputy Secretary had concluded that acquiring difficult and long-lead time elements of the systems infrastructure, such as databases, communications, systems engineering tools and computing power, must be independent of the relatively short-term time span and limited budgets available for individual systems programs. The ELG suggested separating the difficult and long-term elements, to be available from a common telecomputing infrastructure, from the relatively easy and short-term aspects of application designs that met local needs. That meant:

- Providing a standard communications network;
- Establishing standard data elements that are common to all applications;
- Making available standard graphic interfaces that minimize training;
- Creating a high level integration capability within DoD to secure interoperability of applications; and

- Using standard business process models and systems engineering tools.

One goal of CIM was to provide a low-cost technology infrastructure as a generic fee-for-service commodity so that the acquisition process could focus on solutions to unique problems. Instead of building a custom information infrastructure for each major systems program, the expensive and difficult job of constructing shared capabilities would come from a common infrastructure. CIM was to free the information systems from the stranglehold of the acquisition procedures enforced by the procurement bureaucrats whose job tenure was much longer than any of their customers.

By shortening the elapsed time for systems development, control would be returned to the business managers who were directly responsible for supporting defense capabilities. To this end, the acquisition process had to be changed to accommodate a much shorter cycle for making decisions about hardware, software and data management.

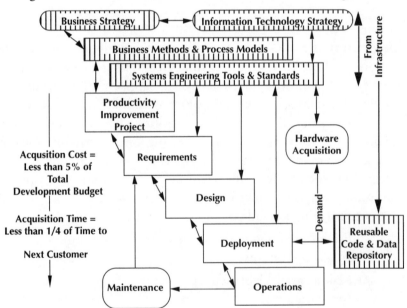

Figure 33.2 The Preferred Acquisition Process

A professionally managed organization charged with the design, operation and maintenance of the DoD technology infrastructure would provide generic hardware, software and communications services to support most standard systems. Customers would then be able to obtain tools to construct their own local applications using hardware, software and communications capabilities already in place. This called for centralizing management and standards of the infrastructure so that local operators could better focus on meeting their varied and unique needs rapidly. The model here was that of the railroads and telephone system, where everybody does not improvise their own networks apart from the rest of the system.

Acquiring the infrastructure's resources and customer-owned computing assets would be kept separate from the rapid adaptation of standard applications to meet local needs. That would allow for incremental growth instead of engaging in giant, decade long acquisitions for each individual systems program. Using the CIM processes would enable any DoD program manager to add fully tested major new functions to an already existing application set for less than $1 million, in less than six months.[277] All technical programs under CIM would have the acceleration of systems modernization and the cost reduction of applications as their unifying theme.

The proposed acquisition schema would work only if the strategies of the enterprise would remain relatively stable, preferably longer than eight years.[278] Only long-term investments generate a steady

---

277. The optimal elapsed time for constructing a new computer application in the military departments had been governed by the Systems Paralysis Cycle, which was equal to 120 working days. In the first six months of a typical two year tour of duty, a new commanding officer learns about what is going on, since he does not have prior systems experience with a similar application. In the last six months, he campaigns for his next promotion. In between, it takes six months to complete the systems reviews with a new set of auditors and get the budget re-authorized. That leaves only six months to get anything accomplished, or 120 working days.

278. Defined here as two consecutive presidential terms. In the case of CIM, all cooperation from the military services ceased November 3, 1992, pending arrival of the new administration. It then took more than another year for the new administration to re-examine CIM sufficiently to declare that it should be continued. With the CIM clock of expected savings running at the rate of about $100 million per month, that gives you the approximate price of a significant change in administration.

stream of profits through conservation of effort. Innovation must come on top of already existing investments put in place by earlier efforts.

Resisting a Common Infrastructure

Early in 1992, it became apparent that systems consolidations guided by the Army, Navy and Air Force would not deliver even a fraction of the expected CIM savings to support rising DoD cutbacks. The military services proceeded to concentrate only on costly physical consolidations of data center operations. They did not simultaneously pursue reduction in the workload through elimination of redundant applications. Instead of approaching their cost-reduction tasks as an inter-related hardware/software campaign, they found themselves waging their attacks separately and sequentially. The total cash savings of the military department-managed consolidations was projected to yield no more than a net of $1.3 billion by 1997, which was less than 8% of the seven-year cost goal.

As projected savings shrunk, a difference of opinion arose about what savings were realistic. What were reasonable productivity gains? What should be the correct benchmarks against which the diligence of the ongoing efforts may be judged?

The unit cost reductions of data services in private industry have been well documented. During the 1980s the computer industry delivered impressive declines in the cost of information technologies through a combination of hardware and software technology innovations. To skillful information systems executives, this has offered enormous opportunities to reduce operating costs. Documented productivity gains from several U.S. commercial firms suggested that annual productivity gains of 20% were available through modernization and continuous quality improvement.[279]

Early in 1992, it became apparent there was something amiss with the 8% seven year savings expected by the military departments as com-

---

279. A CIM study revealed the following seven year unit cost reduction record: Xerox, –81%; Texas Instruments, –54%; J.C.Penney, –76%; EDS-Champus, –73%; EDS-Eligibility, –42%; EDS-Batch Update, –74%; EDS-Batch Reports, –69%; Karastan-Bigelow, –61%; GTE, –75%; Peat, Marwick client survey, –65%.

pared with the 40% to 80% private sector cost reduction performance. The opportunities for tremendous cost reductions in DoD still existed. DoD would be starting from an already excessive cost base that had not received consistent attention to cost reduction. For example, a consultant's comparison of the cost per million instructions per second (MIPS) of some of the best DoD data centers showed their 1992 costs were at least ten times greater than the U.S. industry average. Organizations such as Xerox and Texas Instruments reported ever increasing savings in unit costs during the early 1990s on top of a long history of prior cost reductions during the 1970s and 1980s.

DoD would be downsizing its operations during the 1990s because of changing global geopolitical circumstances. Its transaction volume was expected to come down anyway. However, unless the ongoing consolidation efforts made technology choices which would cut fixed costs substantially, the actual transaction costs would rise by 1997. A smaller volume of transactions would be absorbing the enormous fixed costs that were embedded in the ways that existing systems had been designed. Unfortunately, the military services' consolidation plans were heavily influenced by the proliferation of mainframe data centers that were running a huge collection of technically obsolete and redundant applications. Even after nominally achieving their goals in reducing the number of mainframe data centers by 1997, the services' fixed costs for running existing software and operating uncoordinated data networks would be still excessive relative to the diminished transaction volumes.[280]

Another problem with the military services' cost reduction plans was the cost base from which savings would be realized. The services were pursuing the downsizing of data center operations that were worth $2 billion per year, that represented only a small share of total systems

---

280. The high fixed costs for information processing are not caused only by the high operating costs of DoD data centers. The Defense Finance and Accounting Services charges $10.05 per paycheck, which is five to seven times more than what is charged by commercial operations that specialize in the payroll business. The costs of settling a travel voucher were $40.48 at the DoD, as compared with $7.08 elsewhere. You cannot blame only the computer operations, since much of the processing was dictated by archaic and convoluted administrative rules.

costs. Cost reduction opportunities for interrelated activities increase dramatically when a coordinated approach is used to address connected opportunities simultaneously. In the case of data center consolidation, the most likely place for achieving savings was in the migration of legacy software to successor applications, not in the consolidation of buildings or merger of computer capacity. Yet, the military departments' plans did not link the consolidation of applications to the consolidation of data centers.

In all fairness, I want to note that delays in resolving the selection of successor migration systems by the Principal Staff Assistants in the Office of the Secretary of Defense most likely inhibited the military services from pursuing a more effective approach if they had wanted to choose such a course. The 1990 compromise intended to coax the unwilling military services to accept CIM was flawed because it left too many critical issues unresolved. Politically expedient compromises often offer a temporary accommodation at the price of destroying the capacity to deliver the expected results. In the summer of 1993, the new administration repeated this costly mistake by accepting, as a convenient compromise, the separation of the management of data center consolidation from the control over software development. The politics of service prerogatives prevailed, and therefore remained in conflict with CIM cost reduction objectives.

Command and Control Functional Analysis

Despite the initial injunction to keep CIM out of military command matters it was always clear that the first priority of all defense information systems was to support defense capabilities and not payroll, finance, personnel and medical systems. These functions have legitimacy to the extent that they could support the prime missions of the DoD, which was safeguarding national security. The core information competencies of a defense organization are command, control and intelligence (C^3I), because these systems are becoming one of the primary weapons for achieving success in any warfare mission. Everything else is support overhead.

As CIM came into existence, the importance of C^3I systems was rapidly rising as defense scenarios were shifting from a concentration on resource-intensive strategic warfare to information-intensive low-intensity warfare.[281] To guide the development of new information capabilities, Duane Andrews, the Assistant Secretary of Defense for C3I, needed a fresh look at the military requirements for an era in which the Soviets represented a diminished threat. Following the principle that all statements about combat support information needs should come from the commanders who depend on these systems, in the summer of 1990, Mr. Andrews requested Gen. Colin Powell, the Chairman of the Joint Chiefs of Staff, to outline the command and control requirements of the future.

Fifteen months later, the requested plan arrived. From the standpoint of strategic guidance, it was perhaps the single most important document I received during my appointment in the DoD. In its comprehensiveness, clarity and sharp focus it was as good a statement of objectives as any systems executive could hope to receive from top management. What we got were not only "goals" and "principles," but specific, actionable missions to carry out.

Gen. Powell's recommendations defined the DoD C^{3}I requirements of the future. It was a significant milestone in providing direction for the further evolution of all information systems, including DoD intelligence and business applications. Interoperability between command, control, intelligence and business systems became a mandatory policy of the top military leadership. The recommendations was entirely consistent with CIM. They set the rules for integrating command and control into the CIM model.

Gen. Powell's report defined one-hundred fifteen specific operational requirements that all systems had to meet. It stated why war fighting command and control dictates how intelligence and business support systems fit into a consistent framework that makes information from separate applications available to local commanders at points of use. The following is a partial list of the top ranked actions required:

---

281. "Strategic" warfare is to "low-intensity" warfare as wholesale trade with a few customers is to retail trade with many customers. Low intensity warfare includes actions against insurgencies, terrorism and drugs.

- Restructure defense systems so that any commander can manage his forces directly and immediately.
- Design command and control systems to be modular and interoperable in order to fit into a wide range of missions.
- Assemble command and control systems from standard components. Make them sufficiently interoperable to construct a unique command and control structure with a minimum of delay at a new location.
- Develop command and control systems designs that favor a more centralized and consolidated design approach.
- Increase systems survivability through redundant facilities at widely dispersed locations.
- Provide complete command and control interoperability with automatic data processing for battlefield inquiries concerning personnel, medical, financial, materials, logistics and transportation data.
- Set up command and control functional integration organizations using CIM guidelines and methods.
- Identify and consolidate existing command and control assets for central management in support of decentralized execution, within a standard global command and control infrastructure.
- Strengthen central management and oversight over command and control systems acquisition. Deploy professional staff to provide greater visibility to local commanders about progress of individual programs.
- Minimize the on-site deployment in remote regions of command and control personnel to minimize the risk of casualties and damage.
- Define the additional operating responsibilities of the Joint Staff when this involves allocation of DoD or command resources.

Shortly after receiving the guidance from the Joint Chiefs of Staff, the National Security Council issued a revision to the national military strategy that was in agreement with the recommendations from Gen. Powell:

- The new military strategy shifts its focus from containing communism and deterring Soviet aggression to a more flexible, regionally oriented strategy capable of countering a wide range of potential threats vital to U.S. interests.

- The command, control, communications, computer and intelligence capabilities must support the rapid deployment of Joint or Combined forces.[282]

- A command, control, communications, computer and intelligence infrastructure must be globally available and capable of rapid scaling up to accommodate emergencies. Resources should be interoperable and relocatable from one area to another. The infrastructure must support not only forward-deployed forces, but also crisis response forces, planned contingencies, emergencies, and exercises.

- Develop an information configuration design that supports the national military strategy while staying within reduced personnel and funding levels. Consolidate redundant functions, increase overall system throughput, and merge existing systems to achieve interoperability. This would assist the development of a streamlined "global infrastructure" that reduces overall costs and provides for more efficient uses of scarce resources.

- The command and control of Joint and Combined forces in worldwide contingency operations shall not

---

282. "Joint" forces are combined from individual U.S. military services under a unified military command. "Combined" forces involve U.S. allies as well as local support units.

rely on the ad hoc assembly of service- and country-unique systems. Therefore the new information systems will require a high degree of interoperability in peacetime.

The one hundred fifteen requirements from the Chairman of the Joint Chiefs of Staff and the new national military strategy represented a far-reaching view of the future information needs of U.S. defenses. The challenge was how to proceed with implementation while funds were being drained out of the military budget. Before it could proceed, the CIM organization needed to complete an assessment of the current condition of defense information systems. The following section briefly summarizes publicly available information about prevailing conditions in the DoD early in 1992.

Data Processing Installations

The average age of the installed mainframe computers in over one thousand data centers was over 11.5 years, with some equipment up to nineteen years in operation. Meanwhile, the technology innovation cycle for this type of equipment had shrunk to less than four years. The procurement leadtime for new equipment was longer than the technology cycle, which guaranteed that new mainframe computers would be purchased at the end of their technological life.

Eighty percent of the installed computer capacity was operating substantially below average standards of economic efficiency found in commercial operations. Without exception, all data center operations were immensely labor-intensive. Insufficient money was available for automating data center support functions such as memory management, tape library functions and the handling of paper output.

Average costs per MIPS (million instructions per second) were greater than in industry by a significant factor. This is illustrated in Figure 33.3, in which the best DoD computing centers were compared with industry average and industry best results. Substantial cost savings were available, ranging from 30% to 65%, if DoD operations were brought up to commercial industry standards.

Function	DoD Sample	Industry Avg.	Industry Best	Average Savings	Best Savings
	(MIPS)	(MIPS)	(MIPS)	($)	($)
Print & Distribution	0.368	0.174	0.03	$121,159	$211,878
Tape Operations	0.286	0.237	0.077	$30,716	$130,893
Console Operations	0.245	0.128	0.058	$73,378	$117,268
Administration	0.18	0.09	0.022	$56,313	$98,549
Customer Service	0.169	0.071	0.018	$61,433	$94,709
Schedulers	0.125	0.046	0.016	$49,488	$68,731
13 Other Functions				$124,572	$400,850
Total Savings ($000)				$517,059	$1,122,878
% Labor Savings				30.2%	65.5%

Figure 33.3 Benchmarking Data Center Labor for Savings Potential[283]

With rare exceptions, the DoD data centers could not share work-loads and could not act as emergency back-ups to each other. Their hardware and software configurations were unique because equipment acquisition practices depended on most funding to come from individual programs and not from an overall infrastructure building plan.

Central Design Organizations

DoD business applications were developed and maintained in thirty eight central design organizations with a staff of about six thousand. This staff was supplemented by a large complement of contractors who had previously developed unique applications that continued to require their specialized support services.[284] In addition, systems design and maintenance was conducted at innumerable sites that owned their own minicomputers. There was no way to estimate the size of this "stealth" programming staff, because their occupational titles bore no resemblance to what they were doing.

The central design organizations were engaged mostly in maintaining programming code that was on the average older than the machines on which they ran. A steady accumulation of legacy proce-

---

283. Summary of a 1992 consulting study by the KPM&G company.
284. At some sites, such as at the Wright-Patterson Air Force Base, the buildings that housed systems contractors and subcontractors had more floorspace than those occupied by DoD systems personnel.

dural code, estimated at 1.6 billion lines, consumed most of the available resources.

The central design organizations had the reputation for incurring excessive development time for new applications or program maintenance changes as compared with commercial practices. Some of this delay was caused by insufficient educational and tooling investments in DoD software professionals. Most of it was due to extremely complex procedures for getting anything passed through many layers of management, auditors, checkers and lawyers.

The major cause of inefficiencies at the development centers had its origins in the continued adherence to non-standard systems development methods. Independently contracted applications resulted in the addition of application code to the DoD inventory that required unique skills for making any maintenance changes. The lack of consistent software policies and inadequate investments in systems engineering tools offered to DoD software personnel limited opportunities for modernizing their methods. The central design organizations also suffered from the following disadvantages:

- Top executives, mostly on two year military rotational assignments, had insufficient technical experience to institute major changes in software management practices.

- Systems designs reflected a heavy reliance on support from contractors. New applications were influenced more by the limitations of the scope of the contract award than operational needs for flexibility and adaptability to rapidly changing conditions.

- In the absence of standardized data definitions and data formats, the complexity and costs of development and maintenance were excessive.

Workstations and Terminals

Growth in the workstation and terminals inventory, estimated at 650,000 units, was chaotic and costly because of overemphasis on the original purchase price instead of life-cycle support costs. I ran a survey of the manpower that was required to run isolated local area networks in the Pentagon. Some of the nets required one full time person to keep ten microcomputers in satisfactory operation. None of the networks had more than thirty two microcomputers per support person. In every case I ever examined in DoD, the annual support costs per microcomputer were anywhere from $3,000 to $7,000 dollars while the comparable annual depreciation expense was less than $1,000.[285] The emphasis on the lowest possible microcomputer acquisition costs was clearly misplaced.

The extensive networks of workstations and terminals were only rarely capable of passing electronic mail to each other. Most units of the DoD acquired and maintained their own isolated electronic mail capabilities, passing messages only in teletype formats. You could not distribute formatted documents, graphic materials or pictures using most of these electronic mail systems.

Because of inadequate support services and difficulty in obtaining funds for software, a large number of administrative people became engaged in developing applications for local needs. The sharing of this know-how was accomplished informally, often involving passing disks from person to person. As a result, an audit of personal computers discovered that over half of all software residing in memory had been copied without authorization and probably violated regulations or copyrights. If such practices were allowed to continue, they would represent a serious security risk to the integrity of DoD communication networks.

Long Distance Networks

DoD operated over one hundred separate long distance networks and over ten thousand local area networks. These were constructed to support traffic for particular organizations, individual applications or specific contracts. The utilization of the high capacity links for individual networks was especially poor because the capacity of each sepa-

---

285. In a best practices benchmarking study commissioned by CIM, consultants found that the application of advanced network control technologies would make it possible for one network operator to support 2,400 personal computers for less than $1,570 per year per station.

rate network was designed to cope with peak traffic. Separate networks also meant that there was no way to share traffic-carrying capacity. The networks were not interoperable and often required technical improvisations to connect traffic between two separate sources of information. The networks were exceedingly labor intensive, because few funds were available for investing in coordinated monitoring and control.

Condition of the Defense Information Infrastructure

The existing information systems were not rapidly deployable on defense missions. They were not readily interoperable for passing information across functions or services. The systems were not adequately secure to safeguard the information flows from an increasingly data-hungry population that possessed personal computers with powerful inquiry capabilities.

The operating and maintenance costs were excessive as compared with every commercial benchmark we could find. There was no plan to integrate and reduce the costs of locally developed applications. Except in rare cases, business support applications did not link with those used in the battlefield. I concluded early in 1992 that the quality of support for command, control and intelligence would be the ultimate test of whether or not CIM improved U.S. defense capabilities. CIM not only had to achieve cost reduction, but enhance defense capability under unprecedented conditions facing the U.S. defenses.[286]

A massive dose of modernization was needed. Without modernization, the DoD could not achieve the expected cost reductions. The new defense infrastructure would have to provide automatic links between business, command, control, intelligence and communications functions. Financing the required modernization investments could not be done by increasing funding because the overall DoD budget was

---

286. Any dummy can cut a budget. All it takes is to choke off the flow of money. Without plans to rebuild better capabilities with less resources, indiscriminate budget cutting is like "putting a tourniquet around the neck," or "surgery by chain-saw." Ronald Henkoff (January 10, 1994 *Fortune* magazine) made the identical point: "Continuous downsizing is anorexia. You can get thin, but that's no way to get healthy."

declining rapidly. The necessary cash could come only from swiftly reducing the clearly excessive high operating expenses.

If the pace of implementation was rapid enough, the CIM modernization program had a good chance of delivering the much needed new defense capabilities while at the same time producing substantial net cash savings after the fourth year. U.S. defenses needed an infusion of money to prepare for a different set of warfare conditions. This involved projects such as constructing integrated computer communication links among peace-time bases in the U.S. that reached all the way to combat management via secure satellites anywhere in the world. CIM would not only have to modernize DoD systems for efficiency, but redesign them to make combat effectiveness affordable.[287]

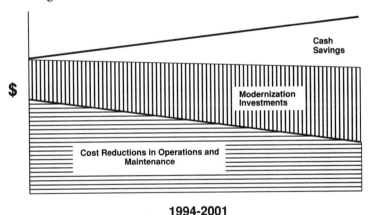

1994-2001

Figure 33.4 Savings to Fund Modernization

Creating a DoD Information Infrastructure

Until the spring of 1992, CIM operated under the assumption that shrinking budgets would persuade the military services to agree to reform their systems' capabilities along the lines defined by the Chairman of the Joint Chiefs of Staff and as advocated by CIM. The logic of

---

287. Each of the military services continued to exempt themselves from interoperability standards and testing by designating their systems as "service-unique." That loophole was finally closed by a directive from the Secretary of Defense.

the CIM propositions was impeccable because the services would have more dollars for weapons. Military readiness could be improved for the price of giving up some prerogatives of systems management.

The opposition to changing the status quo came from some of the key Pentagon senior executive service systems managers and several Generals in charge of C3I in their respective services. They sincerely believed that anything that would enlarge the role of the Office of the Secretary of Defense at the expense of the privileges of the military services could not be trusted. They did not trust the capabilities of the DISA organization to manage extensive joint systems programs. Their anxiety about the possible outcome of the pending presidential election heightened their concerns that the CIM program would expire if a new administration took over. Their opposition to creating a "joint" information infrastructure was overwhelming. They were skilled in the art of participating in committee work while seeking out opportunities to scuttle anything that made real change possible.

Deputy Secretary Atwood, Congressional staff, the GAO and a large number of CIM supporters within DoD and in the industry became frustrated with the relatively slow progress of CIM. This stimulated the single most ambitious CIM effort.[288] The CIM team decided to reexamine the cost reduction opportunities that could become available if one could address the totality of all of the inefficiencies within the entire defense information infrastructure. The initial purpose of this effort was to examine the potential cost reduction if all data centers, all applications development and all communications costs were examined jointly, rather than sequentially and in isolation.

The analytic effort for the CIM defense infrastructure study followed the guidelines established by Gen. Powell and the National Security Council began in May 1992. The first public draft of the analysis suggested that the cost universe for examining the scope of information systems was more than double of what had been previously reported to Congress as "information technology expenditures."

---

288. This ultimately became known as the Information Infrastructure Defense Management Review Decision 918, signed by Deputy Secretary Atwood in September 15, 1992.

This much larger number had already excluded many activities because of unresolved policies in applying CIM to command, control and intelligence systems which were claimed to be "embedded" in battlefield management. Once the new cost basis was established, the cost reduction potential became significantly larger than what the military services had promised when they were allowed to proceed with their own programs.

In the fall of 1992, the CIM organization declared that it would pursue the creation of a new defense information infrastructure that would deliver the following capabilities:

> "Through central technical control and configuration management with decentralized execution the infrastructure will assure an information transfer capability which is protected, interoperable, and cost effective. The information structure supporting the defense mission must provide an end-to-end information support capability encompassing collection, generation, storage, and dissemination of information Department-wide. It must be transparent to its users, improve reliability and service at lower costs, facilitate full implementation of the principles of corporate information management, and be responsive to national security and defense needs in an efficient and effective manner. Further, information, as the vital resource of modern warfare, must be protected commensurate with its intended use. Information systems will be choice targets in future conflicts, and we need to minimize our vulnerability to hostile action."

In drafting the directive that defined the capabilities of the new defense information infrastructure, the primary goal was never efficiency and cost reduction, but improved defense. Existing systems that were wasteful became legitimate targets for extracting scarce cash to fund much needed improvements. At all times we were mindful of the

˞ ꞓnonitions by Martin Van Creveld, one of the foremost contemporary theoreticians of warfare:[289]

> "The conduct of war against an intelligent opponent differs from the management of a large-scale technological system precisely in that efficiency and effectiveness ... are not the same even in the short run. On the contrary, there are any number of occasions when military effectiveness is not only compatible with diminished efficiency but positively demands that it be sacrificed ... In war, however, this advantage has to be balanced against the fact that putting all one's eggs in a single basket is dangerous, is likely to lead to a loss of flexibility and may even give rise to the kind of timidity which, often in history, has prevented precisely the mightiest weapons from being used at all.
>
> Or, take that other mainstay of technological efficiency, standardization. However desirable and even necessary it may be from the point of view of efficiency, in war its result is to make things easy for the enemy. The amount of uncertainty with which he is confronted is diminished. He is put in a position where resources and attention can be focused on a single threat, instead of many different ones. Finally, he is spared the dilemma of having to do two contradictory things at once, which probably represents the most important single way of using technology (or anything else) in order to obtain victory in war."

The Defense Information Infrastructure Proposal

CIM proposed the following initial steps in forming a defense infrastructure:

---

289. Martin Van Creveld, *Technology and War*, The Free Press, 1989, pp. 318-319

- Appoint a single manager for technical control and configuration management so that many of the existing labor-intensive software management task could be carried out as network control functions;

- Establish a single manager for centralized acquisition of hardware and software as a way to streamline the purchasing of technology for the information "utility" and not for individual applications;

- Establish a single manager for centralized management of technical education because the new information infrastructure will have to devote large sums to training and personnel development;

- Assure interoperability, standards enforcement, and security through a high level technical integration and testing organization that would provide ongoing verification of the integrity of the entire DoD information infrastructure;

- Provide funds for making large investments in the modernization and security of information systems operating at military bases to assure that they could be extended for direct battlefield support, if necessary;

- Allow local commanders to own and operate computing systems for local application development, prototyping new applications and experimentation, subject to central technical control on matters related to security, databases and communications;

- Reduce ongoing operating costs for systems by 25%. Conservative estimates for the defense information infrastructure plan were $26 billion savings for the 1994-1999 period, with savings of over $4 billion annually thereafter;

- Establish network control capabilities all the way to the individual keyboards to assure the security of distributed networks;

- Assure the survivability of the defense information infrastructure, especially against terrorist attacks carried out by systems experts;

- Create a $4 billion computer services enterprise as a fee-for-service utility that would offer computing services at rates comparable to the best commercial offerings;

- Move applications from mainframes to distributed low-cost computers for survivability and rapid redeployment. Mainframes would be housed in about twenty five megacenters for network control and archival records protection;

- Conditions would be created for eventual outsourcing of a large share of computing power and telecommunications so that DoD could rapidly augment its capacity from commercial sources if needed.[290]

Security Risks

Analysis showed that creating an integrated DoD information technology utility should yield significant economies. The fragmented, discrete information systems that were so expensive to operate and maintain could not easily share information without causing significant process inefficiencies. However, this fragmentation had provided a sort of protection against attacks on DoD's processes and supporting information systems.[291]

The plan approved by the Deputy Secretary of Defense noted that:

> "Automation, advanced electronics, worldwide communications, advanced sensors, and order of magnitude increases in complexity and capability make

---

290. The technical term for this capability is "reconstitution" of forces. The military history of the U.S. shows a consistent cycle of drastic downsizing of military forces after winning wars, followed by rapid rebuilding subsequent to a military alert.
291. One wag noted "Our own confusion is a form of information security."

information management pivotal to managing the
employment of military forces. Although DoD
spends over $15 billion each year on computing and
communications, there are persistent deficiencies in
the capability to protect, exchange, and combine critical data between and among command and control,
intelligence, combat support, simulation and training, and business systems."

With the creation of a modernized and integrated information
infrastructure this inherent defense-by-proliferation would disappear.
In addition, the transition to standards-based and vendor neutral systems would make it easier to attack and damage the entire information
infrastructure. A portion of the savings that would result from improved
efficiencies would be transferred to mitigating the increase in risk associated with the migration to a coherent DoD information infrastructure.

Creating a protected infrastructure would involve developing and
applying new security technologies, training and educating systems
users and fully integrating systems security measures into the operation
of the DoD information infrastructure.

About two billion dollars of the projected savings were allocated
for boosting the security of information systems. In addition, funds
were provided for indirect security costs, such as designing computer
centers for ease of repair, providing for redundant operations and storing copies of databases on untamperable devices. This would add to the
safety and survivability of the proposed infrastructure.[292]

The Politics of Infrastructure Building

Subsequent to the election in the fall of 1992, which signaled the likely
advent of major changes in defense policies, the military services
retreated to their traditional roles of protecting their own systems bud-

---

292. In 1993, during the time between administrations, the comptroller's office applied these
funds to other purposes. This is an illustration of how information politics without checks and
balances can substitute financial policy for security policy.

gets against damage from budget cuts. Committing to an evolutionary modernization program under CIM would now be out of the question because of the rising uncertainty about what would happen under the new administration which was known to favor major changes in national security policies. The rapidly vanishing investment funds were diverted to protect over ten of thousand computer applications that had meanwhile sprung up from local initiatives. Many of these local applications represented acts of desperation to keep military bases supported by means of rudimentary and often home-grown computer solutions.

In the absence of a unified and generally accepted migration plan for applications, the prospects for proceeding to build a modern and low-cost defense infrastructure were dim. Without a broadly based and widely supported modernization effort, it was likely that any cash savings from modernization would disappear at budget time to pay for essential military equipment. This would leave the existing infrastructure in 1993 with only enough money to support already committed major programs with a little left over for the most urgent fixes. The money that would have been otherwise available for modernization was headed for the maintenance of obsolete systems.

The arguments by CIM proponents in favor of a modernization commitment were listened to, but not heard by the military services. Political realities within the DoD have overtaken the events. The final version of the infrastructure plan approved in December 1992 had a much smaller scope against which to make savings than was initially proposed because of the insistence of military services on the exclusion of many systems costs from the scope of the infrastructure. Nevertheless, the proposal provided for net cumulative savings of $26 billion over a seven year period. The net savings were less than 5.4% of the baseline as compared with a much larger cost reduction potential that was typical of private sector experiences. To maximize the savings, the investment funds allocated for building the infrastructure were small relative to what the DoD would need to support a concerted modernization program to prepare for 21st century information-intensive warfare. This sort of warfare makes enormous demands on making tactical information available at the platoon and even squad levels that previously was provided only to Generals at corps headquarters.

The DoD administration under the new Secretary of Defense, Les Aspin, crippled progress in building the DoD information infrastructure further when it returned control over all software development to the military services. Only the consolidation of largely obsolete data centers into megacenters was retained as the principal CIM accomplishments for the 1993-1994 period. Viewing information management as something that one manipulates through the control of data centers reflects a view that is demonstrably ineffective. What matters is control over software, data, and systems engineering tools, not computing facilities that become obsolete at a rapid rate. The value of the CIM program diminished further when the new administration did not maintain the momentum to capture the savings needed to build an integrated and resilient information infrastructure.[293]

Launching the CIM plan to construct a comprehensive defense information infrastructure was a step in the right direction, but it presently falls far short of being a significant strategic commitment to making information technology a distinct source of combat advantage in "information warfare." Information superiority is perhaps the most cost-effective means to assure the fighting power of much reduced U.S. arms in any warfare scenario of the future. It remains to be seen whether the proposed CIM policy of drastically cutting inefficient operating expenses as a way to fund the much needed modernization of DoD will ultimately prevail.

CIM Lessons

One can learn many lessons from the attempts of the DoD to form a new corporate infrastructure. Financial goals are necessary but certainly not sufficient to launch a comprehensive program to structure information systems to attain competitive superiority. Policy and doctrine must always lead before information efficiency can be set as a goal. Financial incentives and technology planning only work after top exec-

---

293. United States General Accounting Office, "Stronger Support Needed for Corporate Information Management Initiative To Succeed," *Report to the Chairman, Committee on Governmental Affairs, U.S. Senate*, April 1994.

utives reach agreement on a concept of operations and how to change the management processes to reflect the new realities. Most importantly, you must attract a large number of competent managers who will trust their leaders so they can dedicate their energies and careers to reaching out for a distant goal. Such trust does not arise if the leadership vacillates, changes directions frequently and forces progress by dictate instead of broadly based cooperation.

The next few years will show if the actual progress in implementing CIM will match the frequent pronouncements by key officials in the Clinton administration to fulfill the missions that were defined in this program. It will require steadfast leadership, focused objectives and exhaustive efforts to attain progress through cooperation instead of fiat.

A program such as CIM could not avoid becoming a proxy for contention between bureaucratic fiefdoms. Some of the debates concerning the directions of CIM looked more like meetings of the United Nations about Bosnia, where everybody made vague and general pronouncements of good intentions but nobody wished to commit to anything that altered the status quo. For an innovative approach, such as that advanced by CIM, participants must be able to lift themselves above protection of purely parochial interests. Strengthening a federation to achieve a greater unity of purpose need not necessarily result in crippling local capabilities. The basic premise of CIM was always to find ways to modernize the hard-to-do and impossible-to-fund infrastructure. In this way local commanders would become free to satisfy their immediate needs quickly, easily and inexpensively.

The declared objective of CIM was to move over 90% of all computing power directly into the hands of local commanders, because the technology now allows placing mainframe processing capacity into the soldiers' pockets. Low intensity warfare is waged by small squads of soldiers, who need the most powerful and best information technologies to give them better odds in defeating enemies. In low intensity warfare, perhaps the only advantage a U.S. soldier has would be his possession of superior information.

If the services, the agencies, and the Office of the Secretary of Defense don't work together and lower overhead costs of the DoD, Congress will surely do it by drastic means that may degrade U.S. warfare capabilities. Instead of cutting the fat in the "tail" of DoD, the Congress will cut the fighting "teeth" because that is much easier to do. What's worse, the brain – the information systems – that direct the fighting "teeth" will not evolve. Bureaucratic prerogatives, contractual privileges, or regulatory compliance should never take a precedence to enhancing U.S. war fighting capabilities. CIM is not a "zero sum game," where every change in favor of a common infrastructure means there are always some who will become losers. The condition of the existing DoD information infrastructure is sufficiently bad that close interservice cooperation is absolutely essential to make everybody a winner.

Without a financial and managerial commitment to a major modernization program to improve current information management practices in DoD, there is only a limited future for CIM. Without the support of the President and the Secretary of Defense, CIM will degrade to become a vehicle for delivering limited cost reductions and some technology improvements. The CIM program has the capability of supporting the development of U.S. information superiority. This is perhaps the most cost-effective means for assuring the continued power of U.S. arms in any future warfare scenario. That is the promise and potential for what must be done: *Information Superiority for Defense Superiority.*

A Postscript

It is a testimony to the fundamental soundness of CIM principles and programs that after a hiatus of ten months after the inauguration of President Clinton, the new administration appears to have fully reaffirmed its commitment to carry out the CIM initiative on an accelerated basis.[294]

---

294. For an example see J. Endoso, "Paige Moves to Put Teeth in Software Reuse Program," *Government Computer News*, May 2, 1994.

PART V

PERSPECTIVES

If it looks too good, you need better information.

34

Prospects

Fear comes from the unknown, though much of what
is yet to come is already here.

I now turn forward to the global environment of information politics. I believe that the increased complexity of networks, the need for global interoperability, and the demands for security will give rise to computing "utilities," which will deliver services currently hand-crafted by local talent. The transformation of computing from an art to an industrialized commodity is analogous to what happened two hundred years ago when manufacturing migrated from small shops to factories. Much of the computing and networking infrastructure in the future will come from national, and ultimately from international, information services. Then, individual organizations can concentrate on acquiring technologies for serving only their unique needs.

Externalizing Information Politics

The next decade will see the information processing workloads migrate from internal services to marketplace offerings. Political maneuvering will involve re-balancing resources and influence because about half of the current information technology employees will leave their jobs and seek careers and jobs as contractors, consultants, and part-time specialists. Meanwhile customers, such as administrators, analysts, researchers, and engineers, who are accustomed to receiving information processing services without consideration of cost, will be forced to learn how to trade off their requirements against affordability.

The net effect of all this turmoil will be an enormous expansion of computing power at points of use, at substantially lower processing costs. Supercomputer computing and full-motion displays at every office desk, and in every home, are not far off. Competition based on price and new features has already prompted the dismantling of internal monopolistic data processing departments, because they delivered unsatisfactory and obsolescent services. The internal monopolists thrived because they could always get more cash out of the corporate or government agency coffers when no alternatives were available. With the distribution of computing power to network-based computing, the need for company or government-agency ownership of their own tele-computing infrastructure will diminish. The network itself will be the computer, not the way it is today when the telecommunication channels are seen as merely passive means for conveying electronic pulses. Network connectivity, to a wide range of computing services from competing organizations, will dominate the economics of information technology, and will set the price of computing services. Internal monopolies with excessive costs will not survive under such conditions.

Political and economic power will shift from computer makers to network service providers. Network carriers, who persist in marketing the electronic pipes instead of getting into the business of delivering information products, will most likely become obsolete. New entrants into the information delivery business will take advantage of the fixed costs of existing communications channels, burdened by government regulations that limit profits. The new entrants will have the advantage of reaping superior profits by offering new value-added services. When automobiles took over from coaches, the auto manufacturers took advantage of the coach makers and gave them the low profit margin jobs of making seats.

I agree with Max Hopper, the chief information officer of American Airlines, who said: "As technology reshapes the nature of work and redefines organizational structures, technology itself will recede into the background. Eventually, information systems will be thought of more like electricity or the telephone network than as a decisive source of organizational advantage. Only then will our organizations be capable of embracing the true promise of information technology."[295]

Information Services Utilities

The future major new opportunity in the information business will be in delivering systems integration services. The handicraft approach to writing and maintaining applications software will disappear. Instead, major applications will be assembled from pre-tested standard software "objects." Computing cycles and bandwidth will be a commodity, readily available from sources that enjoy enormous advantages in scale and specialized knowledge.

Currently, organizations primarily depend on themselves to satisfy most of their computing needs. They buy their own equipment, select the operating systems, purchase the software, write the applications, and manage the telecommunications links. I do not believe even very large organizations will sustain the required expertise to do all these tasks very well, and certainly not at competitive costs. The future belongs to specialists who market and deliver network services in every way the customer needs them.

I see technical specialists migrating to service providers, while experts with company knowledge will move into management. Every manager will require general systems knowledge and understanding of computing and communications. By necessity, every manager will become a systems manager, with sufficient expertise to choose when, where, and how to buy information services. This implies there will be no Chief Information Officer, because only the Chief Executive Officer can effectively direct and shape the alignment of information with the needs of the business. Nevertheless, such an arrangement will still make it necessary to employ in a key executive post a Chief Information Policy Officer, whose services will be essential in safeguarding the integration and security of a wide range of information services and resources.

---

295. Max D. Hopper, "Rattling SABRE - New Ways to Compete on Information, The Information Infrastructure," *Harvard Business Review*, 1991.

In pre-industrial economies, every village, and in a large town every neighborhood, had its own shoemaker. The shoemakers told their clients what to wear, because they had only limited patterns and little choice in materials. These shoemakers have disappeared. Today, shoe designers are associated with shoe factories, where they engineer increasingly sophisticated and varied footwear. The successors of the old cobblers are managers of shoe factories or shoe salespeople. This transformation has made it possible for consumers to learn just enough about shoes to know what to buy. Shoes are a commodity purchase, and for most people, shoes are sufficiently inexpensive that making the right choice at first is not of major concern. There will always be another pair to try out. I think this pattern will be repeated as information systems evolve from an organization-specific craft to market-provided services.

Effect on Careers

In the same way that shoemakers, blacksmiths, and candle makers can now make a living only at historical landmarks or in undeveloped countries, twenty-five years from now today's corporate information systems organizations will not be recognizable. Therefore, CIOs had better start re-thinking how they will develop technical and management resources, because the skills of their people will become obsolete in the not-so-distant future if their growth and career development are not planned.

There is much confusion about which information systems people to hire and train. That is apparent from the wide divergence of views of CIOs from some of the largest corporations. In a recent article that surveyed qualifications of new hires, one CIO said: "The new hires should have ...general consulting skills. I want generalists in the future who can adapt to any computing environment."[296] At the opposite end was a CIO who wanted only narrow specialists, "My ideal person will know MVS, OS/2, NT and Netware. The network guru should be able to handle SNA, TCP/IP and SPX/IPX, and the programmers should understand COBOL, Visual BASIC and PowerBuilder." Then there

---

296. Susan Cohen, "The Client/Server CIO," *Forrester Research*, September, 1993.

was the CIO who did not care much for technology saying, "My goal is to walk into a room and not know the difference between a systems person and an end user."

Which of the above three views is best is arguable, because it depends on the time horizon of the CIO's own career plans. From the standpoint of a prospective employees, I worry. One of these CIOs is likely to hire the last equivalent of an obsolete guild shoemaker.

Business Procedures as a Political Act

Possessing and using information shape the conduct of business. In turn, business processes determine the importance and justification for more than 50% of the jobs (and 67% of the salary incomes) in an information-based economy.[297] Since information politics is the method for resolving such conflicts, it merits concentrated attention from top executives. The alternative is to allow the seething disputes to remain camouflaged under the screen of arguments about "decentralization," "network control," "user specification," and budget authority for information technology expenditures.

Managing information-based competition is an essential skill for all who aspire to a management position. Formerly, it arose as disputes over minor office procedures, such as who gets to keep the pink carbon copy for their files. These skirmishes preceded posturing for a takeover, and ended up either as acrimonious disagreements or negotiated coexistence. The old ways of information accommodation allowed for flexibility and adaptation, the give-and-take in relationships. Before the advent of pervasive computerization, when two departments claimed equal rights to make a particular decision, they could reach an accommodation by mandating it to be a joint approval process.[298] This solution was not only peaceful but also justified employing additional personnel to negotiate compromises.

---

297. Paul A. Strassmann, *Information Payoff - The Transformation of Work in the Electronic Age*, The Free Press, 1985, Chapter 1.
298. I have participated in decisions requiring eleven mandatory signatures, each representing an authority to postpone or stop a decision.

Information technology has escalated the risks of wasteful bureaucratic warfare. Systems engineers do not know how to design ambiguity into software. When an organization resorts to centrally directed systems management, it often happens in business process improvement, the information flow diagrams readily display information-handling redundancies. Systems design thus becomes the political act of instituting unambiguous procedures. Software code will encapsulate the winner's prerogatives into a workflow sequence that can be overruled only by making changes in the application program. If done well, this should settle intraorganizational disputes, reduce inefficiencies, and speed up responses. However, the new procedures may create a rigid autocracy under the control of the winning party. We may now get both the benefits of efficiency as well as the cost of the inflexibility of limited choices. Once a workflow sequence is programmed, people are stuck. They can not negotiate with a routine defined by the computer if the computer solution makes no sense.

When computers mediate business transactions, software ceases to be a scientifically engineered process, despite the pretensions of systems analysts that they sought "rational" solutions. Software reflects the manager's political choices. Only the mechanics of developing software can lay claims to technical rationality, not its application.

Politicophobia

Corporate politics exist and are on everybody's mind. In a survey of 3,581 senior executives, 41% stated that the "...degree to which company politics, not performance, affects organizational decisions..." is their single largest cause of personal stress.[299] The other stress factors were: Lack of job security, 28%; the degree to which the career was stalled, 25%; volume of work, 21%; and number of projects, 20%. Company politics affects job security, career stagnation, and volume of work assigned. Therefore, corporate information politics deserve attention.

---

299. Barbara Presley Noble, "Job Hunting Isn't Always Goodbye," *The New York Times*, December 5, 1993.

Until recently, it was not polite to talk about politics in information management. Computer people subscribe to thinking rationally, like scientists and engineers. That is why they prefer the metaphors of "architecture," "engineering," and "bridges," that convey the calculated permanence of fixed solutions. Given a choice, they prefer to talk about the physical aspects of hardware rather than the ephemeral characteristics of software.

Engaging in politics has always carried the connotation of bargaining, negotiating, and exercising manipulative instincts for achieving personal gain. Computer analysts are not traditionally, nor by training, comfortable with ill-defined practices, especially if they do not involve mathematics or the laws of physics. The way computer people avoid this topic reminds me of the Victorian attitude toward sex. Although sex was widely practiced openly, discussing it was considered a breach of acceptable conduct.[300]

Conference titles are a sure way to recognize which new topics have moved onto the managerial agenda. Attracting four hundred executives to an exclusive meeting in Palm Springs, California, during the mid-October annual budget rituals requires exciting new subjects. The organizers of *CIO Magazine* satisfied that demand by convening a 1993 conference on "The Politics of Information Technology." It is noteworthy to find out what conversations took place. A summary report said "...the topic was politics, but the talk at the recent conference kept circling back to one point: If you are not adding business value, you are not doing your job." The subject was actually business alignment, not managing political governance. This allowed everyone to avoid discussing an unpalatable subject.[301]

Politicophobia is also reflected in the recent trend for some acclaimed chief information officers to quit to become CIOs for hire. They can then become "...liberated from office politics and to be able to

---

300. A noteworthy exception to politicophobia can be seen in Levine and Rossmoore, "Understanding the Political Threats of IT Implementation," *Proceedings of the 27th International Conference on Systems Sciences*, IEEE, 1994. It includes a case study which can be used by any researcher as an example of how to study organizational politics.
301. Jason S. Casey, "Business or Bust," *CIO Magazine*, December 1, 1993

focus on the substance of their work."[302] Many chief information officers want challenging work with a minimum of political hassle. One should remember that information is the most potent source of managerial power, and managerial power is the exercise of information politics. Therefore, I do not believe that it is possible to walk into a senior systems executive job that is apolitical. A politics-avoiding CIO-for-hire is a technological mercenary, not an executive decision-maker.

Politics Before Technology

Only recently has the primacy of politics over information technology been formally recognized.[303] Davenport, Eccles, and Prusak declare that "...information technology was supposed to stimulate information flow and eliminate hierarchy. It has had just the opposite effect..." They point out that in information-based organizations, information has become too valuable for most managers to give it away without bargaining for an offsetting gain. I agree with their principal arguments:

- In order to make information systems acceptable, organizations must regulate and manage the principal elements of politics: negotiation, compromise, and institutionalization of lasting agreements.

- Today's rhetorical assertions about the coming of "information-based organizations" and "knowledge-based enterprises" are largely overoptimistic and utopian fantasies. The flow of information still reflects the cascading of power through organizational fiefdoms. It benefits office holders rather than being shared by everyone according to their need to serve customers and deter competitors.

- The failure of information systems projects is largely due to the companies' inability or unwillingness to

---

302. Melanie Menagh, "CIO for Hire," *Computerworld*, June 6, 1994, p. 83.
303. Thomas H. Davenport, Robert G. Eccles, Laurence Prusak, "Information Politics," *Sloan Management Review*, Fall, 1992. For a summary, see also the chapter on Managing Information Politics in James McGee and Laurence Prusak, *Managing Information Strategically*, John Wiley & Sons, New York, 1993

treat information management as a political process, rather than a technical one.

- As information becomes the basis for defining organizational relationships, the holders of unique information are less likely to share their information, viewing their knowledge as "...a source of power and indispensability..."

- There are often legitimate reasons for withholding information. In the absence of a due process for making agreements, there are valid differences in opinion what particular information means to different people. Until such dilemma are resolved, individuals and groups have learned to defensively control the sources and evaluation of data.

Davenport, Eccles, and Prusak's define a new agenda for talking about information management. They proposed five models, which use the language of politics rather than the more sterile one of systems analysis. They adopted a historical approach in defining the categories of "technocratic utopianism," "anarchy," "feudalism," "monarchy," and "federalism".

Technocratic Utopianism

"Technocratic utopianism" characterizes what I have experienced with vendors, computer professionals, the popular media, and most academics during most of my career. I can spot technocratic utopians after flipping through their presentation slides. They never assess the existing situation in much detail. They only describe how great business will be when the latest widget becomes fully operational. Costs do not usually enter into their considerations. Benefits, if mentioned at all, are expressed using generalities such as "improving performance by one thousand percent."

Technocratic utopians love to use new abstractions that disguise old practices, such as "entity-relationship models" and "analytic hierarchy simulations." They convey little information about the purposes of such work. That is like taking a blood sample before asking anything about the person who is ill. Utopianism ends up in disaster for any organization that pursues it with reckless abandon. Its proponents are fired only to be hired by one that seeks a utopian solution. Utopian leaders increase their marketability by enhancing their reputation as far-thinking technologists, with a diversity of experience in many firms.

Anarchy

"Anarchy" seems to characterize the most prevalent condition in large organizations since the introduction of the personal computer. It is a technological free-for-all for people who are eager to find a place in the "information society." Everyone becomes an information manager, which really means that nobody manages knowledge sharing. Costs are unknown, because they are obscured inside everyone's budget. Anarchy may be all right for organizations of solo practitioners, such as research and professional organizations. For complex organizations, information anarchy makes cooperation difficult. It is not an improvement over paper-based functional hierarchies, despite its capacity to pass messages faster and in greater volume.

Monarchy

"Monarchy" is what I practiced from 1957 until 1975 as a chief information officer of major corporations. It was the most practical solution at a time when technology was expensive and risky, and executives trusted no one except a few highly placed courtiers. An easy way to spot monarchy is to see if the top computer chief is referred to as the czar.[304] In a medieval monarchy, the crowned head owned all the land. You kept your fief only if the king chose to tolerate your possession. Similarly, the computer czar negotiated the computer budget with the sovereign in charge of all money, and then allocated computer resources based on precedent and personal preference. No wonder assassination, rather then election, was the fastest way to obtain land or a large chunk of the computer resources. Some of the world's largest computer estab-

---

304. I never understood why everybody called the top man "czar" and not emperor, eminence, lord, majesty, king, pope, kaiser, governor, caliph, shogun, sovereign or shah. I guess that the notorious czarist profligacy, incompetence, inability to govern and dismal endings were the fate to wish on the reigning data center monarchs.

lishments have retained monarchic habits by virtue of government regulation. This generalization is particularly applicable to public sector organizations.

Enlightened organizations prolong the life of the monarchy by adopting various forms of "constitutional monarchy," in which the titular head of corporate systems has a small staff to set policy and standards, but has no meaningful control over budgets, priorities, technology development, operations, or alignment of projects with the purposes of the enterprise.

The best example of converting absolute monarchs to a "constitutional monarchy" was establishing IRM (Information Resource Manager) high level executive positions in the U.S. Federal government. With minor exceptions, all of them have only small administrative staffs who mostly engage in wading through a morass of equipment acquisition regulations. Meanwhile, the local magnates run their independent operations as they see fit.

Feudalism

"Feudalism" arose in most large organizations after 1975, when "monarchy" ceased to be workable because the the central data processing establishment could not extract any more funding through "taxation without representation," euphemistically called "corporate allocations." In its new form, feudalism was advertised as "business unit computing autonomy" to make the distribution of excessive corporate costs more palatable to the divisional barons.

Feudal forms are easily recognized by their strong ties to the chief financial officer, who funds an expanding computing budget as a way to decrease his elaborate expenses for cost control. When this happens, finance becomes the only means to bind an enterprise together, thus greatly increasing the influence of all financial people. Marketing, logistics, personnel, and customer service departments are left to wander off to their minicomputers and servers to take care of their most urgent local needs. As was the case in the 12th to the 17th century in Europe, the local gentry enjoys more pleasures and wealth when they have little interference from the king or church. In advanced states of computing autonomy, organizations will progress to "anarchy."

Federalism

"Federalism" is my preferred model for organizing information management in a diversified enterprise. Much of the first part of this book describes how a federated information management structure can offer maximum flexibility to rapidly changing conditions. In this respect, federalism may be superior to other organizational forms, because it can encompass an enormous variety of conditions without compromising the few important principles that hold society together. However, companies at different stages of technological development, or originating from different national cultures, may find other organizational forms more suitable.

Federalism requires a high level of computer literacy throughout the organization, because local management must adapt technology to local needs. People literacy in computers, rather than computer literacy in people, make it possible to delegate complex technical tasks to the information consumers without having to rely on the experts as intermediaries.

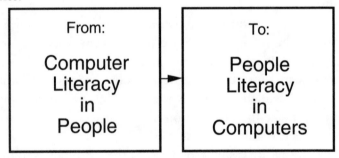

Figure 34.1 Shift in Literacy as a Political Force

Similar theological issues were debated in the 15th and 16th century about the changes in roles of priests and laymen. People-literate computers are becoming available as the increasing power of microprocessors makes it possible to endow every computing appliance with the facility to understand humanly intuitive commands. Previously, humans had to think like computers in order to understand them, which profoundly affected their views about computerization and inhibited the rate at which information technology could be absorbed.

Federalism can exist only if there is mutual trust among co-workers. There must be self-discipline among customers and suppliers against abusing access to shared data. Such trust is rare indeed, especially when jobs are scarce and the threat of unemployment through automation is a source of social unrest.

Companies that must dismiss large numbers of trusted employees due to workflow redesign are likely to regress to feudal, monarchical, or even anarchic forms of governance as the remaining employees seek to protect their jobs. My opposition to the more radical and drastic forms of reengineering comes from a recognition that even though wholesale dismissals may deliver short-term economic gains, the intrusion of fear and dictatorial practices will tear apart the social bonds among people that are prerequisite for cooperation based on negotiated compromise. Organizations that aspire to federated forms of management must sustain mutual trust. It is essential for cooperation, the essence of all organizational survival and a condition for all success.

35

DIVERSITY

The present is only the pre-history of an information-based civilization.

In this book I have addressed the political aspects of information management in information-intensive corporate and government environments found in an economically advanced society. I assume that political conditions will continue to support such institutions. It is likely that this assumption is too narrow and I may be overoptimistic about what the future may bring on a global scale. Patterns that apply in advanced societies may not work for large segments of the world's population, especially less developed countries.

The futurists and authors, Alvin and Heidi Toffler, project that the global population within fifty years will reach ten billion, up from the six billion estimated for 1998.[305] I subscribe to Tofflers' views that a crowded and largely impoverished world of the future will be divided into information-based, industrial-based and materials-based societies and that each will frequently engage in deadly contests:[306]

---

305. "Report on World Population Forecast," *Washington Times*, 4/30/1992, A8
306. Alvin and Heidi Toffler, *War and Anti-War: Survival at the Dawn of the 21st Century*, Little, Brown and Company, New York, 1993

Information-Based Societies

The Tofflers' description of information-based societies encompasses nations and leagues in which the global, services-providing corporations dominate the economy. These societies will include less than a tenth of the global population. They will produce most of the technology, innovation, information, media, and trade. They will reap most of the wealth because they will manage most of the financial and knowledge assets. Per capita incomes may double their present real incomes within twenty years, if peace prevails. The aspirations of these societies will be to become universal, promoting global commercial relations, the rule of international law, trans-national political cooperation, and a culture that recognizes no boundaries in race, religion or geography. Much that I have written in this book reflects these aspirations. However, that is not how most of the world's people are likely to view their own roles in information management and how to apply information technologies.

Industrial-Based Societies

Industrial-based societies are countries in which nationally as well as internationally-based industrial corporations will dominate the economic scene. They will include less than half of the global population, and produce most of the manufactured goods and products. This sector will pursue aggressive and expansive politics, because they will be in a squeeze from the rich information-based societies on top, wishing to extract maximum profits from industrial production, and the resource-based societies on the bottom, struggling to escape out of poverty. The industrial-based societies will continue to rely on the power of the restrictive nationalist state as a way to protect their interests. Foremost among these restrictive practices will be limitations on the flow of information, constraints on information services, and protection of the local means of communication. Their activities will, in many respects, imitate the competition among European states before the first World War. The beginning of the 21st century are likely to see commercial as well as bloody military conflicts between the industrial-nationalistic and information-universalist institutions.

Materials-Based Societies

The Tofflers' materials-based societies includes nations in which local religious, race, tribal, faction and even city-state elements dominate. They will include most of people in the world, because they will have the highest population growth rate. This sector will produce most of the agricultural and raw materials, and will seethe with unrest and a deep sense of social injustice as the readily accessible media reveal its poverty and vulnerability to the more prosperous societies above it.

Local dictators, religious extremists, and warlords will exploit this friction for profit and glory. Such individuals or parties will find it rewarding to control the local sources of scarce minerals or drugs to finance their power by extortion and expropriation. They will provide the seedbed for international terrorism, insurgency, banditry, and piracy that live off the traffic of goods and services shipped between the industrial and information-based societies. These warlord enclaves will create similar devastation as that which preceded the formation of modern European states in the period between the 12th and 17th centuries. Foremost among these practices will be total control over electronic communications, in any form, and preferably by the military or the police. In the future, we will experience attacks by extremists from this sector on the most vulnerable elements of our own institutions. Choice targets will be the global information networks that assist the most advanced global organizations and endow them with the capacity to maintain their dominance.

Diversity in Governance

Information governance for each of these completely different societies will diverge and follow contrary rules. Information feudalism and information monarchy will prevail in the industrial and materials-based societies. Politicians and executives from information-based societies, especially the U.S., will damage cooperation with organizations in the industrial and materials-based societies if the information-haves persist that everyone must follow information management practices of information-rich organizations.

Everyone, worldwide will use the same inexpensive microcomputer and communication technologies just as every military or paramilitary group currently uses similar light weapons. However, the application of the identical information technologies will be different in the same way that similar weapons are now engaged in actions waged by different parties, in pursuit of totally different political goals. The rifles, grenades and land mines used in tribal genocide in Africa and by religious fanatics in Iran are not much different from those used by United Nations peacekeeping troops.

Identical information technologies do not result in identical information management practices. Police state dictatorships will use the same types of computers as the cooperative farm associations. Managers from organizations in advanced information-based societies will find that they cannot transplant information management practices from advanced to backward economies. Only those who understand that information politics precedes information management will successfully negotiate cooperative arrangements with groups whose agendas are fundamentally different.

Future of Information Politics

Corporate information politics will not offer neat distinctions between technocratic utopianism, anarchy, feudalism, monarchy, or federalism. Individual organizations may be able to integrate and tolerate elements of each of these forms within themselves, with some success. For example, the financial establishment in a federated multinational corporation may forever remain a monarchy. Within a global political framework, dictated by the global reach of the information industry's standards and software, there will be room for individual enterprises to articulate their own form of cohesion. These enterprises will do so to the extent that is consistent with the way they manage their operations. Excellence in organizing for information management could become a source of sustainable competitive advantage, just as organization of marketing and logistics used to be the basis of competitive advantage in the industrial age.

When an organization defines its levels of governance, a federated and participative local layer may then coexist with feudalism at the business or process layers. Such arrangement can be successful as long as the boundaries between the layers of governance are clear and there is a due process for settling differences as to who is accountable for what. For example, the responsibilities for information security, if placed at the enterprise layer, could qualify as dictatorship in a structure that is otherwise federated and highly dependent on local authority.

It is possible to grow a global enterprise that fosters local federalism for business units in information-based societies, while accepting monarchy in countries that are emerging from materials- based societies. In this way a global organization can adapt its information systems to different conditions, without having to impose uniformity on the way each unit conducts its business.

In short, the global politics of information management can be designed to accept diversity and deal with messy local circumstances. There is no need to resort to standard information management practices that fit all applications, which is unworkable anyway. As the world becomes commercially and politically more diverse, the inherent capacity of information systems to cope with variety should be used to make differences in local practices affordable, instead of being throttled by the imposition of uniformity using information technology as the excuse for centralized control.

Corporate executives can neither withdraw from information management by delegating it entirely to operating units, nor control it by hiring a dictator chief information officer who will use his charter to front for the headquarters autocrats. Corporate management can neither abdicate information management to a vendor through outsourcing, nor resort to technological self-sufficiency as a way to isolate themselves from outside influence. The leadership of each organization must engage in information politics to make the tough choices that support the path their enterprise has taken toward achieving its objectives.

The Universality of the Telephone

As I contemplate the future of a politically disturbed world, I am encouraged by the enormous accomplishments of information technologies in unifying people, despite their inherent differences. The existing global telephone network is by far the best demonstration of the integrative and apolitical characteristics of information technology.

Any telephone on earth can communicate with any other telephone, regardless of the enormous variety of institutions and technologies that support these connections. Consider the following characteristics of the existing global telephone networks:[307]

- There are over nineteen-thousand local phone exchanges, none of them identical. Some still use over fifty years old technology.

- There are at least fifty thousand different telephone models, made by hundreds of different manufacturers. They vary in function, color, shape, sound, and form.

- There are over thirteen-thousand known calling procedures, such as numbering schemes, ringing sequences, dialing protocols, and identification methods.

- There are telephones in one-hundred ninety countries. Each country has a different legislative and regulatory approach to administering their telephone system.

- Telephone companies settle accounts for international telephone calls in over one-hundred different currencies.

- Twenty different time zones are recognized when recording of the time of a phone call.

- There are at least twenty different types of government involved in negotiating how to administer international phone traffic.

- Although there are at least four thousand known languages, somehow operators can handle international traffic.

- The system offers the capacity for any one person to talk to any other person.

---

307. Based on an AT&T advertisement in *Time*, February 1994

The voice and facsimile networks are interoperable within an enormous diversity of technological choices. This is possible because they solved the relatively simple problem of transmitting analog signals from one handset to another. The existing networks do not care about the contents of the signals they switch through perhaps hundreds of computers and mechanical devices. Their capacity to handle the complexity of voice and facsimile networks resides in the intelligence of their central switches, which remain highly adaptable. The sending devices are dumb.

The major difference between telephones and computer networks is the capability of the sending device. Sophisticated personal computers will become both the sending and receiving devices of the future. Through software, personal computers will perform most of the dispatching functions by giving to each message its autonomous capacity to make self-directed switching decisions through non-homogeneous and non-standard communications channels. The future computer transmission grids will differ from the current telephone network principally by their capacity to inspect some of the contents of a message. This will enable the message to traverse from any one computer to any another, without electronic intermediaries. That involves an enormous increase in cooperative arrangements that will be necessary to achieve such a capability.

For such communications to take place safely, reliably, and economically, requires reaching agreements on how to understand some of the contents of transmissions, instead of relying exclusively on the current practice of imposing tight standards on the format of each transmission. This new approach to worldwide communications will mandate a permanent cooperative relationship between political and commercial organizations on a scale that is totally unprecedented.

Governance and Standards

Visions of how to impose order on rapidly expanding diversity are usually advanced by governments, trade associations and every major vendor. The usual remedy calls for reinstating an orderly and all-encompassing empire, defined by a preferred architecture, where everyone follows identical standards. In most instances this idea is unrealistic because information systems have become instruments of national as well as corporate competitive advantage. There are too many established enclaves of software and telecommunication methods, that any proposal for establishing global uniformity cannot hope to succeed. Not even an intergovernmental treaties can impose information uniformity. From the standpoint of preserving innovation and privacy, any attempt to impose central controls, under the guise of economy and efficiency, is likely to be rejected on social and political grounds. Global uniformity in systems runs counter to the trends that favor free competition and rapid modernization.

Information technologies will become more diverse instead of more homogeneous. Meanwhile, international systems that support electronic commerce will suffer from apparent contradictions. On the one hand, there will be growing globalization of trade. On the other hand there will be an increased proliferation of technology and fragmentation into ever smaller units that aspire to technological autonomy.

The problem with electronic commerce is that it does not follow the precedent of global telephony which succeeded by adopting a relatively small number of standards for defining the format of electronic signals that pass over the wires. Electronic commerce must deal with the content of millions of pieces of data originated by millions of businesses that follow different business practices in generating information that suits their internal needs. Attempting to standardize every data element that any one supplier would ever need, from any conceivable customer, is not feasible, even in the unlikely event the ponderous work of document standardization committees now laboring with the blessing of the United Nations could be accelerated. Achieving universal acceptance of transactions via electronic commerce, by means of standardization of data formats, will not happen in the next few decades. The political and economic interests of the administrative bureaucracies will resist any attempt to displace them through automation or adoption of uniform business practices.

Consider the difficulties of standardization of electronic commerce in international trade. The top five hundred multinationals control about 70% of all international trade, which in turn is about a third of the Gross Global Product. The estimated cost of paperwork for this activity is well in excess of $300 billion per year, which offers prosperous employment to a politically influential fifteen million officials. It is unlikely that this group will encourage elimination of most of its positions as intermediaries in occupations whose job is to negotiate a path through the bureaucracy surrounding all international commerce.

Instead, the acceptance of electronic commerce will arise from recognition that our personal computers are now sufficiently intelligent to understand the contents of messages. The transmission from customer to supplier will need to include not only the raw information but also its application logic – the software – with which the contents of a communication was created. The conceptual differences between managing telephone-to-telephone communications and computer-to-computer exchanges of information are best seen in debates about the adoption of EDI (Electronic Data Interchange) in commerce. Some EDI proponents advocate enforcing tightly defined electronic formats for every conceivable data element that may appear in any commercial transaction. This would generate huge savings if retailers could schedule shipments directly from factories without needing wholesalers. Manufacturers could greatly reduce administrative expenses and inventories by having their production scheduling computers negotiate directly with their suppliers' systems, thus eliminating paperwork in logistics, billing, and payments.

Despite the obvious advantages of removing intermediaries from complex customer-supplier relationships, adopting EDI-based electronic commerce is only making negligible progress. It may account for only a tenth of a percent of transactions in the international trade, and less than that in domestic trade.[308] Progress is remarkably slow despite efforts of hundreds of national standards committees and the involvement of the United Nations, the EEC and the U.S. Government in promoting the adoption of EDI standards. Widespread adoption of EDI will have to wait until the time when software "agents" will carry

---

308. Estimate by the General Electric Corporation, 5th World Congress of EDI Users, Brighton, U.K. 1994

along not only the transaction data, but also the application code with which a receiving computer will be able to fully comprehend the meaning of an incoming electronic message.

Figure 35.1 Let Your Agents Walk the Information Channels

The Universality of Computer-Based Communication

Telephone and video in every form we know today will disappear. The personal computer appliance will take over all voice, data and video functions. The software-driven personal computer appliance will be the successor device because it will be configured to fit a wide range of individual needs. Neither the telephone nor the TV set is adaptable. The victory of the personally configurable personal computer appliance is certain. The current uses of discrete devices to handle facsimile, telephone, videotape, television, radio and radiophone will become increasingly uneconomical and technologically unmanageable because they cannot be used easily to perform a wide variety of jobs. The need to preserve an accumulation of user habits, in the form of learned patterns of person-to-machine behavior will dictate the choice of communication devices in the future. That is a complete departure from today, where each communication device dictates compliance by the user with procedures uniquely suited to that device and which applies only to that device. At present, when a device or software program becomes obsolete, the accumulated learning for using it must be discarded, which destroys knowledge which is becoming more valuable that the device itself.

What journalists now call "multimedia," covers the enhancement of microcomputers to handle facsimile and video capabilities. That description does not really go far enough to help visualize the full future potential, just as adding a gasoline engine to a wagon to become a horseless carriage did not adequately explain the potential of the automobile.[309] What is revolutionary about the automobile is not the motor, but the suburbs, the displacement of railroads, the drive-in movie, car rental agencies, armored vehicles, blitzkrieg, the shopping center, and increased employment mobility.

Encouraging everyone to communicate by electronic mail, as the current rhetoric of the national information infrastructure suggests, diminishes the full potential of wide-band channels to combine all of the existing forms, such as the telephone, cable, television, facsimile and data communication, into a single medium. The personal computer is capable of replacing all of the individual devices that presently take advantage of the characteristics of communications channels separately. The likely evolutionary path will be from multiple communications channels for multiple receivers, to universal communication channels for universal receivers. Enhancing microcomputers with additional capabilities does not just add features. It makes possible devices that serve not only as calculating machines, but as an extension of human senses. In due course such devices will make obsolete many other physical institutions that have served us well, such as classrooms, offices, libraries and the voting booth.

---

309. The inventors of engine-propelled wagons originally called them horseless carriages. The term automobile came later.

An Historical Perspective

The next wave of technological change will arrive faster then anybody can imagine. What used to take a century for social and economic progress now takes only ten to twenty years. Political confrontations concerning taxation, security, and commercial exploitation of multimedia will dominate the economic and legislative agendas for the next few decades. Disputes over control of networks and software will be waged internationally.

Because the U.S. is the leading innovator and producer of much of this technology, this country will carry much of the burden of finding out which institutional solutions will be politically viable domestically, and which ones acceptable internationally. To preserve their leadership position, U.S. organizations must compress learning and experience about managing social and commercial innovation equivalent to two centuries of medieval Florence, one century of mercantile Antwerp, one century of industrial Manchester, and fifty years of machine-age Detroit into the next two or three decades.

Whether the U.S. can retain its current hold over innovation propelling the advent of an information-based society, is an interesting speculation. History teaches us that technological and economic leadership migrates wherever innovation flourishes. At this moment, U.S. dominance over network technologies, computers, and software reigns supreme. However, an unlikely source of change may already be hatching a challenge to what is presently seen as an invincible position. The demise of the leaders thought to be unassailable at one time, to be replaced by previously unsuspected newcomers, has been the pattern of all social change over millennia. There is no reason to believe that we have arrived at the "end of history." There is nothing that would somehow guarantee the retention of U.S. leadership in the information industries indefinitely. Past dominant powers have failed when they forgot that challenges to their power arise from an unexpected periphery, not from opponents who follow rules that had worked well for the leaders.

How do you then identify unconventional threats to the *status quo* that are not temporary disturbances, but fundamentally different alternatives to replace a dominant power? How would the Spanish empire at the peak of its power, recognize that it would be ultimately the under-rated English who would destroy them? How would IBM and DEC have recognized that it would be the microcomputer hobby-toy that would overwhelm them?

The lessons of history suggest that empires first weaken from within when their capacity to meet new challenges atrophies. The external adversary is rarely the root cause of their downfall. The victorious enemy arrives to administer a *coup-de-grace* to an already rotten enterprise. The chances are that the weakening of the U.S. dominance in information capabilities may not come from external competitors, but from our own government seeking to assert control over the application of information technologies in subordination to taxation and social policy.

A Technology Perspective

I believe that the present market segmentation of firms into completely separate communication, entertainment, computer hardware and software markets will not remain viable. Over one billion owners of "extended electronic brains," anticipated in the next decade, will expect delivery of combinations of telephone, video, entertainment, education and computing capabilities through integrated devices. The customers will not be interested in managing disk operating system, visiting computer stores, borrowing video tapes, managing software integration with hardware, or learning the idiosyncrasies of various applications.

Software, hardware, and communication channels that support a billion "extended electronic brains" will become a commodity. Customers will insist on services that respond to their needs whenever, wherever, and in whichever manner they desire. The future of information technology is in information services that relieve customers of technological choices. Those who deliver a wide spectrum of intuitively obvious information services to a wide range of customers will displace the firms that now dominate specialized market segments. The winners will satisfy the rapidly growing taste for more and better information with far less learning difficulty.

Information Technology as a Global Political Force

At the start of this century, large corporations started to replace small local businesses. Small private owners could not generate the capital nor organize the coordination to mass produce and distribute industrial goods. Centrally managed global corporations, which are exclusively based on the control of capital, are now in a decline. They lost economic power because they did not have the capacity to adapt to rapidly changing local conditions in increasingly diverse markets.

With the decline in the capacity of the giant and hierarchically managed corporations to compete effectively, there has been a rise in attempts to circumvent the laws of economics. This is accomplished by forming government-protected enclaves where market competition is not allowed to work and where transition from industrial forms of organization to effective service enterprises is inhibited. The financial losses from attempts at government-managed progress have surpassed anything that competitive organizations could afford. In the absence of bankruptcy and takeovers, state-dominated businesses have accumulated a staggering record of losses while persisting in information management practices from an era that is now gone. For government-controlled information enterprises, the bureaucratic diseconomies of scope negate any benefits from economies of scale. Whatever economic efficiency these organizations gain through information technology, they give up in excessive costs of administration. Whatever they gain under the guise of planned decision-making, they lose in the excessive costs of bureaucratic coordination.

It is an interesting speculation that it may be information technology, not the extension of the political ideas of federated democracy, that will promote the adoption of federalist ideas as the most practical way to achieve global cooperation, regardless of political forms or cultural diversity. The globalization of commerce, information and entertainment, could accelerate this trend without interfering with local culture, identity, and beliefs. Instituting global information governance for safeguarding commerce and security, while not interfering with individual choices, could potentially turn out to be the greatest political achievement of the next century.

Unfortunately, such speculations may be as unrealistic as similar ideas advanced when industrialization started taking over one hundred fifty years ago. The Western vision about the advent of a peaceful world, which prevailed for a century after Napoleonic wars, was based on the premise that universal cooperation will happen through commerce and industry. In retrospect, that euphoria is now understood as setting the stage for massive mechanized slaughter that followed for forty years after that.

Because of the great disparities in wealth and ambitions of societies in the foreseeable future, I see as one likely scenario bitter competition, including warfare against each other's information infrastructure. That outcome need not happen, if we can learn from the lessons of WWI and WWII that conflict may be avoided by making it possible for diversity to flourish, while making sure that the rule of law may not be broken.

A Global Perspective

Federalism is being practiced in few corporations, and even fewer countries. Therefore, the ideas of governance advocated in this book may be only applicable to cultures that subscribe to similar civic values.

There is an infinite number of choices that businesses or states can choose from as the basis for their information governance. The choices do not depend entirely on logic to improve the economic welfare of citizens. Politics is a reflection of human limitations of leadership. The politics of states has origins in warfare, economic development, and cultural heritage, reflecting prejudices acquired sometimes over hundred years ago. The technological homogeneity of much of information technology can therefore never become translated into a consistent pattern how to apply it.

Politics mirrors religion, ethnicity, morality, and social cohesion. All these are becoming more varied, especially in under-developed countries, which include more than half of the global population. The developing and industrializing countries are also not adhering to Western models of governance. They are experimenting with their own ideas of how to adapt information technologies to fit their unique approaches to dealing with the threats as well as opportunities of globalized commerce.

An increasing number of governments throughout the world are exhibiting extreme variations in practices, which U.S.-style information systems management practices cannot readily accommodate. I cannot imagine how to put into operation identical copies of information systems for healthcare or retail banking in Virginia, Russia, Serbia, China, Iraq, and Quebec.

Monarchy, especially if imposed as a military dictatorship, is too unstable to effectively manage information technologies for modern commerce and services. The most notorious example of a failed attempt was the imposition of military intelligence agency controls over the manufacture, import, development, and management of all computing in Brazil starting in the 1970s. The potential economic benefits of computerization in Brazil were set back for many years. Eventually, the grip of military intelligence yield to a more market-oriented approach.

My hope is that the federated information management structures, outlined in this book, may offer to governments in emerging economies flexible options how to accommodate the universality of information technologies to local needs which will always remain unique. A federated structure makes possible protection of national interests, such as security and economic development, without having to impose government restrictions on all information-related activities. Such action would deprive them of the benefits of global technologies, alliances, markets and advancement.

Political Integration

While the daily news reveal increasing incidence of regional, national, and religious conflicts the electronic linking of information sources is advancing at a fast pace. Information networks are encouraging universal communications across all media. The conflict between the universality of technology, finance and commerce, *versus* the nationalistic, tribal, and religious aspirations to retain local political power will remain the main theme for years to come.

I trust that information technologies, especially software, will form the binding that may alleviate the separatist effects of political forces that tend to isolate populations into hostile enclaves. The increasing destructiveness of weapons in the hands of small groups will force collaboration among those who stand for preservation of civilized behavior, where strife would otherwise prevail. A globally federated structure of information management will offer the means for parties with divergent local interests to work together on matters of security and safety just as they work together on communication and commerce.

Concluding Remarks

*Information politics takes precedence over
information technology.*

In this book, my model for information governance follows the principles of constitutional processes, balancing conflicting interests of parties that adhere to disparate information management methods. It is an approach that recognizes that different organizations must learn how to cooperate closely, regardless of whether they operate as federations, alliances, dictatorships, or tend to anarchy. My governance model follows the thinking of Montesquieu, Adam Smith, and James Madison, each of whom held that seemingly random acts of reasonable men, who negotiate out of self-interest, would ultimately tend toward a common good.

I subscribe to the ideas expressed in the *Federalist Papers* which record the arguments that preceded the adoption of the U.S. Constitution. They state that in a large enough community, the various political factions pursuing their goals by legitimate means will ultimately arrive at conditions that will allow them to work together for everyone's gain. For such an equilibrium to hold up requires a separation of governance powers, and institutions that assure proper protection against unwarranted seizure of power by fiat, force or privilege. The purpose of such separation is to not only avoid despotism, but also to restrain unchecked excesses of monopoly power.

When attempting to form rules of governance, there are initially a large number of choices open to negotiation. Every time you make a choice, fewer options remain. Because complexity inhibits flexibility, the initial steps in starting on a process to come up with a system of governance are especially critical. Those first steps in enabling cooperation shape everything that follows.

When changing the rules of governance, beware of engaging complete strangers in guiding your decisions. Consultants are most useful in offering viewpoints about already submitted proposals. These outsiders have the luxury of taking their time in writing a comprehensive report. If it is not applicable, or if their recommendations are impossible to implement, another study can be always commissioned for a good fee. CEOs do not have the luxury of experimentation. Careers, appointments, and budgets reflect policy as it is. When a CEO alters the concepts of operations, that usually happens under pressure and not necessarily with the benefit of well articulated rules.

When a CEO changes a principle or goal of information management, such act leaves an indelible impression on how the organization will behave afterwards, perhaps for many years to come. Therefore, the choices of governance principles deserve the utmost care and deliberation before they are enshrined in rules that guide the practice of management. Everyone key manager who will have to act on these principles of governance should therefore participate in their drafting. Then the politics of information governance turns into the politics of open covenants, openly negotiated, receptive to competitive ideas, tolerant of diversity, and respectful of the morale of those who do the work, because they are the only ones who can make information technology productive.

GLOSSARY

One of the many complaints about computer people is their propensity to express themselves using too much jargon. For that reason, most books about computers include a glossary to explain what should have been spoken in plain English.

To make information politics more understandable, here are terms you may have heard but wondered what they really signify. My explanations are political, not technical:

Application: A replicable collection of accumulated logic. Often discarded when it becomes incomprehensible to those who maintain it, even though it functions perfectly well.

Architecture of Information: Dividing the sphere of influence among contending factions.

Auditors: Experts in guessing the menu from an examination of the digested food.

Awards for Excellence: Industry beauty contests to judge the best public relations department.

Beta Version: Software that might work someday. /See also Release 1.0./.

Budget Cut: Tourniquet around the neck to stop bleeding from the foot.

Business Analysis: Rigorous documentation of why computer technology can be blamed in case of failure of a project.

Business Reengineering: A process to involve employees in recommending how to dispense with themselves.

Business Reengineering Consultant: Shaman qualified to cut jobs because he does not like anyone.

Business Process Redesign: Securing participation of those who know most how to grow a business. Participants are prospective victims.

Buzzword: A new word that masquerades as the solution to an old problem. The repackaging of old buzzwords is a major source of new revenue for consultants and computer vendors.

Catholic Church: An ideal corporation with consistent information policy, long-term employment, niche marketing, preservation of assets, tax exemption, low labor costs, clear lines of authority, little overhead, and concentration on education.

Chief Executive: A person that may be relied on to make wise, intelligent, and strategically prudent decisions after having first exhausted every other possibility.

CIO: Chief Information Officer. An executive who tries to manage what other executives consider their privilege.

CIM: Improving both the brain-to-tooth and the tooth-to-tail ratio. /See also Tooth-to-Tail ratio/.

Client/Server: A data center of their own for those dissatisfied with anyone else's data center. Previously used to describe mankind's oldest profession, which explains its current popularity.

Command, Control & Communications: Electronic methods for solving military problems encountered in the last war.

Computer Budgets: A bag of cash to pay for a dinner where the menu and number of guests are unknown.

Computer Literacy: Converting managers, engineers and scientists to typists and making secretaries into computer experts.

Consolidation: Legitimate hijacking of the budget of one organization by another.

Consultants: Contractors who learn on your job what your own people should have done given the time and money to find out for themselves.

Convergence of Media: Replacing the telephone, television, radio, record player, and videotape with a microcomputer.

Critical Success Factors: Consensus about causes of failure by those who caused the failure.

Data: Raw material of the information age. Usually available only after prolonged digestion.

Decentralization: A method for relieving the burdens of leadership. The redistribution of the central computer budget to where it will show as a hard to trace operating expense.

Defenestration: A way to dispose of losers in palace revolutions. A directed hara-kiri. Also known as a voluntary resignation.

Defense Information System: Pick any one from over 200 choices.

Development Tool: Software that I know how to use.

Digital Equipment Corporation: An organization that forgot that smaller fish can eat bigger fish.

Downsizing: A corporate form of anorexia. Assumes that thinness is the only way to become healthy and profitable.

Electronic Data Interchange: A technique for getting rid of facsimile transmissions. /See also Facsimile/.

Employees: Your most important asset, as stated in the annual report. A disposable resource, as reported in the news.

Encryption: Guaranteed privacy for criminals.

Enemies: Erstwhile friends who have not forgotten what you did wrong.

Espionage: Interviewing the competitor's employees on the pretense of potential employment.

Expert Systems: Complex logical metaphors for shifting the blame for bad managerial judgment onto a computer.

Facsimile: A backward technology but immensely popular because of ease of use. /See also Electronic Data Interchange/.

Floppy Disk: A 3.5 inch opening through which you can lose all your information assets or poison them. Each of your employees has one.

Governance: Rules defining officially tolerated conduct.

Government Regulations: Shifting of control over wealth to the legal profession.

High Performance Computing: The answer is teraflops, but what is the question?

IBM: A corporation superbly educated in the classics, but missed the chapters about the barbarians.

Infoassassination: A crime that leaves no fingerprints.

Information: Something understood by the originator, but not the recipient. /See also Knowledge/.

Information Asset: What companies do not show on their balance sheet. Discovered only after lost.

Information Baron: A bureaucrat who understands that power is control over what information comes and goes.

Information Economics: A method for collecting personal opinions to give them the appearance of analytic findings.

Information Highway: A new way to collect tolls. A bad analogy in that it has no fixed path, occupies no land, erects no structures, does not put up any signs and has no speed limit.

Information Implosion: Collapse of an organization when decision makers talk only to themselves. /See also IBM and Soviet Union/.

Information Resource Management: Entrusting general management responsibilities to a specialist.

Information Politics: The wisdom of recognizing that information management is power.

Information Privacy: Something your government cannot let you have.

Information Productivity: Achieving total customer satisfaction without managers, paperwork, and computers.

Information Security: A ratio of capabilities of infoassassins vs. infodefenders. Currently a multiplier, and rising rapidly.

Information Warfare: Making the enemy deaf, blind, and dumb.

Infrastructure: Critical resources that go unnoticed until they are missed.

Interoperability: Dispensing with messengers, liaison officers, coordination meetings, and hand-carried floppy disks.

Justification of Computers: Not analytically feasible without cheating. Only more productive people can be justified.

Jurisdictional Conflict: A euphemism for turf wars among bureaucrats.

Knowledge: What leaves the building every night.

Legislation: A method for substituting litigation for morality.

Local Area Network: A communication system managed by enthusiastic amateurs.

Legacy Systems: Something for which nobody can be held accountable.

Long Range Systems Planning: A three-ring binder containing recommendations as to when to upgrade computers and software.

Luck: Delivering what pleases management despite fuzzy objectives, inadequate means, and confusing governance.

Macintosh: Name of a fruit. Copied by a computer company that copied a computer design from a company that made good copies but could not sell originals.

Management: People in positions of privilege for admitting to gains, but not to losses.

Management Analysis: A rigorous exploration of why management is not to be blamed for systems failures. /See also Systems Analysis/.

Market Share: The most trustworthy opinion poll, since customers voted with their checkbooks. /See also Quality/.

Methodology: A procedure that I understand and like.

Microcomputer: A device that is like marriage. The acquisition cost is far less than the upkeep.

Microsoft: Proof that the ability to play poker is a prerequisite for engaging in successful information politics.

Military Information Systems: A method of equipping troops with obsolete computers, purchased at excessive cost, and configured for a warfighting scenario conceived at the start of the procurement cycle. /See also Terrorist Information Systems/.

Migration Systems: An application of Darwin's theory of survival-of-the-fittest to information management.

Multimedia: Claims by telephone, computer, publishing, cable, television, movie and radio companies to take over each other's franchises.

Network Control: A means for dispensing with management-by-amateurs.

Object-Oriented Design: Semi-replicable method for transforming alchemy and witchcraft into experimental science.

Object-Oriented Programming: Components that may help transform software from a handcraft to a manufactured product, someday.

Open Systems: A means to extend the economic life of information technologies.

Opinion Surveys: A reflection of what someone wishes others to believe.

Outsourcing: Leaving torn and dirty underwear with a laundry and expecting new clothing in return.

Paperless Office: Something that will happen when people start reading by telepathy.

Password: A means to protect sensitive information that is as good as an umbrella made out of a fishnet.

Pentagon: Where four disparate military services are learning how to win over warlords that have a unified command.

Personal Computer: A machine which is more responsive than the boss or co-workers and therefore loved with possessive passion.

Personal Data Assistant: Advanced technology of no particular use. Performance improves dramatically every month without affecting usefulness.

Policy: Latest memorandum from the chief executive. /See also Chief Executive/.

Polls: Opinions of personnel eager to say what they expect you to expect.

Procedural Programming: Illogical means for the specially initiated to communicate with a device that allegedly possesses logic.

Privacy: A privilege to use company computers to produce resumes, holiday mailing lists, and alibi memos.

Process Model: An analyst's understanding of reality.

Process Reengineering: A game for eliminating employees who should not have been employed to begin with. A method for exonerating past executive misjudgment.

Quality: Something that can be judged only by a paying customer, not by experts.

Reengineering: A widely advertised emetic packaged in expensive perfume bottles.

Reinventing Government: Vinegar in a relabeled old wine bottle.

Release 1.0: The customer pays for the privilege of testing whatever the vendor forgot to test.

Release 3.1: The customer pays for the first version of software that works as originally promised.

Research on Benefits of Computers: Opinion surveys with statistics. /See also Opinion Surveys/.

Return-on-Assets: An assumption that land, buildings, and machines explain profitability. Used in calculating management bonuses.

Return-on-Management: An assumption that the effectiveness of management explains profitability. Never used in calculating management bonuses.

Risk: A dollar amount which tells how bad it could be if everything fails. Never disclosed when asking for budgetary allocation.

Simulation: A technique to imitate the real thing that often becomes confused with the real thing.

Software: Primarily a social process involving participants who have great difficulty in agreeing about what they want.

Soviet Union: An organization with one of the worst information management records in history. Based on secrecy, misinformation, central control, and privileges for a small gang.

Stages of Growth Theory: A way to explain rising expenditures for computers to inquisitive accountants.

Standards: Consent imposed by those who already dominate the market.

Standardization: Choosing on which of many standards you bet your company's money without being blamed.

Stealth Computer Expenses: The cost of financial analysts, administrators, and secretaries doing work previously done by computer specialists.

Strategy: Any proposal to get money for a party where the location, menu, number of guests, and entertainment are unknown. A prerequisite for computer budgeting. /See Computer Budgets/.

Strategic: An adjective used to explain investment proposals that have no other rationale.

Systems Analysis: A rigorous exploration of why technology is not to be blamed for management failures. /See also Management Analysis/.

Systems Failure: An explanation to divert the anger of customers from the incompetence of suppliers.

Systems Paralysis Cycle: After indoctrination, fact-finding, approval of proposed actions, and planning for the next promotion the time left for real work.

Systems Planning: An instant long-term fix, to be repeated at least every year.

Systems Specifications: An attempt at communication between two tribes that do not share the same language, values, or religion.

Terrorist Information Systems: A method of equipping terrorists with the latest technologies, purchased at attractive prices, and configured for an attack scenario conceived at the start of the terrorist mission. /See also Military Information Systems/.

Tooth-to-Tail Ratio: Two hundred thousand fighters told by two million administrators what to do.

Training: An activity that employees with their own personal computers may indulge in while appearing to work.

UNIX: A service that is often confused with functions performed by neutered slaves in harems. A fortuitous label for software that is not trustworthy.

User Interface: Software that substitutes form for substance.

Virtual Reality: A simulation for those who do not like what a simulation of approximation of reality tells them. /See also Simulation/.

Vision: Declaration to visit an unexplored island hoping that somebody will fund for the trip, build a hotel and get others to come and pay for it.

Wide Area Networks: A pathway for professionals to attack networks managed by amateurs. /See also Local Area Networks/.

Xerox: A copy corporation that start-up ventures love to copy. It contributed to the advancement of the U.S. information industry by making duplication easy.

INDEX

Abdication, 18, 204
Academy Awards, 315
Accessing Memory, 206
Acquisition, 75-76, 115, 117, 123-124, 128, 133, 146, 154, 186, 253, 277, 295, 336, 378, 385, 387, 401-403, 408-409, 42423, 429, 434, 438-443, 448, 451, 453, 459, 479, 507
Across-the-board, 223
Activity Based Costing, 421
Ada, 81, 137-138, 291, 394
Adams, John, 45
Addison Wesley, 253
Adobe Systems Corporation, 137
Africa, 486
AIDS, 229, 279
Air Force, 78, 153, 324, 389, 393, 399, 412, 42422, 44444, 451
Air Force Reserve Officer Training Corps, 393
Alliances, 83, 165, 178, 354, 367, 498, 501
Allianz, 324
American Airlines, 349, 470

American Express, 396
American Productivity Center, 174
American Programmer, 254, 256, 295
AMP, 316-317
AMR, 349
AMRIS, 349
Andersen Consulting, 165, 397
Andrews, Duane, 397, 403, 447
Anthropologists, 68, 192, 272
Antwerp, 494
APL, 379
Apple Computer, 190
Appleton, Dan, 420
Application Barriers, 217
Application Level Checklist, 129
Application Level Concepts, 129
Application of Reengineering, 225
Architecture of Information, 7, 52, 204, 31503
Archiving, 144
Arguments, 37, 40-41, 61, 149, 198, 209, 228, 237, 261, 308, 31353, 373, 462, 473, 476, 501
Aristotle, 253

Armour Press, 221
Army Data Management Program, 421
Army Reserves, 402
Army ROTC, 393
Arthur Andersen, 227, 229
ASAP, 234-235
Asimov, Isaac, 37
Aspin, Les, 463
Assistant Comptroller, 172
Assistant Secretary, 383, 397, 402-404, 425, 447
Atlanta, 374
ATM, 142
Atwood, Donald, 385
Auditors, 6, 72, 81, 86, 304, 384, 402, 4144443, 452, 503
Australia, 208
Automated Support, 267, 389
Avoiding Policy-Making, 5-6
Awards, 229, 315, 317, 322, 324, 503
Balance of Power, 36, 43, 84, 187, 397
Baldrige Prize, 253, 304
Ball, Les, 326
Bank of America, 348-349
Bankruptcy, 163, 275, 307, 496
Basic Beliefs, 310
Benchmarking, 62, 103, 143, 306, 341, 398-399, 451, 453
Benchmarking Data Center Labor, 451
Benefits of Computers, 167, 375, 509
Beta Version, 503
Bill of Rights, 210
BlackNet, 209-210
Board of Directors, 31, 61, 89, 204, 317, 332, 343, 384
Boston College, 324
Brazil, 189, 498
British Civil Service, 353
Brooks Act, 408
Brown, Denis, 421
Budget Rent-A-Car, 349
Bull, Computers, 165, 176, 316–317
Bureau of Labor Statistics, 160
Burns & Roe, 172
Burroughs, 165
Business Alignment, 11-13, 75, 97, 475

Business Analysis, 224, 231, 249, 428, 503
Business Barriers, 217
Business Equipment Manufacturers Association, 140
Business Level Checklist, 127
Business Level Concepts, 127
Business Planning, 9, 31, 75, 101, 366, 421, 424
Business Procedures, 104, 113, 257, 291, 473
Business Process Analysis, 224, 428
Business Process Improvement, 110-111, 231, 238, 242-243, 245, 248-249, 338, 368, 39395, 414-415, 419, 421, 423-424, 427, 429-43437, 474
Business Process Redesign, 144, 169, 241, 2534413, 504
Business Process Transactions, 428
Business Reengineering, 17, 226, 233, 241, 25272, 322, 326, 42504
Business Reorganization, 266
Business School Press, 243, 275
Business Week, 169, 265, 315, 379
Buzzword, 61, 233, 504
C3I, 401-403, 411, 446-447, 456
Cadillac, 229
Caldwell, Bruce, 178, 353
California, 223, 475
Canada, 208, 217
Capone, Al, 236
Career Is Over, 231
Carlsbad, 339
Carnegie-Mellon University, 324
CASE, 5, 42, 74, 76, 122, 126, 15153, 161, 163, 169, 203-205, 214, 231, 238, 249, 254, 258, 266, 276-277, 287, 306, 309, 317, 319, 346, 349, 352, 363, 366, 375, 380-381, 385, 39393, 402, 412, 425, 433, 443, 446, 453, 475, 479, 503
Casey, Jason S., 475
Caterpillar, 316-317
Catholic Church, 47, 504
CBEMA, 140
Central Alaska, 351

Central Design Organizations, 451-452
Central Europe, 174
Certification, 109, 254, 34430
Champy, James, 233
Chaos, 4, 37, 39, 73, 135, 146, 179, 329, 381, 396, 419
Chase Manhattan Bank, 324
Cheney, Dick, 386
Chicago Mercantile Exchange, 116
Chief Executive Officer, 18, 89, 471
Chief Financial Officer, 343
Chief Information Officer, 18, 44, 96-97, 107, 172-173, 333-335, 369, 377-378, 470-471, 478, 487, 504
China, 498
CHIPS, 53, 188
Chu, David, 397
CICS, 139
CIM Lessons, 463
CIM Principles, 384, 398, 403, 465
CIM Rules, 430
CIM Share of DoD Cost Reduction Tasks, 390
CIO Magazine, 475
CIO Succession Planning, 362
CIO-for-hire, 476
Circuit City, 275
Clash of Cultures, 175
Clipper Chip, 208-209
Cobb, Lee E., 254
COBOL, 81, 138, 291, 315, 472
Cohen, Susan, 336, 472
Cold War, 159, 163-164, 170
Collective Knowledge, 273
Common Infrastructure, 441-442, 444, 465
Commonwealth of Virginia, 79
Company Structure, 7344
Compaq, 192
Compartmentalization of Organizational Memory, 213
Competitive Advantage, 91, 102, 169, 211, 275, 295, 346, 486, 490
Compuserve, 214
Computer Aided Software Engineering, 393

Computer Budgets, 164, 269, 374, 504, 509
Computer Economics, 339
Computer Hype, 260
Computer Literacy, 72, 177, 48504
Computer Management, 5, 15163, 165, 172, 384, 393, 475
Computer Peripherals, 180
Computer Problems, 68, 392
Computer Progress, 265, 369
Computer Sciences Corporation, 231, 239
Computer-Assisted Training, 281
Computerization, 88, 144, 166, 172-173, 176, 178-181, 187, 249, 29369, 386, 473, 48498
Computerworld, 7104, 166, 231, 234-235, 239, 305, 321, 325, 333, 369, 476
Concept of Operations, 119-121, 123, 125, 127, 129, 131, 133, 35392, 396, 464
Configuration Management, 254-55, 57, 106, 12123, 128, 143, 146, 154, 218, 251, 337, 435, 457, 459
Conflict Resolution, 33, 84
Connor, J. J., 206
Console Operations, 305, 451
Constitutional Convention, 8, 79, 333
Consultants, 5, 8, 113, 18, 35, 51, 65, 78, 112-113, 115, 139, 144, 149, 167-168, 185, 221-222, 225-228, 233, 258, 272, 304, 306, 322, 325, 33332, 336, 346, 351, 358, 38393, 404, 416, 424, 427, 453, 469, 502, 504
Consulting, 225, 71, 85, 108, 165, 203, 211, 23237, 250-251, 281, 306, 33332, 358-359, 381, 397, 44451, 472
Contracting Out, 82, 102, 318-319
Convergence of Media, 504
Copyright, 199, 201
Corning Corporation, 316–317
Corporate Contests, 380
Corporate Implications, 206

Corporate Information Function, 403
Corporate Information Management, 96-98, 105, 188, 206, 219, 383, 387, 457, 463
Corporate Information Politics, 98, 257, 344, 474, 486
Cost Comparison of Alternatives, 246
Cost of Errors, 271
Cost Reduction Objectives, 304, 446
Cost Reduction Potential, 282, 366, 428, 456-457, 462
Costs of Information, 19-2775, 91, 10102, 169, 183-184, 222, 304-305, 338, 409, 446
Counter Reformation, 191-192
Counter-revolution, 35
Coyote Hill, 191
Creating Policies, 417
Critical Success Factors, 394, 505
CryptoCredits, 210
CSC Consulting, 203
CSC Index, 326
Customer Care, 19, 76, 316
Customer Satisfaction, 104, 272, 303-304, 311, 506
Customer Service, 182, 223-224, 226, 246, 316-317, 34451, 479
Customer-focus, 316
Cutbacks, 241, 444
Cypherpunks, 210
Data Administration, 15186-187, 325, 368, 419, 421
Data Malfeasance Cases, 151
Data Management, 58, 69, 105, 12122-123, 151, 153, 336, 338, 421, 43442, 446
Data Modeling, 152, 420-421
Data Processing Installations, 450
Database, 3, 12, 263, 115, 122, 124-125, 143-144, 172, 187, 203-204, 287, 336, 345, 394, 431
Database Package, 12
Datamation, 62, 238, 376
Dataquest, 13
Davenport, Thomas H., 476

DEC, 176, 184, 188, 192-195, 315-317, 324, 495
Decentralization Policies, 107
Declining Administrative Costs, 307
Defenestration, 174, 505
Defense Analysis, 397, 410
Defense Communications Agency, 404
Defense Cost Reductions, 387-388
Defense Executive Level Group, 92
Defense Information Infrastructure, 418, 454, 456-46463
Defense Information Management Policies, 419
Defense Information System, 153, 505
Defense Information Systems Agency, 403-404, 415, 423, 429
Defense Information Technology Services Organization, 423
Defense Intelligence Agency, 403
Defense Investigative Service, 403
Defense Logistic Agency, 324
Defense Management Review Decisions, 386
Defense Mapping Agency, 403
Defense Superiority, 465
Defense Technical Information Center, 410
Defense University, 204
Dell, 192
Department of Defense, 24, 46, 775, 92, 137-138, 324, 351-352, 383, 387, 396-398, 407, 416
Department of Labor, 67, 160
Deputy Assistant Secretary, 404, 425
Deputy Director, 421
Deputy Secretary Atwood, 385-386, 388, 396-397, 403, 456
Design Principles, 110
Detroit, 494
Development Tool, 505
Dhahran, 425
Dictatorial Characteristics, 226
Digital Equipment Corporation, 186, 505
Diplomacy, 84

Director of Defense Information, 404, 407, 41415-416
DISA, 404, 456
Distance Tutoring, 109, 281
Distributing Computing Power, 58, 63, 71
Distributing Tasks, 71
Distribution of Power, 41-42, 63, 260-261, 470
Diversifying Innovation, 357
DMRD, 386, 390-391, 398
DNA, 251
Doctrine, 47, 53, 154, 183, 201, 383, 403, 429-43463
Document Retrieval, 206
Documentation, 45, 131, 143, 145-146, 306, 437, 503
DoD Information Infrastructure, 455, 459, 461, 463, 465
DoD IRM, 409
DOS, 175
Dow Chemical, 316-317
Dow Jones, 214
Downsizing, 167, 242, 254, 26352, 379, 445, 454, 46505
DuPont Company, 438
Eastern Europeans, 198
Eccles, Robert G., 476
ECMA, 140
Economic Value-Added, 12, 17, 71, 97, 99, 101, 103, 15346
Economika, 162
EDI Users, 491
EDI World, 204, 491
EDS, 319, 353, 381, 385
EEC, 491
Egypt, 19
EIS, 173
Electronic Age, 162, 21473
Electronic Data Interchange, 214, 431, 491, 505
Electronic Data Systems, 353, 385
Electronic Meeting Systems, 420
Elements of Information Management, 9
Elements of Information Superiority, 10

ELG, 397-404, 407-408, 441
Emery, Dr. Jim, 421, 422
EMS, 420
Encryption, 122, 207-209, 505
Endoso, Joyce. 465
Enforcement Network, 204
Enterprise Architecture, 51, 53, 81, 201, 422
Enterprise Barriers, 215
Enterprise Level Checklist, 122
Enterprise Level Concepts, 122
Entrepreneurs, 176, 189-19356-357
Entrepreneurship, 338, 356
Erwin, Deane, 425
Espionage, 204, 433, 505
Ethernet, 137, 191
European Community, 72, 14422
European Computer Manufacturers Association, 140
European Economic Community, 72, 140
EVA, 12, 71, 99
Evolutionary Migration Schema, 413
Executive Guide, 204
Executive Level Group, 92, 396-397, 441
Executive Level Staff, 81-82
Executive Office, 401
Executive Ownership, 18
Experimental Prototyping, 11131
Expert Systems, 67, 246, 505
Externalizing Information Politics, 469
Facsimile, 20-21, 178, 313, 363, 489, 492-493, 505
Fannie Mae, 305
Faustian Bargain, 208-209
Favela, J., 206
FBI, 211
FEA, 409-412
Federal Computer Week, 24
Federal Express, 76
Federal Information Processing Standards, 95
Federalist Papers, 37, 501
Federated Governance, 46, 57, 67, 486
Federations, 44, 57, 778, 501

FedEx, 76, 202-203
Ferguson, Gregor, 221
Feudalism, 33-34, 477, 479, 485-486
Finger-tops, 265
Fischer, Dr. Kurt, 422
Floppy Disk, 505
Florence, 494
Forbes, 169, 229, 234-235
Forrester Research, 336, 472
Fort Sill Directorate of Engineering, 427
Fortune, 159-16165, 169, 193, 229, 232, 286, 317-318, 454
Free Press, 128, 458, 473
French Revolution, 187, 238
French Riviera, 141
Ft. Sill Business Process Activity Costs, 428
Fujitsu, 165
Functional Analysis, 409-41419, 446
Functional Barriers, 217-218
Functional Cost Reduction Tasks, 389
Functional Economic Analysis, 409-41419
Functional Modeling, 95
Functional Processes, 47, 106, 12126, 384
Fund Modernization, 455
Future of Information Politics, 486
GAO, 401, 411, 437-438, 456
Garrett, Gary, 397
GDP, 72
GE, 176, 316-317, 414
General Accounting Office, 87, 396, 401, 425, 463
General Counsel, 217
General Electric Corporation, 414, 491
General Foods, 373-376
General Motors, 319, 385, 397, 438
General Services Administration, 401
Geographic Coordinates, 399
Germany, 324
Gerstner, Louis, 310
GITS, 391
Global Barriers, 214
Global Computing Power, 160

Global Political Force, 496
GM, 319
GNP, 72
Gold Nugget, 416, 422
Gorbachev, Mikhail, 162
Governance Cases, 151, 153, 155
Government Accounting Office, 389, 437
Government Computer News, 39465
Government Information Technology Services, 391
Government Regulations, 47505
Governmental Affairs, 39463
Graphic Interface Style Guide, 420
Greek, 3
Gross Global Product, 491
Gross National Product, 72, 291
Groupware, 167, 331
GSA, 401
GTE, 444
Gulf War, 386, 425
Hamilton, Alexander, 37
Hammer, Michael, 233-234, 325
Hancock, Jack, 397
Hanold, Terrence, 173
Harvard Business Review, 184, 236, 471
Hawk, Gilbert, 412
Hays, Laurie, 310
Heathrow Airport, 176
Henkoff, Ronald, 454
Hewlett-Packard, 192
High Performance Computing, 505
High Productivity, 70-71
Hill, David, 397, 400
Hoffman, R., 348
Holy Grail, 422
Home Grown Innovation, 351
Honeywell, 165, 377-378
Hong Kong, 34
Hopper, Grace, 138
Hopper, Max, 470-471
Howard, Mary, 425
Hub Networking, 61
Humphrey, Watts S., 253
Hypercard, 278

I-CASE, 289
IBM, 44, 52, 59, 62, 136, 139, 165, 172, 176, 181, 183-184, 186, 190-194, 198, 229, 31315-317, 324, 329, 359, 374, 377-379, 382, 495, 506
ICAM, 420
IDEF, 142, 420
IDEF95
IDEF1X, 95
Identifying Excellence, 316
IEEE, 206, 42475
Implementation Matters, 12-13, 82, 85
Implementing Business Process Improvement, 423
Implementing CIM, 409, 411, 413, 415, 417, 419, 421, 423, 425, 427, 429, 431, 433, 435, 464
Improvement Through Cooperation, 243
Inclusion Principles, 75
Indian Ph. D., 295
Inductive Reasoning, 227-229
Industrial Engineering, 222, 225-226, 228
Infoassassination, 506
Information Age, 166, 172, 178, 193, 209, 218, 331, 505
Information Alignment, 11, 75, 82, 344, 367, 471
Information Architecture, 7, 51-52, 31336, 341, 42422, 503
Information Asset, 506
Information Baron, 506
Information Channels, 232, 492
Information Configuration Policies, 106
Information Constitution, 32, 45, 47, 49, 52, 56, 74-75, 78-81, 84, 88-89, 99, 109
Information Constitutional Model, 45
Information Effectiveness, 23-24, 10103, 301, 325, 409
Information Hermit, 59
Information Highway, 7, 6168, 506
Information Implosion, 47, 506

Information Infrastructure, 87, 167, 206, 341, 418, 442, 454-461, 463, 465, 471, 493, 497
Information Intrusion, 204
Information Management Doctrine, 154, 429
Information Modeling, 95, 400
Information Payoff, 128, 473
Information Policy Board, 82, 85-86, 97-99, 103, 107-108, 116, 124, 127, 129, 134, 147, 258, 337, 411-412
Information Privacy, 211, 506
Information Processing Standard, 42422
Information Productivity, 12, 71, 91-92, 10506
Information Resource Management, 17, 391, 409, 506
Information Resources Chief, 383
Information Security, 19, 69, 86, 92, 98-10107, 123-124, 128, 144, 187, 204, 209, 214, 336-337, 367, 432, 446, 459-461, 487, 506
Information Services Division, 83, 184, 381-382
Information Services Utilities, 471
Information Superiority, 10-11, 13, 108, 301, 439, 463, 465
Information Systems Agency, 403-404, 415, 423, 429
Information Systems Division, 381
Information Systems Objectives, 19, 128, 304, 313
Information Systems Review Council, 440
Information Technology Reuse Services, 423
Information Warfare, 165, 204, 403, 433, 463, 506
Information Workers, 67, 69, 127, 16175, 193, 198, 222-223, 285-286
Information-Based Societies, 484-487
InformationWeek, 178, 322, 325-326, 349, 353
Inland Revenue, 353
Inspector General, 411, 425

Institute of Management Accountants, 333

Integrated Computer-Aided Software Engineering, 291, 422

Intelligence, 58, 62, 98, 113, 124, 127-129, 134, 153, 182, 194, 201, 203, 205-206, 212, 251, 267, 273, 301, 303, 352, 383, 397, 401-403, 446-447, 449, 454, 457, 461, 489, 498

Internet, 59, 136, 209, 214

Inventory-replenishment, 203

Invisible Hand, 183

Involvement of Auditors, 86

IPX, 472

Iran, 486

Iraq, 425, 498

IRM, 322, 384, 391, 395-397, 401, 403, 408-41416, 479

ISDN, 81

Israel, 208

Issue Work Order Supply Items, 428

J. C. Penney, 444

Japan, 14159

Jay, John, 37

Jeffcoat, Clyde, 423

Jefferson, Thomas, 2, 36-37, 45, 187, 21351

Jell-O, 374

John Wiley, 476

Johnson, Maryfan J, 305, 307

Joint Chiefs of Staff, 397, 447, 449-45455

Jones, Caspers, 232, 276

Jurisdictional Conflict, 506

Justification of Computers, 506

Karastan-Bigelow, 444

Kendall, Cindy, 425

KGB, 208

Kimery, Anthony L., 205

King George III, 198

King Solomon, 76

King, Julia, 239

Kissinger, Henry, 84

Knecht, Ronald, 403

Knopf, Alfred A., 4

Knowledge Based Theory of Labor, 283

Knowledge Repository, 145, 277, 422

Kraft Corporation, 86

Krass, P., 325

Kremlin, 106

Laberis, Bill, 260

Labor Savings, 451

Lawyers, 6, 119, 199-20211, 222, 452

Layers of Information, 47

Leadership, 18, 25-26, 87, 93, 142, 173-174, 176, 189, 194, 212, 221, 223, 226, 234, 238, 243, 249, 267, 274, 295, 297, 299, 308-309, 325-326, 330-331, 359, 365, 368, 386, 391, 397, 403, 407, 417, 421, 447, 464, 487, 494, 497, 505

Learning Assistance, 280

Legacy Software, 125, 256, 446

Legacy Systems, 113, 147, 167, 256-259, 383, 412-413, 507

Legislation, 408, 507

LEGO, 269

Lessons Learned, 154, 195, 357, 384, 421-422

Lobotomy, 235

Local Area Network, 34507

Local Initiatives, 79, 89, 131, 333, 462

Local Level Checklist, 129, 133

Local Level Concepts, 130

Local Politics, 34, 131

Logistics Agency, 398

Long Distance Networks, 453

Long Range Systems Planning, 507

Loss of Power, 333

Lotus Notes, 142, 218

Louis XVI, 187

Low Productivity Companies, 70-71

Loy, Pat, 254

Loyola University, 397

Lublin, Joann S., 234

Lucky Strikes, 229

Lundy, Father George, 405

M. I. S., 71, 327

Machiavelli, Niccolo, 326

Macintosh, 419507

MacWorld, 59

Madison, James, 37, 45, 501

Mafia, 364
Maglitta, Joseph, 321
Mainframes, 59, 76, 184, 259-26328-329, 353, 392, 460
MAISRC, 440
Making Policy, 33, 35, 37, 39, 41
Making Standards, 139, 142-143
Management Agendas, 6, 168, 170
Management Analysis, 507, 510
Management Costs, 16, 19-271, 75, 112, 225, 346, 384, 409, 446
Management Information Systems, 15, 19-254, 71, 75, 77, 83, 123-124, 13172, 251, 294, 319, 344, 369, 396, 419, 448, 49498
Management Review, 145, 236, 386, 396, 456, 476
Management Revolution, 4
Management Services, 12, 76, 103, 105, 108, 129, 317, 470
Management Value-Added, 12, 71, 99
Managing Information Politics, 23, 476
Managing Information Strategically, 476
Managing Standards, 141
Mandarin CIO, 331
Manifesto, 233, 236
Manufactured Software, 295
Marine Corps, 24, 78, 153
Marines, 399
Market Share, 16, 52, 135, 168, 176, 192, 194, 222, 345-346, 385, 507
Markoff, John, 315
Marriott, 349
Marxist-Leninist, 161
Maui, 141
McGee, James, 476
McGraw-Hill, 324
McInerney, Thomas, 24
McPartlin, John P., 326
Medieval, 33-34, 64, 227, 478, 494
Menagh, Melanie, 369, 476
Merits of Alternatives, 70
Mestrovich, Dr. Michael, 415
Meta Software Corporation, 245-246

Microcomputers, 21, 34, 41, 73-74, 176, 188-189, 191-192, 194-195, 198, 201, 261, 288, 303, 306, 331, 355, 396, 435, 453, 493
Microprocessors, 76, 142, 434, 480
Microsoft Corporation, 261
Microsoft Windows, 167
Migrating Legacy Systems, 258
Migration Systems, 366, 383, 412-413, 446, 507
Migration Tree, 414-415
Military Information Systems, 507, 510
Minicomputers, 34, 62, 176-177, 184, 186-188, 329, 347, 451, 479
MIPS, 171, 333, 352, 445, 450-451
Mirabeau, 187
Miss America, 315
Moad, Jeff, 238
Model Constitution, 45, 91, 93, 95, 97, 99, 101, 103, 105, 107, 109, 111, 113, 115, 117
Modernization Program, 421, 455, 462, 465
Monarchy, 45, 378, 477-479, 485-487, 498
Montesquieu, 501
Morality, 236-237, 497, 507
Morrow, William, 193
Moses, 312
Motorola, 316-318
Nabisco, 192
Nanotechnology, 210
National Cash Register, 165
National Dairy Products Corporation, 86, 376
National Institute of Standards, 95
National Performance Review, 24
National Security Council, 449, 456
NATO, 44
Naval Postgraduate School, 421-422
Navy, 78, 153, 389, 44444
Netware, 472
Network Control, 34, 114, 116-117, 126, 128, 173, 204, 218, 321, 341, 432, 434-435, 453, 459-46473, 507
Networked Organizations, 206

Networking Choices, 57, 65
Neumann, P. G., 348
New York Times, 169, 208, 315, 474
Nixdorf, 176
Node Tree Diagram, 244
Northwestern Territories, 361
Norton, David, 397
NT, 141, 472
O'Keefe, Sean, 397
Object-Oriented Design, 508
Object-Oriented Programming, 508
Obsolescent Assets, 287
Occam, William of, 106
Olivetti, 165
Olympic, 147
OMB, 391, 401, 408, 411
Open Configuration Management, 251
Open Systems Interconnection, 57, 136
Opinion Surveys, 5-6, 318, 396, 508-509
Oracle, 336
Order of Priority of Decisions, 400
Organizational Learning, 78, 169, 249, 274
Organizational Memory, 54, 57, 211-213, 215, 217, 275
Organizational Privacy, 201
Organizing Business Process Improvement, 248
Origins of Reengineering, 221
Orwell, George, 205
Outsourcing, 18, 102, 108, 247, 318-321, 334, 342, 364, 381, 385, 46487, 508
Overhead Cost Reduction, 223
Pacificare Health Systems, 260
Pake, Dr. George, 223
Palo Alto Research Center, 191, 223
Paralysis Cycle, 443, 510
PARC, 191, 223
Passwords, 125, 173
Patterns of Failure, 324
PC Week, 59
Peer-to-peer, 48, 58, 61, 64-65
Pentagon, 34, 75, 383, 386, 393, 416, 418, 422, 425, 438, 453, 456, 508

People-literate, 480
People-oriented, 234, 275
Pepsi, 192
Performance Review, 24
Personal Computer, 48, 69, 15193, 198, 214, 217-218, 26352, 475, 478, 492-493, 508
Personal Data Assistant, 508
Personal Privacy, 48, 145, 197-199, 201, 204, 206, 211, 218-219, 308
Personnel Development Policies, 108
Peters, Tom, 4, 231
Pfeffer, J., 275
Phillips, 165, 316-317
Pillsbury, 173
Planning Review, 236, 337
Point-of-sale, 203, 205
Point-of-use, 103, 108, 122, 258, 288
Policy Innovation, 32
Policy Without Governance, 4
Policy-making, 5-6, 23, 26-27, 31-33, 36, 38, 153, 308
Political Act, 38, 4139, 308, 473-474
Political Agenda, 269
Political Astuteness, 346
Political Force, 48496
Political Integration, 498
Political Realities, 26, 462
Political Threats, 475
Politicophobia, 474-475
Politics of CIM, 437, 439, 441, 443, 445, 447, 449, 451, 453, 455, 457, 459, 461, 463, 465
Politics of Control, 38, 435
Politics of Infrastructure Building, 461
Pontius, Harry, 418
PostScript, 137, 465
Powell, Colin, 447
Power Loss, 333
PowerBuilder, 472
Preservation of Knowledge, 276
President Bush, 386-388
President Clinton, 465
Presidential Commissions, 389
Presidential Medal, 223
Presley Noble, Barbara, 474

Press Release, 309
Principal Staff Assistants, 404, 446
Procedural Programming, 168, 508
Process Barriers, 217
Process Flow Simulation, 244
Process Improvement Tasks, 13, 424, 426
Process Innovation, 243
Process Level Checklist, 125
Process Level Concepts, 124
Process Model, 396, 508
Process Reengineering, 17, 241, 243, 25272, 42504, 508
Process Security Barrier, 217
Profitability of Employee Development, 274
Program Analysis, 397, 410
Prolonging Software Life, 289
Property Rights, 105, 199, 201, 204
Protecting Long Term Assets, 289
Prusak, Laurence, 476
Public Sector Reengineering, 232
Quadrillion Calculations, 208
Quebec, 498
R. S. A., 208
RADCF, 410
Randall, R. M., 236
RCA, 165, 176, 375
Re-engineering, 239, 421
Realistic Goal, 302
Reengineering Business Process Modeling, 420
Reengineering Government, 391
Reengineering Work, 236, 238, 241, 243
Reinventing Government, 17, 227, 232, 238, 509
Replication, 115, 217-218
Rescrypt Corporation, 208
Responsibilities of Information Systems Managers, 99
Responsibilities of Operating Managers, 100
Retaliation, 182
Return-on-Assets, 284, 309, 509
Return-on-Management, 12, 71, 509

Reuters, 214
Risk Management, 115, 509
Rossiter, Clinton, 37
ROTC, 393
Rude, Jim, 173
Salomon Brothers, 324
Saudi Arabia, 425
Savings Potential, 339, 451
Schama, Simon, 187
Schottel, David, 412
Scientific Data Systems, 378
Securities Exchange Commission, 71
Security Barriers, 214-217
Security Risks, 62, 81, 434-435, 460
Senate Armed Services Committee, 383
Senate Governmental Affairs Committee, 390
Senior Executive Service, 342, 456
Separation of Powers, 82, 501
Serbia, 498
Services Cost Reduction Tasks, 389
Setting Objectives, 258, 307, 313
Settling Disputes, 85
Shaman, 504
Shell Oil, 396
Siemens, 165
Signal Corps, 432
Signs of Failure, 322
Signs of Obsolescence, 288
Silicon Valley, 19223
Simulating Processing Time, 247
Simulating Staff Utilization, 248
Singapore, 34, 72
Sloan Management Review, 476
Sloan, Alfred P., 438
Smith, Adam, 236, 501
Smith, Roger, 385
SNA, 472
Socratic, 281
Software Agents, 251, 491
Software Assessment, 276, 422
Software Assets, 57, 128, 143, 257, 259, 278, 29326, 382
Software Engineering Institute, 253
Software Excellence, 254
Software Independence, 254-255

Software Maintenance, 2115, 123, 132, 144, 259, 263, 276, 293, 305, 313, 328, 434

Software Portability, 113, 263-264

Software Process Improvement, 253-254

Software Reuse Program, 422, 465

Software Risks, 232, 276

Sony PCX, 315

Soviet Style Computing, 162

Soviet Union, 47, 106, 161-163, 387-388, 506, 509

Spain, 217

Spanish, 494

Sperry, 165, 176

SPX, 472

Stages of Growth Theory, 509

Stalin, 106

Stalinist, 35

Standards Compliance, 139

Standards Documents, 145

Standards Topics, 143

Stealth Computer Expenses, 509

Stealth Technology, 21

Stern Stewart Management Services, 12, 317

Stewart, G. B., 12

Strassmann, Paul A., 128, 184, 473

Supercomputer, 207, 470

Switzerland, 34

Symantec Utilities, 207

Systems Analysis, 367, 477, 507, 510

Systems Concept, 55, 395

Systems Design Policies, 109

Systems Failure, 127, 476, 510

Systems Paralysis Cycle, 443, 510

Systems Planning, 86, 124, 336, 421, 507, 510

Systems Sciences, 206, 475

Systems Specifications, 247, 269, 510

Tape Operations, 305, 451

Taylor, Frederick, 179

TCP, 136-137, 472

Technical Architecture Framework, 52, 420

Technical Integration Management, 421

Technical Reference Architecture, 421

Technical Reference Model, 420

Technocratic Utopianism, 477, 486

Technology Acquisition, 115, 401, 429

Technology Advancement, 97, 112

Technology Adventurism, 347

Technology Agendas, 167, 170

Technology Improvement Programs, 421

Technology Management Roles, 21

Technology Obsolescence, 288

Technology Recycling, 265

Telecommunications, 254-55, 62, 64, 83, 113, 124, 14143, 147, 154, 321, 341, 363, 375, 381, 403, 432, 46471

Telephones, 16, 261, 266, 313, 336, 439, 488-489

Temporary CIOs, 369

Ten Commandments, 78, 93

Terrorist Information Systems, 507, 510

Texas Instruments, 444-445

The Economist, 169

Theocracy, 177, 182

Toffler, Alvin, 193, 483

Toffler, Heidi, 483

Tooth-to-Tail Ratio, 24, 504, 510

Total Quality Movement, 224

Totalitarian Taint, 35

Tourniquet, 454, 503

TQM, 224-225

Transformation of Work, 162, 473

Transition Politics, 39

Tucson Unified School District, 324

Tyson Foods, 275

U. K., 491

U. S. Air Force, 412

U. S. Army, 412, 421

U. S. Army Corps of Engineers, 421

U. S. Congress, 388

U. S. Constitution, 45, 74, 893, 501

U. S. Constitutional Model, 45

U. S. Declaration of Independence, 302

U. S. Department of Defense, 775, 324, 351, 383, 387

U. S. Information Cottages, 193

U. S. S. R., 189

U. S. Senate, 463
Unconventional Thinking, 404
Undersecretary of Acquisition, 403
Unit Cost Reduction Indicators, 305
UNIVAC, 181
Universal Transverse Mercator
  Coordinates, 399
Unix, 81, 139, 142, 510
Unpredictable Leadership, 26
Unstable Leadership, 25-26
User Interface, 510
Utopianism, 477, 486
Value of Information Politics, 8269
Van Creveld, Martin, 457-458
Victorian, 475
Vinegar, 509
Virginia, 79, 498
Virtual Reality, 6510
Viruses, 218
Visicalc, 188
Visionary Consultant, 90
Visual BASIC, 472
VLSI, 77
W. Gunn, Robert, 379
Wal-Mart, 203, 275, 324
Washington Times, 483
Wealth of Nations, 236
Web Networking, 63-64
Whiskey Rebellion, 81
Wide Area Networks, 126, 134, 325,
  510
Wisnosky, Dennis, 420
Workflow, 2167, 243, 245-248, 251,
  293-294, 474, 481
Workflow Diagram, 245, 247-248
Working Group, 391
Working Woman, 218
Workstations, 77, 132, 134, 145,
  26452-453
World Population Forecast, 483
World War II, 389
Wright-Patterson Air Force Base, 451
WWI, 497
WWII, 405, 497
X-Open, 140
X-rated, 218

X-Windows Motif, 167
Xerox, 7, 68, 83, 86, 137, 165, 169,
  176, 182, 184, 191, 193-195, 223,
  309-311, 316-317, 322, 378-382,
  396-397, 414, 444-445, 510
Xerox Data Services, 382
Xerox Information Services Division,
  184, 381-382
Xerox Palo Alto Research Laboratory,
  68
Yoemans, Michael, 427
Yourdon, Ed, 256, 295